Beyond the Arab Cold War

OXFORD STUDIES IN INTERNATIONAL HISTORY

JAMES J. SHEEHAN, SERIES ADVISOR

The Wilsonian Moment
Self-Determination and the International Origins of Anticolonial Nationalism
EREZ MANELA

In War's Wake
Europe's Displaced Persons in the Postwar Order
GERARD DANIEL COHEN

Grounds of Judgment
Extraterritoriality and Imperial Power in Nineteenth-Century
China and Japan
PÄR KRISTOFFER CASSEL

The Acadian Diaspora
An Eighteenth-Century History
CHRISTOPHER HODSON

Gordian Knot
Apartheid and the Unmaking of the Liberal World Order
RYAN IRWIN

The Global Offensive
The United States, the Palestine Liberation Organization, and the Making
of the Post–Cold War Order
PAUL THOMAS CHAMBERLIN

Mecca of Revolution
Algeria, Decolonization, and the Third World Order
JEFFREY JAMES BYRNE

Beyond the Arab Cold War
The International History of the Yemen Civil War, 1962–68
ASHER ORKABY

Beyond the Arab Cold War

The International History of the
Yemen Civil War, 1962–68

ASHER ORKABY

OXFORD
UNIVERSITY PRESS

OXFORD
UNIVERSITY PRESS

Oxford University Press is a department of the University of Oxford. It furthers
the University's objective of excellence in research, scholarship, and education
by publishing worldwide. Oxford is a registered trade mark of Oxford University
Press in the UK and certain other countries.

Published in the United States of America by Oxford University Press
198 Madison Avenue, New York, NY 10016, United States of America.

Library of Congress Cataloging-in-Publication Data
Names: Orkaby, Asher, author.
Title: Beyond the Arab Cold war : the international history of the Yemen
    civil war, 1962–68 / Asher Orkaby.
Other titles: Oxford studies in international history.
Description: New York, New York : Oxford University Press, 2017. |
    Series: Oxford studies in international history |
    Includes bibliographical references and index.
Identifiers: LCCN 2017000719 (print) | LCCN 2017007435 (ebook) |
    ISBN 9780190618445 (hardcover : alk. paper) | ISBN 9780190618452 (Updf) |
    ISBN 9780190618469 (Epub)
Subjects: LCSH: Civil war—Yemen (Republic)—History—20th century. |
    Yemen (Republic)—History—1962–1972. |
    Yemen (Arab Republic)—History—Revolution, 1962. | Cold War.
Classification: LCC DS247.Y45 O75 2017 (print) | LCC DS247.Y45 (ebook) |
    DDC 953.3205/2—dc23
LC record available at https://lccn.loc.gov/2017000719

9 8 7 6 5 4 3 2

Printed by Sheridan Books, Inc., United States of America

To my father, who taught me that the deserts of Yemen are no impediment to success.

Contents

Acknowledgments

I CONSIDER MYSELF fortunate to have received the wisdom and guidance from three pillars of the academic community while researching and writing this book: Roger Owen instilled upon me the wisdom of decades of experience in the field of Middle East History; Erez Manela meticulously and thoughtfully read through many drafts, helping me look beyond the empirical analysis to the much broader world of international history; Steven Caton served as a constant reminder that as international as this narrative became, it was at its core a story about Yemen.

The Center for Middle Eastern Studies at Harvard and my mentor Susan Kahn helped me grease the wheels of university complexities, ensuring that I was always funded and on track to finishing this book on time. Bill Granara provided me with a supportive research home at Harvard for as long as I needed to complete this project. Both Clive Jones and Jesse Ferris offered invaluable help at each stage of my international research and writing. I would also like to thank Simon C. Smith, Tore Peterson, Charles Schmitz, J.E. Peterson, and Timothy Nunan for reading selected book chapters. I am also indebted to Scott Walker at the Harvard Map Department and all of Harvard's librarians. This book could not have been brought to publication without the careful attention of the Oxford University Press editorial team.

The number of archivists and academics who have helped me along the way in Britain, Canada, Israel, Russia, Switzerland, the United States, and Yemen are too numerous to list individually, hardly justice for those who devoted many hours facilitating my intensive archival schedule and pace. This globetrotting research could not have been accomplished without the generosity of the Harry Frank Guggenheim Foundation, the John Anson Kittredge Education Fund, the American Institute for Yemeni Studies, the Society for the Historians of American Foreign Relations (SHAFR), the

Bradley Foundation, the Harvard Davis Center, the Institute of Historical Research, the Harvard Weatherhead Center for International Affairs Canada Program, and the LBJ Presidential Library.

All the research funds and advisers in the world would not have allowed me to finish this book without my children, Binyamin, Eitan, Naftali, and Atara, and their nightly reminders that there are more important things to life. But mostly, without my loving wife Ariela, who has become an expert in Yemen by this point, I would have lost my sanity long ago in some dimly lit archive halfway across the world.

Beyond the Arab Cold War

Beyond Paradigms

AN INTRODUCTION TO THE YEMEN CIVIL WAR

AS NIGHT FELL over the Yemeni capital city of Sana'a on September 19, 2014, a small convoy of pickup trucks carrying hundreds of heavily armed tribesmen belonging to the Houthi rebel movement pulled to a stop in front of the state-run Yemen TV headquarters. Within hours, the world's main source of news from Yemen was in the hands of the Houthis. Within days, the entire city was under Houthi control. These were the first northern tribesmen to enter Sana'a as conquerors since 1962, when the republic replaced the country's thousand-year theocracy. The Houthi tribesmen returned to Sana'a almost fifty-two years to the date after the Yemeni republic had been founded. They arrived along al-Thawra Road, named for the very revolution that overthrew the northern tribal order of the last ruling imam of Yemen in 1962.

The events of September 1962 plunged Yemen into a protracted civil war between the new republic and the deposed imam. This was a battle between tribal and modern national identities, a conflict that continues to define politics in Yemen. Over the next six years this local civil war was transformed into an arena of global conflict that impacted the emerging modern Yemeni state and changed the course of Middle East history. Throughout the civil war, no single power managed to dictate the course of events. The belligerent parties were not allied along Cold War lines and were not dominated by the stark divisions between the Saudi monarchy and the Egyptian Arab nationalist movement. Nor, for that matter, were Yemenis masters of their own destiny. Rather, during the 1960s, Yemen became an open field for individuals, organizations, and countries to peddle their agendas in this remote region of South Arabia, laying the groundwork for subsequent decades of Yemeni and Arabian history.

Deconstructing and Reconstructing
a Yemeni State

Yemen, located in the southwest corner of the Arabian Peninsula, did not exist as a distinct South Arabian state before the twentieth century.[1] Harold Ingrams, a British diplomat in the Yemeni port city of Aden, articulated that "the normal state of *al-Yemen* through history has been chaos. The people and their country have been a regional entity in the Arab world, but never a unified nation."[2] The country's geographic position at the crossroads of ancient spice roads and modern Red Sea routes ensured that Yemen always landed in the midst of faraway regional and global conflicts. Since Roman times, when Yemen was referred to as Arabia Felix, the region has been invaded, occupied, and subjugated by no fewer than a dozen external powers. Between the ninth century and 1962, the succession of Yemeni imams, or religious leaders, adherent to the Zaydi branch of Shi'a Islam, was the only constant among the changing rulers.

September 1962 saw the deposition of Muhammad al-Badr, the last imam of a thousand-year-old dynasty, and the foundation of a modern Yemeni state. During the course of the ensuing civil war, which ran from 1962 to 1968, Egypt and Saudi Arabia were joined by over a dozen countries and organizations in an international civil war that served as a microcosm of global tensions. The Yemen Civil War was an international conflict at a moment when the definition of "international" was radically changing. The 1960s marked the end of an era of European colonialism and the emergence of a new postcolonial order dominated by developing world leaders and countries. Located across the border from the British Empire in Aden, within the sphere of Egyptian expansionist influence, and along one of the most important shipping lines in the world, Yemen found itself at the epicenter of world events: the final days of British colonial order in the Middle East, Cold War competition over imperial remnants, upheaval in the United Nations, and the decline of Arab nationalism.

International intervention brought both destruction and modern advancements to Yemen during the 1960s, establishing a modern political bureaucracy, roads, transportation hubs, a national army, and an increase in revenue with the expansion of existing taxation and postal networks.[3] International organizations were able to cast an unprecedented degree of influence in the absence of a dominant power, and introduced medical care and newfound water resources to areas of the country that still practiced ancient Quranic medicine and where people walked for hours to fetch water. After six years of conflict, a new Yemen emerged as a modern state, independent of three dominant forces in South Arabia: the Yemeni imamate, Egyptian President Gamal Abdel Nasser's Arab nationalism, and British Imperialism in South Arabia, all of which met their demise as a consequence of the internationalized civil war.[4]

The economic and political burdens of Egypt's intervention in Yemen contributed to the downfall of Nasser and the Arab nationalist movement in the Middle East.[5] Egypt's economy and agricultural production could scarcely support its growing *fellahin* (peasant population) and certainly could not bankroll other nationalist movements. As Egypt was reluctantly drawn further into the conflict in Yemen, Nasser sought to fund his quasi-occupation on the backs of local Yemenis and their puppet regime through taxation, printing paper currency, issuing stamps, and exploiting local resources. Nasser, who built his reputation as an anti-imperialist, ironically managed to construct his own model of non-Western colonialism.[6] In North Yemen, he created a colony devoid of the financial resources and investment often associated with European imperialism, yet rife with the requisite corruption, sense of superiority, and boundless exercise of force against both allies and enemies.

The emergence of Yemeni nationalism in the northern Yemen Arab Republic (YAR) inspired similar sentiments in Aden and contributed to Britain's complete withdrawal from South Yemen in November 1967. Violence spilled over the border as Egypt helped arm a growing anti-British insurgency, transforming South Arabia into a new front for the Arab nationalist struggle against imperialism, a battle that had won Nasser public admiration during the 1950s. This final round of the Anglo-Egyptian confrontation in Yemen during the 1960s brought about their mutual defeat and simultaneous withdrawal from South Arabia.

Looking Beyond the Arab Cold War

The Arab Cold War, first published in 1965 by political scientist Malcolm Kerr, conceptualized the Middle East in bipolar terms, divided between Arab nationalists led by Nasser and traditional monarchies led by Saudi Arabia. According to Kerr, the Yemen Civil War was a manifestation of the Arab Cold War and is described as a proxy war between Egypt and Saudi Arabia.[7] Contemporary accounts of Middle East history and politics employ this concept as an assumed paradigm for the 1960s without further substantiating Kerr's theory.[8] Multiple authors continue to describe other contemporaneous conflicts in the Middle East as the "Arab Cold War," such as the Egyptian-Iraqi rivalry in the early 1960s.[9] This term has been further recycled in a twenty-first-century context. "The New Arab Cold War" equates the Egypt-Saudi rivalry of the 1960s to any number of bipolar regional divisions, including the modern day Sunni-Shi'ite divide, tensions between Islamists and authoritarian regimes, the rift between Iraq and the Gulf Cooperation Council, and the Saudi-Iranian rivalry.[10] The term "Arab Cold War" has become so cliché as to render it nearly meaningless, especially when the origins of its first use are not taken into consideration.

The 1962 coup in Yemen culminated decades of indigenous political and social movements driven by their desire to overthrow the autocratic imamate. The Yemen Civil War was a struggle for Yemeni nationalism, nation building, and pan-Arab unity and rhetoric, rather than merely a proxy war between two regional rivals.[11] The Saudi-Egyptian rivalry, at least surrounding Yemen, was not as rigid or warlike as historic and contemporary accounts maintain. Egyptian and Saudi policies toward Yemen were not driven exclusively by the monarchy-nationalist tenets of the Arab Cold War. Instead, they were formulated by a combination of historical conflicts, geostrategic interests, religious grievances, local agency, and pure happenstance.

The prevalence of the term "Arab Cold War" is far overshadowed by the dominant paradigm categorizing half a century of conflict as a Eurocentric "Cold War."[12] The Global Cold War, or the manifestation of the Cold War in the developing world, depicts Soviets as committed to "national liberation movements" in contrast to America's promotion of authoritarian regimes.[13] The political situation in Yemen during the 1960s contrasts with the prevailing notions of Cold War ideological tendencies in the developing world. Prior to 1962, the Soviet Union invested a great deal of time and money in an alliance with Muhammad al-Badr, the heir to one of the most authoritarian thrones in the world. Several months after the September 1962 coup, the United States recognized the YAR and its nascent nationalist movement, forsaking the requests to the contrary of British allies. Ultimately both the United States and the USSR found themselves supporting the same side in a civil war, a particularly striking policy convergence, as it occurred during one of the most contentious decades of the Cold War.

The civil war in Yemen demonstrated the limits of ideologies, as Egyptian-Saudi and US-USSR geopolitics were not as dominant as previously perceived. This international history of the Yemen Civil War combines multinational archival sources in a broader understanding of events on the ground and of a local conflict's far-reaching impact. Rather than taking off the Cold War and Arab Cold War lenses entirely, however, a new set of bifocal lenses incorporates both traditional and innovative perspectives.[14] The newly enhanced vision reveals multiple layers of interactions, conflicts, and themes that are otherwise obscured by the dominance of US-USSR and Egypt-Saudi Arabia competition. Topics of modernity and nationalism in South Arabia, Canadian policy in the Middle East, regional peacekeeping funding crises, the Anglo-Egyptian rivalry, philatelic development, and Israeli-Egyptian confrontations beyond the Sinai border are brought to the forefront of the narrative.

The Yemen Civil War was both a demonstration of the flexibility of US and USSR foreign policy ideologies and of the role played by smaller powers and international organizations during the 1960s. The introduction of additional actors complicates a bipolar understanding, suggesting that the very absence of one or two dominant powers in the conflict left room for others to exercise influence on the outcome, with even individual participants having the power to change the course of history.

1

International Intrigue and the Origins of September 1962

AT 11:00 PM on September 26, 1962, a small column of T-34 tanks and armored vehicles, led by a tank named Al-Marid ("the Rebellious") entered the courtyard of Imam al-Badr's palace of Dar al-Basha'ir ("House of Good Tidings").[1] Al-Badr was sitting in a meeting with Yemeni Colonel Abdullah al-Sallal, who excused himself at the predetermined time and stepped outside.[2] At Sallal's command, the surrounding tanks fired and leveled the top floors of the palace, sending al-Badr and his guards into a panic. Simultaneously, another group of Yemeni soldiers seized the Sana'a radio station, announcing prematurely that Imam al-Badr had been killed and that Sallal and the military revolutionaries had declared the foundation of the Yemen Arab Republic (YAR).[3] In the ensuing chaos, al-Badr fled the palace and made his way north to gather tribal forces for a counter assault on Sana'a.

The attack on the imam's palace was not waged without trepidation. Yahya al-Mutawakil, a twenty-year-old from a prominent sayyid family who had recently been promoted to second lieutenant and the head of a fifteen-man artillery unit, was commissioned with assaulting the palace, and later spoke of the mood among his men the day before the coup. His unit, and the rebelling soldiers in general, saw September 26 as Judgment Day, given the historic taboo against attacking the imam. They saw before their eyes the cadavers of men who had attacked a Yemeni imam littered over centuries of Yemeni history. Believing that this was their last night in this world, Yahya and many of his fellow officers spent their entire month's salary indulging in chocolates in the evening of September 25.[4]

Riding on the shoulders of Yahya al-Mutawakil and his artillery unit were two decades of a growing Yemeni nationalist movement. Opposition to the institution of the imam and the increasing foreign investment in Yemen prior to 1962 formed the foundations of a local civil war that was overrun by foreign interests, interventions, and politics.

Whose revolution?

Throughout the civil war and in academic literature in the following decades, the extent of Egyptian involvement in the planning and hatching of the coup has been debated.[5] There were certainly strategic advantages to Egyptian intervention. By 1962, Egypt was politically isolated in the Middle East, following the breakup of the United Arab Republic with Syria and the formation of a Jordanian-Saudi alliance.[6] Of the major Arab states, only Algeria maintained friendly relations with Egypt, while Iraq, Jordan, Tunisia, Morocco, Syria, and Saudi Arabia remained united in their disdain for Nasser's Middle East machinations.[7] Khaled Mohieddin, a prominent member of the Egyptian military admitted that "The Yemen war was a response to the break with Syria . . . a sign that Egypt's Arab role was not over . . . as Syria was a blow to Egypt's Arab leadership."[8] Mohieddin long believed that "Egypt could achieve far more with propaganda than with tanks" and lamented in retrospect at having "become trapped in so humiliating a situation."[9] According to Anthony Nutting, with a quick and decisive victory in Yemen, Nasser "might have been able to recover the leadership of the Arab world for more than just a fleeting moment."[10]

From a strategic perspective, it is not difficult to understand why Nasser supported the Yemen republic. Backing Abdullah Sallal would give Nasser a chance to regain his stature in the Arab World. Furthermore, the geographic location of Yemen would place Nasser in an advantageous position to pressure the Saudis for economic aid and support anti-British nationalists in the south. Saddling the British with an internal colonial uprising would discourage their Foreign Office from considering another Suez mission and would give the Egyptians unchallenged military and political preeminence over both sides of the Red Sea.[11]

British colonial officials and Yemeni royalists, in an attempt to delegitimize the YAR as a foreign entity, predictably accused the Egyptians of orchestrating the entire event. The British Colonial Office associated the Yemeni coup with Nasser's anti-British agenda on the Arabian Peninsula.

As early as nine months prior to the outbreak of hostilities in September, British intelligence officials believed that there was increasing evidence that Nasser was planning to undermine the Yemeni government. Italian Minister Amedeo Guillet, a close confidant of the Yemeni Imam Ahmad, informed High Commissioner of Aden Charles Johnston that according to his sources, the Egyptians were proposing a "New Operation" in Sudan, Saudi Arabia, and Yemen. The plans supposedly would be coordinated by agents of the Egyptian Intelligence Service.[12] Some British historical accounts claim that the Soviet KGB and their British agent Kim Philby played a role in the coup, although these claims are mostly speculative and without sufficient evidence.[13]

In January 1962, a Yemeni assailant known only as Qunbula, or "the grenade," attacked and injured Ronald Bailey, the UK chargé d'affaires in Ta'iz. Bailey recounted the story and described it as a harbinger of things to come:

Not long before the Revolution . . . the very kind gentleman called El-qunbula or 'the Bomb' put a dagger into me. He knocked at the legation door at about 1:00 in the morning . . . I opened the door and a dagger was stuck straight into my chest. . . . My wife came out of the bedroom in her nightie and she attacked him and threw him down the stairs and he injured himself on his own dagger though he managed to escape.[14]

Italian Minister Guillet concluded that the Egyptians had been behind this attack.[15] The fact that Radio Cairo dubbed Qunbula a "National Hero" further corroborated the suspicions of Egyptian intervention.[16] Qunbula was later found and identified by "two bruises on his buttocks. The distance between the bruises was measured and found to be exactly the same as the distance between the horns of the Consulate's goat, which was assumed to have helped the fellow on his way." Qunbula was imprisoned, released under amnesty, and murdered by an unidentified assailant.[17]

An attack on the German chargé d'affaires on February 8, 1962, continued the spread of rumors that Egyptian intelligence organizations were working to undermine foreign support of Imam Ahmad in preparation for his overthrow.[18] Muhammad 'Abd al-Wahhad, Egypt's diplomat in Sana'a, was believed to have been conspiring against al-Badr and even misled the new imam into allowing additional tanks and armored vehicles to "guard" his palace from a potential enemy.[19] The increased presence of Egyptian advisers and school teachers in major cities throughout Yemen, coupled with militant verbal attacks on Imam Ahmad via Radio Cairo, were later deemed a prelude to the Egyptian participation in the 1962 coup.[20]

In a 1967 interview, Egyptian deserter Qassim al-Sherif further reinforced the British theory that Nasser had orchestrated Sallal's coup d'état in 1962 and sent Egyptian soldiers towards Yemen ahead of the revolution date:

"The soldiers left Cairo on 19th September, 1962 and boarded a ship called "The Sudan" on 21st September (4 days before the revolution started) and told they were going to Algeria. We arrived at Hodeida on 28th September (2 days after the Revolution) and disembarked. Other ships—the *Nile*, *al Wadi* and *Cleopatra*—loaded with weapons and ammunition also arrived in Hodeida on the same day. The ships *al Wadi*, the *Nile* and the *Sudan*, each carried a full Brigade of 1,000 men. The Egyptians' expeditionary force immediately headed for Sanaa [sic] with two Brigades, while other Egyptian troops remained in Hodeida and took control of Manakhah. . . . First fighting broke out on 3rd or 4th October when an agreement with the tribes was broken."[21]

Former Yemeni revolutionaries claimed, based on circumstantial evidence, that the coup was part of an Egyptian conspiracy orchestrated by Nasser's vice president Anwar Sadat and his brother-in-law, the half-Egyptian, half-Yemeni 'Abd al-Rahman al-Baydani, who was working with Yemeni revolutionaries in Sana'a. In a 2004 interview, Baydani told an elaborate tale of acting as an intermediary between Sadat, Nasser, and the Yemeni revolutionaries, using a system of codes for secure communication. He claimed to have sent a message on September 26, 1962, to signal the start of the revolution of which he had been at the center. In explaining the reasoning for his supposed central role in the Yemeni revolution, Baydani pointed to his Egyptian connections as Sallal's insurance policy against rogue revolutionary elements.[22] Baydani's story seems highly unlikely, which is unsurprising considering the description of him offered by Robert Stookey, US counsel in Ta'iz: "Baydani is an incorrigible publicity hound and prone to distort facts and some elements."[23] Seemingly having lost patience with Baydani's penchant for mischief, Nasser arranged to have him arrested during a trip to Cairo in January

1963, keeping him away from Yemeni politics for several months. Baydani was officially accused of "suspicious contacts" with British counterparts during an earlier trip to Aden.[24]

Memoirs of Egyptian officials and military personnel argue that Egypt played at most a minimal role in orchestrating events in September 1962. Instead, Egyptian troops and support arrived, purportedly, in support of a genuine national revolution in Yemen. 'Abd al-Latif al-Baghdadi, an original member of Nasser's Free Officer's movement who had broken with Nasser politically over the intervention in Yemen, argued that war in Yemen came as a surprise. Furthermore, Nasser's decision to send a small contingent of troops was made only after he received the false reports of al-Badr's death and assumed there were no other viable political leaders to support.[25]

Differing from Baghdadi's interpretation, Salah al-Din al-Hadidi, the head of Egyptian intelligence and an early critic of Nasser, claimed to have known about the revolution, but that Egypt made it their official policy not to interfere. Perhaps in an attempt to maintain the innocence of the Egyptian intelligence community, Hadidi claimed that Baydani, acting at the behest of the Egyptians, waited until September 29, 1962, to arrive in Sana'a with a small contingent of Egyptian officers with a direct wireless transmitter link to Cairo.[26]

A particular point of contention between British and Egyptian versions of the events was in regard to the Egyptian ship *Sudan* and the timing of its arrival in the Yemeni port of Hodeidah. According to British sources, four Egyptian ships, the *Nile, al-Wadi, Cleopatra,* and *Sudan* set sail four days prior to the coup.[27] Salah al-Din al-Hadidi, however, claims that the *Sudan* did not set sail prior to the coup. It was waiting in the port of Suez on the night of October 2 under "confidential orders to be equipped with everything deemed necessary by Marshal Amer." The ship set sail as soon as word was received and reached Hodeidah three days later.[28] Hadidi's version of the *Sudan* episode supports his argument that the Egyptian intelligence knew of the plans but consciously declined to intervene, allowing the Yemeni coup to take its course.

British accounts are motivated by a disdain for Nasser and his Yemeni intervention, while Egyptian accounts aim to absolve participants of commandeering a nationalist revolution. Less than three years after the beginning of the civil war in 1962, the number of Egyptian soldiers in Yemen reached an apex of 70,000. The large-scale Egyptian intervention in the civil war has clouded the debate over the origins and organizers of the September coup. The massive number of Egyptian soldiers at the height of the civil war does not presuppose Nasser's role in planning and carrying out the coup. The Yemeni 1962 coup was, in actuality, the culmination of two decades of anti-imam sentiments from a new generation of Yemeni intelligentsia that preceded the rise of Nasser and the Egyptian Free Officers in 1952. A few guns and perhaps some logistical training by Egyptian officers were relatively minor when compared with the historically Yemeni roots of September 1962.

The Famous Forty

In 1934, Yemen and the newly formed state of Saudi Arabia fought a brief war over disputed border territories claimed by both countries. After Yemen's military failure and the loss of the Jizan, Najran, and 'Asir territories, Imam Yahya undertook a project to create a national army, lessening his reliance on tribal militias in the time of war. Taking advantage of a Yemeni Treaty of Friendship with Iraq, Yahya sent students to the Military Academy in Baghdad. Abdullah al-Sallal, the first President of the YAR, along with other members of this group, would later serve as the core of the Free Yemeni Movement (FYM).[29]

Sallal recalled that his time in Baghdad had a great influence on the decision to be involved in revolution in Yemen: "We talked about Arabism and the future of the Arab struggle. And I was thinking while listening to these discussions about my country . . . which was ruled by despotism, in ignorance, backwardness and underdevelopment. Hope began to stir in my chest. . . . Why don't we spread the call for progress when we return to Yemen."[30]

According to historian J. Leigh Douglas, although the FYM can be traced functionally to a few small and scattered groups, it was in reality the embodiment of a new generation of Yemeni urban intellectuals. These were individuals "who held a privileged position in Yemeni society by virtue of their relative wealth, social position and education which allowed them the time and the opportunity to sit and debate questions arising from the foreign literature they were able to obtain."[31] These young educated Yemenis saw that "no country was more in need of enlightenment than their own."[32] The group's designation as a *haraka,* or "movement," connotes a diffuse intellectual force and spread of ideas rather than a tangible political organization.[33]

In addition to the main group of the FYM, several additional Yemeni opposition groups were formed. In 1935 Hay'at al-Nidal (the Committee of the Struggle) met in secret to discuss the need to reforms the imam's government and took the time to recite Arab poetry and literature that had been formally banned from Yemen.[34] Paul Dresch describes Hay'at al-Nidal as the first "modernist" opposition to Imam Yahya as they were a reflection of the young generation's desire to debate the succession of the next imam.[35] Under the same pretext, Fatat al-Fulayhi (the Youth of Fulayhi) met in the al-Fulayhi mosque in Sana'a to discuss concepts of Arab nationalism. Members of this group were known as the *shabbab*, or young men. They formed the core of the young generation's dissatisfaction with rule under the Imam.[36] In the late 1930s, *Majallat al-Hikma al-Yamaniyya* (The Yemeni Review of Wisdom), the only local magazine published at the time other than Yahya's *Al-Iyman* (The Faith), further spread the call for reforms.[37]

In Aden, Baghdad, and Cairo, groups of Yemeni émigrés founded dissident organizations. Among the most prominent of these was the al-Jamiyya al-Yamaniyya al-Kubra (the Grand Yemeni Association), which was formed in Cairo in January 1946 by Ahmad Nu'man and Muhammad al-Zubayri. The two leaders would continue to be prominent revolutionary intellectuals throughout the 1960s.[38] Yemeni émigrés were joined by several hundred young Yemeni men who traveled abroad for secondary and higher education between the years of 1947 and 1959. The "chain migration" from Yemen was encouraged by Yemeni family and tribal networks that had already been established in Aden and Cairo and that facilitated this study abroad.[39]

At the core of these numbers was the Famous Forty, a group of Yemeni students who would return to Yemen in 1962 to lead the republic as government officials, military officers, and cabinet ministers to the new YAR.[40] Imam Ahmad, while still a crown prince in 1947, commissioned scholarships for forty teenage Yemeni students to study abroad. Following Yahya's earlier example, Ahmad understood the necessity of educating a core group of leaders to modernize Yemen's army and domestic infrastructure. One of the students, Mohsin al-'Ayni, was considered a leader of the group, and would rise to become the YAR's first foreign minister and four-time prime minister. Several other students would gain prominence as members of the FYM and the Yemen republic, including Abdullah al-Kurshami, a future prime minister, Abdullah Juzaylan, the future deputy commander of the armed forces during the civil war, and Muhammad al-Ahnumi, a future republican revolutionary officer.[41] Hassan Makki, a future prime minister, was separated from the rest of the group and sent to pursue a doctorate in Italy.[42] According to Robert Burrowes, the Famous Forty constituted the "first-generation modernists" of Yemen.[43]

In the 1940s, leaders of the FYM resolved, albeit reluctantly, to maintain the imamate as it was, in their eyes, more legitimate than a republic. They hoped, however, to decentralize the imam's power through a modern administration, with more power given to the tribes to govern themselves.[44] In February 1948, Abdullah Ahmad al-Wazir, a rival tribal *sayyid*, or descendent of the Prophet Muhammad, of Imam Yahya's Hamid al-Din family, orchestrated the assassination of Imam Yahya with the intention of seizing power. 'Ali Nasir al-Qarda'i and members of the Bani Hushaysh tribes killed Imam Yahya but the plan to simultaneously murder Crown Prince Ahmad in Ta'iz was not carried out.[45] Jamal Jamil, the Director of Public Security and the Deputy Minister of Defense in the post-Yahya regime of al-Wazir, entered Yahya's palace with 2,800 soldiers, killing two of his remaining sons, and carrying out what was considered among the first military coups in the Middle East.[46] By the end of the month, however, the northern tribes, in alliance with the crown prince, looted the city of Sana'a and arrested the perpetrators.

The 1948 coup failed to maintain a lasting new government for a number of reasons. The assassination of Imam Yahya was undignified in the eyes of traditional Yemeni society, particularly when they recalled the elderly imam's last act: diving in front of his young grandson to protect him from a barrage of bullets. Although Jamal Jamil killed two of Yahya's sons, Crown Prince Ahmad escaped the hands of the conspirators and was able to gather tribal support in Yemen's northern highlands. According to Muhammad al-Fusayyil, a veteran of Yemen's revolutions, the 1948 coup failed because the general population did not understand the concepts of "constitutionalism." The core leadership of the coup was elitist and did not engage the local population in the way that it would in 1962.[47] The final missing element of a successful coup was international support, of which al-Wazir received none.

Those conspirators who were not executed following the coup were incarcerated for a number of years at the Hajjah prison located northwest of Sana'a. Prisoners in Hajjah, and in the Middle East in general, were rarely kept in solitary confinement but often met each other on a daily basis. A 1953 list of political prisoners in Hajjah mirrored the list of senior members of the Revolutionary Command less than a decade later as it included Abdullah al-Sallal; Hassan al-'Amri, who served as prime minister; and Qadi 'Abd al-Rahman al-Iryani, the republic's second president, among many other ministers and prominent officials.[48] Sallal later referred to the prison as "the university of Hajja[h]" because of all the political discussions amongst the educated revolutionaries.[49] Among Sallal's reading list in the prison were a number of books on the French Revolution and Nasser's *Philosophy of the Revolution*.[50]

During the 1950s, the FYM continued to operate through its international branches of the Yemeni Union, drawing on the support of the diaspora Yemeni population. For example, Muhammad Abd al-Salih al-Shurjabi founded the Yemeni Young Men's Association in Aden and later published the *Saba* newspaper, a publication focused on anti-imam rhetoric.[51] Muhammad, Ahmad Nu'man's son, and Zubayri published a popular pamphlet called *Matalib al-Sha'b* (The Demands of the People): "Poverty has driven hundreds of thousands abroad. The rulers of the country have been evil, false, and ignorant. . . . No-one is left in towns and villages. All live in fear of robbery, bloodshed and rebellion. Foreign powers hope to occupy, colonise and enslave the Yemen, seeing that the Yemenis have no government . . ."[52]

In 1952, Zubayri, who had been in exile in Pakistan following the 1948 coup, moved to Cairo where he founded a branch of the Aden-based Yemeni Union along with student members of the Famous Forty. Zubayri used members of the student group, including al-'Ayni, as couriers to Yemen to deliver his letters to local FYM supporters.[53] Nu'man joined the group in 1955 after his release from the imam's prison in Hajjah.

On April 2, 1955, Prince Abdullah, the seventh of Imam Yahya's fourteen sons, and Lieutenant-Colonel Ahmad al-Thalaya organized a coup against Ahmad along with six officers and 600 soldiers. On April 4, 1955, when the cars arrived for the imprisoned imam and his family, Ahmad marched from the entrance of the palace carrying a gun in one hand and a sword in the other. He quickly regained the support of his personal bodyguards, commandeered three military cars, and took 80,000 riyals out of the treasury. With these resources in hand, Ahmad managed to rally supporters and reestablish power. Ahmad beheaded the coup leaders along with his own brother, Abdullah.[54]

Although both the 1948 and 1955 attempted coups failed to overthrow Imam Ahmad, the foundation of the FYM would remain at the core of the 1962 coup. The most influential contingent of the Yemeni Union branches was located in Cairo, which constituted the majority of Yemenis studying abroad. Between 1958 and 1961, while Yemen was a member of the UAR along with Egypt and Syria, Nasser curtailed support for the anti-imam Yemeni Union in Cairo. Following the breakup of the union and Nasser's disenchantment with Ahmad, Nasser allowed them to prepare for the September 1962 coup from Egyptian territory. The Cairo and Aden branches of the Yemeni Union worked with dissident elements of domestic military and political circles to prepare for the nationalist coup in Yemen. The most obvious element of cooperation was through Egyptian media. On May 12, 1962, Baydani broadcasted a speech calling for social justice and economic development in Yemen entitled "Blueprint for a Yemeni Republic." In July and August, he gave a series of talks on Cairo radio entitled "The Secrets of Yemen." The popular Egyptian magazine *Ruz al Youssef* published a series of Baydani's anti-imam articles in the month before the revolution.[55] While Baydani and other Free Yemenis made use of Egyptian media, the aid was limited for the most part to broadcast and print.

For those who questioned the extent of Nasser's involvement in orchestrating the coup in Yemen, perhaps it is necessary to reconsider this line of reasoning. The FYM laid the foundations of September 1962 well before Nasser came to power, and it was primarily responsible for its own nationalist revolution. According to the Yemeni revolutionary government's *Al Thawra* newspaper, the 1962 revolution was a third stage of a process that began in 1948 and continued in 1955.[56] Others have gone even further and argued that by September 1962 the traditional Yemeni society had already begun to break down as a social system, and that even without the coup against the imamate the process of disintegration would doubtless have occurred.[57] Egyptian intervention in the Yemeni coup was only one part of a broader local and international involvement in South Arabia that began nearly two decades before the 1962 revolution.

Al-Badr and the Soviets

While the FYM was working to undermine Imam Ahmad's authority, Soviet economic delegations were cultivating a close relationship with Crown Prince al-Badr. Al-Badr was a man of great dreams living in a world of Yemeni poverty, with a lack of modern infrastructure, and international political irrelevance. Desperate to advance his own political interests and his vision for a modern Yemeni state, al-Badr was naively inclined to ally with any nation or organization that promised great things for his country.

Predictably, al-Badr became a self-declared Nasserite, having been cor-ralled by the ideological rhetoric of Arab nationalism and Nasser's person-ality and charisma. When the Soviets approached him with promises of economic development, he was an enthusiastic recipient.[58]

Even his own family members harbored negative opinions of al-Badr's royal qualities and his designation as crown prince. His cousin Abdullah ibn al-Hussein regarded al-Badr as "dissolute, incompetent, and gullible."[59] Al-Badr's character flaws were overshadowed only by his display of pomp and hubris. V. A. Galkin, a Soviet doctor practicing in Yemen in 1961, described a scene in Sana'a of a large retinue of Yemeni soldiers on horse-back followed by tanks in honor of Prince al-Badr, whom he describes as "tall, surrounded by a dense ring of bodyguards dressed in blue who did not step aside even for one minute."[60]

Soviet strategy in Yemen during the 1950s was small scale, long term, and low risk. In 1955, the USSR signed a Treaty of Friendship with Yemen. Imam Ahmad received enough small arms to encourage more hostile anti-British action, but not enough to start a large-scale war that would drag Soviets into the conflict. Moscow's logic in this agreement was that the continued use of Soviet weapons would increase Yemen's dependence on Soviet technicians, spare parts, and additional ship-ments for the foreseeable future. In supplying Yemen's army, the Soviets encouraged Ahmad to attack the British, a position that he likely would have taken regardless of Soviet support. There was little chance for a British victory and a high likelihood that Yemeni attacks would weaken the British position in Arabia.[61]

Furthermore, Moscow envisioned Yemen as a staging ground for Soviet expansion into the Arabian Peninsula at the expense of Western interests.[62] Vladimir Sakharov, a Soviet diplomat to the YAR who defected to the United States in 1971, explained that Moscow had no diplomatic relations with Saudi Arabia or any of the other oil sheikhdoms at the time. North Yemen, and South Arabia more generally, were envisioned as a Soviet entry point into both the Arabian Peninsula and the Red Sea.[63]

In 1956, as per the terms of the Yemeni-Soviet trade agreement, planned projects were launched for cement, leather, juice, and metal packaging factories; a depot for oil storage; and a new port at Hodeidah. Soviet trade delegations in January and March of that year oversaw the implementa-tion of these projects.[64] In addition, a credit of $3.5 million was granted to Yemen. In July 1956, al-Badr led a well-publicized Yemeni delegation of twelve Yemeni ministers to visit Moscow and formalize military and economic cooperation, marking the first visit of an Arab leader to the USSR.[65] Al-Badr received "permission" from his father to embark on a world tour to the People's Republic of China (PRC), the USSR, and other Eastern European countries only after he proved his worthiness by rallying tribal allies after the 1955 coup.[66]

The first Soviet mission opened in Ta'iz in January 1958 and the ambassador to the UAR was asked to serve as chargé d'affaires for Yemen as well, warranting a second Yemeni delegation to the USSR in 1959.[67] In the months following the second visit, China sent engineers and laborers to build roads in Yemen, while the Soviets sent specialists to begin work on the port in Hodeidah.[68] In 1957 there were only 50 Soviet and Chinese specialists in Yemen, while in 1959 there were 600 Chinese and several hundred Russians, and by 1960 there were over 1,100 Chinese laborers working on Yemeni roads.[69] The Hodeidah port, named Port Ahmad, required 300,000 tons of modern construction material for the port and facilities to create the capacity for storing 9,000 tons of oil. The area around the port was to be equipped with electricity, mechanized factories, cars, and Soviet technicians and specialists. In addition, the Yemenis were granted $2 million credit to facilitate these projects.[70] Soviet media covering the arrival of tractors, excavators, and other heavy machinery to the port construction site noted that: "While working together, the Soviet-Yemeni friendship widened, fraternal cooperation is growing, and they have achieved together a new brightness in the completion of Port Ahmad—a port of peace and friendship."[71]

The Soviets had given their support to Ahmad despite his "feudal" country and absolute theocracy. His personal character trait of frugality and good intentions were exemplified by the state of his palace, which the Soviets deemed "modest," and his sincere efforts to improve public health. The real target for Soviet foreign policy, however, was al-Badr, who preferred rapid Soviet-supported modernization.[72] In the spring of 1962, al-Badr organized another trade delegation to Moscow, this time to accept a Soviet agreement to use Yemen as a transit point for oil shipments to Africa.[73] Al-Badr's affinity for the Soviets was apparent during a speech that he gave in June 1962 at the opening ceremony of the Ahmad Port in Hodeidah, less than four months before the start of the Yemeni revolution. He opened with lengthy poetic verses about the triumph of the Yemen people in the construction of the port. Amidst this long oration, he dedicated several elaborate sentences of praise and gratitude to the Soviet Union for their aid in funding and constructing the port: "We and the Soviet People—Brothers, you are the most true and faithful of our friends . . . Many thanks to the Soviet government for their generous help to Yemen."[74] Several pages of text later, al-Badr returned to the subject of the Soviet-Yemeni cooperation in greater detail:

> "I am happy to be among you on behalf of his Majesty the King . . . at the opening of port Ahmad. This immortal project was until recent times a dream of many and it seems a utopia far from imple- mentation . . . and here this port that speaks for itself, here this high building ascends to the heaven, and here is mastery and mecha- nism. This great work continued day and night. Colossal efforts given by our Yemeni sons and brothers in a joint operation with our Russian friends cause us great respect and wonder. I send you a thousand welcomes and respect. Port Ahmad is the first of projects that are needed to carry out the service for the benefit of our own country . . . thank our dear friends, to share in the opening of our first grand project . . . "[75]

Al-Badr's Port Ahmad speech referred to this as merely the first of many future Yemeni-Soviet projects, a clear indication of his visions for a long-term relationship between the two countries. In a speech eulogiz- ing his father, the late Imam Ahmad on September 21, 1962, al-Badr even claimed that his father's dying wish was to "adopt socialist economic, mili- tary, and political standards for the people."[76] Khrushchev echoed al-Badr's sentiment and described Ahmad in his condolences as having "made a worthy contribution to the cause of consolidating the political and eco- nomic independence of Yemen."[77]

Armin Meyer, the former American ambassador to Iran, best described the plight of al-Badr, whom he referred to as the "red prince": "He had been impatient with [the] West, had gone to Moscow, been wined and dined, and delightedly embarked on arms procurement road with Soviets. Months later, when he was murdered by recipients [of] those arms, Soviets shed no tears but cynically and quickly recognized his successors."[78] David Holden, the Middle East correspondent for the *Guardian,* described al- Badr in equally unflattering terms: "Al-Badr was, in fact, what is usu- ally described as a wooly-minded liberal, sincerely anxious to reform his country without much idea of how to set about it or what passions reform might release. He was full of good intentions which ultimately, and appro- priately, paved the way to his downfall."[79]

Al-Badr and Nasser

Anti-Ahmad plots were not limited to the fringe members of tribal opposition or the FYM, but may have included al-Badr himself.[80] According to al-Badr's account of events, he was recruited by Nasser to overthrow the leadership of his own father and establish an Egyptian hub on the Arabian Peninsula.[81] In a long conversation with British MP and mercenary Neil McLean during the Yemen Civil War, al-Badr confessed to the extent that his naiveté, trustworthiness, and hubris almost caused him to sacrifice his father and the independence of his country for empty promises. During al-Badr's many trips to Cairo, Nasser had been cultivating him as a protégé, hoping to secure a Nasserist ally in South Arabia.

In all likelihood, some details of al-Badr's personal accounts were exaggerated and intended as a justification of his former pro-Egypt and pro-Soviet positions. The fact that these stories were told at length to British MP Neil McLean, and intended for transmission to the rest of the British mercenary network operating in Yemen, was further evidence of al-Badr's intentions to justify his past misdeeds. Nonetheless, al-Badr's "confession," as McLean termed it, clearly matches his travel itinerary and provides context for meetings that certainly took place, but for which no official transcript is available. More important than the accuracy of every utterance is the dual significance of this confession in delving into the psyche of Imam al-Badr and his British supporters. Al-Badr preferred to present himself as an unwitting victim of Nasser's scheming, while the British endeavored to convince critics of their policies that their imperfect ally had whole-heartedly repented for his previous sins of anti-British and pro-Nasser policy and was now worthy of their support.

Al-Badr and Nasser first met in 1954 during a two-month visit to Cairo after which Nasser announced a large aid program for Yemen. During a subsequent trip to Cairo in 1955, al-Badr met with the local branch of the Yemeni Union, developing a contingent of supporters among the FYM.[82] During his third visit to Cairo to sign the Jeddah Defense Pact with Egypt in 1956, al-Badr promoted thirteen Yemeni cadets from the Egyptian military school to first lieutenants. Following graduation several months later, the newly promoted cadets set out for Yemen and were greeted personally by al-Badr at the Hodeidah port. 'Abd al-Latif Dayfallah, a future Yemeni prime minister and one of the thirteen returning, remarked: "The thirteen Yemeni officers—by the way the same number as the Egyptian Free Officers—was quickly being molded into the Egyptian model. The

Egyptian Free Officers movement which overthrew the monarchy in Egypt was something we emulated."[83] Dayfallah and Abdullah Juzaylan, who was also one of the thirteen, were instrumental in forming the Yemeni Free Officer movement in 1960. The group of young officers would be at the core of the September 1962 overthrow of the imam.[84]

After Yemen officially joined the UAR in 1958, al-Badr made a trip to Damascus to meet with Tito, Nasser, Syrian President Shukri al-Quwatli, and a cohort of Egyptian officials including Ali Sabri, 'Abd al-Hakim Amer, and Anwar Sadat, among others, to discuss the planning of a revolution against his father, Imam Ahmad. Nasser explained that he envisioned turning Yemen into a base for Arab nationalism and anti-imperialism in Arabia. He promised to send al-Badr two cases of pistols, Egyptian £25,000 (approximately $79,000), and an additional £50,000 sterling after completion.

Later that year, Nasser called al-Badr on the private wireless transmitter that Nasser had installed in al-Badr's palace in Sana'a, and instructed him to meet 'Abd al-Salam 'Arif, the Iraqi Arab nationalist leader and Nasser supporter in Baghdad, for further instructions. In a series of comical episodes, Iraqi Prime Minister 'Abd al-Karim Qasim incessantly interrupted al-Badr's meetings with 'Arif, refusing to leave them alone for even five minutes, perhaps fearing that they were conniving against his own rule. 'Arif's final attempt at passing a letter to al-Badr was intercepted personally by Qasim, punctuating an unproductive visit to Baghdad.[85]

In 1959, al-Badr was again called to Alexandria, where he was spirited off on a lengthy car ride to an isolated house near the town of Borg el-Arab.[86] Al-Badr arrived in time to see off a group of men who Nasser explained were Saudi dissidents looking to overthrow King Saud. In what was no doubt a planned charade, Nasser led al-Badr to believe that he had plans for overthrowing the Saudi royal family and perhaps restoring the honor and land that the Yemenis had lost in 1934. Al-Badr and Nasser then returned to Cairo to meet with leaders of the Algerian FLN, Ferhat Abbas and Benyoucef Benkhedda, who explained the role envisioned for Algerian commandoes and saboteurs. The plot thickened when Soviet naval agents proposed sending a fleet to Hodeidah to block off any attempts at American or British intervention during the Yemeni revolution.[87]

According to Neil McLean, Nasser came to an agreement with the Algerian FLN to send volunteers to Yemen and organize terrorist activities against Aden through extensive training camps in Egypt. In the first phase of his plan, he would occupy Yemen and set up a government ready to become a member in the UAR.[88] Then, as part of the second phase, he would undermine Saudi monarchs and arm opposition parties in Aden and Saudi Arabia, thereby fomenting an Arab Socialist revolution on the Arabian Peninsula. For the third and final phase, Egypt would occupy the Persian Gulf, thus gaining access to oil money. The Russians and Chinese had purportedly approved this plan, as it suited their own idea of weakening Arab-Western ties.[89] Portions of this version were later corroborated in October 1962 by a wounded Egyptian paratrooper who had been told by Nasser that they were going to Yemen to fight the British in Aden.[90]

At the urging of al-Badr, Imam Ahmad's Italian doctors declared him incapacitated because of a morphine drug addiction.[91] From April to August in 1959, the ailing imam flew to Rome for medical treatment, leaving his son al-Badr in charge. Al-Badr invited Egyptian advisers and technicians to the country[92] and made promises of a substantial pay raise to army officials. These promises precipitated a political crisis once the Yemeni officers realized that al-Badr did not have sufficient funds in his possession to meet these promises. Ahmad flew back and ordered the withdrawal of all Egyptian advisers, fearing that they had orchestrated a coup against al-Badr in his absence. He called Ahmad Abu-Zeid, the Egyptian Ambassador to Yemen, and warned him that unless the Egyptians ceased their plotting against him, he would forcibly remove Egyptians from the country permanently, as his father Imam Yahya had done before him. To punctuate the statement, during a face-to-face meeting with Abu-Zeid, Ahmad tore up the civil air agreement recently signed between the two countries, which has allowed Egyptian airlines to fly over Yemeni airspace.[93] He also tried to secure the repayment of bribes given by al-Badr to the tribes, but managed only to further alienate his tribal alliance, which had become more amenable to the tenets of the FYM.

The remaining years of Ahmad's life were punctuated by multiple unsuccessful attempts to assassinate him. The imam had managed during the last year of his life to make enemies of both local tribes and Nasser, a combination that would be disastrous for his unprepared crownrince.[94] Making matters worse for al-Badr, following his failed attempt at reform and based on suspicious evidence of al-Badr's dealings with the Soviets, Ahmad essentially grounded his son and refused to grant him permission for international travel.

According to al-Badr's confession, as documented by McLean, in late 1961, al-Badr again spoke with Nasser, explaining that he was grounded, monitored by his father's confidants, and not at liberty to coordinate the revolution. Nasser responded that he would "take care of it" and arranged for Chinese laborers to ship unmarked boxes of guns and explosives disguised as construction equipment for one of the road building projects. In the spring of 1962, the Egyptians prematurely spread a rumor that a plot against the Yemeni Imam was impending. Nasser sent an urgent telegram to al-Badr asking him to kill his father Ahmad. In way over his head, al-Badr finally confessed the details of the intrigue to his father, who forgave him, but instructed him to leave his relationship with Egypt behind. Instead, he should invest his energies into improving Yemeni relations with Saudi Arabia and Jordan and perhaps join the Pact of Ta'if recently signed between the two kings. Several weeks prior to Imam Ahmad's death, al-Badr did, in fact, lead a Yemeni delegation to Saudi Arabia to negotiate Yemen's entry into the Ta'if Pact. Meanwhile, Ahmad expelled the Egyptian ambassador, leaving only the Egyptian diplomat Muhammad 'Abd al-Wahhad behind. On the day of his father's death, al-Badr received an ultimatum from Nasser and a personal visit from 'Abd al-Wahhad demanding an immediate union with Egypt. Before al-Badr had time to consider his options, however, his palace was shelled; the time for his naiveté had expired.[95]

According to Ali 'Abd al-Rahman Rahmy, an Egyptian officer who served in the Yemen Civil War, "In Cairo, al-Badr was attracted by Nasser, to a point where he was convinced he had Nasser's personal friendship ... and wished to emulate the Egyptian leader as much as possible."[96] Similarly, Aden High Commissioner Kennedy Trevaskis remarked in 1961 that al-Badr was seen by both British colonial officials and Zaydi tribal authorities as a protégé of Nasser.[97]

Al-Badr developed an open diplomatic policy of what he referred to as "positive neutrality", or as Rahmy explained it, "a modernist on friendly terms with Russia."[98] Prior to September 1962, it was apparent to any observer that Imam Ahmad's son, Crown Prince al-Badr, was sympathetic to both Soviet machinations and Nasser's Arab nationalist plans in Yemen. From the perspective of the Soviet Union, al-Badr was an Arabian leader who expressed enthusiasm for Soviet construction and development efforts and had functionally granted them the keys to the Red Sea through the port of Hodeidah. Given the potential and actual benefits of a closer relationship with the Yemeni royal family, it mattered little whether al-Badr was a communist, a capitalist, or an autocratic dictator. From the vantage point of the Soviet Union on the Arabian Peninsula, economic and political strategy were more significant than ideology in determining their foreign policy. Nasser viewed al-Badr as a naive and spineless ruler who could be cajoled into supporting even the most outlandish of his Arab nationalist schemes. Al-Badr himself was both hubristic and trusting, as was evident from his confession of globetrotting and plotting at the behest of Nasser's Arab nationalist vision. While one might add "fanciful story telling"to his repertoire, there is no denying that both the Soviets and the Egyptian were tempted by the malleability of al-Badr's leadership in Yemen. Their eventual support of Sallal and the YAR, however, was mainly a product of circumstances in the days following the outbreak of the Yemeni revolution in September 1962 rather than a preordained plot to overthrow both Imam Ahmad and al-Badr, as will be detailed in the next chapter.

The US Attempt to "Locate" Yemen

At the same time that the Soviets were investing economic and political capital in Crown Prince al-Badr, their US counterparts could scarcely find Yemen on a map. President Dwight Eisenhower's Middle East policy, known as the Eisenhower Doctrine, supported and united the conservative Arab regimes of Iraq, Jordan, Kuwait, Lebanon, and Saudi Arabia, placing them as an ideological counter to "Nasserism." By June 1957, Eisenhower succeeded in polarizing the Arab world and creating a "royalist axis" of conservative regimes that were willing to counter and criticize Egypt and Syria.[99] The 1958 coup in Iraq and the US military intervention in Lebanon conversely discredited US intentions in the Middle East and strengthened Nasser as the anti-imperialist. After abandoning the failed Eisenhower Doctrine in 1958, the administration decided to seek political accommodation with the Nasserist movement. Toward the end of the Eisenhower presidency, Soviet-Egyptian tensions arose over Nasser's policies targeting domestic communist parties, presenting an opening in US-Egyptian relations.[100] Upon entering office in 1961, President John F. Kennedy was therefore inclined to consider not only US obligations toward Saudi Arabia, but a continuing effort to court Nasser's friendship. Gulf oil exports and the stability of the Saudi Arabian government lent an added level of importance to every policy decision made in the region.[101] The United States had no comparable strategic interests in Yemen.[102] Prior to the civil war, relatively few Foreign Service officers and Arabic speakers had served in Yemen.[103]

The following demonstrative episode occurred during a meeting between Chester L. Cooper, the CIA liaison officer to National Security Council staff; Allen Dulles, the director of Central Intelligence; and William Putnam "Bill" Bundy, a member of the CIA and Kennedy's foreign affairs advisor, best illustrates the importance, or lack thereof, of Yemen in the eyes of US officials:

"When Bundy and I were discussing the next day's NSC meeting, we were interrupted by an unexpected visitor . . .

Dulles's secretary came in to say that the head of the Middle East Division was calling. "He says it's urgent." Allen reached for the phone. I crossed my fingers. Bill rolled his eyes.

"Yemen?" Dulles asked. "Who's he? . . . Oh. Is it really important? . . . Well, send him up." And up he came . . .

"Well?" Dulles stared at the obviously frightened analyst. "Yemen?" he asked again. "What's the Yemen? . . . A country? . . . Never heard of it. Where is it?"

The expert pointed with a shaking finger to a small speck on the edge of the Red Sea. "There, Mr. Dulles."

"I can't see it. But what's happening there that's so important?"

"It's the Imam sir."

"Imam? Never heard of that either."

"It's a person, sir. A religious person. He's the head of the government—the imam of Yemen."

Dulles's eyes were wandering. He looked first at Bundy, who shrugged. Then at me, who was trying to keep a straight face. Then at his watch. "All right. What about him?"

"He's leaving the country, sir. The first this has ever happened— the imam leaving Yemen. There may be a coup."

"Where's he going? Moscow? Beijing?"

"No, sir. He's going to Switzerland. Zurich."

"Very nice. A holiday?"

"No, Mr. Dulles. He's going to see a doctor. A specialist."

Dulles suddenly became interested. "Oh, why?"

"He has syphilis, sir."

"Well," sighed Dulles, "you've finally told me something that will interest members of the NSC. Thank you. Good night."[104]

Yemen was barely on the radar of US foreign relations in the beginning of the 1960s. In fact, even on November 14, 1962, during a meeting regarding the Yemeni Civil War, British Prime Minister Harold Macmillan recorded in his diary that President Kennedy had said, "I don't even know where [Yemen] is."[105] The ignorance of world leaders and what they do not know is as important as what they claim *to* know when it comes to decision making.

Despite the relative obscurity of Yemen in American foreign policy circles, there was an American presence in Yemen prior to the Yemeni coup, albeit through the operations of private oil companies. The extent of Soviet investment in the Yemeni port of Hodeidah and the Soviets' developing relationship with al-Badr set off a flurry of activity focused primarily on understanding Soviet plans for the Arabian Peninsula. During the 1950s, American diplomatic officials had virtually no presence in Yemen under the rule of Imam Ahmad, who prided himself on limiting the penetration of foreign powers in his country.

The first significant contacts with the Yemeni royal family were made in December 1955 by the Yemen Development Corporation (YDC), a small oil exploration company formed in cooperation with the CIA for the express purpose of infiltrating North Yemen. At the core of the YDC were veteran Texas oilman John Alston Crichton, a former US intelligence officer with the Office of Strategic Services during World War II; Walter S. Gabler, a Washington, D.C. investment banker consultant; and George Wadsworth, US ambassador to Saudi Arabia and Yemen. Gabler, who had previously negotiated American oil concessions in Egypt in 1951, raised $20 million to purchase oil and mineral exploration rights from Imam Ahmad.[106] Aside from this agreement with the YDC, a German oil company stationed in the country's Tihama coastal region was the only other foreign entity to have secured exploration rights in Yemen. In a subsequent meeting with Imam Ahmad, Ambassador Wadsworth noted that Ahmad assumed this agreement would lead to further agreements for economic cooperation between the two countries, specifically in regard to expanded road networks and privately financed factory projects. Ahmad threatened to otherwise accept the Soviet overtures of economic assistance.[107]

Crichton later explained that the company had the explicit support of the State Department, which expressed a sincere interest in American commercial activity in Yemen to counter the rising Soviet interests in Arabia. In November 1955, the YDC signed a thirty-year agreement with Imam Ahmad giving him a 50 percent stake in an oil profits.[108] In return for the concessions, Crichton recounts that Ahmad was given "$300,000 in bonus payments and a bullet-proof Cadillac so he could take the ladies of the harem for rides."[109]

Founded as a base for American intelligence gathering, the YDC unsurprisingly accomplished very little actual oil exploration. By 1957, they had run out of money and were sold off to Resource Associates, an investment group that included Wallace Whitaker, the president of the Intercontinental Hotel chain, and William Casey, who later became the director of the CIA. Hatem al-Khalide, an American-educated Lebanese geologist, remained with the company in Yemen throughout its transition and later wrote his own book based on his experience with the company, divulging the company's supposed involvement with the US intelligence community.[110]

The State Department was reluctant to relinquish control over the Yemeni oil concessions for fear that it would be open to the Soviet techni-cians already present in the country and that the United States would lose a vital intelligence source in the region. The actual prospects of finding oil were exceedingly remote and operating a mission in the inaccessible areas of eastern Yemen where oil deposits were most likely to have been found was cost prohibitive. Nonetheless, British reports agreed that the mere presence of either American or British oil companies in Yemen offered "an additional avenue for infiltration" into Imam Ahmad's closed society. Their absence would only serve to present similar opportunities to Soviet oil engineers.[111] The British Foreign Office declined to grant exploration rights to British Petroleum or Shell for fear that they would be presenting Imam Ahmad with easy hostages in the event of a border conflict with the Aden Protectorates.[112]

When other options such as Standard Oil Company of New Jersey remained reluctant to resume oil exploration in Yemen, the US State Department admitted that maintaining the oil concession "was only to preserve the US position on the Arabian Peninsula and not for commer-cial reasons.[113] After the departure of the YDC team, the State Department convinced John Mecom Oil, based in Houston, Texas, to assume responsi-bility for oil exploration in Yemen. John Mecom (see Fig. 1.1), a prominent Texas oilman, was well known for pioneering commercial oil exploration in the Middle East in countries including Libya, Jordan, and Yemen.

Perhaps at the behest of the American Overseas Investment Corporation, which was funding the expedition, Mecom Oil's exploration team moved to a location only thirty-four miles north of Hodeidah, near where the Soviets were currently constructing Port Ahmad.[114] British offi-cials were asked by the US State Department to vouch for Mecom's oil

FIGURE I.I John Mecom Sr. standing to the right of King Hussein of Jordan in 1964. (This photograph currently hangs on a Mecom Oil office wall in Houston, TX, and was shared with the author by his grandson John Mecom Jr.)

business, which they did despite harboring reservations as to the sincerity of the exploration.[115] On April 17, 1961, Imam Ahmad met with John Mecom Sr., the president of Mecom Oil, and granted his company permission to conduct explorations for oil in the region of Salifa and in other regions of Tihama.[116]

Despite John Mecom's high expectations, no oil was found, much to the ire of Imam Ahmad, who had grown jealous of Saudi oil riches.[117] In an interview on May 3, 1962, Mecom was forced to account for the delays in the progress of the search for oil in the region of Tihama: "He explained that the delay in the exploration was due to natural conditions and promises to resume drilling after the arrival in Yemen of a new more powerful drilling rig."[118] John Mecom did not have much time to fulfill or renege on these promises as the country was thrown into turmoil four months later, making oil exploration impossible for the rest of the decade. Oil was finally discovered in 1981 in the very same locations where YDC and Mecom Oil teams had explored in the 1950s and 1960s. The arrest of Muhammad Galeb Farakh, a Yemeni university student and an employee of Mecom Oil, on charges of spying for the United States, served to further suspicions of the presence of American intelligence agents amongst the oil exploration teams.[119]

Throughout his six-year flourishing relationship with Nasser and the Soviets, al-Badr formulated a policy of socialist reform and anti-British rhetoric. US onlookers were concerned that al-Badr would consciously or unconsciously open the doors of the Arabian Peninsula to Soviet penetration. Prince Hassan, al-Badr's uncle and Imam Ahmad's brother who was deemed to have been "less militantly anti-Western," was the ideal Anglo-American choice as a successor to Ahmad. According to a 1958 CIA intelligence assessment, in the event of a succession crisis al-Badr was likely to receive the military support of the Egyptians and perhaps Soviet intervention as well.[120] British observers were particularly alarmed by al-Badr's claim to the Aden Protectorate and his declared interest in expanding the anti-British border attacks that had begun under his father Imam Ahmad. Alan Lennox-Boyd, the first Viscount Boyd of Merton, briefed British Prime Minister Macmillan on joint British-American plans for a Yemeni coup to replace Imam Ahmad with his brother Hassan, thereby preventing the anti-British al-Badr from coming to power.[121] Hatem al-Khalide as well makes reference to American attempts at befriending Hassan and orchestrating the assassination of Ahmad and al-Badr.[122] Imam Ahmad had long suspected that the US government was supporting his brother Hassan as an alternative to his son.[123] Even after Imam Ahmad's death, however, the US Foreign Office refused to intervene in support of Prince Hassan lest "Yemen should veer too far in the direction of the Soviet Union."[124]

The events of September 26, 1962, were the culmination of decades of popular anti-Imam sentiment, planning, and failed coups at the hands of the Free Yemeni Movement and their affiliates. Two decades earlier what began as struggle between Yemeni traditionalists and modernists by the end of 1962 had become an armed conflict that drew the interests and involvement of major powers. Behind the scenes of national Yemeni revolutionary politics Egypt, the USSR, and the United States were making political inroads into Yemen, forming alliances with members of the royal family. With the success of the 1962 coup and the foundation of the YAR, the broader international community was pulled into Yemeni power politics by a weak revolutionary central government that sought to replace its lack of tribal legitimacy with international support. In so doing, the Americans, British, Egyptians, Saudis, and Soviets found themselves supporting sides in the conflict they would not have considered only days earlier. What followed was a series of political divisions and alliances dominated by historical irony and ad hoc diplomatic decisions. As will be discussed in the next chapter, the fateful decisions made by Abdullah al-Sallal in the first days of the coup and the ensuing international divide over the recognition of the new republic set the stage for a lengthy and costly internationalized civil war in Yemen.

2

Recognizing the New Republic

YAR PRESIDENT ABDULLAH Sallal must have realized relatively quickly that al-Badr's body was not among the rubble of his palace when midnight struck on September 26, 1962. He committed the errors of his rebel predecessors from the 1948 and 1955 coups by failing to carry out the complete regicide of the Hamid al-Din family. By this point, al-Badr was on his way north to rally tribal support for an assault on Sana'a. The YAR could last no more than a few weeks unless Sallal could elicit foreign assistance. Given al-Badr's popularity with Nasser and the Soviet Union, it seemed unlikely that Sallal would receive their recognition if either power knew that the imam was still alive.

Although he failed to kill al-Badr, Sallal's forces managed to capture the Sana'a radio station and telephone exchange, a success that was key to the survival of the fledgling republic.[1] Upon hearing the first shots fired, Yemeni revolutionary officer Hassan al-'Amri led an assault team to seize the communication stations and inform groups of co-conspirators in Ta'iz, future YAR prime minister Hamoud al-Jaifi in Hodeidah, and other urban centers that the coup had been successfully launched.[2] With the radio and telephone in Sana'a in his possession, Sallal controlled domestic and global access to information about events on the ground in Yemen. Furthermore, his supporters captured al-Wusul palace, a reception area for foreign dignitaries who had been waiting for an audience with the new Imam. In the weeks following the coup, Sallal and his revolutionary council would conceal the truth of the events on September 26 in an attempt to secure international recognition and support prior to the organization of an opposition to the republic.

Yahya al-Mutawakil, who commanded one of the artillery units surrounding the palace, explained that al-Badr was saved by the heroic efforts of one of his guards. Upon hearing the first tank shells hit the palace, the guard "managed to climb onto the roof and pour petrol onto the lead tank in the column heading towards the palace. It burst into flames in a narrow lane, and stopped the other tanks from moving forward. Everybody began to panic with the road to the palace blocked. . . . Adrenaline pumping, we threw everything we had at the palace. Within a few minutes we had gone through our entire stock of 45 shells."[3] Al-Badr took advantage of the mistakes made by the anxious artillery men and escaped the palace through the rear exit.

According to al-Badr's version of the night's events, he had been presiding over the new Council of Ministers in the royal palace compound. When he stepped out into the hallway, Hussein al-Shukeiri, the deputy to Sallal, attempted to shoot him from behind, but the rifle trigger jammed. He ended up shooting himself in the chin while al-Badr's guards were trying to arrest him. The palace's electricity was cut off, followed by an exchange of gunfire. Al-Badr claimed that the resistance lasted for twenty four hours, during which time he escaped from a hidden passageway out of the building. Al-Badr's account adds that a Yemeni officer named 'Abd al-Ghani was the principal ringleader and the main contact for the Egyptian Embassy. Conveniently for al-Badr's tale, al-Ghani was killed during the initial exchange of fire and Sallal was given command of the coup.[4]

Amedeo Guillet, the official Italian representative to Imam Ahmad's funeral a week earlier, was staying in al-Badr's palace as an honored guest while the coup was taking place. After having been awoken by the shelling of the palace, Guillet ventured into the hallway just in time to see al-Badr and several of his half-dressed followers running in his direction, frantically loading their weapons. Al-Badr led his followers through Guillet's open door, and jumped down from his balcony window, which led directly to the back of the palace grounds and the garden below. Guillet misled Sallal's guards, informing them that al-Badr was under the rubble in the front section of the palace. With a sense of irony, Guillet recalled hearing news reports of his own death in addition to the death of al-Badr in the days following the coup. Guillet, who was a dear friend and confidant of both Imams Ahmad and Yahya, recalled losing many close friends from the imam's circle on that day, and immediately took a position in opposition to Sallal and the new republic.[5]

Claude Deffarge and Gordian Troeller, two French journalists who witnessed the first stages of the Yemen Civil War, summarized Sallal's September 26, 1962 radio broadcast: "Armored units and tanks, acting on the orders of the military high command, have surrounded the royal palace and asked the tyrannical dictator to surrender. Upon his refusal, artillery opened fire on the palace. The next morning, the monarchy collapsed. The tyrant was dead, crushed under the rubble of his palace."[6]

As the newly appointed deputy prime minister of the YAR, 'Abd al-Rahman al-Baydani managed to dig a deeper political hole for the new republic with his penchant for storytelling. During a radio address on October 11, Baydani declared that Yemeni forces had defeated Hassan's supporters in the city of Sa'dah and had seized all the national territory of Yemen. He boldly stated that any aggressive action on the part of Saudi Arabia would be construed as an act of war.[7] Deffarge and Troeller pressed Baydani on the issue of confirming al-Badr's death during an interview one week after the coup. He emphatically dismissed rumors that al-Badr was still alive. Baydani explained that "Yemenites like stories. They will grow weary of them quickly."[8]

Baydani was not alone in stretching the truth of facts on the battlefield. During an October 15 rally in Sana'a, Sallal declared: "We have defeated the rotten monarchy. The revolutionary regime is recognized by 20 countries. Anyone who tries to restore the monarchy in Yemen is the enemy. Our troops entered Sa'dah. They have defeated the enemy and send King Saud and King Hussein retreating."[9] Later that month Sallal reiterated his ambition to establish a "Republic of the Arabian Peninsula," further increasing Saudi suspicions of the new republic's aims.[10]

To make matters worse, on October 19, Sana'a radio announced the death of Crown Prince Hassan, who had assumed the role of imam after the reported death of al-Badr. The YAR government ordered his property and that of fifteen other members of the royal family confiscated, in all approximately 40,000 acres.[11] As the world soon found out, aside from requisitioning royal property, none of these pronouncements was true.

Baydani and Sallal's declarations did not last beyond November 12, 1962, when there was an official media confirmation that al-Badr was alive and leading the counterrevolutionary forces in the north. French journalist Jean-Francois Chauvel conducted a public interview with al-Badr, during which al-Badr was photographed, confirming that he was alive and along the Saudi border.[12] In the interim, however, both Egyptian and Soviet sources believed that al-Badr, their once stalwart ally in South Arabia, was presumed dead. In the confusion of the coup, al-Badr's relatively pro-American Uncle Hassan declared himself imam of the exiled monarchy. Egypt and the Soviet Union were further persuaded to recognize the new

Yemeni republic, in place of their former "red prince" al-Badr, and salvage what they could from their previous foreign policy investments and visions for the region. The Saudis, on the other hand, were compelled by historical and strategic circumstances to support Hassan and the Yemeni imamate.

Within months, Egypt and the USSR found themselves supporting a weak and unproven state, while Saudi Arabia was supporting a loose coalition of stateless tribes along its border. The US intervened in a situation rife with historical and political irony, offering the Saudis and Egyptians a diplomatic solution to their mutual strategic conundrums. Negotiating the withdrawal of reluctant foreign support for the Yemen Civil War would become the dominant theme throughout the next two years of the conflict.

The Egyptian Pledge of Support

Although Nasser played a supportive role in overthrowing Imam Ahmad, the decision to support the YAR was not inevitable. Nasser and the Egyptian population did not have favorable opinions of the Yemenis, whom they generally regarded as violent and uneducated bedouins.[13] The following satirical story illustrates the skepticism that many Egyptians held toward the new Yemeni government:

> "The story went around Cairo that Sallal sent a telegram to the Egyptian government saying, now that the war is succeeding the greatest need of revolutionary Yemen is education. Please send us 500 schoolteachers. The next week came another telegram saying, the greatest need in revolutionary Yemen is still education. Please send us 20,000 schoolbooks. The third week there was another telegram saying, the greatest need in revolutionary Yemen remains education. Please send us 50,000 students at once."[14]

Between September 29 and October 4, 1962, a series of actual telegrams were exchanged between Sallal and Nasser, which included a formal request for recognition, the UAR recognition itself, subsequent offers of aid, and finally a YAR response thanking Egypt for recognition and aid.[15] Egyptian General Ali 'Abd al-Hameed was dispatched to Sana'a for an investigative mission on September 29. After seeing the alarming state of the revolutionary council and the armed forces supporting the state, Hameed asked Nasser for a *sa'aqah*, or special force battalion, which arrived on October 5 and acted as Sallal's personal bodyguard.[16]

In the midst of, or perhaps in response to this correspondence, on October 1 Muhammad Zubayri, the new YAR minister of education, and 'Abd al-Rahman al-Baydani made an important trip to Cairo to enlist Nasser's help.[17] It was clear from the urgency of this first foreign trip for the new republic and the timing of it so near to the start of the revolution that Nasser's support for Arab revolutionaries was not taken for granted. It took until October 6 for an Egyptian steamer to arrive in the Soviet-constructed port of Hodeidah with soldiers in uniform.[18] While there was certainly speculation that Egyptian soldiers had arrived in Yemen within hours of the revolution, the October 6 arrival was the first widely documented demonstration of Egyptian support and might well have been a reaction to Zubayri and Baydani's visit several days earlier.

In a cable sent to Nasser on October 3 Sallal declared that, as a representative of the Yemeni government, he was invoking the collective defense clause of the tripartite Jeddah Military Pact of 1956 made between Egypt, Saudi Arabia, and Yemen. In his response Nasser assured Sallal that "the UAR is pledged to live up to every pact it has concluded and moreover, emphasize that the UAR put the Jeddah Pact into effect at the very moment it received news of the Yemeni people's revolution."[19] Mahmoud Riad, Egyptian Ambassador to the United Nations, explained that the Egyptian intervention was a response to Saudi assistance given to royalists rather than an Egyptian invasion.[20] In justifying Egyptian intervention in Yemen, Nasser cited the collective defense clause in Article 2 of the Jeddah Pact:

> "The contracting states consider that any armed aggression upon any one of them, or upon its forces, is an aggression directed against all of them, and hence, in conformity with the legal right of individual and collective defense for their existence, they are all bound to hasten to the relief of the country aggressed upon, and to take at once all necessary measures, by contributing resources and armed forces to repel the attack, and re-establish security and peace."[21]

Using the Jeddah Pact as justification for Egyptian intervention in Yemen was both halfhearted and in contradiction to the wording of the pact. First, when Nasser issued a declaration of military support on October 3 there was no foreign presence in Yemen. In fact, the supporters of the imam had not even publicly declared their opposition until two days after Nasser's own declaration of support. Furthermore, the pact called for the collective action and agreement of all three parties, including Saudi Arabia, which Nasser did not consult prior to making his declaration.[22] Muhammad Heikal further elaborated on this justification in a November 1962 *Al Ahram* article: "We did not go to Yemen to start a war but to prevent a conflict."[23]

The identification of the legal Yemeni state that was party to the Jeddah agreement was an added layer of difficulty. In justifying Nasser's legal right to intervene in Yemen, historian Alf Ross explains that "although the military occupation of one state by another is a violation of the law of nations, the prior or simultaneous consent of the existing government legitimates the intervention." This means that Nasser referred to earlier agreements made with the imam's government, despite the fact that Egypt was supporting the imam's deposers.[24]

Nasser might have offered legal justifications for military intervention and support of the new Yemeni republic, but the truth is that Baydani and Zubayri simply showed up at the right time. Defarge and Troeller claimed that "the Yemeni operation was a miracle for Nasser," and may have temporarily saved his political isolation in the Arab world.[25] As the historian Eli Podeh explains, origins of Nasser's intervention in Yemen were found during the Iraq crisis in 1961. On June 25, 1961, 'Abd al-Karim Qasim, the prime minister of Iraq following his coup d'état against the monarchy in 1958, declared his intentions to incorporate Kuwait as part of Iraq. This announcement, six days after the British granted Kuwait independence, precipitated a regional crisis as British and Arab armies dispatched troops to protect Kuwait's sovereignty. According to Podeh, the 1961 Kuwait-Iraq Crisis was the first Arab dispute "neither initiated by Nasser nor in which he played a leading role . . . Iraq's bid for Kuwait may be construed as a bid for Arab leadership as well, though Qasim would have not necessarily admitted it." Following a military coup d'état in Syria in September 1961, the new Syrian military regime withdrew from the UAR. Ostensibly to prepare his troops for a possible intervention in Syria, Nasser prematurely withdrew Egyptian soldiers from Kuwait on December 20, 1961, leaving him politically isolated in the Arab world.[26] Although Egypt remained the only member of the UAR after 1961, Nasser continued referring to his country as the UAR until his death in 1970.

The Yemen Civil War was a foreign policy opportunity for Nasser to become relevant once again. Khaled Mohieddin, a member of the

Egyptian Free Officers Movement and a close confidant of Nasser, stated emphatically that "The Yemen war was a response to the break with Syria ... a sign that Egypt's Arab role was not over."[27] Nasser's intentions in Yemen were not limited to mere support for the YAR. Rather, he envisioned Sana'a as a base through which he could extort economic aid from the United States, Saudis, and Soviets while scoring political points against the British in Aden.[28] The relationship between Egypt and the YAR was formalized when a five-year mutual defense pact was signed by Sallal and Anwar Sadat in Sana'a on November 10, 1962, and ratified by Nasser the next day.[29] According to an *Al Thawra* article in December 1962, even Yemeni republicans began to view their own revolution as part of Nasser's grand vision.[30] This vision was codified in the April 17, 1963, Cairo Charter signed by Iraq, Syria, the UAR, and the YAR that outlined the process for forming a unified "fertile-crescent" and larger "Arab federal state."[31]

Nasser made the decision to support the YAR and Sallal under the assumption that al-Badr was dead. In later years, 'Abd al-Latif al-Baghdadi argued that Nasser would not have supported Sallal and the YAR if al-Badr had been confirmed alive at an earlier date.[32] Mahmoud Riad, Egypt's representative to the UN and Minister of Foreign Affairs during the 1960s, concurred and added that "Egypt would not have intervened in Yemen because al-Badr was an open-minded Imam and wanted to bring about a real change in Yemen."[33] While Baghdadi and Riad may have been advocating a self-serving analysis of Egypt's decision to intervene, it certainly seems likely that had Nasser received word from al-Badr during his meeting with Baydani and Zubayri, he would not have offered his support to an untested leader and to a republic that had yet to exhibit popular and tribal support. On this matter, Riad readily blamed Baydani for intentionally feeding Egyptian officials with misinformation. Anwar Sadat, Baydani's brother-in-law, particularly "relied on Baydani's analysis of the situation in Yemen." Riad explained that "because Sadat did not like to read, al-Baydani was able to control his mind."[34]

John Badeau, US ambassador to Cairo under Kennedy, provided his own interpretation of Nasser's opportunistic intervention in Yemen: "There is some reason to think that the revolutionary groups both within and outside Yemen may have expected Egyptian support if they mounted a potentially successful coup d'état. Yet the decision to enter the Yemen struggle was largely a pragmatic one, made at the time of the revolt and in the light of its particular character."[35]

Initially, Nasser sent a small contingent of forces to support the YAR with the intention to maintain only a short and limited Egyptian presence. Former Egyptian General Muhammad Fawzi, who served as minister of defense during the 1960s, explained that Egyptian support was originally conceived as "a limited action comprising political, moral and material support—by no means was it envisaged as an action that could drain our resources." Nasser sent two battalions of special forces and an aircraft squadron, a force that he described as "symbolic." However, by 1965 the Egyptian commitment to Sallal had expanded to some 70,000 troops on the ground.[36]

Saudi Arabia and Tribal Loyalties

The 1934 Treaty of Ta'if between Saudi Arabia and Yemen brought an end to the first modern conflict between the two Arabian states. The Saudi war effort in Yemen had been led by Crown Prince Saud ibn 'Abd al-Aziz, who served as king during the outbreak of the Yemen Civil War. The first article of the treaty brought hostilities to an end and created the foundation for a peaceful coexistence between the two countries. Article 18 added on to those foundations and guaranteed that both parties would not support or recognize any armed opposition to either monarchy.

Article 18: In the event of insurrection or hostilities taking place within the country of one of the high contracting parties, both of them mutually undertake:

a) To take all necessary effective measures to prevent aggressors or rebels from making use of their territories.
b) To prevent fugitives from taking refuge in their countries, and to expel them if they do enter.
c) To prevent his subjects from joining the rebels and to refrain from encouraging or supplying them.
d) To prevent assistance, supplies, arms and ammunition reaching the enemy or rebels.[37]

In 1937, Saudi Arabia, Yemen, and Iraq, the first three independent Arab states, signed a mutual defense pact further solidifying the relationship established by the 1934 Ta'if Agreement. During both the 1948 and 1955 coups in Yemen, the opposition to the Hamid al-Din family asked Saudi Arabia for aid and recognition. In both instances the Saudis refused to recognize their new regime, citing the first and eighteenth articles of the Ta'if Agreement.[38] During the 1950s, King Saud and Imam Ahmad forged a close relationship, punctuated by the 1956 Jeddah agreement and a continuously expanding trade relationship across a porous border to the north.

As part of the Ta'if agreement, Imam Yahya ceded the northern Yemeni territories of Najran, 'Asir, and Jizan to Saudi Arabia for a period of sixty years (see Fig. 2.1). Although Sunni Arabs constituted the majority of these territories, a significant minority consisted of Shi'ite Zaydi Arabs who were ethnically Yemeni and who adhered to the authority of the Zaydi Yemeni imam.[39]

According to Article 22 of the Ta'if Treaty, the tenets of the agreement would be in effect for twenty lunar years, after which either Yemen or Saudi Arabia would be able to demand arbitration in the case of a border dispute. In 1954, Imam Ahmad allowed the twenty-year limitation to lapse without introducing arbitration. Upon ascension to the throne, al-Badr had no intentions of calling for arbitration, either. It was not until the founding of the YAR that Sallal made a public declaration calling for an arbitration of the border dispute.[40] The YAR government announced its specific intentions to regain the former Yemeni province of 'Asir. The Egyptian air force began flying missions over Saudi Arabia, dropping caches of small arms for use by local "freedom fighters." Rather than use the weapons against their government, however, local Bedouins sold the arms on the market or directly to the 'Asir Government.[41]

Parker Hart, US ambassador to Saudi Arabia in 1963, retold a similar story describing Nasser's anti-Saudi intrigues:

"One of the highlights of this episode was the dropping of 108 bundles of ammunition and weaponry on the Saudi coast in February of '63 in the expectation on Cairo's side that the Bedouins and others would pick these weapons up and go after the government. They misestimated the whole situation—the Bedouins turned the weapons in to the police. And there was no party of revolutionaries to pick up the enormous quantity of weaponry, ready-to-go-weapons, put the clips right in and start firing. I saw them, inspected them myself. . . . This weapons drop deepened, of course, the feeling of distrust in Washington of Nasser's intentions."[42]

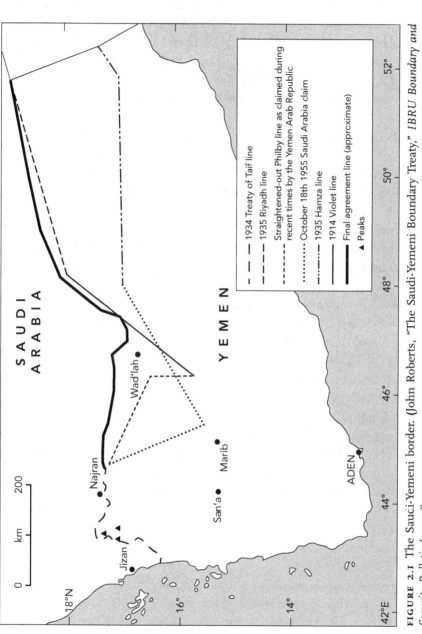

FIGURE 2.1 The Sauci-Yemeni border. (John Roberts, "The Saudi-Yemeni Boundary Treaty," *IBRU Boundary and Security Bulletin* [2000])

YAR Deputy Prime Minister Baydani, having also spread false rumors about al-Badr and Hassans' deaths, broadened his path of rhetorical destruction by declaring a state of war against Saudi Arabia. He ordered the closure of the Yemeni legation in Saudi Arabia and publicized a hostile stance toward the Saudi monarchy: "We have taken all measures to move the battle to the Saudi territory itself and to Riyadh itself, if necessary."[43] On December 27 Sallal echoed Baydani during a parade in Sana'a and declared that "the Yemeni National army would liberate the entire Arabian Peninsula."[44]

According to a US intelligence bulletin, Baydani "charged that Saudi actions in the present situation were tantamount to aggression, and stated that Yemen therefore considers itself to be in a state of war with Saudi Arabia." According to the CIA analysis, "this statement, while certain to add to the tensions in the area, appears to be primarily an attempt to justify the presence in Yemen of Egyptian forces. It follows frequent recent assertions by Cairo that the UAR, under the old "Jidda Pact" signed in 1956 by Egypt, Yemen, and Saudi Arabia, would defend Yemen against outside aggression."[45]

Yemeni Prince Hassan and Saudi Prince Faisal were sitting together in New York at a UN meeting when news of the coup arrived. Faisal immediately told Hassan, al-Badr's uncle who was appointed interim imam following the announcement of his nephew al-Badr's death, to fly straight to Saudi Arabia and appeal to King Saud for aid in defending in the imamate.[46] As members of the Hamid al-Din family began crossing the border into Saudi Arabia, King Saud and his brother Prince Faisal did not turn them away. The official Saudi position was described as an adherence to the Muslim and Arabian honorable custom of *sharaf,* offering refuge to the deposed imam's family. This response was further grounded in the historical tenets of both the Treaty of Ta'if and the Jeddah Pact. Similar to Nasser's legal approach, the Saudis claimed they were adhering to the military alliances stipulated in both agreements. Nasser and the Saudis differed only in the identity of the legitimate Yemeni state, whether it was the YAR or the imam.

From the Saudi perspective, supporting the imam had two major strategic advantages over similar support for the YAR. The northern tribes, bordering Saudi Arabia, were staunch advocates of the Yemeni imam and were not likely to support the republic. The northern highlands themselves were a particularly difficult terrain for Nasser's mechanized army and would likely serve as a partial buffer between Egyptian troops and

Saudi territory.[47] Additionally, by supporting al-Badr the Saudis avoided domestic tensions in the border regions of 'Asir, Najran, and Jizan, where there was a sizable minority of Zaydi tribesmen tracing their ethnic origins to pre-1934 Yemen. Saudi Arabia's southern border was further destabilized by an unspecified number of Yemeni refugees who crossed into the border regions as a result of the conflict.[48] Avoiding internal tribal conflict was particularly important as the ruling structure was entering a two-year succession crisis that lasted from 1962 to 1964.[49]

In January 1963, Egyptian military commanders Field-Marshal 'Abd al-Hakim Amer and General Ali Amer made an extended visit to Sana'a, where they discovered a failing republican military campaign. Royalist forces were moving southward, threatening republican positions. Nasser responded with a bombing campaign on the Saudi border in spring 1963, in an attempt to destabilize royalist bases in Jizan, Khamis Mushayt, and Abha. One of the bombs was reportedly dropped on a hospital in Abha, killing thirty-six patients. Egyptian targeting of Saudi border regions caused further unease and alarm among the members of the Saudi royal family.[50]

The Egyptian bombing campaign was accompanied by anti-Saudi propaganda. During the Aswan High Dam Celebrations in January 1963, Nasser shared embellished accusations, rivaling only Baydani's fanciful tales. According to Nasser, Saudis and royalists were being armed by Pakistan who was providing planes and daily shipments of 500 guns to the Ta'if airport. This trope epitomized the first months of Nasser's anti-Saudi propaganda, a campaign of rhetoric that would continue throughout the war.[51]

The Formation of an Opposition

During the shelling of his palace, al-Badr slipped out of Sana'a to the nearby village of Hamdan. Following the precedence of his forefathers and his own actions after the 1948 and 1955 coups, al-Badr fled north to rally the tribal militias. In 1948, his father Ahmad had fled to the northern village of Hajjah, where he rallied the tribal armies for a successful assault on Sana'a within three weeks of the coup.[52] In 1962, however, Abdullah Hussein al-Ahmar and Sinan Abu Luhum, principal sheikhs of the powerful Hashid and Bakil Federations, supported the republic despite their traditional allegiance with the imamate. Imam Ahmad had overseen the execution of their close family members, garnering a great deal of recent animosity between them and the Hamid al-Din family.[53] Al-Badr's northward journey, therefore, took a somewhat different path as he was pursued by bands of republican supporters for the entire journey, an additional sign that Sallal and Baydani must have known he was not killed in the shelling of his palace.

When word arrived that al-Badr had been killed, Mujahid Abu Shawareb, a prominent tribal leader from the town of Kharif, gathered 500 men and headed for Sana'a. His tale gives additional details as to al-Badr's northward journey: "Halfway there a messenger met us to report that it seemed al-Badr had not died after all. He said the Imam had managed to flee the palace dressed as a woman and was making his way north to Saudi Arabia. We turned northeast in order to find him and prevent him from rallying support to his cause. Marching from village to village, they told us in one place that al-Badr and his supporters had passed through only five hours earlier. We tracked him for two weeks, without success, and he finally made it to Saudi Arabia."[54]

However, according to the earliest known account, al-Badr did not make it to Saudi Arabia until October 8. In his absence, opposition to the YAR was declared. On October 6, the same day that the first official Egyptian troops arrived in Yemen, a royalist radio station operated by Hassan and his supporters on Saudi territory broadcast an announcement that members of the royal family had fled to Saudi Arabia and were organizing an armed opposition to Sallal and the YAR.[55]

In forming the opposition, al-Badr convinced many of the northern Zaydi tribes to declare their support for his anti-Egyptian efforts. He declared that "Yemen would be a graveyard for the Egyptians just as it was a graveyard for the Turkish."[56] Muhammad Sa'id al-Attar, a French-educated Yemeni who founded the Yemen Bank for Reconstruction and Development and served as the YAR Minister of Economics, explained the historical and political reasoning behind the formation of a northern opposition to the republic. Historically, given the difficulty of the terrain, the northern highlands could not be conquered by a foreign army, whether Egyptian, Turkish, or Saudi. Although the core of the allegiance to al-Badr was religious, as the number of Egyptian soldiers increased, the northern tribes fought for independence against what they perceived as a foreign invader.[57]

Al-Badr's supporters were dubbed "royalists," a designation with which al-Badr did not agree, as he made clear in a later interview: "Royalists . . . I do not like that word, because it causes false associations. We fight for our beliefs, for our tradition, for our home—not for the crown, but for a new world order. Who can lead our people and our suffering people from [Nasser's] war to freedom? Have a look at us, my brothers and I, we live with our people."[58] There is no consensus as to the origins of the term "royalists," although perhaps it was conceived by the British, who had developed their own alliance with the "feudal" sheikhs and sultans in South Arabia.[59] The term "royalist" may have been an attempt by British media to link US support for Saudi monarchs (royalists) to their counterparts in Yemen. Imam al-Badr's supporters referred to themselves, instead, as "loyalists" and their territory as "Free Yemen."

Once al-Badr was confirmed alive, Sallal's claim of legitimacy in the absence of a significant royalist opposition was no longer viable. According to a report from the Soviet embassy in Yemen, the Yemeni revolution itself was in danger of being lost entirely and Sallal was trying desperately to go on the defensive: "Al-Sallal said that the goal of Saud, Hassan, and British imperialists was the restoration of the reactionary regime in Yemen.... The Prime Minister had previously refuted the rumors that Prince Hassan was in Sa'dah and al-Badr of the Hamid al Din family was in Hajjah. He said that the Yemeni revolution had already destroyed the reactionary Hamid al Din dynasty."[60]

The initial momentum of al-Badr's opposition and the relative weakness of Sallal's military effort and political support drew an increasing number of Egyptian soldiers and resources into the conflict. Despite Nasser's commitment of troops and resources, he was confounded by Yemeni tribal politics. In the first weeks and months of the civil war, tribal sheikhs were continuously switching allegiances, accepting bribes from either the royalist or the republican camps, and forming their own inter-tribal truces. Although fighting was at times intensified and casualties were exacerbated by the presence of the Egyptian army, certain necessities of life trumped all other political considerations. For example, the Hajjah region village of al-Ahnum's *qat* (a wildly popular narcotic leaf) trade continued unabated throughout the war, "under agreements guaranteed in common by men who on other grounds were at daggers drawn."[61] Much to Nasser's chagrin, the success of the YAR began to encapsulate the success of Nasser and his vision of Arab nationalism. Having declared his public support for the YAR, Nasser could not forsake his powerless ally, even after al-Badr was discovered alive.

Deffarge and Troeller argue that Sallal was a last-minute addition to the revolutionary council that was led primarily by young officers without comparable revolutionary qualifications and history. "His personality is not the decisive element of this revolution, for it was not intended that he be made the leader of the group ... he was only a last minute choice." Furthermore, with the Republic only a week old, Sallal had been dubbed by foreign media with nicknames such as the "dictator," "Moscow's man," or "Nasser's agent."[62] To be fair, Deffarge and Troeller held similarly condescending opinions of al-Badr: "Everyone knows that al-Badr is an idiot.... . Every time his father turned his back, he was going to the Egyptians. Was it not he who appointed Sallal the commander in chief of the Yemeni army?"[63] In the following years of conflict, the two parties of the Yemen Civil War came to be dominated by ineffectual and unpopular leaders, who in turn were dominated and overshadowed by the interests of regional and international powers.

Soviet Relations with the YAR

Prior to 1962, the Soviets had invested a great deal of political, economic, and industrial capital into cultivating a relationship with Yemen. Soviet presence in South Arabia was an important element in the USSR's grand strategy for the Red Sea and the Middle East in general. In an attempt to explain the Soviet vision for South Arabia the French journal *Perspective* printed a prophetic observation of Soviet efforts in Yemen and its place within their overall Middle East strategy: "Since the North African phase of Soviet expansion was completed, now begins the new stage which will lie in the complete subjugation of the entire Arabian Peninsula and especially out towards the Indian Ocean and the Persian Gulf. This is a much more reasonable goal than Cuba."[64]

The historian P.J. Vatikiotis described Soviet relations with Egypt and by extension in Yemen in similar terms: "The Soviets throughout the sixties considered Egypt, whether under Nasser or his successor, the essential center of their hoped-for power position in the Mediterranean. This, in turn, is linked to their emerging global naval strategy that encompasses the Indian Ocean. It gives them not only a deterrent against the US Sixth Fleet, but affords them also several potential political advantages, apart from the Middle East, in southern and western Europe and Africa."[65]

As noted in the previous chapter, Crown Prince al-Badr was open to greater Soviet penetration and was an advocate of socialist reforms in Yemen. While the French journal *Perspective* might not have compared al-Badr (or Sallal for that matter) with Fidel Castro in the same fashion that Yemen was equated with Cuba, it is likely that the USSR would have maintained its relationship and support of al-Badr, had they known he was still alive. For the entire month of October, both *Izvestia* and *Pravda* referred to al-Badr's death in dozens of articles and did not even entertain the notion that he might still be alive. With the pronouncement of al-Badr's death, the Soviets rushed to be the first (arguably the second, behind Egypt, although this was a point of mutual contention) country to recognize the new republic. While the continued cultivation of a relationship with the Yemeni people could potentially secure Soviet investment in the port of Hodeidah, the speed and degree of the Soviet reversal in policy from supporting al-Badr to vilifying the imamate was remarkable.

During 1961 and 1962 articles published in *Izvestia* and *Pravda* made every effort to praise Imam Ahmad and the blossoming relationship between the USSR and Yemen. Published letters between Khrushchev and Ahmad praised Soviet-Yemeni friendship, port Ahmad, and Ahmad's progress in fighting colonialism and advancing reforms.[66] On October 10, 1962, however, *Izvestia* began portraying Prince Hassan, the Hamid al-Din family, and the royalists as tools of the Saudis and Western oil companies like ARAMCO.[67] Indeed from the ease with which Soviets switched allegiances, it appears that their objectives in Yemen were opportunistic and pragmatic rather than guided by an overarching national ideology.[68]

Soviet Premier Khrushchev's initial telegram recognized the YAR on October 1, 1962, and offered moral and political support, but was reluctant to include a military commitment. The Soviets, who understood the important problems that could arise from the local war and the difficulties of achieving peace and complete disarmament, preferred to avoid a military commitment, investing instead in non-military areas of Yemeni society. According to a pre-revolutionary study, most Yemenis lived on less than $100 a year, 95 percent of the populace was illiterate, and there were serious deficiencies in the national health care.[69] This concise description of severe problems in Yemeni society would become the Soviet "to-do list" in order to garner the loyalty and appreciation of the local populace and the ruling class.

Beginning in early 1961, teams of Soviet engineers and technicians began to open schools, factories, hospitals, and other vital infrastructure, garnering a great deal of fanfare at each stage. In doing so, the Soviets treated Yemen as another of the politically neutral countries of Africa and Asia that participated in the 1955 Bandung Conference, focusing their aid on social welfare, an area that would "win the hearts and minds" of the general populace. The USSR staffed a large contingent of technological advisors and providing political, military, and economic aid while funding these national projects. When Sallal assumed the presidency of the YAR, he continuously maintained an outwardly positive view of the USSR in rhetoric as well as action.[70] During his first trip to Cairo, Sallal spoke highly of peaceful Soviet initiatives and expressed support for Khrushchev's message.

According to a CIA intelligence report, by October 19, 1962, the Soviets had in turn placed their full support behind the YAR, calling the coup a "national liberation movement" rather than a "people's revolution," as it had originally been termed. A Soviet official described the Yemeni people to Sallal as "struggling selflessly for the freedom and independence of their motherland." This semantic upgrade in Yemen's status was a response to the USSR-YAR "technical-aid agreement" signed just two days earlier, and announced publicly by Sana'a radio.[71] From the Soviet perspective, it seemed that Sallal might be able to, at least temporarily, fill al-Badr's role in Yemen as an ally of the USSR.

On November 8, 1962, a Yemeni delegation traveled to Moscow and returned without an official Soviet military commitment to the YAR as the USSR. The Soviets were initially reluctant to issue an open aid package to the YAR, preferring instead to "extend its long-range reconnaissance capacity." In as such, the Soviets invested in the construction of an airport near Sana'a large enough to handle the Egyptian TU-16 bombers.[72] At the time there did not seem to be a need for a major airport in Sana'a. The Yemeni air force had been inaugurated less than one year before and there were only a minimal number of nonmilitary flights. The Soviets had conceived the new Yemeni airport as a significant strategic asset in South Arabia, rather than simply a service to Yemeni civilian aviation.[73] Without an official guarantee from the USSR, Sallal signed a defense pact with UAR on November 10. "The USSR could rest assured that they would have relatively unimpeded access to Hodeidah and Sana'a airport as long as the UAR was governing Yemen, and the UAR certainly remained the dominant force in that country."[74]

During the reign of Imam Ahmad, the USSR provided Yemen with economic and military aid, as detailed in the previous chapter. Under Sallal, however, any direct Soviet military presence in Yemen receded to an advisory role after the Egyptian army intervened. Although weaponry continued to be supplied from Soviet sources, Egypt acted as a middle-man supplier and trainer of Yemeni troops. There remained, however, a core group of 75 Soviet military advisors designated to train a modern

Yemeni army and modern technological specialists as well as thirty-two Soviet advisors for economic development.[75] In March 1963, nine Soviet specialists in hydrology and agricultural specialists along with twenty doctors (fourteen to Hodeidah, four to Sana'a, and two to Ta'iz—mostly used for Soviet personnel) arrived in Hodeidah. In addition, the USSR sent specialists and teachers in higher education. A total credit of $60 million was granted to Yemen, for which the Soviets agreed to delay repayment for five years. In 1963 there were $2.3 million worth of Soviet exports to Yemen (such as technology, sugar, cement, soap, matches, oil products, and machines) and $1.5 million of Yemeni export to the USSR (including coffee and cotton).[76] In essence, the post-coup saw a significant expansion of Soviet-Yemeni relations, even without an official commitment from Khrushchev.

Komer's War

The United States was a latecomer to the emerging international arena in Yemen. President Kennedy and his Foreign Office had previously given little thought to this remote, impoverished region and were perfectly content to allow a motley group of oilmen and intelligence agents to represent US interests in Yemen. Ironically, it was this lack of interest in Yemen that allowed US decision makers to forestall recognition of the regime as they weighed both local factors and the interests of British and Saudi allies. By the time the United States was ready to recognize the regime, al-Badr was discovered alive, further complicating the Yemeni situation. The uncommitted position of the United States in Yemen allowed its Foreign Office to act as a mediator between Egyptian, Saudi, and Yemeni interests during the first months of the conflict. Peter Somerville-Large, an Irish journalist reporting from Yemen during the civil war, observed that, despite the official recognition of the YAR, Americans were equally as popular with royalists because the tanks and military hardware used by Egyptians were all Russian, not American. He explained that "because the Americans did not openly help the republicans it was assumed among the [r]oyalists that they secretly supported the Imam, and had only recognized the new regime for devious diplomatic motives."[77]

During the Yemen Civil War, decision making on the Yemeni situation was moved from the State Department to the White House. Concern regarding the possible repercussions of the Yemen Civil War for US oil interests in Saudi Arabia gave this local conflict an inflated sense of importance for the Kennedy administration. Kennedy soon became so heavily engaged in forming Middle East policy that senior staff member of the National Security Council Robert W. Komer claimed that Kennedy was functioning as his own Secretary of State.[78]

Robert Komer collected all the information disseminated from the Saudi and Egyptian Foreign Offices and local intelligence relating to the Yemeni crisis. In this role, he formulated US policy with the full approval of Kennedy and sent the president summaries detailing events in Yemen several times a week. As nearly every piece of material that came in or out of the White House relating to Yemen had Komer's "RWK" signature affixed to it, members of the Kennedy administration often referred to the Yemen Civil War as "Komer's War." Phillips Talbot, the assistant secretary of state for Near Eastern and South Asian affairs, gave his assessment of Komer and the extent of his influence: "Komer is a tremendously vigorous man. . . . He was the key man over in the White House on Middle East things. Mac Bundy, I believe, worked basically from Komer's analyses and recommendations, and these went to the President in that direction."[79] In his biography of Komer, Frank Leith Jones explained that Komer was nicknamed "Blowtorch Bob" because his "resolute determination to have the direction of his superiors carried out was akin to having a blowtorch aimed at the seat of one's pants."[80]

Komer himself admitted, however, that he was appointed to this position by sheer coincidence of being in the room when the conflict first broke out, having had no previous exposure or knowledge of Yemen.[81] The fact that Komer was not an expert on Yemen specifically, but was rather "more a coordinator with a special eye for Kennedy," underscores the broader scope of the Yemen Civil War in the eyes of American policy makers in the 1960s.[82] Komer's lack of experience regarding Yemen was by no means the exception in the Kennedy administration. Kennedy was very clear from the beginning of the civil war that from the US perspective, Yemen itself was not particularly significant. Komer, in very illustrative terms, summed up how Kennedy felt about Yemen, that is, once he was able to locate it on the map: "If this place was on the moon or the center of Africa and the Russians or Egyptians or other people were not involved, we couldn't care less what went on in Yemen. It could be a head-hunter fight in the depths of New Guinea. As long as it didn't impinge on our interests, no problem."[83]

Although prominent American politicians did not give thought to Yemen prior to the revolution, Soviet machinations in Hodeidah were clearly noticed. US policy throughout the Yemen Civil War consisted of a single word: containment. The only question was how best to prevent an escalation of the civil war that could potentially engulf the entire region. Official US aims in Yemen were outlined by Phillips Talbot:

1. To keep the Yemeni conflict and its repercussions from spreading and endangering vital US and Western interests in the Middle East, outside of Yemen, particularly in Saudi Arabia and Jordan.
2. To prevent the development by the Soviet bloc of a predominant position in Yemen.
3. To encourage the prospects for a relatively stable and independent Yemen.[84]

Imams Ahmad and al-Badr did not have many fans in the Kennedy administration. The CIA had become concerned by the increasing number of arms shipments and the amount of economic aid arriving in Yemeni ports from Soviet and Communist Chinese sources during the 1950s.[85] Sallal's coup, on the other hand, seemed to have genuine intentions to modernize Yemen. Robert Stookey, the US chargés d'affaires ad interim to Yemen in 1962, was of the firm belief that the Yemeni imamate was "ignorant, bigoted, venal, and avaricious."[86] In a telegram to the secretary of state's office in October 1962, Stookey justified US support for the revolutionaries: "If ever a country needed revolution, that country is Yemen. Its new regime's stated policies we cannot possibly quarrel with. We have opportunity here [to] align ourselves only reluctantly with forces of justice, reform and progress. Let us seize it."[87]

In isolation, the new regime would have been hailed as a great achievement. The Egyptian support of the revolution, however, complicated the matter. King Saud of Saudi Arabia justifiably believed that Nasser's presence in the Persian Gulf presented a direct threat to the Saudi seat of power. On October 23, 1962, Cairo Radio warned Crown Prince Faisal: "the sons of all the Arabian Peninsula lie in wait for you and your family . . . Faisal, nothing but death awaits you".[88] Additionally, Saud voiced fears that the success of Nasser's revolution might inspire a similar Nasserist coup in Saudi Arabia, possibly orchestrated by the large Yemeni workforce in Saudi Arabia; a potential fifth column. King Hussein of Jordan was equally concerned with the stability of his own regime and feared a Nasser-supported Palestinian revolution in his own country.[89] Although the Saudi and Jordanian concerns may have been somewhat exaggerated, they managed to garner the attention of US policy makers in the Middle East.

The Soviet recognition of the YAR, followed in turn by the rest of the Eastern bloc, brought the question of recognizing the YAR to the forefront of US foreign policy.[90] The potential repercussions of US recognition were summarized by McGeorge Bundy, Kennedy's National Security Advisor: "Our immediate concern is less with what transpires inside Yemen than the prospect that our failure to recognize the new regime will lead to [an] escalation of the conflict endangering the stability of the whole Arabian Peninsula. Likewise, failure to recognize will result in termination of an American presence in Yemen and is likely to lead to a considerable increase in Soviet influence."[91]

Saudi Deputy Foreign Minister Sayyid Umar al-Saqqaf expressed his personal concern for the repercussions of Saudi support for al-Badr to Parker Hart on October 25, 1962. The deposed imam lacked both the popular and military support to bring the civil war to an end, and would only attract a more protracted Egyptian attack against the royalists and their Saudi backers.[92] It was unlikely that Saudi Arabia's poorly trained 15,000 troops would stand a chance against Nasser's 13,000 troops, who had arrived in Yemen within one month of the coup.[93] Under these circumstances, it appeared that recognition of the YAR and a diplomatic agreement for the withdrawal of Saudi and Egyptian forces from Yemen would be instrumental in securing the Saudi regime. Saudi Arabia needed an exit strategy that would allow King Saud and his brother Faisal to withdraw from the conflict without giving the perception of being defeated by Nasser. As John Badeau recounted in his memoirs, lacking another realistic option, the Kennedy administration resigned to supporting Nasser after slightly ameliorating their perception of his communist leanings: "Nasser was not an ideologue. He was a highly pragmatic man indeed; he took some things from the communist system and some things from the capitalist. At that time it was quite strongly represented in the Department that this was kind of a vaccination, if you will, against a real onslaught of a worse disease."[94]

It was determined that Nasser's support for the revolutionary state would obviate Sallal's need to turn to the Soviets.[95] Mahmoud Riad, a prominent Egyptian diplomat and ambassador to the UN from 1962 to 1964, noted that "during the Yemen Crisis, the Russians did not offer any opinions, and did not bargain with us [Egypt]. Their main goal was to find a foothold in Yemen."[96] Riad's perspective, while certainly tinged with elements of self-interest, highlighted a disconnect between the Egyptian offensive and Soviet policy. Although continuing to give Nasser a blank check in their support of the YAR, the Soviets did not seek to control the Egyptian policy. Rather, they were waiting for the opportunity, presumably during the political instability which would follow Nasser's withdrawal from Yemen, to assume a dominant role in the YAR. Nasser "jealously guarded his clients, thereby preventing the Soviet Union from gaining any credit for their efforts" and shielding the Yemen Civil War from Soviet dominance.[97]

Nasser was accepted by the United States as the lesser of two evils and even as a potential obstacle to a Soviet Republic of North Yemen. While Foreign Offices and media outlets attempted to decipher the Egyptian rationale in Yemen, the French *La Gazette* made the observation less than two weeks after the start of the revolution that "[i]t may be that Gamal Abdel Nasser is fighting a battle at once in the vast distances of Saudi Arabia, England, and Russia."[98] While certainly not intending to fight a three-front battle, Nasser's very presence in Yemen essentially discouraged Saudi Arabia, the British in Aden, and the Soviet Union from expanding their influence over South Arabia.

Following the Cuban Missile Crisis in October 1962, neither Kennedy nor the US public had much patience for further brinksmanship in the Middle East. Both Nasser and Sallal managed to placate US foreign policy concerns by publicly announcing their intentions to adhere to the US vision for the resolution of the conflict. On December 17, 1962, Sallal announced that the YAR intended to honor its international obligations and live in peace with its neighbors. The following day Nasser made a pledge to withdraw Egyptian troops from Yemen gradually, but only once Saudi Arabia and Jordan withdrew their own support for royalists.[99]

The December 19, 1962, US recognition of the YAR, unsurprisingly, did not stabilize the conflict. Although agreeing in theory to disengage Egyptian troops from Yemen in exchange for US recognition of the new regime, in January 1963, Nasser claimed that a "token force" of 30,000 troops was necessary to ensure the stability of the new regime.[100] Jordanian officials were upset with US recognition and threatened to "reconsider the utility of dealing with Communist bloc nations ... Jordan might accept Soviet aid missions as a prelude to the establishment of formal diplomatic relations with the USSR." While this scenario was unlikely, the Jordanians believed it was essential to increase their "nuisance value" to get the United States to pay attention to their views.[101]

Komer optimistically suggested a continuation of the current course of diplomacy: "I conclude that a bird in the hand is worth two in the bush. Advantages of trying to keep war from flaring up again in first place outweigh those of getting out from under a faltering disengagement scheme. More preventative diplomacy just looks better than risking another blow-up."[102]

Reports of Egyptian and YAR incursions into Saudi territory and the British-administered Aden Protectorate continued to arrive at the State Department throughout the first few months of 1963, threatening the spread of conflict into neighboring territories.[103] Nasser began contingency military preparations, which included placing naval units, including submarines, motor torpedo boats, and destroyers, in an advanced state of readiness. The UAR was also continuously moving military equipment and personnel to Yemen in preparation for air and naval attacks on towns along the Saudi Red Sea Cost and the Saudi-Yemeni border. The Egyptian airfield Rad Banas, less than 300 miles across the Red Sea from Jeddah, was modified to accommodate MIGs and IL-28s. The Saudis also prepared for a military confrontation by ordering troops to Red Sea coast positions, improving anti-aircraft defenses for towns and airfields and shifting nationalguard positions to southern border area.[104]

Internally, the YAR was in serious financial trouble, needing significant aid "until it can get house in order and begin to satisfy revolutionary promises."[105] The "house," however, was in complete disarray. A military stalemate necessitated additional Egyptian reinforcements, as Sallal's regime was not able to subdue the royalist force in the north and northeast tribal areas. The rising frequency of Egyptian air raids on royalist strongholds continued to foster virulent anti-Nasser sentiments among the northern tribes. It seemed reasonable to conclude that Sallal's regime could not survive without continual Egyptian military intervention. According to a CIA estimate, with a premature UAR exit the Soviets were poised to gain unrestricted access to Yemeni airfields, and so set up a staging ground for communist penetration in Africa.[106] The instability of Sallal's regime cast further doubt on the ability of Yemenis to govern Yemen, leading some members of the Kennedy administration to advocate a permanent Saudi presence in Yemen as an obstacle to Soviet expansion.[107]

Despite the bleak CIA assessment, Komer, representative of the minority opinion in the administration by that point, maintained a level of tepid optimism, declaring: "I'm convinced that if we can keep the Saudis turned off and the Egyptians from being stupid, we have a controllable situation which can be gradually damped down." US policy objectives were subsequently restated as: "preventing Yemen war from spreading into full-fledged intra-Arab conflict (with risk of overt US/USSR involvement), and protecting our Saudi clients from their own folly while still not compromising our overall UAR policy."[108]

The US mission to the UN at first suggested dispatching to Yemen the Italian diplomat Pier Pasquale Spinelli, former UN representative to the Middle East in 1958. UN Secretary General U Thant rejected the request because he did not want to seem too closely aligned with US interests. U Thant's developing-world proclivity and predilection for nations such as the UAR and YAR would continue to serve as an impediment to UN operations during the Yemeni conflict. He feared being accused by Soviets of supporting his predecessor's (Dag Hammarskjöld's) pro-American policy. In as such, U Thant insisted that the entire Security Council (the United States and USSR included) agree to any UN action taken in Yemen. Following the UN refusal to act, the United States then sent its own mission led by James Terry Duce, the vice president of ARAMCO and a personal friend of Saudi Crown Prince Faisal. Faisal refused to agree to a withdrawal of support for royalists, citing worries over Egyptian meddling.[109]

From February through April of 1963, Ellsworth Bunker, the seasoned US mediator and Kennedy's special emissary, dedicated an intense six weeks of "shuttle diplomacy" between Egypt, Saudi Arabia, and New York to negotiate a disengagement settlement.[110] Diplomacy during this conflict was no easy task given the diverging Egyptian, Saudi, and Yemeni national policy goals. Nasser wanted the Saudis to cease their aid to the royalists immediately and promised a gradual withdrawal at some time thereafter. Nasser's logic in forcing the Saudis to withdraw support first was to finish off pockets of royalist resistance prior to his own withdrawal, thereby securing the YAR.[111] The Saudis demanded Nasser's simultaneous withdrawal specifically to avoid this scenario.

Sallal, who had been consulted by UN representative Ralph Bunche, wished for the sky by asking for a complete Saudi withdrawal, the exile of the entire Hamid al-Din family from the Peninsula, and firm assurance that Britain and Saudi Arabia would withdraw all "rebel" infiltrators from Yemen and recognize the YAR, all which essentially amounted to winning the Yemen Civil War on his behalf. In return, Sallal would not intervene in Saudi Arabia or Aden, actions that his fledgling republican army was hardly in a condition to carry out in any event.[112] Further negotiations avoided consulting with the YAR as a reaction to both Sallal's audacious requests and the Saudi protests over the unwillingness of mediators to speak with the Imam al-Badr and his royalist opposition. To make matters worse, Bunche's meetings in Yemen had gotten off to a bad start in February 1963 when a "qat-chewing crowd of Yemenis" began to rock his car in protest upon his entry to the city of Ta'iz.[113]

Kennedy's updated policy, outlined by National Security Memorandum 227 issued on February 27, 1963, called for a special presidential emissary to the region and the dispatch of a US Air Force squadron to Saudi Arabia.[114] In an effort to placate Saudi security fears, Kennedy commissioned Operation Hard Surface, a squadron of eight US planes stationed in Dharan, a major oil administrative center in Saudi Arabia's Eastern Province and the headquarters for ARAMCO.[115] Komer explained that the presence of the US squadron, although under strict orders not to be used in combat, was meant to send a clear message to Nasser that the United States would not tolerate continued incursions into Saudi territory.[116] Nonetheless, Kennedy told Komer, "I don't want the squadron out there until after we are 99 percent certain it won't have to be used."[117] Secretary of State Dean Rusk concurred when he told Bunker before he left to the Yemen mission: "Be sure to tell Faisal that we will not be dragged into his little war in the Yemen."[118]

In the beginning of April 1963, during a meeting in Nasser's home in Manshiyat al-Bakri, Badeau and Bunker secured Nasser's commitment to gradually disengage the Egyptian military from Yemen with a simultaneous Saudi cessation of aid to the royalists, although he insisted on leaving some remaining Egyptian "military advisors."[119] Bunker conferred the success of his diplomatic mission to U Thant and stressed the importance of an immediate UN mission to oversee the disengagement process.[120] Having secured Nasser's commitment to the interim withdrawal agreement, Bunker flew to Riyadh where he received Faisal's approval on an eight-point proposal. This included the termination of support and territorial refuge to royalist troops in exchange for the UAR's simultaneous withdrawal of an undetermined number of troops. The UAR would be barred from taking any punitive actions against remaining royalists as a punishment for previous resistance and a demilitarized zone of twenty kilometers would be established along the Yemen-Saudi border with impartial observers on both sides.[121] The Bunker agreements were signed on April 10, 1963, and were subsequently passed on to the UN for mediation.

Robert Komer advocated continuing the slow-moving negotiations between the Saudis and the Egyptians, saying that "while they're talking they'll at least be less inclined to start shooting."[122] George Ball, Kennedy's undersecretary of state for economic affairs, and Averell Harriman, Kennedy's assistant secretary of state for Far Eastern affairs, both expressed concern that "forcing substantial UAR withdrawals would leave Yemen in chaos with Soviets waiting to fill the vacuum."[123] In fact, in March 1963, the Soviets had signed an aid agreement with the YAR worth approximately $20 million and offered the Yemenis education grants to study in the USSR.[124] The Italian minister to Yemen claimed to have counted 147 Soviet personnel and Soviet-sponsored agricultural and industrial projects in the port city of Hodeidah.[125]

Nasser himself assessed that his premature departure would jeopardize Sallal's government because 30,000 Egyptian troops alone could not completely subdue the royalist imam supporters.[126] Even a partial reduction in the number of Egyptian troops would have been interpreted as a withdrawal of UAR support for the revolutionary state, potentially shifting Yemeni support to the royalists.[127] Nasser's adamant efforts to remain in full force in Yemen were sanctioned by US foreign policy. Kennedy still harbored visions of extending a hand in friendship to Nasser, although there were ulterior motives in keeping Nasser intensely involved in Yemen. It appears evident from the exchanges in the Kennedy administration that no one actually thought they could negotiate the withdrawal of Egyptian forces from Yemen. As will be discussed in later chapters, allowing Nasser to remain in full force in Yemen was in fact the underlying rationale behind US policy in Yemen. Not only would the Yemeni conflict be confined to Yemen, but Nasser's army and activities would be confined to Yemen as well, preventing him from undertaking concerted military effort elsewhere in the region.

Robert Komer eloquently described Nasser's plight in Yemen from the US perspective. "Nasser is trapped in Yemen. It's bleeding him, but he can't afford either the sharp loss of face in letting go or the risk of confronting us by starting on the Saudis again. . . . On top of this, Nasser has deep economic trouble at home, and now an open fight with the British. Nasser cornered is a dangerous animal, and we want to be mighty careful how we handle him."[128]

Komer's assessment of the Egyptian economy was not entirely accurate. In 1963 Egypt was still in the midst of a five-year plan for rapid modernization.[129] The cost of the Yemen Civil War and the foreign-service pay for 70,000 soldiers certainly contributed to the growing Egyptian deficit during a period that saw an increase in Egyptian GDP and over-all higher living standards. Nonetheless, Yemen was only one of multiple aggressive Nasserite policies, which included agricultural and industrial expansion, a massive propaganda machine, and an expansive social wel-fare network.[130]

Economist John Waterbury further dismisses the widespread notion that the Yemen misadventure led to economic disaster in Egypt, pointing out that no official accounting of Egypt's military expenditure in Yemen has been made public. Furthermore, the Yemen intervention had little bearing on the 1962 payment crisis, although it did have an impact upon similar crises in 1965 and 1966. The major culprit of Egypt's economic troubles was the trade imbalance that continued to deteriorate during the 1960s, with falling rates of Egyptian export and "the gross inefficiencies of a public sector called upon to do too many things: sell products at cost or at a loss, take on labor unrelated to production needs, earn foreign exchange, and satisfy local demand."[131]

Komer's expertise as an economist aside, he explained his optimism about eventually resolving the Yemen crisis: "Let them all bleed to death. Egyptians are having their forces bogged down, Saudis are spending their money, and the Yemenis are suffering. When worn out, they will finally reach a settlement."[132]

During the fog of war that characterized the first weeks of the Yemeni conflict, information was at a premium. Sallal's capture of the radio sta-tion allowed him to recover from his initial blunder of letting al-Badr escape Sana'a alive. Sallal and Baydani proceeded to propagate an inter-national charade claiming al-Badr's death and the imminent victory of the Yemeni republican forces. Nasser and Khrushchev wasted little time in recognizing the YAR, under the assumption that their stalwart ally was dead. The Saudis cited treaty agreements, tribal politics, Arabian *sharaf*, and strategic advantages in declaring their support for the Hamid al-Din family that showed up at their border. Al-Badr's miraculous resurrection and the momentum of the royalist opposition movement, however, turned a domestic succession crisis into a global conflict. Saudi and Jordanian alarm at Nasser's intentions and their own domestic instability drew the United States into the conflict as the mediator intent on pleasing all par-ties involved.

The unfolding scene in Yemen was not one that could have been pre-dicted by the ideological proclivities of either the United States and the USSR or Egypt and Saudi Arabia. Nasser and the Soviets offered support to an untested nationalist regime after forsaking their Nasserist and pro-communist ally al-Badr. After careful consideration, Kennedy declared support for a nationalist government, joining ranks with the USSR and the Eastern Bloc, while at the same time London and Riyadh withheld their recognition. No single foreign power or political entity in Yemen exercised decisive control over local events; each party peddled its own agenda. Foreign conflicts were transposed onto Yemen, further exacerbat-ing the civil war and complicating the world's comprehension of events in South Arabia. This global political baggage continued to burden diplo-matic efforts in the subsequent years.

3

Local Hostilities and International Diplomacy

THE EGYPTIAN ARMY, which grew in size over the course of the civil war, peaking at 70,000 soldiers, was the largest and most significant presence when compared with the long list of countries, organizations, and individuals who played major roles in the Yemeni conflict. Nasser's military staff quickly understood that the northern highlands of Yemen were indeed the "graveyard of empires," reminiscent of similarly difficult topography in the foreboding Khyber Pass in Afghanistan.[1] The successes and failures of Nasser's counterinsurgency efforts in Yemen and subsequent royalist counterattacks reverberated among the parties involved, the impact of which was felt most pointedly in international diplomatic efforts. While Egypt fought with royalist forces and their allies on the local level, a second civil war was being waged in the global arena, where local events and foreign agendas competed for prominence in South Arabia.

During the first two and a half years of the conflict Egypt developed a comprehensive counterinsurgency strategy. Egyptian military manuals captured by Israel in 1967 and the publications of Bruce Condé, a news correspondent aiding the royalists, provide the basis for the analysis in this chapter. With every victory in the battlefield, Nasser appealed for international diplomacy and a ceasefire to secure the gains made by republican and Egyptian forces. Egyptian attempts to determine the terms of disengagement from Yemen commenced almost as soon as the first Egyptian battalion arrived, and remained a constant part of the regional politico-military process.[2] Significant efforts were made by the US and UN over that period to bring the UAR and Saudi Arabia to a diplomatic agreement and a withdrawal from Yemen. Imam al-Badr and the royalists, on the other hand, were not recognized as a state and not included in international diplomatic negotiations. As a nonstate entity, the royalist tribal armies were able to continue military operations unabated and without fear of international sanctions or retribution. Appeals for international diplomacy were followed by royalist counter-offensives that rolled back many of the Egyptian territorial gains and imperiled the sustainability of Sallal's regime. Nasser's ultimate about-face and refusal to withdraw Egyptian troops in accordance with multiple international agreements was a response to the reality of the battlefield rather than a premeditated diplomatic ploy to buy time for his troops.[3] This depiction of events in Yemen runs counter to the narrative of the civil war from US, British, and UN perspectives, which instead accused Nasser of manipulating international parties with false promises of withdrawal.[4]

Mutual Limitations and the First Weeks of the War

The first Egyptian soldiers to arrive in Yemen in October 1962 landed at the Red Sea port of Hodeidah with no maps, no previous military experience in mountainous terrain, and no understanding of the tribal opposition to the republic. What Nasser did understand was that without Egyptian help the YAR army and tribal supporters of the republic would not be able to secure the capital city for longer than a few weeks.

Upon their arrival, the Egyptians validated rumors of the decrepit state of Imam Ahmad's weapons supplies and armed forces. Yemen's navy consisted of only two motor boats in Hodeidah. A reported fifty Yemeni cadets were training in Italy as paratroopers or pilots, but at that point they had not graduated into regular service in the Yemeni army. Imam Ahmad had ordered the dismantling of the few Yemeni planes that had been shipped, and stored the various parts in caves around Sana'a.[5] The airports in Sana'a, Hodeidah, Ta'iz, and Sa'dah (see Fig. 3.1) were little more than dirt runways and in need of serious modernization.[6]

Fearing they would be used against him, Imam Ahmad had ordered artillery shells hidden in practically inaccessible large caves on the top of Jabal Nuqum, the tallest mountain near Sana'a. The supplies could only be transferred down by camel, which could carry only two cases of ammunition on two round trips per day, maximum, down the mountain.[7] Had the Egyptians not arrived with their own munitions, this would have been the only method, albeit laborious and time consuming, to arm the

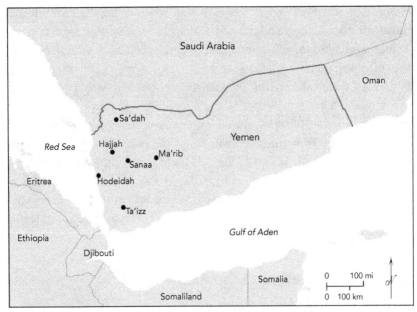

FIGURE 3.1 Map of Egypt's strategic triangle. Created by author.

republic's armored units consisting of thirty-one tanks and ninety-five armored vehicles, which had already used much of their ammunition in the shelling of Imam al-Badr's palace. Egyptian technicians were equally surprised to discover that the spare parts for artillery pieces in Sana'a were stored in a warehouse 200 miles away in Ta'iz. Large-scale UAR efforts were underway to locate, document, and repair these artillery pieces to working condition. Chief of Staff of the Egyptian Army, Field Marshal Muhammad 'Abd al-Hakim Amer, founded artillery schools in Sana'a and Hodeidah to train Yemeni soldiers in artillery use, as the majority of the YAR army had little experience with such weaponry. The Yemeni army was deemed antiquated and far behind the rest of the Arab world, and in need of significant Egyptian military aid, with the eventual goal of transferring security responsibilities to a modernized Yemeni republican military.[8]

During the first phase of the war, urban areas were the focus of republican and Egyptian attention for multiple reasons. The Free Yemeni Movement and the 1962 coup were fomented and supported by a largely urban population. Rural and village areas, on the other hand, tended to associate more readily with the religiously conservative allegiance to the imam. Cities in Yemen were built on mountaintops with outer houses built of stone with slots for firing, a defensive asset to forces holding the city. Large villages and cities were located near significant sources of drinking water, of utmost importance to the increasing size of the Egyptian military presence. In order to secure an urban network, road engineering projects were needed to connect the cities and villages and prepare them for motorized military transport, as most of the roads in Yemen were then only capable of supporting animal transport.[9] The three cities of Sana'a, Hodeidah, and Ta'iz constituted the "strategic triangle" at the crux of Egyptian military control and Sallal's political and economic strength. All other offensive and defensive strategies focused on the security of this triangle and the maintenance of its interconnected road network.

Battle for Sa'dah

The republican forces entered the first weeks of the revolution with a clear military plan in what would amount to a race against the clock until Imam al-Badr was able to gather a sufficiently organized tribal opposition to Sallal. The northern cities of Sa'dah and Hajjah were traditionally the epicenters of the Imam's support during times of political crisis. Following the 1948 and 1955 coups, Imam Ahmad and his supporters established a strategic base in the Hajjah fortress and from there led a tribal army in an attack on the capital city of Sana'a. Given the importance of these two cities to the counter-revolutionary movement, they became among the most important targets of the first republican offensives and were essential to garnering early support for the YAR in 1962.

Within two weeks of the coup, Prince Hassan captured Sa'dah, Ma'rib and other centers in the northern region of al-Jawf. Following numerous royalist military triumphs, additional tribes announced their opposition to the republic and their allegiance to the imam. Hassan continued moving his troops southward, preparing for an attack on Sana'a and on the republican ruling apparatus. Egyptian intervention and the arrival of aerial support for republican troops turned the tide of the battle, stemming the royalist advance on the capital.[10] The most representative battle for the military significance of the Egyptian army occurred in Sa'dah in the second half of October 1962.

At the end of October 1962, a unit of Egyptian paratroopers arrived in Sa'dah to establish an airfield and secure roads for Egyptian troop movements to the northern city. Part of the 18th Egyptian paratrooper brigade arrived in Sa'dah without incident and established an Egyptian base. On the way back toward Sana'a to link up with Egyptian ground troops, the paratroopers were ambushed by tribesmen from the Hashid federation and were forced to return to the relative safety of Sa'dah. Within days, tribal militias loyal to the imamate placed a siege around the Egyptians in the city. Aided by Sa'dah locals who had declared their support for the YAR, the paratroopers repelled numerous royalist attacks on the city.[11]

On November 8, 1962, the rest of the 18th paratrooper brigade arrived from the coast to reinforce the Egyptian position in Sa'dah. Royalist forces, however, took control of the main roads, thus preventing reinforcements from reaching the city, and concentrated artillery fire on the Sa'dah airport in an attempt to cut off the Egyptian air supply as well. The royalist coordination and tactics were more organized than the paratroopers had anticipated, causing one Egyptian officer to claim: "The enemy's tactics were based on sound military reasoning; evidence of foreign leadership behind it, planning its missions, providing it with funds, weapons, ammunition personnel, and specialists."[12] In reality, foreign mercenaries fighting for the royalists did not arrive in Yemen until many weeks later.

On November 27, the 18th brigade, supported by an Egyptian armored division that had arrived from Sana'a, launched an offensive to retake the main road into Sa'dah and break the siege. The brigade was split into four groups equipped with three-ton trucks carrying 37mm cannons and 1.5-ton trucks equipped with machine guns. The first group secured two shoulders of the main road in a nighttime raid that relied on heavy fire from 82mm mortars. The group's progress was halted when they found four barriers two hundred to three hundred meters apart with rows of antitank spikes in between. Engineers attempted to disable the barriers, but when one armored 4x4 vehicle exploded from a roadside bomb, the air force was called in to strafe the road and destroy the barriers. By the afternoon, the group managed to secure a hilltop fortress overlooking the city, where they established a defensive position. The next evening, the second group of Egyptians was forced to halt midway on the evening of November 28, in the face of heavy fire from the royalist-held pass of al-Amasiya, manned by 500 tribesmen armed with guns, cannons, mortars, and 75mm recoilless rifles. Heavy Egyptian return fire forced the tribesmen to retreat from their position to the nearby mountains. Egyptian troops then made the error of chasing tribesmen into the mountains and were ambushed; they suffered heavy losses. Egyptian commanders again blamed the losses on foreigners serving the imam, claiming to have found dead foreign soldiers, foreign papers, gold lira, and foreign currency—evidently proof that foreigners were behind royalist success.[13] They were not willing to believe that Yemeni commoners could outdo the Egyptian army. In reality, Egypt's army, trained for desert warfare, was ill-equipped to conduct mountainous combat.

The third and fourth groups were sent to subdue the estimated 1,500 royalist forces guarding the al-San'ara pass, a winding and narrow road that was the only approach to the city of Sa'dah from the south. As the Egyptian scouts approached the pass, they came under heavy fire that cut off their wireless connection with the rest of the brigade. Another scouting unit was sent and suffered casualties, losing several armored vehicles in the process. Although unable to establish a wireless connection with the two frontline scout units, the Egyptian officers were, to their great fortune, able to make contact with the besieged paratroopers in Sa'dah, who described the location and strength of the tribesmen from behind enemy lines. With this timely positioning information, Egyptians bombarded enemy positions with artillery fire, forcing them to retreat and open the pass.[14] With the al-San'ara pass open, Egyptian heavy artillery were transported to frontline positions, overwhelming the southern remnants of the Sa'dah siege and delivering a blow to the royalist attempt at securing the northern capital. On the morning of November 30, UAR troops entered Sa'dah and established a defensive perimeter.[15]

The battle of Sa'dah ended in a virtual stalemate. Egyptian troops held a garrison in the city itself and on an overlooking hilltop. Royalist tribesmen held several other overlooking hills, with neither side able to drive the other from their defensive positions. At this early stage in the war, the royalist tribes were able to confront the Egyptian army directly in the battlefield, as both sides had access to heavy artillery and munitions. For the Egyptian army, it became clear that success on the battlefield in Yemen was contingent upon their ability to amass a greater advantage in munitions and to utilize air cover as often as possible. The lessons learned in the Sa'dah battlefield factored into a more concentrated Egyptian attack as part of the Ramadan Offensive in 1963.

From the perspective of the United States and Western European nations, the initial gains made by republican and Egyptian forces were sufficient to recognize the new Yemeni republic on December 19, 1962, as it seemed that the YAR was in control of the majority of the country with the exception of a few border areas. US officials noted in particular that the republicans were in possession of the major urban areas and the majority of Yemen's population. Although royalists held larger swaths of territory, these constituted mostly tribal, rural, and desert areas of sparse population.[16] In December 1962, Nasser agreed to disengage Egyptian troops from Yemen in exchange for US recognition of the new regime. His commitment would, however, be short-lived.

Royalist Counteroffensive: December 1962–January 1963

Imam al-Badr's "resurrection" in November 1962 inspired northern Yemeni tribes to contribute to a royalist offensive against Egyptian troops. Al-Badr's uncle, Hassan, along with other members of the Hamid al-Din family (see Fig. 3.2), led tribal militias in recapturing Ma'rib and Harib pushing the frontlines westward towards Sana'a. The royalist military effort was supported by monetary aid and arms shipments from the Saudi monarchy to the north.

The main Hamid al-Din royalist generals were uncles and first cousins to al-Badr. Hussein, one of former Imam Yahya's sons, had six sons of his own: Muhammad, Abdullah, Hassan, Ahmad, Ali, and Yahya, with the surname "al-Hussein." Abdullah, who was a third-year student at the American University of Beirut (AUB) in 1962, led the battle in al-Jawf. His brothers Ahmad, who trained in an Egyptian military school, and Ali, who was studying political science at AUB and drafted al-Badr's constitution, were killed in action. Al-Badr controlled the royalist army in Yemen's north- west regions, while his uncle Hassan controlled the northeast. Hassan's six sons each took leadership roles in the royalist army.[17] The hereditary slave guards of the royal household, supposed descendants of Christian Ethiopians who were cut off from retreat across the Red Sea after the failed fifth- and sixth-century occupation of Yemen, were the most trustworthy supporters of the imam. They were in charge of the royal motor pool and transporting supplies and soldiers to front lines.[18]

Two battles marked a shift in the momentum of the battlefield in the imam's favor from the end of 1962 through the beginning of 1963. In Sirwah, located twenty-five miles west of Ma'rib, royalist eyewitnesses described the slaughter of the 180-man Egyptian parachute jump (three planes of sixty each) near the Sirwah battlefield. Many paratroopers missed their mark entirely while others were shot in midair by royalist tribesmen on the ground.[19] In Arhab, twenty miles north of Sana'a, twelve Egyptian tanks attacked royalist lines of communication. The Egyptian armored

Mutawakkilite Family Members of Direct Relevance to the Civil War

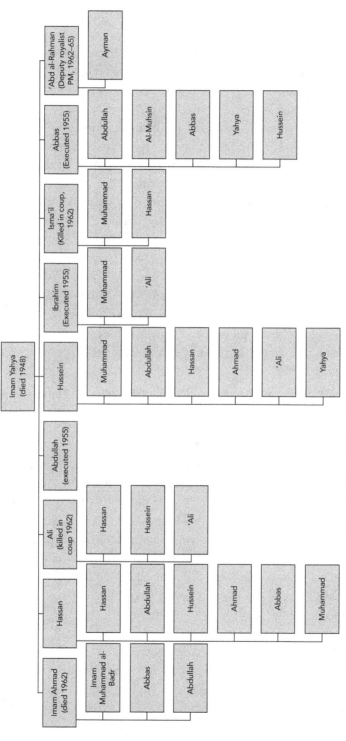

FIGURE 3.2 Hamid al-Din Family tree in 1962. Created by author.

units did not position accompanying troops to protect their tanks, leaving the tanks' blind side open to attack. Arhabi tribesmen approached the unguarded tanks and physically overturned them with tree trunk levers, then burned them and the soldiers inside. The accompanying soldiers fled in terror back to Sana'a, cutting the assault short.[20] The royalist offensive demonstrated to Nasser early in 1963 that the war was far from over.

In some instances, outdated Ottoman cannons were brought out of storage in a last-ditch effort to repel an Egyptian offensive. Shaharah, a large mountaintop village in the northern district of 'Amran, was the location of an early clash with Egyptian soldiers. The hilltop town was armed only with Ottoman-era weaponry captured by Imam Yahya after destroying an Ottoman army of 15,000 led by General Faidhi Pasha in 1919. The 1904 oversized Ottoman field gun known as "al-Bisbas" (the pepper) had a large supply of shells stored in the village. Al-Bisbas was brought out of retirement to repel an Egyptian attack in December 1962. Observers remarked on the historical significance of using an Ottoman-era gun against a modern enemy: "The Turks were the best soldiers in the world, and the Egyptians are about the worst."[21] Foreign observers described Egyptians as "inept, and helpless to cope with guerilla mountain warfare conditions, suffering losses of ten to one man-to-man infantry engagements."[22]

What made matters even more difficult for Nasser was that Yemeni tribesmen loyal to the republic could not be counted on to support Egyptian military plans. Although local tribes were given bribes in exchange for their continued allegiance to the republic and small arms in exchange for their military service, few of the tribesmen or arms ever made it onto the battlefield, and when they did, they were disorganized and hardly considered an asset.[23] Mark Millburn, one of the British mercenaries who aided the royalists, ridiculed the republican army: "I am fairly certain that the Republicans do not notice anything short of an army passing through, unless their Egyptian masters are around." On another occasion he remarked: "Gone are all my illusions about the lean, hawk-eyed warrior defending his all against the aggressor. In his place arises a picture of a shifty idle character, brutal to weaker beings and inferiors, out for what he can get, yet servile and cringing when his bluff is called."[24]

Tribal sheikhs and militia (see Fig. 3.3) preferred to hoard the weapons for their own use and under their own terms of engagement. For example, during an early 1963 campaign to uproot a royalist position along the Sana'a-Hodeidah road, a group of a thousand Hashid tribesmen under the command of Sheikh Abdullah al-Ahmar, along with thirty-five Egyptian soldiers, were given the responsibility of capturing an outpost on Jabal Masur. Even after aerial bombardment and artillery fire on the position for an entire week, the republican tribesmen were reluctant to attack the weakened royalist position. Rather than follow the Egyptian-led battle plan, they were more interested in attacking one house at a time and pillaging the local population. The UAR army was forced to assume the sole responsibility of reconquering Jabal Masur and its environs.[25]

While royalists paid the tribesmen one dollar per day of fighting, the Egyptians expended a great deal more to secure the tenuous alliances with profiteering sheikhs who often collected bribes from both sides. One tribe was reported to have collected two million dollars from Egyptian authorities for their military assistance, yet "before every battle sent messages assuring the Imam they would shoot to miss." An Egyptian officer was quoted complaining that "we can never trust the Yemenis who come to fight on our side.... [t]hey're always likely to turn their fire suddenly

FIGURE 3.3 Prominent republican Sheikh Sinan Abu Luhum, the leader of the Nahm tribe in the Bakil confederation. (JFK Library, NSF, Yemen, 9/63 Box 209)

against us."[26] Republican tribesmen were not even allowed to ride in armored vehicles with Egyptians.[27]

Patrick Seale, a correspondent for the *New Republic*, shared a description of the tribal stance toward the war that helps explain the difference between tribal loyalties to the imam and those to Egypt:

> "Whereas the Egyptians seem uncertain why they are there, the Yemeni tribes are ... enjoying opportunities for loot on a scale probably unparalleled since the incense caravans of Sheba. I met a man who had acquired 80 Egyptian blankets; another had a couple of hundred cans of excellent Egyptian beans; children were dressed in rags of parachute silk and every royalist camp was littered with captured weapons, bazooka bombs, boxes of grenades and Egyptian cigarettes."[28]

Despite his commitment to withdrawal, in January 1963 Nasser claimed that 30,000 troops were necessary to ensure the stability of the new regime.[29] Although Nasser was accused of deluding the United States with promises of withdrawal, a superficial analysis of the map of Yemen in the beginning of December 1962 may have led Nasser to conclude that the civil war was indeed over and that the YAR could survive without heavy Egyptian military presence. The strength and organization of al-Badr's opposition was, however, greatly underestimated, as was the significance of the nonurban terrain and rural population of Yemen.

Egyptian Strategy and the Ramadan Offensive

To raise the morale of Egyptian troops fighting in Yemen, Nasser offered higher compensation for service and the ability to purchase products through the tariff-free Aden port and transport them to their families in Egypt, duty-free. Soldiers and officers returning from Yemen would often bring refrigerators, gas ranges, and televisions along with them. Higher salaries for service in Yemen provided Egyptian troops with additional disposable income to purchase goods on the black market. Upon returning to Egypt those soldiers who had served in Yemen would be given privileged positions in the government for themselves and their relatives.[30] New hotels, upscale accommodations, and grandiose shopping centers were constructed in Hodeidah to accommodate Egyptian officers and their comparatively lavish lifestyles.[31] The fringe benefits offered for service in

Yemen perhaps lends truth to Nasser's claim to have received many letters from military officers, with requests to transfer to Yemen, purportedly "for the sake of fighting for Arab nationalism in Yemen."[32]

The chief of staff of the Egyptian army, Field Marshal 'Abd al-Hakim Amer, envisioned Yemen as his own "military fiefdom," away from Nasser's oversight in Egypt. Service in Yemen among senior officers became a rite of passage to higher echelons in the Egyptian government. Anwar Sadat, President of Egypt from 1970-1981, for example, was a central planner of the Egyptian occupation of Yemen from the first days of the republic through his connections with Baydani. Hosni Mubarak, President of Egypt from 1981-2011, headed an air force squadron with troop transport and long-range bombing responsibilities in Yemen.[33] Omar Suleiman, Mubarak's short-lived vice president in 2011, also served as a senior officer during the Yemen Civil War. General Anwar al-Qadi, the Director of Operations during the 1967 War with Israel, first commanded Egyptian forces in Yemen from October 1962 through November 1963 and was instrumental in reconceiving Egyptian military strategy in Yemen.[34] Al-Qadi had originally envisioned a five-year mission to Yemen to secure the revolution and create a stable Yemeni national army.[35]

There were other elements of political intrigue lurking behind Amer's "fiefdom" and the growing Egyptian military presence in Yemen. Amer's rapid rise in the Egyptian military and ruling revolutionary council constituted a potential threat to Nasser.[36] The outbreak of the Yemen Civil War presented Nasser with an opportunity to send Amer and his most loyal commanders into the midst of an unwinnable guerilla war from which there could be no political benefit to Amer. Nasser thus presented Amer with an untenable position, as the sought-after stability in Yemen could not, realistically, be achieved, and an ignominious retreat would have ended Amer's political career. By perpetuating the quagmire in Yemen, Nasser managed to keep his most powerful rival at a distance.

Despite the potential political pitfalls, over a two-month period from February through March 1963, Amer began to construct a counter-guerilla strategy called the Ramadan Offensive. This campaign consisted of trial-and-error tactics aimed at securing the strategic urban triangle of Sana'a, Ta'iz, and Hodeidah, and responding to the royalist counter-offensive. The Egyptian army increased the troop numbers to over 30,000 and embarked on a bold campaign to regain areas ceded to the imam in the previous weeks. Royalist positions were to be pushed further north and east of the triangle, specifically to target the imam's supply lines and mountainous strongholds. The tactics, supply lines, and overwhelming artillery and aerial power made the Ramadan Offensive the most successful of the Egyptian occupation and a future model for international counterinsurgency operations.

The indiscriminate use of artillery shells and air power required endless shipping and transport of munitions and fuel from bases twelve hundred miles away in Egypt. The main port of entry for the country was in Hodeidah, where large cranes, storage facilities, and a capacity of 4,500 tons of fuel were used continuously by the Egyptian military. Two to three weekly shipments carrying three thousand to eight thousand tons of supplies set out from the Egyptian port of al-Adabiya to Hodeidah. Aerial transport by Ukrainian Antonov planes carrying five to seven tons (aside from the weight of fuel) arrived in Yemen twice a day in addition to periodic Ilyushin-14 shipments. Once unloaded at the port or the airport, a large number of trucks and pack animals carried the supplies to areas north and east of Hodeidah and Sana'a. Supplies were delivered to inaccessible areas by helicopter, parachute, or small aircraft. During the first year of the war, eighteen Egyptian vessels (aside from fuel tankers) conducted 122 shipments—an average of 2.34 per week.

The Hodeidah port entrance could only accommodate one ship at a time, while the pier had room for four small ships or three medium-sized ships with a separate area for fuel shipment. The Hodeidah port had three cranes, each with a five ton capacity. Smaller twenty-five to thirty-ton ships carried supplies from the larger vessels to the smaller ports north of Hodeidah. Deliveries from Hodeidah to Sana'a consisted of forty trucks operating on a three day cycle: two days for a roundtrip and one day rest and repair. Forty trucks, carrying forty-five tons, on average, over thirty days translated into an average of fifty thousand tons of equipment being transported from Hodeidah to Sana'a each month. Trucks carrying twenty-three tons each made daily trips to other secondary outposts from Hodeidah in the same manner.[37]

Frequent use of the Red Sea to transport equipment necessitated a sizeable navy to patrol the 1,200 miles from the al-Adabiya Egyptian naval base to the Hodeidah port and the 200 miles of YAR coastline from Bab al-Mandeb northwards. Naval responsibilities included patrolling shipping lanes, monitoring coastal security in Yemen, particularly in the north, where royalists tried running supplies along the shore, and maintaining a security perimeter around the Hodeidah port. In essence, the Egyptian position in Yemen extended the Suez Canal security zone over

1,200 miles south to the Gulf of Aden. Large numbers of patrols around port areas and up and down Red Sea coast and the required naval escort for each military and commercial vessel constituted a substantial number of ships in the Hodeidah port. The Hodeidah port, however, had limited capacity, thus creating long lines of military and civilian ships.[38] The Hodeidah radar base monitored approaching aircraft and coordinated the increasing sea traffic related to Egypt's war effort. Major hydrographic surveys of the Yemeni coastline provided the first modern detailed maps and of sea lanes along the Red Sea coast, facilitating smaller-scale naval operations in the ports of Mocha, Midi in Hajjah province, and al-Luhayyah.[39]

The Egyptian air force was equally as important to the success of the Egyptian occupation of Yemen as was the navy. Most UAR missions used Russian MiGs from airfields initially based in Hodeidah and then in Sana'a by 1964. Russian-manufactured Tupolev Tu-16 bombers flew twelve hundred miles from bases in Egypt to bomb buildings and fortifications in Yemen ahead of UAR offensives. Several Ilyushin-28 jet bomber aircraft were stationed in a small airport nine miles north of Sa'dah with a 1.5 mile runway, but were forced to relocate to Hodeidah because of the constant danger of attack near Sa'dah. The Egyptian air force took to dropping time bombs, as the delayed detonation frightened the locals who understood these only as random explosions without planes in the vicinity.[40] Taking further advantage of the tribal unfamiliarity with planes, Egyptians equipped twelve Yak-11 single engine planes with the standard four rockets and two additional .303 caliber machine guns. Tribesmen would count the rockets and unknowingly assume the danger had passed after the fourth bomb was dropped. The planes would then make a second turn strafing the enemy tribesmen who had come out to inspect the damage with a barrage of gunfire significantly increasing the deadliness of Egyptian air raids.[41]

Antonov An-12 four-engine transport aircraft served as an "aerial bridge" between Egypt and Yemen. The planes originally shipped to the Sana'a civilian airport before shifting direction and transporting supplies directly to the Sa'dah airport. Given the tenacity of the intense fighting in the Sa'dah region, the airport would need to be "reconquered" every night in order to secure the landing strip for morning shipments. The fuel supply in Sa'dah was low and the Antonovs were required to carry sufficient fuel for a roundtrip flight from Aswan, to avoid depleting the local supply in Sa'dah.[42]

During the first months of the war, four temporary airport facilitates and seven heliports were constructed. Given the dearth of proper maps and unfamiliarity with the terrain, pilots were reliant on navigational equipment and radio communication. In order to accommodate the increasing number of aircraft in Yemen, a massive effort was undertaken to pave new runways and light them in order to facilitate use in day and night and even after rain storms. In addition to the main airports in Sana'a, Hodeidah, Ta'iz, and Sa'dah, eight additional airports of smaller size were placed strategically within range of contentious fronts. Helicopters with 12.7mm machine guns were stationed at each landing strip and airport and proved decisive on many battlefronts.[43]

The first examples of this new battle strategy which featured overwhelming firepower occurred in al-Jawf, a neighboring region northwest of Sana'a. Al-Jawf had traditionally been a refuge for mercenaries and brigands and in December 1962 became a source of munitions for royalist troops. UAR troops encamped in al-Hamidah, a village north of Sana'a, in preparation for an attack on al-Jawf with three battalions and one armored unit. The first attempt at conquering the al-Fajra pass into the al-Jawf region was a disaster, as the secondary forces lost their way. Subsequent overflights pinpointed the enemy location, and the night was spent bombarding the enemy by air and with heavy artillery. The next morning tanks and troops with flamethrowers followed behind to extract enemy troops from cave hideouts. The Egyptian offensive continued south of al-Jawf, conquering the city of Ma'rib as well, intimidating local tribes with a display of heavy artillery along the way. In the process the imam's army learned quickly the degree of inadequacy of their artillery pieces.[44]

Part of the Egyptian strategy involved deceiving royalist units into exposing their hidden location. For example, Egyptians soldiers lit fires two kilometers from a royalist mountain outpost near Ma'rib and shined lights as if there were a full assault on their position from that direction. The royalist unit began feverishly firing their cannons and mortars in the direction of the oncoming "assault," divulging the location of their artillery and subjecting themselves to subsequent Egyptian bombardment. In the capture of al-Hazm, the capital of Jawf, the Egyptians even managed a successful thousand-man parachute drop to capture the city in February 1963.[45] This successful parachute drop was in stark contrast to the failed Sirwah mission only a few weeks earlier.

Even with the advantage of aerial reconnaissance, pinpointing the exact location of these outposts was difficult. As a result, Egyptian artillery teams were instructed to excessively bomb a wide area with long-range artillery and smoke grenades.[46] Collateral damage was not a consideration. While large-scale bombing certainly had a demoralizing effect on enemy troops, the real and tangible utility of the artillery fire was actually hitting the target. The key, according to the Egyptian strategy, was to draw premature fire from royalist positions, note the coordinates, and communicate the positions to supporting aircraft and artillery. In February 1963, for example, Egyptian intelligence received word that the imam's forces had obtained shipments of 75mm cannons and mortars to Arhab in preparation for an assault on a major Sana'a corridor. Two companies of paratroopers equipped with sizable artillery units were sent to verify the approximate location and destroy the enemy. During the first night, a small group of scouts detached two headlights from a truck, attached them to batteries, and placed the lights in a wooden box half a mile from the approximate enemy base. The scout group, standing under cover a fair distance from the headlights, flashed them on and off intermittently, giving the impression that there was an approaching vehicle. Surprised to see the "vehicle," the enemy bombed the area, revealing to the Egyptians a count of at least four 81mm mortars and one cannon. When the royalists sent a patrol party to investigate, the Egyptians quickly left the area, having noted the approximate location of the artillery.

The following night scouts planted four diversionary sets of vehicle headlights in a similar fashion. This time, however, four armored vehicles, with headlights off, were to approach from a different direction. A second group, with two 120mm mortars that had a maximum range of 7200 meters, camped a mile from Arhab. Once the location was reestablished using the headlight deception tactic, Egyptian artillery bombarded the royalist artillery location and the four armored cars approached Arhab with their lights off. As enemy fire began to subside, perhaps after one or two artillery units were damaged, Egyptian 120mm mortars began firing beyond the enemy position, giving the impression that they were missing the location while also covering the movement of the four vehicles. Assuming it was safe to emerge for a moment, members of the royalist artillery unit exposed themselves and were captured or killed by the armored vehicles that had by that point reached the royalist defensive position in Arhab.[47]

This developing strategy of heavy artillery was not without its difficulties and inadequacies. Moving artillery between stations was a challenge, and there was a preference for artillery with greater range, albeit inferior accuracy. Heavy artillery, for instance, would often get stuck in the road to Sa'dah, where the 25mm cannons needed to be pulled by rope. Even when the Egyptians were able to move the cannons freely along the road, the shaking was so incredible that it would cause damage to the artillery pieces. The forward progress of artillery shipments was therefore limited to six to nine miles per hour, leaving the slow-moving units vulnerable to sniper fire and ambush. The 120mm mortar could only ride on the back of a truck for this reason. At least half the artillery movement was dependent upon air travel and trucks, increasing the expense and difficulty of transport, especially given the difficult terrain.[48] In order to avoid excessive transport over unfriendly terrain, the Egyptian army adopted a policy of decentralization of arms depots, which ensured supply and independence of action by local commanders.[49]

While Yemen's mountainous terrain was an obstacle to heavy transport for the Egyptian army, it was an asset for the imam's army, whose soldiers spread themselves thin in hidden outposts situated strategically in caves along the sides of the transport arteries. Stone barriers twenty to twenty-eight inches wide, designed to deflect shrapnel, were constructed in circular form on mountaintops or as straight walls in open fields, and surrounded by pits.[50] The royalists moved their artillery pieces and cannons out of hidden locations and caves only for a short period of time to fire and then hid them away again, moving the weapons freely from place to place, making them very hard targets for Egyptian fire.[51] The UAR planned nightly sporadic bombardments with incendiary munitions, phosphorous shells, and flare launchers to frighten locals, draw groups of fighters from hiding, and deprive enemy troops of rest before a major confrontation.[52]

Egypt's counterinsurgency, superior firepower, and impressive demonstration of large-scale naval and air logistics translated into significant victories and territorial expansions. Armed with confidence following the successful Ramadan Offensive, Nasser agreed to the Bunker agreements and committed to withdraw Egyptian forces in April 1963. This success did not last long, however, as many of the YAR gains were lost during Saudi-aided royalist offensives in the subsequent months. This forced Nasser to maintain troop levels despite commitments to the United States and UN. Even when his own Lieutenant General Anwar al-Qadi, an early proponent of a lengthy occupation, approached him in May 1963 and recommended that Egypt withdraw from Yemen, Nasser dismissed the suggestion.[53]

Modified Royalist Tactics

The Egyptian army was trained to fight in an open desert; guerilla war with an elusive enemy in a mountainous setting proved a challenge. Heavy artillery and aerial bombardment may have succeeded in temporarily scattering the enemy, but when the Egyptians withdrew, royalist forces emerged from hiding and retook the lost territory.[54] The Ramadan Offensive forced the royalist tribesmen to modify their tactics, particularly in mountainous regions, and avoid structured military assaults against an enemy with far superior aerial and artillery firepower. The imam's army preferred to cut Egyptian communications and ambush convoys, saving frontal assaults for advantageous terrain and superior numbers.

The royalist base in al-Qarah, located in the al-Jawf region, was named Camp Mansur, and the "Free Yemen Loyalist" (royalist) armies were named "Mansur Armies," which matched al-Badr's adopted title of "al-Mansur Bi'allah" (victorious through God). From Camp Mansur, al-Badr communicated with troops on the front lines through coded radio messages from his bomb-proof bunkers.[55] Many of them were trained as snipers and marksmen, and so preferred small arms to heavy artillery.[56] Farm-boy tribal volunteers learned to use Degtyarev-Shpagin 12.7mm Soviet anti-aircraft (50-calibre) machine guns either captured from massacred Egyptian forces, bought from republican soldiers, or received as gifts from "defector elite units of Sallal's 'National Guard.'"[57] Yemeni tribal sharpshooters were rumored to have "picked off fifty Egyptians with fifty rationed bullets in a single day."[58] They were stationed in groups of six, and occupied outposts along the road; they communicated by lighting bonfires, drumming sounds, or firing guns.[59] Their small units, subsistence rations of barley and raisins, and light munitions allowed royalist commanders to maintain a mobile and barely discernible armed force with the ability to inflict heavy casualties on Egyptian armed forces. The impact of aerial bombing on royalist positions was not as potent as the Egyptians had intended. The dispersed nature of the royalist bases and their ability to hide in a vast network of mountainous caves made the imam's tribesmen difficult targets for the UAR air force. For example, the Egyptian bombing of al-Qarah never came closer than a mile to hitting the imam's base and cave, despite reportedly dropping sixty-five bombs in the area. Royalist witnesses claimed the total damage was only "one stray dog killed and one farm wall knocked down." The inaccuracy of Egyptian bombing campaigns was partly attributed to the three-thousand foot altitude observed by most planes for fear of anti-aircraft ground fire. Royalists have derisively referred to the Egyptian bombing raids as the daily "milk-run."[60]

As the Egyptians began to secure urban areas and the road networks connecting them, al-Badr envisioned a strategy that would place a virtual siege on every republican-held city. He planned to starve the inhabitants into submission by attacking road shipments into and out of the city and by conquering an agricultural region that had acted as a vital supply of food for urban dwellers. In June 1963, following the imam's conquest of the Wadi Dahr grape-growing region to the north-northwest of Sana'a under Prince Yahya al-Hussein (5th army), there was a republican shortage of raisins and almonds, which "rank[ed] next to sorghum as Yemenite food staples." Jabal al-Loz (the almond mountain) and the surrounding almond-growing region directly east of Sana'a had long been held by Prince Abdullah al-Hassan, which further exacerbated the food shortage in Sana'a and elsewhere. In addition, Egyptian bombing in royalist areas had destroyed dwellings, crops, orchards, herds, and flocks with machine-gun fire and incendiary bombs, resulting in widespread loss of food supplies in a country that scarcely had enough for basic nutrition. Imam al-Badr's Yemen was not a UN-recognized country and was therefore not eligible for food aid, relying instead on their own hoarded supplies, a camel caravan trail from Saudi Arabia, and meager proceeds to purchase food.[61] There was therefore little to offer in trade to the country's urban areas. The YAR, on the other hand, was eligible for US PL-480 wheat sales (the food aid program created in 1954 to dispose of domestic agricultural surplus) and became further reliant on the UAR and the USSR for their daily sustenance.

The roads themselves, particularly those frequented by Egyptian military vehicles, were mined using M35 small mines. Additional explosives were placed under the earthen floors of houses and lavatories to "upset enemy morale" and perpetuate the notion that few locations were safe for Egyptian soldiers. According to royalist reports, sixty-three mines were placed from September 1963 through January 1964 killing an estimated 2,585 Egyptians and republicans and destroying thirty tanks and nineteen armored cars.[62] What emerged in the first months of 1964 was a stalemate between superior Egyptian munitions and al-Badr's effective and elusive tribal guerilla force. In the summer of 1964, Nasser would make one last major effort to end the war on his terms.

Haradh Offensive and the Hunt for al-Badr

The royalist offensives in early 1964 forced the retreat of republican positions to the extent that the vital Sana'a-Hodeidah road was again cut off, besieging the capital city. Although a heavy Egyptian military presence reopened the road in March 1964, periodic royalist ambushes threatened supply lines. As the situation grew more desperate, Nasser made his first impromptu visit to Yemen on April 23, 1964, and announced an increase in the size of the Egyptian garrison to over 36,000 in preparation for a massive offensive in the summer.[63]

On August 14, 1964, Nasser launched a determined push on the imam's base in al-Qarah with a massive bombing campaign emanating from the new Soviet-financed and -constructed al-Rahaba airport in Sana'a. The Egyptian pincer movement on al-Qarah consisted of troops moving south from Sa'dah and north from Sana'a and converging on the imam's stronghold. Without the regular supply of munitions from Saudi Arabia during the tenure of the UN observer mission, al-Badr was forced to abandon his cave in al-Qarah. Merjan bin Yasser, a member of the "royal motorized pool," drove Imam al-Badr in his Dodge Power Wagon to the furthest northern point on the Harad-Mushaf front, where the imam proceeded on foot to al-Mushaf. From there al-Badr split his force of 1,500 tribesmen, sending half to the Haradh front to join the Royal Guards and half northeast to Jabal Razih. Following the departure of UN observers in September 1964, supplies began to cross the Saudi border once again. By the end of the month, tribal soldiers were rearmed and sent into battle; they advanced to within thirty miles west of Sana'a. Fourteen thousand tribal levies claimed to have massacred Sallal's troops, destroyed twenty Soviet tanks and twenty armored cars, shot down three planes, and sent six hundred wounded Egyptian soldiers packing for Port Said.[64]

Aside from hunting al-Badr, Egyptian and republican forces endeavored to close the border with Saudi Arabia. The main thoroughfare from Saudi Arabia into royalist territory was through the Ma'jaz pass, flanked on either side by the mountains of Jabal Razih and Jabal Sha'ar. The Egyptian offensive targeted each mountain stronghold separately before taking control of the pass, albeit for a short period of time. The unique part of the offensive was that republican troops constituted the majority of the soldiers for one of the first times since the early days of the Yemen Civil War.[65] Although al-Badr remained at large, at the close of the Haradh offensive, royalist forces had been pushed back to the border with Saudi

Arabia. Nasser approached King Faisal during the Arab Summit in September to propose a ceasefire and a resolution to the Yemeni conflict.

The aftermath of the Haradh offensive followed the pattern of local battles and international diplomacy since 1962, as Nasser jockeyed for an opportunity to dictate the terms of Egypt's withdrawal from Yemen. Nasser appealed for diplomacy after each successful offensive, hoping that international pressure would help the UAR and the YAR hold on to their territorial gains by establishing a ceasefire. At each diplomatic juncture, royalists came back down from their mountainous refuge and pushed the Egyptian frontline positions back to the general confines of the strategic triangle of Sana'a, Ta'iz, and Hodeidah. Rather than face negotiating from a position of relative weakness inflicted by the royalist counteroffensive, Nasser repeatedly renewed his offensive, reneging on international commitments for a ceasefire and troop withdrawal. In the first month of the civil war in 1962, Egypt captured Sa'dah and established control over the majority of urban areas in the country. Imbued with misplaced confidence of an impending victory, Nasser committed to withdrawing his troops in exchange for US recognition of the YAR on December 16, 1962. The first royalist counteroffensive led by al-Badr quickly reversed Nasser's intentions. Egypt's massive Ramadan Campaign in 1963 was so successful that Nasser agreed to the presence of UN mission to oversee the withdrawal of all foreign assistance from the Yemeni conflict. Modified royalist tactics and an emphasis on guerilla war tactics scaled back Egypt's military gains and warranted Nasser's visit to Sana'a in support of plans for the Haradh Offensive, which began as the UN mission was leaving in September 1964. The offensive's measured success convinced Nasser once again to pursue a diplomatic resolution with the upper hand and conduct, over the next two years, a series of international conferences aimed at reconciliation.

4

The UN Yemen Observer Mission (UNYOM)

THE RAMADAN AND Haradh offenses and subsequent royalist counterattacks dominated the narrative of events emanating from the local scene in Yemen. In the concurrent international sphere an entirely different battle was taking place between the old European guard of the UN and the emerging influence of the developing world. This global struggle was transposed upon Yemen from 1963 to 1964 and impacted the conduct of diplomatic efforts and their later historical accounts.

In 1963, UN Undersecretary Ralph Bunche and senior US diplomat Ellsworth Bunker embarked on separate efforts of "shuttle diplomacy" between Yemen, Saudi Arabia and Egypt with the intention of establishing the basis for the withdrawal of international players from the Yemeni conflict. The UN Yemen Observer Mission (UNYOM) was commissioned to oversee the implementation of these agreements over a fourteen-month period beginning in July 1963. Contemporary and historical accounts of the UN mission have described it as a failure from diplomatic, political, and tactical perspectives.[1] Other accounts have minimized the importance of the mission in the overall narrative of the Yemen Civil War by relegating it to a footnote or a few paragraphs at most.[2]

Critics note that rather than a withdrawal during the mission, there was a notable increase in the size of the Egyptian military presence and that Saudi military aid continued to arrive, albeit through more clandestine and varied geographical locations. The overall mission was further criticized for its apparent failure to approach al-Badr and the royalists with similar diplomatic entreaties. The supply and hygiene of UN quarters were deemed dangerously inadequate, which contributed to the low morale of personnel. Many of the journalistic and historical accounts of the mission were further skewed by the negative US and British opinions of the UN. For example, Michael Crouch, the British resident adviser in Aden, summed up the way his cohort felt about the UN mission in Yemen, describing it as "the mission from the UN anti-colonialist committee . . . sitting on the other side of the border making mischief."[3]

Recently available UN and Canadian archives challenge the perceived "failure" of UNYOM. In the pages of the archives, UN personnel continuously reiterated the explanation that the stated goal of the mission was to "observe" the withdrawal of Egypt and Saudi Arabia. Simply stated, at a certain point in the mission, there was no withdrawal to observe, a failure on the part of the two belligerent countries rather than the UN mission. The actual purpose of the mission was not to force an end to hostilities, but rather to maintain a symbolic presence in the region, the fruits of which would not become clear until after the series of peace conferences that followed the mission's termination.

UNYOM marked the beginning of a new era of UN missions during the 1960s and 1970s that were hampered by diplomatic and financial obstacles. In structuring UNYOM, UN Secretary General U Thant endeavored to create a mission that was both uncontroversial and low cost, a clear departure from previous UN operations of lavish expenditure. An ameliorated picture of the mission emerges from the archives, one that is starkly different from the depraved conditions described by detractors. Reports and complaints of inadequate supplies and low morale were more a protest against Thant's attempts to redefine the place of peacekeeping in the UN rather than an objective testament to reality on the ground. UNYOM was in fact a valiant effort to maintain a benign and limited international presence in the midst of an intractable internationalized conflict, thereby confining the global repercussions of the civil war and laying the foundations for subsequent efforts at reconciliation.

The Emergence of Regionalism and a Financing Crisis in the UN

When Swedish UN Secretary-General Dag Hammarskjöld died in a plane crash on September 18, 1961, it marked the end to a "heyday era of a free-wheeling secretary-general" and an aggressive UN peacekeeping policy.[4] From 1946, Hammarskjöld and his Norwegian predecessor Trygve Lie had exercised an agenda controlled by the United States and Western

Europe and were guided by the priorities of the emerging Cold War global conflict. The UN peacekeeping missions were dominated by a collection of mid-level countries, including Canada, Sweden, and Denmark in what Canadian Secretary of State Howard Charles Green termed the "Scandi-Canadian axis in the UN." Lester Pearson, who served as Canada's prime minister during the Yemen Civil War, is known by historians as the "father of peacekeeping" and the public face of Canadian international diplomacy. His championing of peacekeeping encouraged a Canadian contingent of pilots to join the UN mission in Yemen.[5]

By the end of 1960, however, following a period of rapid postcolonial independence in Africa and Asia, non-Western countries constituted the large majority of the General Assembly. This new Asian-African regional bloc called for a decentralization of UN leadership and a shift in focus from the East-West conflict to the regional economic development of the Southern Hemisphere.[6] Brian Urquhart, a former undersecretary of the UN, explained that the emergence of the Third World in the UN transferred discussion and significance from the Security Council to the General Assembly, a situation with which neither the West nor the USSR was comfortable.[7]

This regional movement gained a voice in 1955 at the Asian-African Conference held in Bandung, Indonesia, bringing together twenty-nine regional states to formulate joint principles of economic development and international relations. The Non-Aligned Movement, the group's official title, met in Belgrade in September 1961, at the First Conference of Non-Aligned Heads of State, to formalize their commitment to avoiding military agreements with the superpowers while continuing to support national independence movements. Nasser was an integral part of the movement's leadership and would later use this context to justify support for Egyptian intervention in Yemen.[8] In June 1964, the "Group of 77" formed the largest intergovernmental organization of developing countries in the UN under the pretext of promoting their collective economic interests.[9] The regional politicization of UN power dynamics during UNYOM's mandate had a profound effect on the limited diplomatic latitude offered to planners of the mission and observers on the ground.

In the search for a new secretary-general following Hammarskjöld's death, the impetus was to choose a candidate from the Afro-Asian bloc of nations. U Thant, ambassador to the UN from Burma, perceived as a third-world country not involved "in a festering conflict that could alienate any of the great powers," was appointed for the position and served his first term until April 1963. Thant was sensitive to Soviet charges levied against Hammarskjöld's Western proclivities, and sought to develop a persona of neutrality and impartiality. This philosophy did have its limits, particularly in relation to what Thant perceived as the "historic injustices perpetrated against third world nations."[10] During his tenure as secretary-general, he oversaw the transition of the UN from an East-West Cold War arena to an institution forced to grapple with the priorities and concerns of the developing world. The mission to Yemen and the UN stance toward the conflict were greatly influenced by Thant's preference for the developing nations of the UAR and YAR, his desire to appease the Soviet Foreign Office, and perhaps an effort to secure support for a second term as secretary-general after April 1963.

In the midst of this geographic transition in the UN, a crisis broke out in the newly independent Congo, drawing the intervention of a UN peace-keeping mission, known as the UN Operation in the Congo (ONUC), amounting to twenty thousand troops over a period from July 1960 to June 1964. UN forces racked up exorbitant bills and suffered many casualties, including Hammarskjöld himself, whose plane crashed on the way to a ceasefire conference. The chaos of the emerging civil war in Congo embroiled ONUC in a complex domestic conflict that went beyond normal peacekeeping duties. ONUC was forced to take sides in a country divided into four rival camps and was accused of having facilitated the overthrow of Congolese Prime Minister Patrice Lumumba.[11]

ONUC's mandate was established nearly four years after the beginning of the UN Emergency Force (UNEF), a peacekeeping mission stationed along the armistice demarcation lines in Sinai between Israel and Egypt. The financing of these two operations and of peacekeeping missions in general was a contested issue in the UN, with four distinct opinions disagreeing over the responsibility for financing UN peacekeeping. Soviet Union Deputy Foreign Minister Vasiliy Kuznetsov argued that the aggressor nations should be responsible for maintaining their own international peacekeepers. Representatives from Latin America argued that the permanent members of the Security Council should fund the missions because "they have a primary obligation for the maintenance of peace and security under the charter." Latin American and Asian delegates also offered an opinion that either wealthy nations or the countries with the greatest economic interests in the region should pay the bills. Finally, the Canadian delegates, representatives of one of the largest contributors of peacekeeping forces, advocated a "compulsory payment principle," as they envisioned peace and security as a collective responsibility borne equally by all UN members.[12] Lacking consensus on the responsibility for financing the missions, Hammarskjöld established separate budgets for each mission, to be funded by voluntary contributions from all UN members.

1963, the year UNYOM was approved by the Security Council, was the most expensive year for UN peacekeeping costs, with the continued administration of UNEF, ONUC, and an annual peacekeeping budget exceeding $195 million, an amount ten times larger than the UN's first annual budget in 1946. This contributed to the overall UN financial shortfall of $110 million in 1963.[13] Members of these two missions were later sent to Yemen to fill administrative roles in UNYOM, bringing along with them their grudges and political tensions from Congo and Sinai. The deficits incurred as a consequence of financing UNEF and ONUC placed further pressure on U Thant to run the mission to Yemen frugally and to secure funds from the aggressor nations themselves, rather than from UN resources. To make matters worse, the Soviet Union and France refused to pay their share of assessments for UNEF and ONUC, further deepening the financial crisis of UN peacekeeping missions.[14]

Ralph Bunche compared the crisis in Yemen to that in Congo and stressed patience in bringing about results.[15] He would later term this limited-budget approach as "tin cup peacekeeping," a sure recipe for futility.[16] Beyond the financial constraints imposed on the proposed UN mission to Yemen, U Thant had "to ensure that each new mission was sufficiently uncontroversial that no state would use its existence to justify further attacks on the UN."[17]

A Rough Beginning

Conscious of the need to both keep costs down and propose an uncontroversial mission to Yemen, U Thant sent Swedish Lieutenant-General Carl von Horn, then serving as the Chief of Staff of the United Nations Truce Supervision Organization (UNTSO), to Egypt, Saudi Arabia and Yemen to ascertain the potential needs of a group of UN observers. Von Horn, described as "prestigious but stormy," was to join UNYOM after having served in Congo for six months in 1960 and almost two years in Jerusalem.[18] Following a long and illustrious UN career highlighted by comfortable office positions, the rustic field mission to Yemen was seen by von Horn as a personal offense bestowed upon him by U Thant.[19] In 1962, von Horn's wife Scarlett died in Hadassah Hospital in Jerusalem, leaving von Horn alone with their fourteen-year-old son Johan. His personal tragedy was confounded by his disdain for U Thant and the new African states that had recently joined the UN. Upon arriving in New York to accept his Yemen assignment, von Horn noted: "The old ambience was gone. The new states were reveling in the politically inspired largesse of the great powers, and had discovered how well it paid to shout and snarl and be abusive." In condescending terms, he described members of the nonaligned nations as "enjoying influence without responsibility ... using their inflated importance to band together to become a pressure group." Von Horn felt that the Americans and Soviets must have regretted allowing their rivalry to open the door to these countries, as he believed they were a "great embarrassment to themselves in the United Nations where the balance of power had been seriously upset ... contributing to the organization's eventual decline."[20] Von Horn had great respect for and friendship with former Secretary-General Dag Hammarskjöld, feelings that he did not exhibit toward U Thant, a matter that would impact von Horn's stance toward UNYOM. He later accused Thant of seeming "almost entirely preoccupied with the political implications of virtually every step which peacekeepers took in the field."[21]

Thant had originally conceived the mission in terms of "not more than 50 observers, with suitable transportation, aerial and ground, for patrol purposes."[22] In May 1963, von Horn returned from Yemen asking for two hundred personnel, a million-dollar budget, and four months in which to oversee the agreement.[23] This divergence in opinion on the size of the UN mission marked the beginning of a stormy relationship between von Horn and Thant that ended with von Horn's premature resignation in August 1963. The Soviet Union insisted that a UN mission should not be sent to Yemen without explicit approval from the Security Council, setting the timetable for the mission even further behind schedule.[24] As if to reiterate his disdain for Thant, before the official start of the mission von Horn had already submitted a request for two weeks of personal leave in July 1963.[25]

On June 11, 1963, the UN Security Council issued Resolution 179, which called for the formation of UNYOM with the limited function of observing the disengagement and reporting back to the UN Security Council via the Secretary General:

The Security Council requests the Secretary-General to establish the observation operation as defined by him; urges the parties

concerned to observe fully the terms of disengagement set out . . .
and to refrain from any action which would increase tension in
the area.

Saudi Arabia and Egypt agreed to split the cost of the initial two months
of the observer mission, an effort that eventually cost a total of $1.8 mil-
lion.[26] The YAR refused to contribute to the mission, claiming that they
were the "injured party."[27] The initial outlay amounted to a $200,000 con-
tribution by each country for a two-month observer mission.[28] A speech by
Saudi Ambassador Rashad Pharaon, explained Saudi Arabia's willingness
to support the UN mission to Yemen:

> The United Nations has justified its existence and shown the value
> of its work on various occasions of international conflict recently in
> Yemen. The conflict in Yemen is one between brothers, and it should
> be settled, as Saudi Arabia has suggested from the outset, in accor-
> dance with the aspirations and desires of the Yemeni people, for my
> country is convinced that ultimately it is they who will decide their
> own future. In view of the traditional friendly relations and spiritual
> ties between the Yemeni and Saudi Arabian peoples, my Government,
> which has sincerely collaborated with the United Nations, is prepared
> to give its honest and loyal support to any effort designed to produce
> a peaceful, just and equitable solution to this problem. We are sure
> that the efforts made by the Secretary General of the United Nations
> will help to put an end to this conflict and to similar conflicts which
> might threaten peace in different parts of the world.[29]

Under the terms of the agreement, the Saudis would cease aid to the
royalists and the Egyptians would begin a withdrawal of its forces from
Yemen. A twelve-mile demilitarized zone (see Fig. 4.1) would be established
on either side of the YAR-Saudi Arabia border, within which UN observers
would be stationed to ensure the implementation of the Bunker agreement. Another group of UN observers would keep track of the Egyptian
military withdrawal from the airfield in Sana'a and the port in Hodeidah.
The purpose of the mission was to "check and certify on the observance by
the two parties of the terms of the disengagement agreement." In as such,
the mission was not tasked with an official peacekeeping role.

At maximum strength the mission had 189 military personnel, including 25 military observers, 114 military officers, and 50 members of the

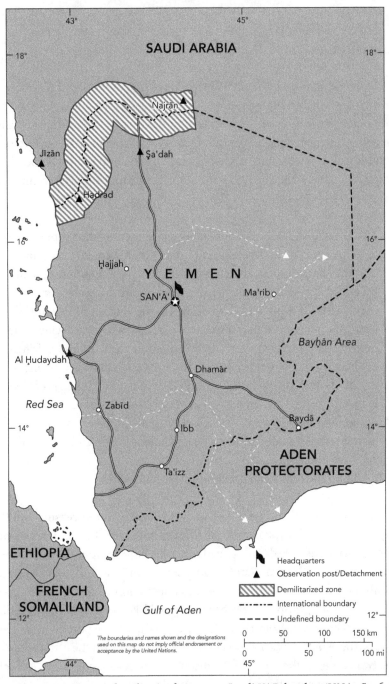

FIGURE 4.1 UNYOM demilitarized zone on Saudi-YAR border. (UNA, S-0656-0003, UNYOM DMZ map)

Royal Canadian Air Force (RCAF), supported by international and local civilian staff. The majority of the staff was from Canada and Yugoslavia, but others hailed from Australia, Denmark, Ghana, India, Italy, Netherlands, Norway, Pakistan, and Sweden. The troops were stationed in Jizan and Najran, Saudi Arabia, and Sa'dah, Yemen. The air unit consisted of 50 RCAF officers and pilots employing Caribou and Otter aircraft based out of Sana'a, Jizan, and Najran.[30] It was presumed that royalist arms arrived in Yemen by sea via the Red Sea shores of Jizan and by land through Najran.[31]

The Canadian Cabinet agreed to contribute to the mission on June 13, 1963. The Canadians provided twenty-three RCAF fliers and two Caribou aircraft based in El-Arish, Sinai.[32] Paul Martin, the Canadian secretary of state for external affairs, stated during the parliamentary approval of the UN observer mission:

It is hoped that this will bring about the termination of a situation in that country which has become increasingly acute since the establishment of the present republican government in September of last year, and will help to avoid the danger of the internal conflict in that country developing into more widespread hostilities throughout the area.[33]

Thomas Clement Douglas, a Canadian member of Parliament from British Columbia added:

I wish to congratulate the government on having accepted this responsibility, and to say that . . . we shall always give our support to any contribution which Canada may make through serving under the United Nations for the maintenance of peace throughout the world and supplying part of a world peace force.[34]

From the perspective of Martin, Douglas, and much of the rest of the Canadian Parliament in June 1963, it seemed that UNYOM had the potential to bring about "world peace," or at the very least to contain a local conflict. While it might be tempting to dismiss the perceived potential benefit of UNYOM as another case of misplaced Canadian optimism during the 1960s, there was in fact a shared hope among the UN and the United States that the Saudis and the Egyptians would be willing to adhere to the tenets of the April 1963 Bunker agreements. The war was proving to be a constant drain on the Egyptian economy and political apparatus, and the Saudis were in the midst of a transfer of power between King Saud and his brother Faisal. Canadian optimism was, however, dampened before the observer mission even began.

As if in a prophetic omen of things to come, during an overflight of Yemen on June 19, 1963, in preparation for the start of the Yemen mission, von Horn's aircraft sustained damage from an unspecified source of ground fire en route from Sa'dah to Sana'a. The immediate reaction was one of alarm over the substantial risk of using low-flying single-engine aircraft, vulnerable to ground fire from sporadic hostilities.[35] Von Horn sent Thant a vitriolic letter describing the incident and blaming Thant for the lack of air support. Furthermore, von Horn argued, others should have been doing the reconnaissance, as the task was beneath his dignity.[36]

In the aftermath of this incident, Canadian and UN officials suggested that reconnaissance flights remain above a certain altitude in order to stay clear of errant ground fire from belligerents. While the safety and wellbeing of peacekeeping forces was of utmost concern, there was a perception that the absence of low-flying observation would seriously detract from the overall efficacy of the aerial observation mission. Those advocating riskier, yet more effective flight regulations, purportedly believed that royalists and republican forces alike would immediately recognize the UN peacekeeping planes and respectfully redirect their fire. Skeptics on either side of this argument continued to make their cases on issues of aviation and ground reconnaissance throughout the interim of the mission.

The debate over the relative safety of UN peacekeeping pilots was not, however, limited to their flight altitude. Following the incident with von Horn's aircraft, U Thant requested that, for the safety of pilots involved, no UNYOM missions should operate in areas other than those openly observing a ceasefire.[37] Prior to the start of the mission, there was no actual ceasefire between the royalists, republicans, and Egyptians. The only "ceasefire" zone was the demilitarized border area between the YAR and Saudi Arabia. The limitation of observation to this area served to further distance UNYOM from actual events in Yemen.

Following U Thant's amended guidelines for peacekeeping pilots, Canadian officials began to recognize the futility of this ill-defined mission. It was becoming apparent that the "aim of the operation is to provide a face-saving cover for this Saudi-UAR disengagement which would prevent a direct confrontation from possibly engulfing the whole Middle East in war."[38] UNYOM was not intended to bring a stop to hostilities between republican and royalist forces, but was rather a context within which the Egyptians and Saudis could respectfully disengage without conceding defeat.

Within days of arriving at the UN Headquarters in Sana'a, there were already grievances from the personnel. Canadians complained of a lack of provisions and believed that the water had been poisoned by Yemenis who threw their dead bodies into wells utilized by UN officials. Multiple requests were sent to UN headquarters for an immediate airlift of drinking water. Brian Pridham, an official from the Arabian Department of the British Foreign Office, expressed a great deal of skepticism toward these tales of water issues: "The story about the water, as well as the water itself, takes some swallowing. The lowest plain around Sana'a is renowned for its wells, and even if the Yemeni had been so un-Arab as to pollute their own water, it would have been far simpler to tap any local mountain spring than to fly water in."[39]

On July 2, a briefing was received from Sana'a: it complained of the inability to boil water at a high enough temperature in high elevation to purify water of high bacteria content.[40] While in reality drinking this partially boiled water would likely not have harmed the personnel, the fact that this briefing was one of the first major issues from the mission to Yemen is indicative of more serious problems in preparing for conditions in Yemen. It was as if the troops had arrived from their previous UN posts in Congo and Sinai only to discover, much to their surprise, that Sana'a was set atop a mountain rather than a plateau.[41] The purity of water in Sana'a was representative of the greater difficulty of transitioning UN personnel to the shoestring mission in Yemen, a new model being advocated by U Thant.

The Mission Continues to Unravel

In protest of the unsatisfactory administrative arrangements for UNYOM, General von Horn submitted his urgent resignation on August 20, 1963, effective officially on August 31. He remarked in his letter of resignation: "When my duty-bound representations so often are boomeranged as "unwarranted remarks" I feel having [sic] lost your confidence and therefore I have no other choice but to herewith tender my resignation."[42]

Von Horn highlighted several specific areas where he thought the mission was particularly problematic. The purported goal of UNYOM was to observe the withdrawal of Saudi Arabia and Egypt, a task the current

mission was not capable of completing. Based on the mission's reconnaissance, the Saudis were no longer aiding the imam's forces across
the Yemen-Saudi border, although this did not preclude tribal groups
from conducting their own trade. In a meeting with UK Ambassador
Colin Crowe, acting Saudi Deputy Foreign Minister Sheikh Muhammad
Ibrahim Mas'ud explained "that Saudis have ceased all aid through official
channels, but cannot account for illicit arms trade." In addition Mas'ud
reiterated that Jizan and Najran had functioned for centuries as markets
for the local Yemeni economy and as such attracted significant movement
of nonmilitary goods. This created further difficulties for the UN as there
was a need to distinguish between contraband and legal trade.[43]

Additional impediments along the Saudi-Yemeni border further limited the mission's ability to observe, as for logistical reasons aerial and
ground reconnaissance could only be carried out during daylight hours.
Given the intense heat during the majority of the year in Yemen, however,
much of the travel was conducted at night when there would be no UN
observers on site. Although UN peacekeepers solved this issue by maintaining a fixed-observer position alongside a main road for forty-hour
shifts at a time, von Horn did not deem this sustainable for a successful
mission. For example, a UN ground patrol at one point observed eleven
camels and sixteen donkeys loaded with sacks and wooden boxes passing through the Saudi Arabian border town of Nahuga. When asked, the
leader of the convoy explained that all he was carrying was food. Believing
him, the observers let him through without having him checked or questioned further.[44]

Von Horn complained that he could not verify Nasser's claim to have
withdrawn 8,300 troops through independent observation. UNYOM personnel did not have access to Egyptian troop transport facilities in Hodeidah
or the Egyptian garrisons in Sana'a. He believed that the apparent movement of Egyptian soldiers was merely a rotation of troops rather than an
effectual withdrawal. In essence, from von Horn's perspective, Nasser was
making a mockery of the mission and his agreed withdrawal. As if to add
salt to the wound, Nasser continued unrestrained aerial bombardment and
continuous encroachment on the "demilitarized zone."[45] According to the
eyewitness account of a USAID worker in July 1963, at least six hundred
Egyptian troops were seen disembarking in Hodeidah. Yugoslav Deputy
Commander General Branko Pavlovic added that despite the fact that
UNYOM observers were required to oversee Egyptian troop withdrawals, UAR officials actually had asked UN observers to leave the premises

during troop movements on numerous occasions. Unsurprisingly, during these instances, reports confirmed the arrival of additional Egyptian soldiers to replace those who had been sent home as part of the usual troop rotation.[46]

The second major concern noted by von Horn was the difficulty of securing financial support for the mission. In agreeing to fund the UN mission, the Saudis provided money while the UAR promised only the equivalent value in logistical support.[47] Von Horn refused on numerous occasions to use UAR transports or facilities, as doing so would have compromised the neutrality of the mission.[48] This difficulty in maintaining a neutral and uninvolved position is best highlighted by the following two incidents. On July 23, 1963, reports were sent to UN headquarters that UAR aircraft were following UNYOM Caribou aircraft during flights from Sana'a to Sa'dah. In a second incident in July 1963, UN aircraft were seen bringing wounded Egyptian soldiers to Sana'a for treatment. Canadian Secretary of State Paul Martin released a directive indicating that the transport of non-UN personnel should be limited to situations in which lives were in danger and no other aircraft were in the region. Any extensive airlift of Egyptian or Saudi troops on UN aircraft would not only cast doubts as to the neutrality of the mission, but might actually put UN personnel in danger. Either side might otherwise consider UN aircraft as troop transports for one of the belligerent parties.[49]

UN aircraft was competing with the UAR for airspace, particularly around Sana'a, where the old airport had no control tower and only a single runway that was in essence a 14,000-foot-long gravel surface.[50] These circumstances were part of a deliberate attempt by the Egyptian air force to use UN observers as a cover for bombing raids over royalist territory in Yemen and Saudi Arabia. Close encounters with UAR aircraft were additionally a consequence of the language barrier between the Canadian pilots and the Egyptians in the control tower who spoke no English. The Egyptian air force was, however, able to communicate the need for priority access to the airfield, barring UN aircraft from the field during Egyptian maneuvers.[51]

In November 1963, Saudi Prince Muhammad ibn Nayef and Corporal Saher ben 'Abd al-Amer reported seeing two aircraft passing over the Jizan checkpoint before hearing explosions in al-Kuba, a Saudi border town. The attack occurred on Thursday, November 21, a traditional regional market day during which four thousand people gathered on the banks of the local wadi. When two airplanes approached from the west, people ran for cover.

After the planes circled once, they left toward the north, clearly displaying their white color and UN emblem. When two more planes approached from the southeast ten minutes later, the locals did not run, assuming that these were UN aircraft as well, and then the bombing began. The attack lasted thirty-five minutes and targeted five trucks parked in the middle of the market with bombs and gun fire. Among the dead were children, women, and men from both Saudi Arabia and Yemen. UN Major Paul Paulson recounted having visited al-Kuba numerous times and not seeing any suspicious Saudi military activity, claiming that the only purpose of this UAR attack was "terror."[52]

A third element to von Horn's grievances was more personal. Von Horn's requests for airlift of material from Rafah were rejected because of expense. Much to his ire, material would be sent via sea. Von Horn perceived this rejection as a personal affront by Indian General Indar Jit Rikhye, who was serving as military advisor to U Thant. General Rikhye also rejected von Horn's request for extra leave for his personnel as compensation for the difficulty of operating in Yemen. This was part of a larger debate that included the level of personnel salaries, sufficient supplies, and hygienic accommodations, which von Horn and others deemed insufficient.[53] Sargeant Robert McLellan, a member of the UNYOM personnel, sent a formal request to UN headquarters taking up the same issue of compensation and requesting an increase in salary given the risk entailed in the UN mission in Yemen. McLellan insisted that he was not being greedy in asking for more money, but that he was only advocating for fairness.[54]

On September 1, 1963, Yugoslav Deputy Commander General Pavlovic took over from von Horn as interim commander of the UNYOM. He had previously served in this capacity during von Horn's two-week absence in July. Pavlovic faced additional difficulties, however, because of linguistic barriers (he spoke little English) and so was replaced by Indian Lieutenant General P.S. Gyani before the end of the month.[55]

During this leadership transition, Yugoslavia announced the withdrawal of its ground forces from Yemen, following the end of the four month original proposal made by U Thant. Without a presence on the ground, the entire observation mission became reliant on aerial reconnaissance. Furthermore, the declining effectiveness of the four single-engine Otters (see Fig. 4.2) in the hot and mountainous Yemeni climate forced the RCAF to rely on the larger Caribous which fly at a higher altitude, providing even less "observation," although at a safer distance and with greater reliability in the Arabian climate.[56]

FIGURE 4.2 UNYOM personnel inspecting a damaged wheel of a Royal Canadian Air Force Otter aircraft. (UNA, Photo 159707, UNYOM, June 1, 1963, Najran, Saudi Arabia)

In an attempt to find a solution to the absence of a Yugoslavian military presence, Gyani planned for Saudi military representatives to be stationed at checkpoints along with UN observers. Saudi patrols were not, however, to accompany UN observers into Yemen territory. The Saudi soldiers were responsible for checking the contents of the convoy with "a thorough scrutiny" while the patrol commander merely observed and made notes for his report. UN observers could only ask Saudis to stop vehicles and requisition contraband or ammunition, but the observers were instructed not to inspect convoys themselves and certainly not without Saudi officials present. The observers' handwritten reports, found covered in a layer of sand after decades stored in their archival folders, detailed the movement of troops in the demilitarized zone, convoys between Saudi Arabia and Yemen, air activity, hostile military activity, and personnel and equipment redeployment; they made no indication of UAR withdrawal.[57]

After insistence by U Thant, the Canadians agreed to continue supplying members of the RCAF for a primarily aerial observer mission. Pier
P. Spinelli, the acting undersecretary and director of the European Office
of the UN, was brought on to serve as the civilian special representative
to the secretary general and head of the mission in Yemen. Although no
effectual Egyptian withdrawal was noted, it seemed that the very presence
of the UN in Yemen, even in a limited capacity, was a deterrent to full-scale
UAR assaults on the royalists or on Saudi Arabian territory. With this in
mind, Thant managed to secure five additional two-month renewals, continuing the mission until September 4, 1964. According to Thant's reports
to the Security Council in 1964, while fighting continued in Yemen, air
attacks on Saudi border villages had subsided, with only a few exceptions.[58]

Although direct confrontation between Saudi Arabia and Egypt may
have been avoided, munitions transports across the border were growing more brazen. Heavy transports were seen traveling through the Saudi
border towns of al-Jara'a and al-Kuba, but vehicles were not checked by
observers, "owing to the hostile attitude shown by the drivers and vehicle
guards." The trucks were, however, observed to be carrying "war materials
and soldiers."[59] The town of Jizan was also being used as a transport location for munitions to royalist forces in the north and as a destination for
Yemeni tribal refugees.[60]

Prior to the end of the UNYOM mission, General Rikhye observed
that rather than reducing troops, Nasser seemed to have been preparing
to make a large-scale assault on royalists just as the UN mission was
due to expire on September 4, 1964.[61] UN observers gathered information indicating substantial Egyptian and republican troop deployments
in the planning of further large-scale assaults on royalist positions.[62]
The Saudis, however, did not need this report to realize that Egyptian
troops were not withdrawing from Yemen and were reluctant to continue funding UNYOM, finally bringing an official end to the belliger-
ent-funded mission.[63]

UNYOM—More than Meets the Eye

The UN mission in Yemen has been criticized not only for its failure to
end hostilities in the region, but also for restrictions placed on contact
with royalists, the limited observation mandate, and the conditions for
personnel.[64] Recently available UN archives have shed light on multiple
aspects that counter these three perceived deficiencies of the mission. The

criticism of the mission was more a result of international controversy than the actual situation on the ground in Yemen.

The principal complaint against UNYOM was its failure to engage royalists, thereby hampering the mission's ability to mediate a peaceful agreement that took all sides into account.[65] In reality, there were multiple visits to royalist bases aimed at familiarizing Yemeni tribesmen with the blue helmets and white planes of UN personnel. For example, in August 1963, Saudi Prince Turki ibn Abdulaziz al-Saud (seen Fig. 4.3), the governor of Riyadh Province at the time, was asked by UN headquarters to make contact with royalists in Jizan on behalf of UNYOM. The announced purpose of the meeting was to explore royalist reactions to UN personnel and determine whether they would offer them protection.

The meeting took place on August 21 in the Sa'dah area, where UN Major Larry David, an American fluent in Arabic with years of experience in the Middle East, met with royalist Hassan ibn Hussein. Together they crossed the Yemeni border at al-Kuba, transferring to a royalist Dodge

FIGURE 4.3 Prince Turki meeting with UNYOM observers in Jizan, July 1963. (UNA, Photo 159705, UNYOM, June 1, 1963)

Power Wagon, as the UN jeeps could not handle the terrain. Major David was received hospitably, and royalist officials assured him that al-Badr would order the tribes not to harm UN officials and not to fire upon white planes. Royalist soldiers offered their own assessment of the power of Egyptian air supremacy in the Yemeni conflicts: "If the UAR aircraft were withdrawn from the Yemen, the royalists would solve the problem of the withdrawal of Egyptian troops." This implied that Egyptian air support was the republic's only tactical advantage over royalist forces.[66]

In October 1963, Major Nicholas Doughty, a member of the UNYOM personnel, traveled from Najran to the Yemeni district of al-Hashwa for a three-day meeting with Prince Ali, the twenty-two-year-old first cousin of al-Badr who spoke English, having learned the language while spending a year studying economics in the American University of Beirut. Ali described an apparent UAR military build-up northeast of Sa'dah and offered to escort UN observers to the outskirts of the Egyptian military site. In addition, given that UN officials were already arbitrating between Egyptians and royalists on prisoner exchange matters, Ali expressed a willingness to have UNYOM observers stationed on a semipermanent basis in royalist areas. He pledged to circulate the word to tribesmen not to fire on white UN aircraft, although he admitted that "it was often difficult to ensure disciplined acts by the tribesmen."[67]

In his assessment of the meeting, Doughty suggested continuing talks with royalists, as they occupied a central geographic position with access to the specific areas that appeared to be the focus of the UN mission's attention. He suggested maintaining contact with Prince Ali and other royalists, while still retaining an unofficial status, in accordance with U Thant's directive to avoid internal politics of the Yemeni conflict. Doughty felt there was a need to increase "at least an awareness of what UN people look like, particularly among the tribesmen." Furthermore, Doughty surmised that "if UAR were notified of UN presence in Hashwa area, the regular bombing might cease." Nonetheless, he admitted that there were some difficulties in maintaining regular contact with the royalist camp. The rough terrain of the al-Hashwa region would require the purchase of new vehicles for UN personnel and there was always a danger of UAR bombing despite UN presence. Doughty's visit was highlighted by hours of dancing with royalist hill tribesmen. He showed off the blue UN helmets to three hundred chanting tribesmen who were "in line abreast coming down the wadi, each line led by a group of dagger waving dancers."[68]

Aside from David and Doughty's accounts, several additional visits were had with royalist representatives. Pier P. Spinelli met with Imam al-Badr's foreign minister in April 1964,[69] and UN and ICRC representatives visited with al-Badr in August 1964 to negotiate a prisoner exchange.[70] André Rochat, the head of the delegation from the ICRC in Yemen, maintained continuous contact with royalists and reported regularly to UN officials who in turn provided occasional air transport for Rochat.[71] The ICRC field hospital in the royalist-held northern territory of Uqd was also a direct line of communication with royalist officials, as ICRC personnel utilized frequent UNYOM flights between Sana'a and Jeddah to transport people and supplies by Caribou.[72]

Nonrecognition of al-Badr's royalists was limited to the official halls of the UN. On the ground, UNYOM officials coordinated their mission with royalists and made efforts to regularly visit their remote encampments. The demilitarized zone situated in royalist territory contained observer outposts, the ICRC hospital, and many other instances for official and happenstance interaction with royalist officials and members of the tribal militias.

The "observer" designation of the UNYOM has also been given as a reason for the mission's failure as there was no Egyptian withdrawal to observe. In reality, the UN mission was called upon to observe much more than just the planned withdrawals of Egyptian troops and Saudi support. An addendum to the responsibilities of UNYOM included the investigation of regional incidents "where appropriate and possible." These included UAR offensive actions against royalist positions and accusations of Saudi aid being delivered to royalists in Yemen.[73]

The presence of UNYOM acted as a safety valve for Saudi Arabia and the UAR to let off steam without engaging each other. According to the UN observer log, both countries submitted dozens of complaints to local UN observer personnel. Most of these grievances sounded more like familial bickering, with half of Saudi communications naming a camel as the primary victim of a UAR bombing run.[74] To ease regional tensions, UN observers or Yugoslavian military representatives would be sent to "investigate" at least half of the submitted allegations, a process that amounted to writing a few notes in an incident log.[75] Despite the lack of actionable responses to any of these incidents, the complaints continued to arrive at UN bases, a sign that even meager international attention was sufficient for the parties involved. Beyond the role of sanctioning diplomatic finger pointing, the UN observers were able to foster a working relationship with local officials with whom they consulted during their investigations.

June 1963, while the mission was only in a preliminary stage, was nonetheless a particularly busy month for UN military observers. UN observers responded to UAR accusations of Saudi weapons transfers by documenting ammunition and gasoline dumps near towns along the Saudi-Yemeni border. UN observers responded to reports of UAR bombings in the Saudi border villages of Tamniah, al-Abha, and al-Hadira, where UNYOM representative Major Brage Schaathun was accompanied by Saudi Lieutenant Colonel Hassan Katlan and Prince Abdullah al-Madi for thorough investigations (see Fig. 4.4). The team examined bomb fragments and interviewed survivors to put together a detailed report with photographs of property destruction and injury to civilians.[76]

On August 27, 1963, the village sheikh of al-Atam wrote to Saudi officials to report that their cattle had been subject to artillery fire. Saudi officials passed on the information in the form of a formal complaint. UN Major David arrived on site, where he was shown shell fragments from the

FIGURE 4.4 UN Major B. Schaathun (center) investigating UAR bombings at al-Abha, June 27, 1963, with Saudi Lieutenant Colonel Katlan (left) looking on. (UNA, S-0057-0001, Folder 1, June 27, 1963)

artillery fire. Nearby, other UN observers toured the evacuated village of Halfa to investigate reports of an earlier bombing. While they were on site Egyptian artillery started shooting in their vicinity, and UNYOM officers had to lie on the ground and crawl toward the Ta'ashar Valley, from where they withdrew.[77] In another investigation on November 21, UN observers recorded the testimony of locals that UAR planes had raided the Harah market, south of Jizan. Bombs and machine guns targeted the market, causing injuries and damage to property. Onlookers claimed that the UAR planes followed a UN overflight by five minutes and flew back over UN headquarters in Najran "at a low altitude as if challenging the observers."[78]

These examples represent only a small number of the total complaints investigated by UN observers, who served additional roles beyond observing the withdrawals of Egypt and Saudi Arabia. The perspectives offered by UN and Canadian officials' accounts run counter the image of a dysfunctional mission. The UNYOM that emerges from this newly informed investigation is of a mission that did in fact play a significant role in mediating the Saudi-Egyptian conflict and managed to incorporate all sides involved.

Von Horn and other critics of the UN mission have highlighted the meager rations and paltry conditions at UN bases and outposts in the demilitarized zone between Saudi Arabia and the YAR. Von Horn blamed what he referred to as the "paucity of transport planes" for leading to the "near starvation" of UN personnel.[79] During a visit with Canadian pilots in December 1963, Flight Lieutenant Peter Kelly, a medical officer for the Canadian Air Transport Command, claimed that the supplies and conditions were so poor that "we in the RCAF have reached the peak of our endurance in the filthy living environment of Yemen."[80] Kelly's comments came at a time of heightened UN tensions: Yugoslav ground forces were withdrawing, leaving the bulk of the mission's responsibility in the hands of the RCAF, much to the indignation of the Canadian public, which was losing patience with their country's continued role in global peacekeeping.

In reality, the rumors of conditions in Yemen were greatly exaggerated, leading UN officials and critics to believe the situation in Yemen was far worse than it actually was. RCAF Flight Lieutenant George E. Mayer, a twenty-two-year-old pilot serving in Yemen, recalled hearing rumors about working conditions in Yemen prior to his arrival. The flying was dangerous, the food was terrible, and the "Yemen gut" traveler's diarrhea and vomiting was even worse. He had been told that "the outposts made the TV program M*A*S*H locations look like the Chateau Laurier."[81] Upon arrival in Sana'a, another Canadian pilot remarked that in fact the accommodations, located in an old palace that had been home to Imam Yahya's harem, were primitive, but certainly acceptable for UN standards.[82]

While there is no doubt that operating in temperatures that topped 125 °F during the daytime can hardly be considered comfortable, the UN staff was not lacking, especially when the dire poverty experienced by most Yemenis is taken into consideration. The base in Najran, for example, received weekly North Star air deliveries of mail, fresh fruits and vegetables, and other supplies from the UNEF base in El-Arish.[83] A close analysis of the shipment orders in the UN archives reveals a picture far different from the purportedly depraved conditions under which the UN staff lived.

The main complaint in many of the telegraphs from Najran, Hodeidah, and Sana'a was of the staff's boredom rather than lack of resources. In response to several requests for reading material and entertainment, headquarters granted six copies each of weekly newspapers including *Life*, the *New York Times, Time*, the *Herald Tribune, Newsweek*, and the *Daily Telegraph* (London). Along with the newspapers, UN headquarters also sent eight films, including *Bye Bye Birdie, In the Piazza, Big Red, Come Fly with Me*, and *Ambush in Cameron Pass*.[84] A follow-up request procured a new movie projector, loudspeakers, a cinemascope lens, spare parts, and a transformer.[85] The projector came along with an additional collection of movies, including *The Running Man, Wives and Lovers, The Mouse on the Moon, Come Blow Your Horn, Murder at the Gallop*, among other hit movies from 1963.[86] The UN base in Najran would occasionally host a barbeque of roasted gazelle and movie viewing for ICRC officials located across the Yemeni border in Uqd.[87]

In addition to being entertained with daily newspapers and current movies, UNYOM staff also developed a penchant for heavy drinking and smoking. Telegrams from the various UN outposts in Yemen requesting shipments of beer and alcohol to be charged either to UNYOM's cash account or to their individual expense accounts were sent at least once a week. On several occasions UN headquarters responded: "Forwarding two Tuborgs [beer] ASAP."[88] One telegram to headquarters, perhaps in preparation for a night of heavy drinking, read: "Please increase whisky request to four bottles for each of us." Some orders did not specify brand name, but sufficed with a general request for beer, whisky, vodka, or "any other alcohol."[89] Other orders, however, were made by UN officials with a more epicurean taste. For example, Major Paul Paulson, who worked as a liaison officer in Jeddah, requested an emergency airlift of two bottles of Rémy

Martin, a particularly expensive brand of cognac. Paulson deemed this airlift, which was to include gin, vodka, and pipe tobacco as well, an appropriate restitution from UN headquarters for not agreeing to ship the UNYOM
station in Jizan a Christmas tree in December 1963.[90] Requests for beer
and spirits were surpassed only by orders for cigarettes, specifically Phillip
Morris brand.[91] Aside from a special meal order for Christmas dinner in
December 1963, the content of these telegrams did not convey a desperate
need for food or any other staples. UN personnel in Yemen seemed to have
plenty of leisure time, during which they would drink and smoke heavily,
watch movies, and read regularly—hardly indications of a demoralized and
depraved crew. Even General von Horn himself was often accompanied
by the two things that "never strayed far from his side: a beautiful blond
Swedish secretary and bottle of his favourite malt beverage."[92]

After spending two months in the desert Najran observation point,
the UN radioman Kenneth Woskett was transferred to Jeddah to run the
UN radio station and staff the UN liaison office, which served as a transit point for personnel. While there, the commanding officer in Sana'a
ordered him to rent a locked storage space in the part of the Jeddah airport where international flights departed and arrived. This area served as
the transit point for alcohol arriving from Jerusalem twice a week, which
was then sent along with personnel on transfer to Sana'a. Woskett, who
served as the gatekeeper for this locker (he was the only one with a set of
keys), ensured that the booze was off-loaded from the aircraft with the
full knowledge of the Saudis and locked in the storeroom in the "international" area. The room also stored other necessities such as soap, combs,
toothpaste, and the like. Radio transmissions from Yemen would place
alcohol requests with Woskett the night before the C-130 transport plane
left Jeddah with the replacement staff. In Sana'a the spirits were off-loaded
and taken to the UNYOM headquarters, which had a small basement bar
for social occasions. Generally an average of about six bottles, mostly gin
or whisky, were sent with each shipment. There was no Yemeni government agency to make UN personnel accountable, and the Saudis did not
press the issue.[93]

Upon arriving in Sana'a, George Mayer was treated to four cold Amstel
beers to make him feel at ease. He recounted a comical anecdote that
demonstrated the centrality and importance of beer for UN personnel
during his later stationing in Najran: "The focal point of Najran was the
450lb. kerosene fired double door fridge strategically located in the shady
party area. On the left side was the Danish beer Tuborg and on the right

side, my favourite Dutch Amstel beer. You were obliged to bow or salute whenever you passed it by! It was the junior man on the outpost that was charged with keeping it stocked and worth his hide if he didn't!"[94]

Any demoralization of the group could be attributed to the Montreal Canadiens' playoff loss in April 1964. The Canadian pilots staffing UNYOM in 1964 spent a great deal of their leisure and work time receiving updates on the scores and standings of the Montreal Canadiens and Toronto Maple Leafs during the course of the National Hockey League (NHL) playoffs. Over fifty telegrams were sent to UN bases in Yemen detailing the outcome of the most recent playoff game, the performance of the Detroit Red Wings hockey great Gordie Howe, and the eventual Stanley Cup victory of the Toronto Maple Leafs.[95] Despite the complaining, it seems that at least Canadian hockey fans had their priorities straight. The accusation of UNYOM limitations, failures, depravity, and shortages were in fact reflections of broader disenchantment with the peacekeeping model and the evolving face of the UN rather than the reality of the mission to Yemen.

Understanding UNYOM in Context

The stark differences between von Horn's description of the barebones conditions of the UN outposts versus the college dorm–like environment of drinking, movie watching, sports fandom, and smoking during leisure time portrayed in the archives was, as Canadian pilot Doug Poole explained, a matter of psychological perspective. Poole claimed that Canadian airmen were spoiled, as "they have always been accustomed to going about the business of war, well-lodged, well-fed, well-clothed and clean shaven. This mission would tax their mettle to the limit. The environment and the hygiene conditions found in this inhospitable climate would not be their only problem. It would be harder, and take them longer to cope with the mental challenges."[96] The sign welcoming new recruits to the mission's base in Sana'a, referred to the impressive three-story structure as "The Twilight Zone," despite the fact that the building was staffed with a personal chef, water purifier (albeit somewhat late in coming), electricity, and an acceptable latrine, amenities of which the local population could only dream.[97]

The negative outlook of UN personnel was more likely the result of disgruntled reactions to abusive UN leadership and general despondency with the UN mission. Although he declared himself an advocate of UN staff and resigned from his post in protest over their conditions, General Carl von Horn was known to have had a short temper and was often verbally abusive to UN personnel. During a preflight inspection of his Caribou in Sana'a, Doug Poole noticed a fresh bullet hole that caused him some concern. When von Horn arrived to ascertain as to the delay in takeoff, the following demonstrative episode occurred:

> "The Wing Commander took him around to the back of the Caribou and showed him the bullet hole. The General had got out of the wrong side of the bed and wasn't in a very good mood. He seldom was. He asked if the aircraft was alright to fly. The Wing Commander assured him it was. He told the General, the bullet had gone in on one side of the aircraft and out the other, "without hitting anything important." ... The General frowned and replied: "Then get in the God damned thing and fly it, what the hell do you think you're being paid for?"[98]

Kenneth Woskett took particular note of von Horn's entitled attitude toward his staff. Woskett recalled being reprimanded by von Horn for trivial incidents related to the official UN car. On one occasion, Woskett, who had recently arrived at UN headquarters as a radioman, accidentally parked his car in the senior staff parking spot in front of the UN laundry site. Von Horn took the time out of his schedule to call Woskett to a meeting to discuss the severity of the parking offense and to reprimand him.[99]

Beyond the confines of their headquarters, UN personnel reported being shocked by the disdain Egyptians harbored toward Yemenis. The thought that the UN mission was aiding the Egyptian cause, even indirectly, cast a negative light on UNYOM in the eyes of its personnel and critics. Doug Poole reported driving by two Egyptian guards on the way to the Sana'a airport and noticed them pointing and laughing at a decapitated head of a Yemeni, mounted on a plank; they had placed a cigarette to dangle from the severed head's mouth.[100] Ian Umbach, who served as George Mayer's commanding officer in Yemen, noted "the appearance each morning of a freshly severed head over the main gate to the city," a sign, according to Umbach, that Yemen was still in the Middle Ages.[101] On a different occasion, a group of four Canadian pilots was shocked by the abuse that a senior Egyptian administrator in Sana'a inflicted upon his Yemeni barber. The Egyptian reprimanded him for being late, then slapped him and kicked him multiple times in a demonstration of what Poole noted was an imposed hierarchy of Egyptians over Yemenis.[102]

Many UN officials and personnel felt that the General Assembly and the United States had "stumbled into premature recognition of Sallal's republic" and was now in a political bind as supporters of the perceptibly weaker side of an internationalized civil war.[103] Although they may have felt uneasy about the organization's political stance, U Thant's political options regarding the royalists were constraints by UN protocol. Following the US recognition of the YAR on December 16, 1962, the UN had been given the green light to recognize the Yemeni republic as well. On December 20, the General Assembly voted seventy-four to four, with twenty-three abstentions, to approve the Credential Committee's recommendation to seat the YAR delegates as the official representatives of Yemen. Given the official UN decision recognizing the republicans, Thant and UNYOM could not openly incorporate royalist officials and opinions into the specifics of the mission without violating the General Assembly's decision. Lieutenant General P.S. Gyani needed to be reminded of this fact by Ralph Bunche when he assumed the head position of UNYOM in September 1963: "Limit contact with royalists out of concern that the UN might be legitimizing other government than YAR."[104]

Serving as a window into the thinking of Thant's inner circle, Gyani noted that UAR military action had made the republic even more unpopular to the extent that the YAR could not even collect taxes to pay full salary to its employees. He suggested that the UN could serve in an advisory role to the YAR in the place of Egypt, seeing this as an alternative to the UNYOM mission in its present form.[105] It is evident from Gyani's suggestion of stationing a permanent UN financial consultant in Yemen that he understood the true purpose of UNYOM: simply having a presence in Yemen.

After two months as interim head of the mission, Gyani was replaced in November 1963 by Spinelli, the first civilian UN official to lead a military mission. U Thant's logic in appointing Spinelli was further explained in his grand vision for UNYOM: "It was desirable that the mission of military observation with its limited mandate should be complemented by a United Nations political presence, which, by exploratory conversations with the parties concerned, might be able to play a more positive role in encouraging the implementation of the disengagement agreement and peace and security in the region."[106] In appointing a civilian, U Thant was also thinking beyond the UNYOM, to perhaps maintaining a permanent

UN aid mission in Yemen dedicated to the establishment of health and education facilities. However, Sallal and Baydani later rejected this offer, fearing that a UN presence would undermine Egyptian support for the republic.[107]

In the early months of the mission Thant indicated to the Security Council that he had envisioned the mission as an "intermediary and endorser of good faith on behalf of the parties concerned."[108] In hindsight, although there was an increase in the number of Egyptian troops in Yemen, the withdrawal of the UNYOM mission was followed by a series of direct diplomatic negotiations between Egypt and Saudi Arabia and royalist and republican camps. Mediation efforts that included Bunche, Bunker, von Horn, Spinelli, and other UN officials acted to reduce inter-Arab tensions and keep open the possibility of a diplomatic solution. The model offered by international diplomatic efforts would be at the core of the eventual Saudi and Egyptian withdrawal from Yemen in 1967 and served to underscore, despite having been hampered by global conflicts unrelated to local events, the true benefit of UNYOM.

5

Nasser's Cage

AT THE SECOND Arab Summit in September 1964, following the withdrawal of UNYOM and the measured gains of the Haradh offensive,
Nasser and the Saudi monarchy once again declared their desire for
mutual withdrawal. Rather than renew the Egyptian offensive when the
royalists attacked in October 1964, Nasser chose to hold onto defensive
positions and organize additional meetings that included representatives
from both the republican and royalist camps. The peace conferences,
highlighted by the Saudi-Egyptian Jeddah Pact in August 1965 and the
Yemeni National Conference in Haradh in November 1965, created expectations for reconciliation.

By the end of 1965, however, Nasser's policy in Yemen reversed course,
renewing the Egyptian occupation in what he called the "long-breath strategy." UAR troops garrisoned the strategic triangle and interconnecting
road network, relying on an intensive aerial bombing campaign that would
feature the indiscriminate use of chemical weapons to subdue royalist
tribal supporters. The reversal of the Egyptian withdrawal from Yemen
has been described as a reaction to British colonial policy, Saudi-Iran relations, and renewed royalist attacks against Egyptian troops. Alternatively,
it may be argued that the United States and the USSR played a role in
encouraging Nasser to remain in Yemen in an effort to confine Egyptian
military power. Even amidst Cold War tensions, US President Lyndon
B. Johnson and Soviet Secretary Leonid Brezhnev found themselves following similar policies toward Nasser in Yemen in an effort to forestall a
superpower nuclear confrontation over an Egyptian-Israeli war. Foreign
agendas, once again, dominated the course of the Yemen Civil War and
placed local events into an arena of international conflict.

Haradh Conference and Political Turmoil in Yemen

After reopening diplomatic relations in the months following the first Arab Summit in Cairo in January 1964, Nasser and Faisal declared their willingness to bring the Yemeni conflict to a resolution.[1] The Montaza Palace in Alexandria, Egypt, served as the venue for the second Arab Summit in September 1964. This was intended as a demonstration of Arab unity and reconciliation. According to a Soviet account of the September 1964 Summit, although the topic of normalizing Saudi-YAR relations was discussed, no definitive actions were taken. There was, however, universal agreement on the Arab anti-imperialist stance and support for anti-British nationalist forces in Aden, Cyprus, and Oman.[2]

The Arab Summit came on the heels of the success of the Egyptian Haradh Offensive and the capture of the royalist base of al-Qarah in August 1964. Nasser was intent on establishing a ceasefire in order to secure the territorial gains north and east of the strategic triangle. From October 30 through November 4, Nasser and Faisal met in the summer hilltop resort in Erkowit, Sudan to negotiate the mutual withdrawal of Egyptian and Saudi support from Yemen according to similar parameters of the original Ellsworth Bunker agreements of 1963. The royalists were represented by Ahmad Muhammad al-Shami and the republicans by Muhammad Mahmud al-Zubayri, one of the founders of the original Free Yemeni Movement. All parties agreed on a ceasefire, which was to take effect on November 6, 1964, with a Yemeni National Council planned for November 23. There was an understanding among the attendees that both Sallal and al-Badr would be forced to step down during the process of forming the new Yemeni government.

On the ground in Yemen, however, another reality was unfolding. As had been the pattern in the prior two years, royalist forces that had previously retreated to the northern highlands came back down from the mountains to reclaim territory lost during the Egyptian Haradh Offensive. The description of these battles in Western media was analogous to a heroic Maccabean effort of the few royalists against the many Egyptians. For example, during the battle with Egyptians on the northeastern mountain of Jabal Razih, royalist forces numbering only 1,600 tribesmen faced three times that number of Egyptian soldiers and armor. The royalist assault was able to recruit seven thousand additional Hajuri mountaineer militiamen in five hours by "ordering the Hajuri tribal war drum mobilization message to be circulated," and capturing the last two northern Egyptian strongholds at the top of Jabal Razih on December 31, 1964.[3] This battle epitomized the futility of the Haradh Offensive, originally intended to capture or kill Imam al-Badr by any means necessary. Although the summer of 1964 had been Imam al-Badr's "blackest days," during which he developed a "nagging neurosis and a raging carbuncle," he emerged triumphant in December 1964 to declare yet again that "Yemen will be Nasser's graveyard."[4]

Nasser's setbacks were not limited to the battlefield, as segments of Yemeni republicans considered moderates were growing increasingly frustrated with the ongoing civil war and the continued presence of Egyptian troops in Yemen. Several leaders formed opposition parties to Sallal's regime, constituting the movement that became known as the "third-force." Sayyid Ibrahim Ali al-Wazir, descendant of the historic rival clan to the Hamid al-Din family for the position of imam, led an opposition to Sallal in the form of the Union of Popular Forces, an ill-structured and short-lived political party.[5]

Al-Zubayri, who had served as a minister in Sallal's cabinet, subsequently formed the Party of Allah and left Sana'a to recruit tribal supporters in the northern and northeastern Yemeni highlands. The stated goal of Zubayri's party was to rid Yemen of the Egyptian military occupation and oust Sallal and his government. Zubayri and his third-force supporters envisioned retaining the structure of a republic equally divided between royalist and republican supporters. Although groups within the third-force suggested reviving the concept of a constitutional monarchy, most agreed that the Hamid al-Din family should not remain in power.[6] Qadi 'Abd al-Rahman al-Iryani, who later served as the YAR head of state from 1967 to 1974 and oversaw Yemen's reconciliation, was considered, along with Ahmad Muhammad Nu'man and Zubayri, as one of the founding fathers of the concept of a Yemeni republic and a leader of the "third-force." His formal title of *qadi*, or religious judge, underscored his role as the bridge between the traditional imamate and the modern Yemeni state.[7]

Several secret meetings between royalist and republican representatives took place between November 1964 and March 1965. Egyptian authorities reportedly became alarmed at the content of these meetings, and arranged for the assassination of Zubayri on April 1, 1965,[8] in the hopes that removing him would bring the third-force movement to a premature end. Other accounts of Zubayri's assassination blame Hassan ibn Yahya, who may have been alarmed by Zubayri's popularity among the royalist tribes.[9]

Popular protest and the Hashid and Bakil tribal federations' threats of marching on Sana'a in the aftermath of Zubayri's assassination pressured Sallal to appoint Ahmad Nu'man as prime minister of the YAR, in the hopes that it would appease the opposition. As prime minister, Nu'man wrested much of Sallal's presidential power and organized a national peace conference in Khamir, a hilltop village thirty miles north of Sana'a, in May 1965.[10] YAR Prime Minister Mohsin al-'Ayni expressed a great deal of optimism for Nu'man's government and the success of the national conference, as he believed an Egyptian withdrawal would follow.[11] This belief was based on a letter received from Nasser around the time of the Khamir conference. In the text of the letter, Nasser made it unequivocally clear that he intended to withdraw Egyptian forces as early as July 1965.[12]

The goal of the Khamir Conference was to form a united Yemen, with the exclusion of Egypt and with limitations on Sallal's power.[13] The conference featured more than five thousand tribal notables and produced the first modern constitution intended for the whole Yemeni state. Yemen would become an Islamic republic, with a strong assembly that could overrule the president, and would raise an eleven-thousand-member people's army to replace the Egyptian forces on which the current YAR was dependent. Iryani, the chairman of the conference, planned to seek Saudi recognition and support, supplanting Egyptian forces, Sallal's regime, and al-Badr's source of financial and logistical support. Rather than acquiesce to Nu'man's political demands, Sallal rejected the power-sharing measures, a clear sign that he was reluctant to compromise with the third-force.

While Nasser's assassination of Zubayri was intended to remove the major political opposition to the Sallal regime, this brash political move was not accompanied by immediate plans for an Egyptian offensive to regain lost territory north and east of the strategic triangle. The royalist offensive continued unabated from March through August 1965, driving Egyptians away from Jawf and Mishriq and leaving them with only two surrounded outposts in Sa'dah and Hajjah.[14] Rather than immediately reinforcing his troops in Yemen, Nasser began the gradual withdrawal of his army and traveled to Jeddah for yet another meeting with Faisal. Before setting out to Saudi Arabia, Nasser gathered Nu'man and his supporters for a frank conversation about the future of the Egyptian presence in Yemen. At the end of the meeting even Nu'man, a vocal opponent of

Egypt's occupation, sincerely believed that Nasser intended to bring the war in Yemen to a close and withdraw his troops.[15]

The Jeddah Pact, signed on August 23, 1965, between Nasser and Saudi King Faisal, seemed to be Nasser's appeal for respite from the war.[16] Although there were reports of Egyptian troops massing on the Saudi border for an attack on Jizan, a principal source of royalist munitions and support, these seemed highly unlikely and were at most a demonstration of military strength prior to negotiations with Faisal.[17] The Egyptian military was hemorrhaging funds, munitions, and soldiers, and had little tangible success to show for it. According to the agreement, Egyptian forces would withdraw by September 1966 and Faisal would deny Saudi territory and resources to royalist armies. Plans were put in place for a second Yemeni tribal meeting in Haradh in November 1965, with a Yemeni plebiscite scheduled for November 1966. Al-Badr reportedly ordered his troops to maintain an offensive ceasefire without ceding any of the gained territory until after the outcome of the second Haradh conference. Sallal responded in kind by freeing political prisoners, although he was soon forced to leave for medical care in Cairo after purportedly being shot by "irate Yarimi tribesmen while staging a bogus 'save the republic' rally at Dhammar replete with imported 'applause' and slogan-shouters."[18] The atmosphere at the November 24, 1965, Haradh II Conference was optimistic, as Nasser had visibly been withdrawing troops, and the mutual ceasefire was being upheld by both sides. Spirits were not dampened when republican and royalist delegates could not agree on the future of the Yemeni imamate after a month-long meeting; they planned to reconvene after Ramadan on February 20, 1966. However, the second rounds of talks never occurred.[19] Within weeks of the Haradh II Conference, Egyptian reinforcements were sent back to Yemen and Nasser's offensive began once again in earnest.

In September 1965, Sallal traveled to Cairo, ostensibly to recover from an illness, but in reality to come under Nasser's watchful eye lest he be overthrown by the growing opposition. When Sallal finally returned to Yemen eleven months later, on August 12, 1966, Egyptian tanks lined the road from the airport to central Sana'a, a testament to the fear that YAR Prime Minister Hassan al-'Amri and opposition leader 'Abd al-Rahman al-Iryani had designs to depose Sallal. Yemenis had begrudged the fact that every Yemeni army officer had an accompanying Egyptian officer: "a Siamese twin empowered to overturn the Yemenis' decisions if they failed to concur with Egyptian thinking."[20] On September 9, Egyptian authorities evidently stooped to new lows by dropping leaflets all over Sana'a accusing al-'Amri of taking money from the United States and embezzling YAR funds. Egyptians encouraged republicans to reject any peace overtures, arguing that the Egyptians must stay in Yemen until the British left Aden, "to protect the republic." Several other prominent officers and officials were accused of being royalist sympathizers or were placed on trial for high treason and either publicly executed or given long prison sentences.[21]

An enraged al-'Amri demanded a face-to-face meeting with Nasser. Acquiescing to al-'Amri's request, Nasser sent two aircraft to Ta'iz to bring al-'Amri and an estimated fifty ministers who opposed Sallal for a meeting in Cairo. Following a meeting at the Officers' Club in Cairo on September 16, 1966, Nasser arrested al-'Amri, al-Iryani, and Nu'man, and kept them under house arrest while the other ministers were sent to a military prison in Cairo's Heliopolis neighborhood. With a single act of political treachery, Nasser successfully lured Sallal's opposition out of the country for the duration of Egypt's presence in Yemen.[22] During the months of imprisonment, Ahmad Nu'man's son Muhammad wrote to the International Red Cross in Geneva, requesting an inquiry into the well-being of his father and political constituents imprisoned in Cairo. In March 1967, André Rochat, the head of the ICRC delegation to Yemen, was entrusted with Muhammad's letter to his father and subsequently used this as an excuse to open additional lines of communication with Egyptian authorities.[23]

Nasser's Change of Heart

As the Egyptian army was rolled back from its positions north and east of the strategic triangle, Nasser appeared to be withdrawing from Yemen with the intention of redeploying his troops in Sinai for a confrontation with Israel.[24] He wanted to prepare for an attack on Israel, but also needed to uphold Egyptian defensive positions during the withdrawal. Several reasons have been suggested to account for the sudden reversal in policy at the end of 1965 and the subsequent failure of the Haradh II peace overtures. Republican intransigence and refusal to compromise with royalists on the republican nature of the state has often been cited as the primary reason.[25] The declared "ceasefire" itself was officially broken by royalist forces, partially as a reaction to the barring of Hamid al-Din families from the Haradh I and II Conferences. Nasser's renewed offensive in 1966 was a response to the insulting nature of royalist attacks on a withdrawing army in order to improve their postwar position.[26] The renewed offensive has also been attributed to Marshal 'Abd al-Hakim Amer, who purportedly sabotaged the Haradh II Conference to give his military solution to the conflict another chance.[27]

Other accounts of the war have blamed the Saudi diplomatic overtures with the Iranian Shah in December 1965 and the attempts to form an Islamic alliance against Arab Nationalism even as King Faisal was negotiating a peace settlement with Nasser.[28] In 1966 Saudi Arabia was the recipient of large and unprecedented military contracts from the United States and Britain.[29] The Anglo-American air defense program from 1966 to 1967, worth $400 million, offered the Saudis a package that included forty British Aircraft Corporation (BAC) Lightning planes, radar and communication equipment, 150 American Hawk surface-to-air missiles (SAM), and British training and support service. While the defense program was being installed, Faisal also purchased thirty-seven British Thunderbird I SAMs and fifteen former RAF planes to be flown and serviced temporarily by British pilots. Although the defense system failed to prevent UAR aerial bombing of Saudi border territory, the large arms purchase presented a potential challenge to Nasser's military supremacy in the region.[30] According to David Stirling, founder of the British SAS regiment and representative to the Saudi government, Faisal was reluctant to openly engage Nasser before the "magic carpet" air defense system was operational.[31]

Saudi Arabia was not the only regional power to recognize Nasser's weakened position, both in Yemen and in the Middle East in general. Responding to a royalist visit to Tehran in 1963, Muhammad Reza Shah Pahlavi sent the first group of Iranians to Jabal Ahmar in Yemen on April 30, 1965, ostensibly to observe the circumstances of the civil war.[32] Royalist Prince Muhammad ibn al-Hussein made his own trip to Iran in October 1966 to ask the Shah for heavy weaponry, Iranian military trainers, and space for royalist training in Iran. In addition, Prince Muhammad broached the possible use of Iranian airlifts and parachute deliveries in order to resupply besieged royalist troops. The shah agreed to the requests and pledged to organize three parachute drops and the transport of heavier materials by land through Saudi territory. Royalist tribesmen were invited to Tehran to be trained in medical, combat, and sabotage missions, while Iranian trainers were sent to royalist camps in Yemen.[33] Iranian aid for the royalists was concerning for both Nasser and the Saudis, who expressed their willingness to forsake al-Badr and his supporters for the sake of Arab unity.[34] British MP Neil McLean conducted his own trip to Tehran with a substantial request for military aid. A portion of this shipment was received in October 1967, during a period when Iran was acting as the sole supplier of royalist forces.[35]

The most repeated explanation for Nasser's decision to maintain a large contingent of troops was the issuance of the British 1966 Defence White Paper, which declared a withdrawal from Aden and the Federation of South Arabia (FSA) by 1968. Nasser allegedly perceived the impending British withdrawal as a way to salvage an otherwise disastrous military expedition by expanding his influence over South Arabia following the British withdrawal.[36] This theory was supported by the reported redeployment of Egyptian forces to the southern border with the FSA.[37]

There is no denying the fact that, as John Badeau described: "Most Arab countries seemed content to let President Nasser wrestle with his own difficulties in Yemen and watched King Faisal's increasingly effective opposition to the UAR with quiet approbation."[38] Focusing solely on regional actors, however, neglects to consider the broader geostrategic interests of the United States and the USSR as a major factor in convincing Nasser to remain in Yemen. For the first years of the civil war, Soviets supported the Egyptian occupation of Yemen with air munitions, loans, and diplomatic capital for the defense of UAR actions in the UN. In contrast, the official US position under President Kennedy advocated withdrawal, containment, and mediation even as Nasser's continued military presence in Arabia was quietly sanctioned. Rather than championing the Haradh conferences and the Jeddah Pact as the culmination of years of international diplomacy in the region, the administrations of Johnson and Brezhnev renewed support for Nasser and indirectly encouraged him to maintain a continued presence in Yemen, further draining Egypt's economy and caging Nasser's Arab nationalist foreign policy. Even at the height of the Cold War, the two superpowers may have realized the danger of unleashing Nasser's unbridled military on the Sinai Peninsula and the politically charged conflict with Israel.

Ibrahim al-Wazir, a prominent member of the Yemeni third-force, was one of the few to understand the significance of this policy: "Both East and West are now kindling the resumption of the war in Yemen, paying no heed to who kills whom. The Communists are supplying the Egyptians with weapons whereas some Western countries are supplying them with wheat and dollars."[39] Al-Wazir further charged Nasser with cowardliness by keeping his army in Yemen in an effort to avoid a confrontation with Israel.[40]

Soviet Relations with the YAR

The Soviet Foreign Office envisioned Yemen as a base and staging post for further Soviet expansion into the Arabian Peninsula and postcolonial Africa at the expense of Western interests.[41] The completion of the Hodeidah port by 1961 and the construction of a modern airport near Sana'a in 1963 were an essential component.[42] On March 21, 1964, a treaty of friendship between the USSR and YAR was signed in Moscow as a reaffirmation of the original treaties signed in 1928 and 1955.[43] Over the course of the civil war, republican officers were sent to train at the USSR Officers Infantry Academy in Solnechnogorsk, twenty-five miles northwest of Moscow, before returning to Yemen to train new recruits. By 1965, the YAR army totaled ten thousand troops. Despite a continued reliance on tribal militias and the presence of tens of thousands of Egyptian soldiers, the YAR army earned the Yemeni republic some semblance of independence, the underlying intention of Soviet investment.[44]

The Soviet naval base in Hodeidah was a manifestation of the doctrine of Sergei Gorshkov, the admiral of the Soviet fleet from 1956 to 1985, known by many as the "father of the modern Soviet navy." Gorshkov's published articles, later republished in his celebrated 1976 book *The Sea Power of the State,* had a profound influence on Soviet naval strategy in a similar manner that Alfred Mahan's *The Influence of Sea power Upon History* had on US naval doctrine in the early twentieth century.[45] Like Mahan, Gorshkov argued that the future of the land empire of the USSR was at sea. Only with a powerful navy could the USSR protect the revolution and support liberation movements across the globe. Naval staff stationed at these ports functioned as cultural ambassadors, organizing sports and other activities for the local population.[46] He emphasized the peacetime military-political role of the Soviet navy in "protecting state interests," specifically Soviet state economic, political, and military interests in the developing world.[47] The Hodeidah port and the Soviet presence in South Arabia was part of Gorshkov's vision of a strong naval presence in the Red Sea region and near the Horn of Africa. This Indian Ocean region was envisioned as the "epicenter of the national liberation movement."[48]

Soviet diplomat Oleg Peresypkin explained that because Soviet ships were going from Odessa to the Far East via the Indian Ocean, "we need to have friendly relations with the littoral states. We had, and do have, some economic interests there. We had, or have, trade offices in Hodeida, Jidda, Massawa, Djibouti and Port Sudan—some of them were set up as early as the 1920s."[49] As Soviet admiral, Gorshkov personally oversaw the expansion of Soviet naval influence in the region and joint Egyptian-Soviet strategic interests in the Mediterranean and Red Seas.[50] The Mediterranean Sea and Indian Ocean also became scenes of Cold War tensions, as in 1962 the United States deployed nuclear submarines, the *Polaris* and the *Poseidon*, which had the capability to target Soviet cities.[51]

Until his presumed death during the coup on September 26, 1962, Moscow had been cultivating a close relationship with al-Badr, with the intention of securing its financial investment in Hodeidah. The coup and the subsequent Egyptian intervention complicated Moscow's long-term strategy for the Red Sea region. Rather than serve as a facility solely for the Soviet navy, the Hodeidah port was backlogged with Egyptian shipping and military transport. Similarly, the airport in Sana'a was also being used as a base for Egyptian aerial operations in Yemen.

Nikita Khrushchev was removed from power in October 1964 and replaced by Leonid Brezhnev as first secretary of the Communist Party of the Soviet Union. Khrushchev had been accused by members of the Soviet politburo of indiscriminate support for nationalist governments, such as the UAR. There was considerable concern among Nasser's administration that military and economic aid would be curtailed and that Brezhnev might demand loan repayment. During a speech on December 24, 1964, Alexander Shelepin, the former head of the KGB, laid these concerns to rest by making it clear that Soviet support for the UAR would continue unabated.[52]

Following the August 1965 Jeddah Pact with Saudi Arabia, Nasser flew to Moscow and obtained a massive military aid package in which the Soviets offered to underwrite Nasser's continued military presence in Yemen. Two more shiploads of Soviet munitions, including 50,000 machine guns and an additional six thousand Egyptian troops arrived in Hodeidah while the Haradh II Conference was still in session. The UAR became the first country outside of Eastern Europe to receive MIG-21D jet fighters (twenty of them in total). The USSR wrote off Egyptian debt of $400 million for military equipment and concluded a trade agreement that promised Egypt shipments of Soviet machines, minerals, oil, wheat, and wood.[53] According to Muhammad Heikal, Nasser's confidant and a prominent Egyptian journalist, the debt forgiveness was granted after Nasser demonstrated to Leonid Brezhnev that these were expenses directly related to arms purchases for the war in Yemen.[54] Some Yemenis were of the opinion that the Soviet Union played its role in the failure of the Jeddah Pact and in "keeping the pot boiling" in Yemen. By writing off some of Cairo's debt to Moscow for the equipment used in Yemen, and giving E£200 million in financial aid before Nasser's visit to Moscow at the end of August 1965, the Soviet Union encouraged the Egyptians to continue their occupation.[55]

The Soviets may have been relieved to have Nasser occupied in Yemen, as a similar stance of aggression against Israel would have involved the USSR in another high-stakes confrontation with the United States.[56] By 1965 Egypt was no longer as asset to Moscow, but rather had become a burden. Nasser had outlived his usefulness after helping the USSR establish a foothold in South Arabia and Africa, and was now deemed expendable.[57] Moscow could not turn its back entirely on its unpredictable Egyptian ally out of concern that Nasser would foster a closer relationship with Chinese Prime Minister Zhou Enlai, whom he met in late 1963.[58] With one hand Moscow was pushing Nasser back into Yemen and with the other it was developing a closer relationship with Yemenis through direct military and economic aid in preparation for the post-Nasser Yemen republic.

The continued Egyptian presence secured Soviet access, albeit somewhat limited, to both Hodeidah and the Sana'a airport in the short term, but the instability of Sallal's regime created a level of uncertainty in Moscow about the long-term strategy and access to Yemeni facilities. After succumbing to successive political and military crises, the Soviet Foreign Office began to explore other, more reliable, Soviet allies in the YAR administration to replace Sallal.

It did not take long for Soviet officials to begin to question continued support for the forty-eight-year-old Sallal. Sallal had taken part in the failed 1948 revolt and was a longtime member of the Yemeni Free Officer group. He was considered a revolutionary hero by some Yemenis, a title that was reinforced by his continued rhetoric against British imperialism and the deposed imam. In the months following the revolution, however, Sallal's popularity was subdued in response to the increasing corruption among Yemeni officials, tense tribal relations, and the continued presence of Egyptian troops in Yemen. According to Russian historian Alexei Vassiliev "[Sallal's] dependence on Egypt was absolute. He visited Cairo so frequently that he became a figure of fun. In some areas of Yemen Egyptian officers acted as virtual governors and often engaged in black marketeering, snatching away a portion of foreign trade from local merchants. Moreover, the Egyptians' condescending attitude even riled a good number of republicans."[59] Sallal's reliance on Nasser vicariously weakened the Soviet position in Yemen, as their approach to the YAR was contingent upon a middleman relationship with Egypt, an unpredictable regional ally.

In an official assessment of the economic and political situation in Yemen, the Soviets observed that Sallal relied mainly on his disorganized army and the aid of the UAR, but had little or no domestic popular support. Rather than address those inequities, Sallal retained unrealistic plans for a Yemeni army of 28,000 in order to create a presidential security state. Furthermore, his government did not manage to carry out a single economic reform, yet repeatedly made statements regarding restricting large estates, expanding the construction industry, improving living standards for the population, and other ambitious projects. The Yemeni government's only salvation came from foreign financial and economic assistance, primarily from the USSR and UAR. The Soviets concluded that without help from the UAR, "it will be difficult for Sallal's government to strengthen its position and its republican regime in the country."[60] Even Nasser himself, in a conversation with John Badeau admitted the futility of the YAR government: "You would not believe what goes on in Sana'a. Half of the Ministers never go to their offices and the other half don't know what to do when they get there."[61]

On March 31, 1964, Nikita Khrushchev and Vasiliy Kuznetsov, the First Deputy Foreign Minister, met with Sallal and YAR Foreign Minister Hassan Makki during a planned visit to Moscow. Khrushchev and Sallal exchanged letters of formality thanking each other for their respective invitations, travel, and hospitality, and reiterating the friendly intentions of this meeting. Kuznetsov considered this visit a positive sign of Soviet-Yemeni friendship, despite serious misgivings toward the sustainability of the Sallal regime.[62] The emergence of the "third-force" several months later forced Sallal to make further compromises to the opposition leaders and granted them a political council to form the "Progressive Yemeni Republic." Sallal was only able to maintain his political position and control over the army by using coercive military force against his own population.[63] His precarious political situation left the USSR with little choice but to consider alternatives to Sallal's leadership, for fear that continued access to strategic assets in Yemen would otherwise be endangered.

In anticipation of the collapse of Sallal's regime, Soviet intelligence reports listed five potential replacements, highlighting in particular their respective stances toward the USSR. The Soviets planned to install a puppet leader so that the YAR could be corralled into the Soviet sphere in the aftermath of an eventual Egyptian withdrawal. Until that point the "Soviet five" could also be counted upon for continued Soviet intelligence and support within Sallal's regime itself. The list of possible replacements included 'Abd al-Rahman al-Iryani, Hassan Muhammad Makki, Hussein al-Dafa'i, Abdullah Dobbi, and Saleh Ali al-Ashwal.

'Abd al-Rahman Al-Iryani, the YAR Minister of Justice and a prominent member of the "third-force," assumed control of the YAR presidency in 1967. Iryani, a judge prior to the coup, had spent fifteen years in prison after being implicated in the 1948 coup against Imam Yahya, and was an ardent opponent of the Egyptian occupation and foreign interference in internal Yemeni affairs. Yet, in February 1964 he was appointed a member of the politburo in recognition of his positive attitude toward the Soviet Union.[64]

Hassan Muhammad Makki, the YAR deputy prime minister and foreign minister during the 1960s, was in contact with Soviet embassy employees in Ta'iz both before and after the coup and had been instrumental in strengthening the Soviet-Yemeni relationship. He was believed to have had a warm opinion of the political relationship with the USSR and was initially the Soviet Foreign Ministry's top candidate to replace Sallal.[65] Makki ultimately became the YAR prime minister in 1974.

Hussein al-Dafa'i, who served as YAR minister of war, minister of the interior, and ambassador to the Soviet Union, was one of Sallal's closest and greatest confidants in addition to being a pro-Egyptian Arab nationalist. During his tenure as ambassador to the USSR from 1965 to 1966, Dafa'i developed a friendly relationship with the USSR and openly praised the Soviet military help for the YAR and the work of the Soviet military specialists in Yemen. He often spoke of developing a closer relationship and alliance with the Soviet Union.[66] Sallal was alarmed by Dafa'i's relationship with the Soviets and had him arrested under suspicions that Dafa'i was subverting Sallal's regime. Dafa'i was later appointed Yemeni minister of state in 1977.

Abdullah Dobbi, the former minister of war and a YAR military commander, had earned a military degree in Baghdad along with Sallal and others of the Yemeni Free Officers group and was one of the most active and influential revolutionaries. Dobbi had a relatively long history with the Soviet Union dating back to Imam al-Badr's 1958 Moscow trip, and served as national security director in Hodeidah during the period of the Soviet port construction. In February 1963 he was named the personal presidential consular to the Soviet premier, and cultivated a friendly relationship with Soviet officials throughout the civil war.[67] As Sallal's agent for the arrest of targeted political opponents, Dobbi developed his own network of security personnel stationed around the country.[68]

Saleh Ali al-Ashwal, the longtime YAR Ambassador to the USSR, was one of the first YAR officials to visit Moscow in November 1962, by invitation of the Soviet minister of defense. He personally handed Khrushchev a message from YAR President Sallal in recognition of the forty-fifth anniversary of the Great October Socialist Revolution. During their stay in the USSR together with the delegation, al-Ashwal was taken on tours of Kiev and Leningrad and developed a close relationship with Soviet officials. At the 1962 meeting and throughout his tenure as ambassador, he was reported to have divulged confidential and valuable information about the internal political situation in Yemen.[69]

The Soviet Foreign Office understood that increasing the military aid and debt ceiling for Nasser would encourage him to maintain a military presence in Yemen, thereby securing Soviet access to Yemeni port and air facilities and redirecting Egyptian foreign policy away from a high-stakes confrontation with Israel. Relying on Nasser's independently minded machinations was not a sustainable long-term solution for the broader Soviet aim of securing a stable naval and air base in South Arabia. Throughout the civil war, Yemen continued to play an important role in Soviet grand strategy in the Middle East. The "Soviet five" stood at the center of plans for a post-Sallal and post-Nasser regime that would secure Soviet interests in the region.

Yemeni "Hearts and Minds"

As the Soviet Foreign Office was planning for a post-Sallal Yemen, they were also overseeing a shift to a direct diplomatic and aid relationship with the YAR, so that they would not have to rely on an Egyptian intermediary.[70] While the United States was cutting aid to Egypt and improving relations with Saudi Arabia through official visits and the presence of an air squadron for protection, the Soviets were cultivating a very different relationship with the Yemeni people. Rather than focus solely on military and strategic aid, the Soviets invested resources in education, infrastructure, and entertainment in an attempt to win the "hearts and minds" of local Yemenis.

In October 1964, for example, the first group of Soviet tourists arrived in Yemen and included teachers of Middle East history, culture, and languages; journalists; artists; and religious Muslims. During their guided tour they became acquainted with the way of life of the Yemeni people, along with the country's history and culture.[71] The following month, a group of Soviet musicians gave their first concert in Sana'a in front of an audience of two thousand, filling the hall to capacity. The attendants included YAR Vice President Hassan al-'Amri and other important ministers.[72] This effort to win Yemeni "hearts and minds" was deemed a success, at least according to one barometer. The Yemenis observed that the Soviets called themselves *tovarishch*, or comrades. In turn, the Soviets working in Yemen noticed that the Yemenis began to call themselves *sadik*, a rough Arabic equivalent of "comrade." This was taken as a sign of positive Soviet influence on the Yemeni public and the foundation of closer Soviet-Yemeni relations.[73]

The port city of Hodeidah, long envisioned as the base for Soviet operations in the Red Sea and the Middle East in general, continued to undergo major infrastructure and civil engineering projects that went well beyond the confines of the port facilities. The majority of these efforts were focused on the area of the city known as New Hodeidah, a newly constructed urban area built over parts of the original city of Hodeidah that were destroyed in a fire in 1961. Soviet specialists, sent to the YAR for two-month rotations, included architects, quantity surveyor engineers, geological engineers, construction engineers, and doctors.[74] The main projects included the construction of hospitals, schools, roads, telephone lines, and an electrical grid within and between the cities of Sana'a, Hodeidah, and Ta'iz. These projects were seen as a rival to the American $500,000 investment into the reconstruction of the Ta'iz water supply system, which was called the Kennedy Memorial Water System.[75]

The stated goal of the Soviet education program in Yemen was "that the Yemenis should leave the darkness of the Middle Ages and take the road towards progress and civilization."[76] Prior to the revolution in 1962, there were only nineteen elementary schools and a reported illiteracy rate of 98 percent. By October 1964, more than nine hundred elementary schools (grades one through six) and four secondary schools (grades seven through nine) were open for enrollment. The subjects taught included Arabic language and literature, religious education, history and society, math, drawing, painting, sciences (physics, biology, chemistry, and nature), labor education, and music. There were over thirty hours of school per week, starting in first grade, during a school year that extended from October 1 through the end of July. In Hodeidah, the schools dedicated six hours a week to Russian language beginning in third grade in a plan of study approved by the YAR Ministry of Education.[77] As a testament to the popularity of the Russian language classes, the program advisor placed an urgent request to the Soviet Ministry of Education for an airmail delivery of an additional sixty copies of Arab-Russian textbooks for the upcoming school year as many more students had enrolled than initially expected.[78] In addition to investing in local education, 5,500 Yemeni students were given scholarships to study in the USSR in December 1965.[79]

The Soviets contributed politically and economically to the Egyptian mission in North Yemen, but preferred small-scale relations with the Yemeni people. The paradox is that the Egyptians received the brunt of Yemeni hostility as a reaction to their military occupation and forced model of a socialist state, while Moscow was spared similar criticism, leaving Soviets in a position to benefit from the new Yemeni state once the Egyptians withdrew.[80]

US Policy: Irrigating the Yemeni Countryside

The US Agency for International Development (USAID) looked upon Yemen not as a future state in the American orbit, but as a blank slate where their most ambitious visions for modern development could be implemented. As US Deputy Chief of Mission David Newton remarked: "Yemen was the darling of USAID as they perceived it as starting from nothing." The USAID mission began in Ta'iz, where they stored heavy equipment used for the road construction and later the Kennedy Memorial Water System.

Soviet and Chinese construction teams had already completed construction on their own road projects in Yemen. In playing catch-up to Communist efforts, USAID undertook construction of the Mocha-Ta'iz-Sana'a road, arguably the most difficult road project in Yemen given the mountainous terrain. In order to scale down construction and maintenance costs, the US engineers built a gravel road, which in retrospect was a political disaster, as Yemeni drivers did not abide by the speed limit and would often skid off the gravel road. Locals nicknamed the road "the American death road," hardly an achievement for US propaganda.[81]

Aldelmo Ruiz, a water engineer trained at Virginia Tech, was brought to Yemen in 1962 to begin a new era of USAID projects, which had shifted from road-building to urban and village water supply projects. Ruiz recalled finding out how dire the situation was upon his arrival to the USAID guesthouse in Ta'iz. After lengthy travel with his wife Maria and their young daughter Stella, Ruiz remarked to the attendant that he would love to take a shower. With a smile, the Yemeni attendant answered: "Mr. Ruiz, that's the reason you're here—to provide us water. We don't have any water now. You can wait until the truck comes—we'll order some."[82]

The initial construction of the Kennedy Memorial Water System in Ta'iz was completed in December 1963.[83] By 1965, USAID had connected the main water pumps to over 6,400 houses in Ta'iz, a city with approximately 25,000 residents at the time.[84] After the completion of the major road and Ta'iz water system construction, Ruiz orchestrated a self-help water project with surrounding villages. The village sheikhs would provide the manual labor, land allocation, and partial financing, while Ruiz and USAID would provide the machinery and technological expertise. Water projects were seen as a way to utilize the existing machinery and provide a reason to maintain workshops, facilities, and a general American diplomatic presence in the YAR.[85] In addition, periodic local draughts in Yemen were exacerbated by indiscriminate water consumption by Egyptian occupational forces during the 1960s.[86]

USAID personnel and property became an outlet and target of Egyptian frustration with the perceived US foreign policy. Sana'a and Ta'iz, the two main centers of US presence in Yemen, were transformed into an arena of conflict and competition between the United States and Egypt. Marjorie Ransom, who worked along with her husband David in the US consulate in Yemen during the 1960s, explained that Yemen was practically the only place where Nasser could retaliate against US international diplomatic slights.[87]

There was no single moment that triggered this rift, but rather a gradual escalation of tensions between representatives of the two countries. There were, however, several episodes that served as markers for a deteriorating relationship between US and Egyptian personnel in Yemen. In 1966, USAID employee Michelle Hariz was accused of spying and given twenty-four hours to leave the country. Hariz, a Lebanese-American, was indeed a contact for the CIA, a fact that was well known by everyone in the mission.[88]

Another incident occurred in February 1967 while David and Marjorie Ransom were working for the US Information Services (USIS) in Sana'a. One evening, both were alerted to the screams of the USIS budget and fiscal officer as she saw several Egyptian soldiers stealing the official USIS car. The car was attached to an old and slow-moving Russian truck. David Ransom, an ex-Marine, was able to jump onto the bed of the truck and follow the Egyptian soldiers. They had only properly fastened one chain to truck, leaving the car to swerve wildly as they drove away. The swerving car slammed into an electric pole, knocking out the lights to what seemed like all of Sana'a. When the truck eventually stopped, Ransom swiped the keys before the Egyptian officials could arrest him, and presented them as evidence the next morning when the Egyptian military tried to deny the whole incident. When the pieces of the Egyptian cover story started to unravel, Ransom was sent home rather than stand as witness to the rest of the embarrassing episode. The following day, other US political officers rather shamefacedly shared stories of their own cars having been stolen the night before by the Egyptian military. What became clear was that the Egyptians had intended to plant weapons in the back of US officials' cars, photograph them, and then use them as propaganda to foment anti-American sentiments among Yemenis. The relative chaos and power vacuum in Yemen allowed even junior Egyptian officers to manufacture international incidents and their American counterparts to singlehandedly foil their plots.[89]

April 1967 marked the apex of crises for the USAID mission in Yemen. One evening, two British intelligence agents infiltrated and bombed an Egyptian military compound in the city of Ta'iz. The agents had parked their getaway car outside of the city limits in preparation for a quick retreat. However, with Egyptian soldiers in pursuit, the two agents took a shortcut through the USAID compound, located on the outskirts of Ta'iz, on the way to their getaway vehicle. Egyptian soldiers cut the electricity to the USAID compound, forcibly entered, and gathered any sensitive material they could find. In their report, the Egyptian military implicated the USAID staff in the attack and declared nearly their entire staff personae non gratae. They were given twenty-four hours to vacate the premises and leave Yemen.[90] Aldelmo Ruiz recalled his frantic trip through Ta'iz collecting passports from the USAID officers, who were completely unaware of the circumstances of their deportation.[91] Marjorie Ransom conjectured that the deportation notice was really only a formality. Egyptian authorities, who controlled the radio and media in Yemen, had already broadcasted their version of events and encouraged mob riots against US citizens.[92] The US State Department independently reached the decision that it was no longer safe to retain a mission that included approximately sixty USAID staff, forty legation employees, and twenty children.[93] Only six US representatives remained in Yemen after April 1967 and all were evacuated after Egypt cut diplomatic relations with the United States in retaliation for Israel's victory against Egypt in the June 1967 War.

Wheat Conflicts with Egypt

Congressional disapproval of US aid programs to Egypt grew exponentially as Egyptian rearmament continued, even during the UN observer mission. Alaskan Senator Ernest Gruening led the Senate opposition to Kennedy's third world military and economic aid policy, which had already racked up a bill upwards of $1.8 billion by the end of 1963. David Bell, Kennedy's former budget director and new administrator of USAID, received the brunt of the criticism, primarily from Democratic liberals such as Frank Church, who had defected from Kennedy's leadership in the party. Church noted that by 1963, all but eight noncommunist countries were receiving some form of US foreign aid, demonstrating that the United States tried to "do too much for too many, indiscriminately." Senator Halpern of the Senate Foreign Relations Committee claimed that the PL-480 shipments to Egypt were causing "Yemen mass murders subsidized by our economic assistance."[94] When the Senate passed the Gruening amendment in October 1963, one month before Kennedy's assassination, it was clearly seen as a criticism of his policy with Nasser. The amendment terminated all forms of US aid to any nation "engaging in or preparing for aggressive military efforts" against the United States or its allies.[95] This included Kennedy's economic aid to Egypt through the Public Law (PL)-480 wheat sales. Although the Gruening amendment was only the first step in a series of political maneuvers to increase Congressional control over foreign aid, it significantly hampered Kennedy's ability to repair his coveted relationship with Nasser.[96]

According to economist John Waterbury, Egypt's growing population was increasingly reliant on the import of wheat specifically from the United States: "Like arms supplies, there are only a handful of countries that can regularly export wheat, and all of them are Western . . . keeping Egyptians alive, if not well-fed, is a matter settled in international grain markets or through bilateral trade agreement with the U.S. Every man, woman and child in Egypt receives an average of 100 kilograms of imported wheat per year or about 70 percent of their total consumption. Egypt's jugular vein runs through Iowa, Nebraska, and the Dakotas."

A combination of Nasser's intransigence and US Congressional dissent forced Kennedy to reconsider his relationship with Nasser and Arab nationalism, which in turn compelled Egypt to look eastward to secure economic and military aid from the Soviet Union.[97] In 1962, Kennedy was under the assumption that Nasser was the predominant ideological force in the Middle East. In 1963, however, two Ba'thist coups in Iraq and Syria presented a challenge to Nasser's monopoly of the Arab revolution and weakened Nasser's position in the eyes of the Kennedy administration.[98]

When Lyndon B. Johnson took office on November 22, 1963, he retained few of Kennedy's affinities for Nasser and did not hesitate to portray the Yemen Civil War as it was: a cage for Nasser and Arab Nationalism. As he wrote to King Faisal less than a month after taking office: "On its present course, the UAR is gaining little, losing much in Yemen. UAR problems are many. Yemen's drain on UAR resources is great. UAR is not winning popular support among the people. Yemen can well prove to be a trap for those who would seek to dominate it."[99]

Two foreign policy crises in Egypt further soured Johnson's opinion of Nasser. On Thanksgiving Day in 1964, Congolese protestors in Cairo stormed the newly dedicated JFK Library in Cairo in protest of US policies in Congo, burning the building to the ground. Egyptian police who knew of the riots in advance did not inform the US Embassy. Weeks later, on December 18, 1964, Texas oil man John Mecom's plane was shot down near Egyptian airspace. Although Egyptian officials claimed it was an accident, Mecom was a friend of LBJ and one of his biggest financial supporters; thus the incident further tarnished Nasser's image in Johnson's eyes. US Ambassador to Egypt Lucius Battle warned Nasser that he would not receive aid from Johnson "because first you burn his libraries, then you kill his friends."[100] The efforts of Bushrod Howard, an American lobbyist for the royalist cause, continuously criticized the economic aid to Nasser, further pressuring the Johnson administration to reconsider any form of economic aid to Egypt.[101] Johnson was not amused by Nasser's lack of gratitude for US economic aid. In a particularly anti-American Port Sa'id speech in December 1964 Nasser mused: "The American Ambassador says our behavior is not acceptable. Well, let us tell them that those who do not accept our behavior can go and drink from the sea. If the Mediterranean is not enough to slake their thirsts, [the Americans] can carry on with the Red Sea."[102] Nasser's appeal to the Egyptian people to throw US aid into the Red Sea was countered with further Congressional limitations on aid to Egypt.[103]

Robert Komer, the LBJ administration's Yemen Civil War guru, feeling unrestrained by Kennedy's courting of Nasser, explained to McGeorge Bundy that Yemen had become a perpetual military disaster for the Egyptian army. As long as the United States did not force Egyptian disengagement and continued to dangle PL-480 wheat sales to the "bellies of the *fellahin*", it was safe to assume that Nasser would not threaten US and UK bases in Aden and Libya and would not succumb to complete Soviet domination.[104] Komer explained to LBJ: "At this point it may serve our interests better if Nasser has to keep a third of his army tied up there, since this will enforce restraint vis-à-vis Israel."[105] The United States was "just as happy to have 50,000 UAR troops in Yemen rather than deployed against Israel." All that remained to be done was to periodically reassure Faisal's security in order to protect the billion-dollar oil investment and encourage Faisal to purchase US aircraft over the British and French options.[106] In conversation with his British counterparts, Parker Hart admitted the US mistake in recognizing the YAR, but "compared Nasser's position in the Yemen to that of a fly stuck on fly paper for Nasser was caught in the Yemen and could not escape from it and would slowly die there like the fly on the flypaper."[107]

In a speech to Palestinian (PLO) delegates in 1965, Nasser explained the logic of his inaction against Israel: "Is it conceivable that I should attack Israel while there are 50,000 Egyptian troops in Yemen?" After the 1956 Sinai War, the UN negotiated a ceasefire and positioned a peacekeeping force in Sinai. According to Michael Oren, the absence of a realistic military option against Israel while the Egyptian army was bogged down in Yemen ameliorated Nasser's stance against the presence of UN peacekeeping troops on Egyptian territory.[108] Many Egyptians viewed Nasser's colonization of Yemen at the expense of war with Israel as "national treason."[109] Although only a temporary respite from Egyptian and Israeli hostilities, Nasser's commitment in Yemen carried with it an inherent inability to pursue military expeditions elsewhere. In fact, the Egyptian efforts in Yemen became "so futile and fierce that the imminent Vietnam War could have easily been dubbed America's Yemen," just as Yemen was "Nasser's Vietnam."[110]

The realization in 1965 that Nasser might actually be pulling his troops out of Yemen led Johnson and others in the State Department to argue that it was in the US national interest to send economic aid to Egypt, if only to keep Nasser in Yemen. On June 22, 1965, Washington resumed wheat sales to Egypt and allowed nongovernmental organizations and charities to gift an additional $11.6 million worth of agricultural equipment. Johnson was able to circumvent the limitations of the Gruening amendment by issuing a direct presidential order for the resumption of aid. On January 3, 1966, the United States sold Egypt an additional

$55.7 million of agricultural surplus in an effort to alleviate the economic strain of sustaining an army of significant size in Yemen.[111]

Faisal's June 15, 1964, letter to LBJ expressed "supposed alarm and revulsions" at Soviet intentions and Nasser's violation of Saudi airspace.[112] Later that year, Faisal continued to drop buzzwords about global communism and expressed concern about "the dangers of anarchy and Communist activity in Yemen." He said that "today, virtually every facet of international communism, including the Russians, Chinese, Poles, and Czechs, are at work in Yemen."[113] Faisal's Soviet alarmism was nothing more than a game to gain the goodwill and support of Johnson. Johnson visibly appreciated Faisal's anticommunist rhetoric and continued to perceive Saudi Arabia as the cornerstone of American policy and oil interests in the Middle East. This perception was evident in the great deal of preparation and care invested in King Faisal's Washington visit in June 1966.[114]

Despite calling him a communist and urging Nasser's immediate departure from Yemen, Faisal secretly rejoiced at the sight of Nasser expending huge sums of money on a futile war. A combination of covert British operations, Saudi support for royalists, and the popularity of Zubayri's Party of Allah made it increasingly clear that by 1965 Nasser was simply trapped in Yemen and was unable to establish a republican regime loyal to the UAR.[115]

In a June 1966 meeting with Faisal, Secretary of State Dean Rusk clarified the relatively lax attitude toward Nasser's troop presence in Yemen. The return of over 40,000 troops to Egypt would threaten the stability of the entire region: "With more troops in Egypt, the possibility existed for the U.A.R. to move toward the east, which would result in a full scale war; to the west, where we had our important base in Libya; or to the south, which would create a large problem with the Sudan and would not be welcome by the Africans."[116]

According to CIA intelligence estimates in May 1966, Nasser was not prepared to suffer a humiliating withdrawal from Yemen and was forced to accept the realities of the intractable stalemate. His failed five-year economic plan, combined with the strain of financing a large army abroad, led to a plethora of economic problems in Egypt. Domestic economic woes and self-inflicted foreign affairs blunders encouraged popular opposition to the cost and casualties of the war in Yemen.[117] In essence, there was no longer a need for an expedited Egyptian withdrawal from Yemen, as the continued occupation was destroying Nasser's regime from within.

Nasser's policy reversal in 1965 and his decision to maintain Egypt's occupation of Yemen were encouraged in part by continued Soviet and US support and the abandoned efforts of international diplomacy. Neither Brezhnev nor LBJ was eager to have Nasser's army completely withdrawn from Yemen and free to exercise an aggressive foreign policy agenda elsewhere in the region. At the same time, both the United States and the USSR endeavored to win the "hearts and minds" of local Yemenis, hoping to secure an ally in South Arabia. What emerged during the height of civil war tensions was a conflict in the developing world that found the two superpowers not only supporting the same Yemeni republic, but pursuing parallel policies in the region.

6

Chemical Warfare in Yemen

BY 1966, NASSER had been cajoled back into the cage of Yemen, reluctantly defending the YAR, having been persuaded by a combination of international pressures, encouragement, and opportunities. His military presence, however, had ceased to be focused on large-scale offensives. Nasser retreated to Sana'a, Hodeidah, and Ta'iz, the triangle of strategic cities that formed the administrative and military centers of Egypt's occupation. By the time Nasser implemented his defensive strategy at the end of 1966, he did not need to worry about internal opposition undermining his position from within the triangle. Sallal's opposition was securely imprisoned in Cairo and would not be allowed back to Yemen until after the last Egyptian departed. The Egyptian occupation was focused mainly on repelling royalist attempts to breach the defenses of the strategic triangle.

The Egyptian "long-breath strategy," a defense of the strategic triangle and road network, was sustained by an increased presence of the air force, hindering royalist troop and supply movement and demoralizing the local Yemeni population. In addition to unguided, precision, incendiary, and delayed-explosion bombs, the Egyptian air force began to employ poison gas bombs in large numbers in 1967. This use of chemical weapons was a calculated part of the Egyptian effort to depopulate the countryside through a "scorched-earth policy designed to eliminate support for the royalist guerillas."[1] The international community failed to censure Egypt's use of poison gas in Yemen. National, economic, and political interests, in addition to the ramifications of wars half a world away from South Arabia, impeded the world's ability to directly engage Egypt's violation of the norms of warfare.

Egypt's poison gas bombings were first investigated by British Minister of Parliament (MP) Neil McLean, then serving on a team of British mercenaries in the northern highlands of Yemen, during his visit to the Yemeni village of Jabal Bani Awar in July 1963. McLean disseminated the first of many gruesome testimonies and photographs that characterized Egypt's use of poison gas in Yemen, a tragedy that has since been largely forgotten. Decades before the more well-known chemical attacks by Iraq in the 1980s and Syria in the 2010s, Egypt's use of chemical weapons in Yemen during the country's civil war was one of the first large-scale and substantively documented military uses of poison gas following World War I.[2] Nasser's first foray into chemical weapon use in Yemen began in 1963 and was limited to rudimentary tear gas bombs. Early experiments with poison gas evolved into a more sophisticated and deadly aerial campaign that by 1967 used phosgene and mustard gases.

The absence of a global response to Egypt's war conduct in Yemen demonstrated the limitations of the international community's ability to respond to the use of chemical weapons and served as a further example of how global conflicts impacted the conduct and reaction to the local war in Yemen. US General John J. Pershing famously stated that "chemical warfare should be abolished among nations, as abhorrent to civilization. It is a cruel, unfair and improper use of science. It is fraught with the gravest danger to noncombatants and demoralizes the better instincts of humanity."[3] In reality, the supposed moral indignations and concern for weapons proliferation that the United States and Europe had associated with the use of poison gas took second stage to issues of national interest, reinforcing the observation that "morality in foreign policy is simply politics by other means."[4]

The historic taboo against chemical weapons was first codified in the text of the Geneva Protocol of 1925: "Whereas the use in war of asphyxiating, poisonous or other gases, and of all analogous liquids, materials or devices has been justly condemned by the general opinion of the civilized world, and Whereas the prohibition of such use has been declared in treaties to which the majority of the Powers in the world are Parties." As Richard Price explains in his seminal book on the subject, chemical weapons continue to defy the path to normalization taken by other new forms of weaponry. Other weapons such as tanks, submarines, and missiles are collectively more deadly than poison gas yet have gradually become an accepted means of war. However, chemical weapon use continues to be reviled by policy makers and public opinion as an inhumane and immoral method of warfare.[5] The use of chemical weapons by Egypt in Yemen and the lack of international condemnation challenged the tenuous nature of a taboo whose existence was either merely theoretical or whose immorality had been diluted by the passage of time following the poison gas battlefields of World War I. The supposed taboo was not universal and the fear of its violation did little to deter Egyptian generals in Yemen.

Following the passage of the 1925 Geneva Protocol the signatories debated the interpretations of the language used and the applications of the protocol's restrictions. One of the most contentious divergences was the categorization of chemical agents and whether they included "harassing" and "incapacitating" agents like tear gas and herbicides. Prior to the outbreak of the civil war in Yemen, the United States was concerned that "aerial spraying techniques to destroy crops in Vietnam might give rise to Communist propaganda that the United States was embarking on chemical warfare in Asia."[6] International media did not often distinguish between the various categories of "poison gas," readily using this single term to refer to both innocuous tear gas and deadly mustard gas. This painted Washington's policy in Vietnam in an even darker light as both the US army and the South Vietnamese forces frequently used tear gas for riot control.[7]

Critique of Washington's Vietnam policy appeared in newspapers and as meeting agendas for international organizations around the world. The United States was not only using tear gas in Vietnam as a riot control method, which was considered by some to be a "humane" use of gas. Rather, it was clear that tear gas was being used as a "force multiplier" to increase the effect of lethal weapons. Similar to the methods used by Egypt, tear gas was used by the US Air Force to flush the Vietcong out of their caves so that they could be attacked with artillery and aircraft.[8] The similarities in chemical warfare tactics employed by both Egypt in Yemen and the United States in Vietnam gave a new level of credence to Nasser's observations that Yemen was "his Vietnam." Ibrahim Ali al-Wazir, a prominent Yemeni politician who spent the majority of the civil war as an exile in Beirut, commented that "what is going on in Yemen is by far worse and more horrible than what is going on in Vietnam."[9] Although Egypt's use of poison gas was a clear violation of the 1925 Geneva Protocol, the United States could not take the lead on censuring Egypt. As historian Barbara Keys explains: "As long as the [Vietnam] war went on it branded the United States as a major source of oppression and violence in the world, making it impossible to propose the [US] champion a crusade against those evils elsewhere."[10]

On the face of it, international reaction to Egypt's use of chemical weapons was yet another example of human rights limitations in the foreign policies of the United States and Europe, subject to the hurdles of coordinating multilateral action, overcoming cumbersome legislative formalities in the UN and other international organizations, and accounting for domestic public opinion.[11] The emerging field of human rights literature, and specifically the work of those scholars focusing on instances of chemical warfare, often highlights specific moments where interventions could have been made to prevent atrocities or chemical attacks. For example, George Baer argues that closing the Suez Canal to Italian shipping in 1935 would have economically pressured Benito Mussolini and forced him to abandon a poison gas campaign against Ethiopia that same year.[12] In his book on the Iraqi chemical attack on the Kurdish city of Halabja in 1988, Joost Hiltermann argues that a strong condemnation of Saddam Hussein's early chemical attacks against Iran in 1983 could have prevented further chemical attacks that eventually took the lives of over 50,000 victims.[13] Yemen truly was a unique situation in that, even in hindsight, there was no realistic diplomatic, military, or economic effort or defining moment that could have prevented Egypt's use of chemical weapons.

Although human rights talk had become the lingua franca of international affairs as early as the 1940s, the politics and enforcement of its tenets remained weak.[14] The 1960s was a dead zone for international efforts to condemn human rights violations. The United States was mired by the moral baggage of an ongoing Vietnam War. Britain, despite rapid postwar decolonization, was still associated with the remnants of the British Empire. By the early 1960s, the Afro-Asian bloc of decolonized nations and the Soviet-led communist bloc came to dominate the UN General Assembly. In this new diplomatic reality, it was unlikely that Egyptian President Nasser, a prominent leader of the nonaligned movement and an ally of the USSR, could have ever been censured by the UN, in essence granting Egypt's occupation of Yemen (1962 through 1967) a great degree of latitude.

Presenting another obstacle to addressing the use of chemical weapons was the fact that the attacks were perpetrated against the royalists who were unrecognized by the international community and resided in one of the most remote areas of the world. The YAR, and by extension their Egyptian overlords, were seen as the legitimate suzerains in Yemen, while al-Badr and his tribesmen were perceived by foreign leaders as rebels and readily associated with beheading, torture, and other arcane methods

Chemical Warfare in Yemen 133

of punishment. Defending medieval tribal armies, who were themselves supported by British imperialists and Saudi royalists, would most certainly have garnered a great deal of negative public opinion. Making matters more difficult were the Cold War politics, economic considerations, the Vietnam War, continued British imperialism, and legal obstacles at the UN and International Committee of the Red Cross (ICRC) that were transposed onto the Yemen conflict and presented additional limitations to any concerted effort at condemning Egypt's war conduct.

The Emergence of Chemical Weapons in Yemen

Egypt's counterinsurgency campaign in Yemen remains a primary historical example for considering the difficulties of hunting rebel tribesmen in inhospitable terrain using modern weaponry. Yemen's mountainous topography, however, proved the greatest obstacle for an Egyptian army that had been trained and equipped for desert warfare. Armored vehicles had great difficulty navigating the rough terrain and mountain passes in a country that lacked modern transport infrastructure. Given the limited mobility on the ground, the Egyptian army relied increasingly on its air force to target the tribal forces of Imam al-Badr. The incessant Egyptian air raids drove tribesmen and supplies into a system of caves that pockmark the mountains of north Yemen, which provided both men and supplies with reliable cover from air raids, further frustrating the Egyptian military strategy.

In June 1963, Egypt began employing makeshift tear gas bombs with the intention of extricating tribesmen from the cave system before bombing them with conventional weapons. US General Alden Waitt of the Chemical Warfare Service (CWS) had advocated the use of chemical weapons against Japanese tunnels and caves on Pacific islands during World War II, remarking that gas was "the most promising of all weapons for overcoming cave defenses."[15] According to British intelligence reports, Nasser employed a strategic logic similar to Waitt's in order "to overcome heavily fortified defenses which did not succumb to attack by high explosive or fragmenting weapons." Many of the air raids were done in pairs, such that the first wave would drop concentrated tear gas near the entrances to the caves and a second wave would bomb the tribesmen who had exited the cave for air.[16]

The use of poison gas in Yemen first gained the world's attention in June 1963 when the British Yemen Relief Committee brought Muhammad

Nasser, a twelve-year-old Yemeni boy from the village of Jabal Bani Awar who suffered from a perpetual cough and deep blister wounds, to London for hospital examination. Richard Beeston, the *Daily Telegraph* correspondent in Yemen, reported that the boy was suspected to have been sickened by an Egyptian poison gas attack. Beeston assumed that the production of simple chemical weapons was beyond the capabilities of the Egyptian scientist and proceeded to perpetuate a rumor that the Soviet Union was supplying Egypt with advanced chemical weapons in Yemen.[17] Media hype had died down by the time the boy was released from the hospital with a clean bill of health. There was no definitive evidence from the boy's medical report that his symptoms were caused by inhaling poison gas. Competing correspondents, such as Desmond Stewart of the *Spectator*, wasted little time in ridiculing the quality of evidence used by Beeston and other alarmist journalists who were quick to utilize unconfirmed chemical attacks as anti-Egyptian propaganda.[18] American and British audiences moved on from the 1963 suspected Egyptian chemical attacks as quickly as they first came to hear of their existence.

The poison gas incident in 1963 was Egypt's first attempt at chemical warfare in the battlefield. However, Nasser's malicious intentions were hampered by Egypt's poor laboratory capabilities. As Raymond Titt from the Chemical Defence Experimental Establishment (CDEE) Munitions Research Division observed: "There is evidence of an ingenious malevolence supported, however, by only rudimentary knowledge of chemical weapons."[19] British labs at the CDEE at Porton Down, the UK government military science park, concluded that the bomb used in June 1963 was not originally manufactured as a chemical weapon. Dr. E.E. Haddon, the director of CDEE, observed that "the markings on the bomb and the shape of its nose, point to improvisation rather than a factory-made product."[20] According to CDEE conclusions, these manufactured weapons that used old British teargas grenades "represents an ingenious and competent piece of ad hoc engineering, but a very poor piece of basic design." The modification allowed the grenades to attach to the inside of the bomb, "in a somewhat misguided after-thought to make the fire bombs even more unpleasant, and this is consistent with the evidently ad hoc nature of the assembly." The CDEE findings were verified independently by US laboratories in Langley, Virginia, and by UN officials who obtained their own samples from the attack site.[21]

In July 1963, the US Ambassador to Egypt John Badeau confronted Nasser on the issue of poison gas in Yemen. Nasser initially claimed that only napalm was being used. When Badeau pushed further and indicated that the United States had evidence that actual poison gas bombs were used, Nasser then said that "'a bomb' was being used which had been manufactured in UAR, of which he did not know [the] precise chemical content." When Badeau warned Nasser of the self-defeating use of unconventional weapons, which were probably militarily ineffective and would most likely only open Egypt to international criticism, Nasser claimed "he could not sit in Cairo and direct military operation in Yemen as to specifics of weapons and tactics. If [a] military commander in Yemen felt air bombing and support was necessary for troops, the decision would be his."[22] Robert W. Komer argued that there was no need to take a lead on "public noises," as the United States should wait until the investigations into the Egyptian alleged poison gas use were complete. President Kennedy also mentioned to Komer that he would prefer that others lead the investigation and censure out of concern that it would harm US policy in Middle East.[23]

Just a few months earlier in 1962, Kennedy had authorized Operation Ranch Hand, the large-scale herbicidal warfare in Vietnam. At the same time that the Egyptian air force was experimenting with poison gas weapons in Yemen, the US air force was flying sorties over forests and farmland in Vietnam, Cambodia, and Laos, dropping "rainbow herbicides" and defoliating large swaths of Southeast Asian territory.[24] In March 1963, the US Embassy in Vietnam expressed concern over the growing negative news coverage and Communist bloc propaganda on the use of poison gas in Vietnam.[25] A CIA intelligence cable observed how the use of nonlethal poison gas in Vietnam negatively impacted the country's image in the UN in particular: "The image of the United States is at its lowest ebb . . . "[26] Kennedy's, and later Johnson's, administration were subject to harsh criticism from domestic and international media as well as their voting constituency.[27] The mounting opposition against herbicidal warfare in Vietnam certainly played a role in influencing Kennedy and Johnson's decision to shy away from a confrontation with Egypt over the use of poison gas in Yemen.

The UN was equally quiet and scarcely addressed the allegations against Egypt's war conduct in Yemen. As U Thant explained to William Yates of the House of Commons: "the often confused and obscure nature of the situation in Yemen makes it difficult to provide such information with any certainty of its remaining correct. Indeed, a part of the trouble in Yemen stemmed from detailed and highly colored reports on what goes on there, which are not always in accordance with the true facts or nature of the situation."[28] U Thant backed away from Yemen, claiming that tribal and political dynamics of the civil war were far too complicated and that the sources of information were unreliable and often dismissed as mere anti-Egyptian propaganda.

U Thant's approach echoed Nasser's defense against British allegations during a public statement on July 8, 1963 that turned allegations of Egypt's misconduct into an attack on British imperial actions in Aden. Nasser claimed that the media attention for poison gas use in Yemen was a "campaign of slander" and that newspapers were printing these sensationalist stories "without any attempt made to verify the facts of the story.... . The British, being aware of the far reaching repercussions of this vicious campaign, knew that such a harrowing allegation would soon catch the spotlight in some newspaper and international wire services.... The inventive and slanderous campaign are a desperate attempt to cover up the aggressive, provocative and imperialistic actions carried out by the British forces on the Southern Boundaries of Yemen."[29]

British Conservative backbenchers such as Patrick Wall took advantage of the momentary public attention on the Egyptian use of poison gas to pressure their party to take a more anti-Egyptian stance.[30] However, aside from internal British political pressure and short-lived media coverage, the suspected Egyptian use of poison gas in 1963 went largely unnoticed internationally. The absence of definitive scientific evidence likely contributed to the lackluster international response. Yet, the lack of an effective Egyptian censure in 1963 undoubtedly led Nasser to take bolder actions later in the war.

In implementing Nasser's long-breath strategy, the Egyptian air force strategically deployed both conventional and poison gas bombs against tribal positions to forestall a serious offensive against the strategic triangle.[31] The sites of the attacks were chosen for their proximity to royalist leadership or other significant military sites. The royalist cave network of bases often abutted local villages which served as supply depots for water, food, staples, and nonmilitary manpower. The psychological impact of an unfamiliar and deadly new weapon contributed in part to delaying the royalist advance on Sana'a.

As can be seen from the map below (see Fig. 6.1), nearly all of the reported major chemical attacks that took place from January through the end of May 1967 occurred north and northwest of the capital city of Sana'a. These attacks occurred a far distance from Nasser's strategic triangle, a

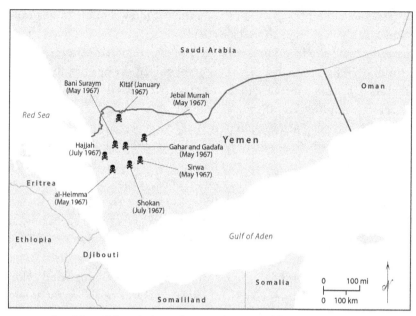

FIGURE 6.1 Map of chemical attacks in 1967. Created by author.

reflection of the fact that the northern rural areas of the country remained beyond the control of the YAR central government. Nasser preferred to utilize Egypt's air superiority by using conventional, incendiary, and chemical bombs to attack the imam's tribal forces rather than send an Egyptian armored division into the inhospitable enemy territory.

Following Egypt's defeat by Israel in June 1967, Nasser's strategy in Yemen changed dramatically. Rather than trying to prolong Egypt's presence in Yemen until the complete British withdrawal from Aden scheduled for the beginning of 1968, Nasser began a rapid transfer of his troops from Yemen to the Sinai border with Israel. Egyptian troops and munitions were transported from the battlefield directly to the Soviet-constructed port of Hodeidah and from there to Egypt. As Egyptian troop strength receded, the royalist tribal armies continued their march southward in a concerted effort to retake the city of Sana'a as soon as Egypt withdrew. The chemical attacks, in addition to the conventional air raids, in July 1967 took place closer to Nasser's strategic triangle and in some cases south of Sana'a itself, combating the tribal militias who attempted to cut off the main roads leading to the capital. Where earlier air raids had been a concerted effort to destabilize royalist cave headquarters and terrorize Imam al-Badr's tribal supporters, these bombings was seen as a desperate attempt by Nasser to cover the withdrawal of his troops from Yemen. This new set of large-scale chemical attacks was intended primarily to forestall the imminent royalist advance and to cover the Egyptian withdrawal. Rather than a cessation of all poison gas attacks, there were reports of a sizable increase in the number of conventional and chemical bombings in June and July.[32]

Chemical weapons were reported to have been used in at least a dozen instances between January and August of 1967 and were of a more advanced nature than the tear gas bombs used in 1963. Two-thirds of the attacks were documented as having used phosgene gas, and one-third had used mustard gas. Several US media outlets that received information from contacts at CIA laboratories claimed traces of a nerve agent present as well.[33] At least 800 Yemenis were killed, a high proportion of them women and children. While civilian casualties may not have been intentional, the instability of poison gas clouds and the changing winds often spread the gas to nearby villages, causing mass hysteria and terror among local tribes. This hysteria drew the attention of international media, which brought the issue of chemical attacks in Yemen to the desks of Western politicians.

Kitaf, a small northern Yemeni village of about a thousand inhabitants, was bombed by Egyptian aircraft on January 5, 1967. The number of casualties was estimated to be one hundred to two hundred, and the testimonies of the survivors pointed toward the presence of chemical weapons. The village of Kitaf was likely the unintended victim of a strike aimed at the nearby royalist military headquarters of the imam's Prime Minister Emir Hassan bin Yahya. The gas from bombs dropped near his cave must have drifted toward the village as well.[34] The major difference between the bombing of Kitaf and earlier tear gas bombings in 1963 was the geographic location of Kitaf, just thirty miles from the Saudi border town of Najran. From early 1964, the ICRC, previously based in the Yemeni desert region of Uqd, had been forced to move the base of its Yemeni medical facilities across the border to the Saudi town of Najran in response to safety and supply issues.[35] The ICRC delegation, led by André Rochat, was able to reach Kitaf within days of the reported bombing and obtained greater sample sizes for laboratory testing and bodies for autopsy. The same was true of technicians from the United States and Britain, in addition to foreign correspondents, who were able to reach the relatively accessible site at Kitaf. The ICRC investigation and subsequent reports were particularly significant, as the ICRC was considered the only neutral organization able to speak with and treat the patients of both sides of the civil war.

Nonetheless, Rochat was not a particularly reliable spokesman and as a result, ICRC policies and terminology were often misinterpreted. In an interview with the Saudi newspaper *al-Medina* in February 1967, Rochat expressed his frustration with Egyptian media and their incorrect interpretation of the ICRC report and Rochat's public statements. He cited a particular incident with Salah Jabadiyya, a correspondent for the Cairo-based newspaper *al-Akhbar*, who referred to the ICRC report and quoted Rochat in saying that the Egyptians had not used poison gas in Yemen. Jabadiyya claimed, instead, that all of the Yemeni casualties had simultaneously died of tuberculosis rather than Egyptian gas. Rochat denied the validity of the article to the Saudis and reiterated his commitment to the neutrality of the ICRC. This episode demonstrated the potential for serious misunderstandings when utilizing careful terms of neutral scientific analysis.[36] In this case, Jabadiyya understood the ICRC statement of "no conclusive evidence" to mean that Egypt had been absolved and that poison gas had not, in fact, been used.[37]

ICRC's neutrality was an asset in a climate that was overpoliticized by Cold War tensions, media hype, and Anglo-Egyptian rivalries in Arabia. Yet that neutrality also hampered the ICRC, as it limited the organization's ability to criticize Egypt for fear of a loss of impartiality.[38] Rochat admitted that the ICRC was powerless to impact Egypt's war practices, as the organization's very presence in South Arabia was contingent upon Nasser's continued approval. In a 2009 documentary film, Rochat seemingly continued to toe the line and attempted to historically defend and whitewash the ICRC's inaction by contradicting his previous claims and emphatically stating that Egypt had never used chemical weapons and that no condemnation was ever necessary.[39]

Even the possibility of distributing gas masks to Yemeni civilians was hindered by the politicization of the Egyptian chemical war.[40] William Norman Hillier-Fry, a diplomat in the Aden Department of the Foreign Office, praised the potential distribution of gas masks as having "publicity value." The delivery of gas masks would in essence substantiate the initial claims that the Egyptians were using chemical weapons. Hillier-Fry was concerned, however, that delivering direct aid from London to the royalists might result in unintended political consequences, as the UK would be accused of aiding a belligerent party in the civil war.[41] What was missing from these deliberations was any mention of Yemeni civilians or the moral necessity of granting defense measures to a population subject to poison gas attack. The idea of providing Yemeni civilians at risk with gas masks petered out as it became clear how much it would cost to refurbish the British surplus masks in storage and how little the propaganda value might actually be.[42]

Gas mask distribution was only the first of many politically marred issues that would arise over the course of 1967, but it was most demonstrative of things to come. Moral indignation and humanitarian concern for Yemeni victims of poison gas scarcely factored into calculated political decisions. In the case of poison gas in Yemen, respective national interests trumped all else.

"Passing the Baton"—National Interests vs. Human Rights

By March 1967, there was little doubt among British policy makers that poison gas had been used on the Yemeni village of Kitaf on January 5, 1967. Both the prime minister and members of both houses of the Parliament were willing, at the very least, to support a Saudi initiative condemning the Egyptian use of poison gas in Yemen. Many were even willing to pressure Secretary General U Thant to have the UN Security Council consider the issue. However, British condemnation of the UAR was limited by several factors.

Royalist officials had submitted complaints, but U Thant could not take action because the royalists did not occupy the Yemen seat at the UN. Saudi delegates to the UN were hesitant to bring the complaint, lest their enemies vote them down or the evidence prove to be too stale to be definitive by the time the UN would organize a fact-finding mission. Saudi delegate to the UN Jamil Baroody presumed, at least in February 1967, that "[Saudi] enemies at the UN would anyway outvote them in any case."[43] Nonetheless, he did log a complaint in the UN regarding the alleged UAR bombing campaign, in the process making a strong claim against Nasser's entire endeavor in Yemen: "We hope for amicable solutions, but President Nasser seems to think he is the arbiter of the Arab World, that he can impose a government on the Yemen ... "[44] U Thant unequivocally rejected Baroody's initial attempts to press for UN action on the grounds that only the YAR representatives, and not the imam's royalists, could request an investigation: "I am bound by the actions of the United Nations in matters involving official status and accreditation of governments. On matters relating to Yemen, therefore I deal only with the representative of the government of the Yemen Arab Republic whose credentials have been accepted here." Furthermore, U Thant explained that the UAR had already denied the use of poison gas and therefore concluded that "[t]here is no further action on this matter that I can properly take at this time."[45]

The British assumed that U Thant would not undertake action unilaterally, unless invited to do so by Saudi Arabia or the UAR, because he was "afraid of being dragged into an Egyptian propaganda exercise." This was despite the fact that UN Charter Article 99 granted the secretary-general the power to bring to the attention of the Security Council any matter that in his opinion might threaten the maintenance of international peace and security.[46] The UK mission to the UN was particularly disturbed by the overall double standard that they perceived in the halls of the General Assembly. "It is also in general a bad thing that delegations in New York should be allowed to close their eyes to a most flagrant example of 'imperialism' merely because the perpetrator is an 'Afro-Asian.' "[47] UK Ambassador Richard Beaumont echoed similar sentiments later that same year: "the "imperialist" powers came under constant criticism for "atrocities" but apparently the Afro-Asian states could never commit any sins."[48]

It was also not entirely clear which UN commission would be most suitable to undertake the investigation. The Security Council would have been best suited to address an act of aggression by the UAR, but this was not an option as the Soviets would most likely have vetoed any anti-Egyptian resolution. The British were concerned that "raising the matter in the Human Rights Commission (HRC) might encourage the UAR to support Amnesty International's allegations of torture in Aden." There was further debate over the nature of the HRC, which "is concerned with the relationship between individuals and their governments, not between individuals and the activities of a foreign government." In this case, Egypt was a foreign government supporting a legitimate state government, and it was not clear that the HRC would be an appropriate venue for this issue. Nonetheless, more optimistic members of the British Foreign Office assumed that "the charge of use of poisonous gas is so serious that it would not be understood if the HRC declined to discuss it." Furthermore, the Egyptians might very well have put pressure on Amnesty International's investigation in Aden regardless of whether the British supported a UN investigation of poison gas.[49]

Assuming that the HRC or the Security Council would have actually considered a condemnation of the UAR, it is not clear that Egypt would have been found guilty of violating the 1925 Geneva Protocol, which specifies the prohibition against "the use in war of asphyxiating, poisonous or other gases." In a legal sense, Egypt was not technically "at war," but instead was merely aiding the republicans in their war against the royalists.[50] There remained a possibility of issuing a general resolution condemning the use of chemical weapons, similar to the December 5, 1966 resolution, co-sponsored by Hungary, which reiterated the need for "strict observance by all States of the principles and objectives of the Geneva Protocol." The 1966 resolution was partly intended as a censure of Washington's use of poison gas in Vietnam. There was a recognized danger in another broad resolution emphasizing the general human-rights aspects of Egyptian gas usage, as "attempts might then be made to turn the 'attack' by indicting the United States use of napalm in Vietnam, and the use of tear gas by [the UK] in colonial territories."[51] The use of napalm in Vietnam had already been cited by Arab newspapers in their critique of the ICRC's investigation in Yemen, while at the same time the UN declined to investigate the US conduct of war in Vietnam: "hence its avowed concern in this incident whilst it stands idly watching American massacres in Vietnam."[52]

Daniel J. McCarthy, a British diplomat attached to the Aden High Commissioner's office, highlighted "the important humanitarian considerations involved and the advantage from the point of view of our position in South Arabia of bringing discredit upon the Egyptians for their activities in the Yemen, it is most unfortunate that the UAR are getting off lightly."[53] Not everyone in the British Foreign Service agreed with McCarthy's perspective. Peter W. Unwin, a British diplomat, argued that the UAR was not getting off lightly, as press reports of poison gas use against Yemeni civilians had served to discredit the UAR in the Arab world: "Although there is no official UN condemnation, I think the point has gotten across." Unwin was additionally hesitant to lead a political attack against Egypt's use of poison gas for "fear of arousing great Egyptian hostility towards us" and "the fact that if we lead a critical chorus we will be accused of attacking the UAR not on the merits of the gas attack but because of our imperialist antipathy to them."[54] In essence, Unwin ironically seemed to have been concerned that the British Empire would be accused of being imperial, especially regarding its policy toward Egypt.[55]

Unlike his American and British counterparts, Jamil Baroody, a Lebanese-born New Yorker who served as the Saudi UN ambassador, knew how to play the diplomatic field and navigate the UN General Assembly, as he had been a member of the UN since its founding in 1946. Baroody had Saudi King Faisal's total confidence and was at liberty to speak his mind on the floor of the UN. There seemed to be no one more suited to challenge Nasser and U Thant in the UN than Jamil Baroody, who earned the nickname "unguided missile" for his ability to "derail trains of thought, [discomfit] the orthodox, and [disrupt] debate."[56] The results of a Saudi lab report released in March 1967 convinced Baroody that he could take complaints to the UN, as the scientific evidence was accurate. The report, an analysis of Egypt's chemical attacks,was published by the Saudi Arabian Ministry of Health and included forensic medical eports from the military hospital in Ta'if where acutely ill Yemen patients were transferred from the border village of Najran.[57]

In his first oral complaint to U Thant, Baroody labeled the Egyptian use of poison gas in Yemen a "silent genocide."[58] In subsequent correspondence with U Thant between February and April of 1967, Baroody logged similar complaints against the UAR. Baroody declared that he planned to "wrap U Thant like an octopus" on the subject of chemical weapons in Yemen with his intense letter writing campaign.[59] U Thant on his part managed to delay any action by sidestepping Baroody's complaints, claiming that there was insufficient evidence of Egypt's use of chemical weapons. On April 1, 1967, Baroody wrote out of frustration: "if God forbid, should lethal gas be used in another region of the world, no United Nations representatives should keep silent."[60] In continuing his critique of U Thant's double standard, Baroody highlighted the UN's censure of the US conduct of war in the Far East while ignoring the Egyptian war in Yemen. In response, U Thant continued to refer to the fact that UAR representatives to the UN have "flatly and repeatedly denied" the use of poison gas, evidently giving him no further reason to press the matter. To this Baroody reiterated the convincing evidence presented by the ICRC and Saudi reports, claiming that the UAR is taking "refuge in denials."

In some of his letter writing to U Thant, Baroody, one of the original delegates to the League of Nations, assumed the role of the wise old man offering advice to a younger generation. In his April 1 letter, he left U Thant with strong final words: "The tendency has always been to rationalize one's inaction on the ground of legal niceties or juridical intricacies whence the better part of valor takes refuge in caution and prudence. The United Nations can no longer afford such a policy, for if it does, there is no assurance that it will not founder like the League of Nations had done before it." Baroody later continued that "if no warning is sounded that the use of lethal gas constitutes an act of genocide and should be forbidden under all circumstances in wars whether declared or undeclared, there henceforth shall be no deterrent for ultimately plunging mankind into suicide."[61] Despite his oratory prowess, Baroody was unable to sufficiently pressure the hesitant U Thant to take a strong stance against Egypt's use of chemical weapons. Just as Baroody predicted, failure to censure Egypt's first attack on Kitaf would serve to encourage further attacks in the following months.

Post-1967 War and the "Let-someone-else-do-it policy"

In the aftermath of Egypt's war with Israel, Baroody's correspondence with U Thant and Saudi Arabia's condemnation of Egypt quickly died down. Several Conservative British MPs argued that "we are going too far along the line of doing practically everything to placate Egypt."[62] The majority of MPs, led by Secretary of State for Foreign Affairs George Brown, however, were reluctant to continue efforts to condemn the Egyptian chemical warfare as they felt that "the present is hardly the time to take such action, since we should probably be accused of simply seizing another stick with which to beat President Nasser." It also seemed unlikely that Saudi Arabia "will wish to risk more cracks in the face of Arab solidarity" by continuing its campaign against the Egyptian use of poison gas in Yemen.[63] Without the support of Saudi Arabia, or any other Arab country, it did not seem expedient for the UK to continue its international campaign against Egyptian war tactics

The staunch anti-Egyptian stance of the British Conservative party had seen a change of face following the 1967 War. Even Donald McCarthy, who had advocated earlier in the year for a harsher censure of Egypt, ameliorated his position toward the poison gas issue in Yemen. In justifying his changed position, he highlighted the "big lie" (following Egypt's defeat in June 1967, the Arab press falsely accused the United Kingdom and the United States of playing a role in Israel's victory, giving birth to what became known as the "big lie") atmosphere in the Middle East, making any British protest against Egypt inherently counterproductive.[64] In McCarthy's view, the British response needed to be limited to "sympathy but unwillingness to take drastic action."[65]

Echoing McCarthy's thoughts, William Hillier-Fry explained that if British involvement in any poison gas censures was discovered, "it would be widely believed that we were simply indulging in a vindictive attack upon the Egyptians."[66] There was additional concern in the British Foreign Office that any British-led anti-UAR initiatives had the potential to adversely affect British interests in Libya, Kuwait, and the Emirates, which were all still under British colonial control in 1967.[67]

George Brown's talking points for August 8, 1967, were a demonstrative sign of how British policy toward the Egyptian poison gas issue had changed after June 1967. Britain would not take the lead on UAR condemnation because it was unlikely to succeed in stimulating action by UN Security Council, General Assembly, HRC, or the Economic and Social Council. British involvement would only be a "propaganda gift" to the progressive Arab countries, who would assume the initiative was part of the UK vendetta against the UAR. Secretary Brown concluded his remarks with a statement absolving Britain of any further responsibility for holding Egypt accountable: "While I sympathize very strongly with the victims of what has happened, I must keep the British interests as a whole in mind in any action I take or attitude I adopt."[68]

On the other side of the ocean, even though CIA labs had confirmed the presence of a nerve agent in the battlefield samples from Kitaf, it was not until the end of July 1967 that the US State Department officially acknowledged the use of poison gas in Yemen.[69] Hermann F. Eilts, US Ambassador to Saudi Arabia, was one of the lone government voices advocating greater US involvement on the poison gas issue. "UAR continues [to] indiscriminately use poison gas in Yemen. On our part we [are] no longer seeking [to] obscure this fact . . . we here are also discreetly urging Yemeni royalists give wider, more effective publicity to these poison gas attacks." On one occasion, Eilts tried to convince the State Department to supply two hundred gas masks to royalists.[70] Leading up to the June 1967 war, the United States had been concerned that excessive pressure on Nasser related to his war conduct in Yemen would push him into a war with Israel. As Eilts pointed out, that war had already occurred and these constraints were no longer a factor in US policy toward Egypt's chemical warfare in Yemen.

Secretary of State Dean Rusk did not agree with Eilts's approach. In his response to ICRC's request for gas masks, Rusk demonstrated the impact of the politically restrained US policy toward Egypt's chemical war in Yemen. He first blamed the complicated nature of using a gas mask and the supposed ineptitude of Yemeni civilians: "effective use of masks, medicines, and equipment requires training or supervision of type not easy to arrange in conditions of this area. Many Yemeni are illiterate and would require oral instructions in use of masks. Yemenis are known to fear injections and would be hard to train to make proper use of medical kits."[71]

When British officials asked why the United States had not made a public statement on the Egyptian use of gas in Yemen, Rusk replied that "this information would have greater impact internationally if it came from the Red Cross rather than from the US."[72] British officials recognized that by this point in the Middle East conflict US officials were facing similar constraints in that "the United States cannot take the lead in any action against the Egyptians because any such initiative would undoubtedly be attacked as a "pro-Israel" maneuver by the United States."[73] Rusk's hesitance may also have been driven by the fact that by mid-July 1967, the Ranch Hand herbicidal warfare missions in Vietnam had reached their all-time peak in terms of defoliating agent volume and the number of sorties.[74] General William Westmoreland made it clear in 1967 that he wanted all his officers and their Vietnamese counterparts to make use of tear gas during combat operations, citing several years of successful tactical deployment. Tear gas was particularly effective at flushing enemies out of hiding, denying guerillas access to terrain or supplies, and during search-and-rescue operations.[75] Rusk had always been a vehement opponent of Kennedy and Johnson's defoliation policy, fearing that the United States would be charged with biological and chemical warfare despite the fact that herbicides were not officially prohibited by international law. He recommended several times that the Ranch Hand program be terminated.[76] Washington could therefore not hope to contribute to the censure of Egypt's chemical warfare in Yemen without receiving an international critique of their own use of chemical agents in Vietnam in return. As Harold Beeley, the former UK ambassador to Egypt, noted: "The Soviet bloc would certainly exploit the item for attacks on the use of gas, lethal or not, in Vietnam by the United States. We should then have a sterile propaganda debate, which at the best would waste time and at the worst would erode the present East-West détente . . . "[77]

Given the political limitations of Cold War tensions and the restrictive environment following the June 1967 war, Britain, Saudi Arabia, and the United States offered only supportive roles in investigating the use of poison gas in Yemen. Officials from the United States and Britain were desperate for another country to take the lead in a censure of Egypt. Roscoe Drummond, a reporter for the *Washington Post,* ridiculed US Ambassador Arthur J. Goldberg and US inaction against Egypt in the UN as a "let-someone-else-do-it-policy."[78] Numerous attempts in August and September 1967 to find another country or organization to lead the attack against Egyptian chemical warfare failed to find the metaphorical sacrificial lamb.

During a meeting that appears to have taken place in front of a map of the world, British foreign officers went through continents, eliminating entire regions while highlighting several countries that could be portrayed as "neutral" and that could be relied upon to broach the poison gas issue in the UN. The entire continent of Africa was ruled out for a multitude of reasons, including Nasser's prominence in the decolonized world and the issue of African solidarity with Egypt. In Asia, evidently "only Ceylon, Indonesia and Malaysia, whose attitudes in recent months has been reasonable, could avoid accusations of commitment and are also free to act." Yet there remained a reasonable doubt whether any would take the lead against Egypt. This left only the Latin American and Scandinavian countries, or perhaps a willing NATO member.[79]

In an attempt to find a neutral Western country to lead a censure of Egypt, US and British diplomats approached the Portuguese delegation to NATO, who rejected the request, as they believed that the use of poison gas in Yemen was an inter-Arab matter that should be dealt with among the Arab foreign ministers in Khartoum, Sudan, rather than one of the NATO countries. They referred specifically to Saudi Arabia and Egypt, whose delegates would be at the center of the upcoming Arab Summit in Khartoum on August 29, 1967. When approached with the same request, the Turkish delegates to NATO suggested that continued public media attention and condemnation would be more effective than a UN resolution.

US Ambassador Goldberg was initially optimistic that one of the Scandinavian countries would accept the responsibility to lead the political attack against Egypt's war in Yemen, given their recent history in supporting UN peacekeeping forces as a neutral Western power. Following a meeting with representatives of the Norwegian government, Goldberg's initial optimism seemed somewhat misplaced. British foreign officers met with their Norwegian counterparts and expressed serious skepticism:

"Norway considers that it enjoys at present a certain measure of goodwill with the Afro-Asians in the United Nations and is ready to play an active part in peacekeeping in the Middle East if called upon to do so . . . The Norwegian Government will therefore not be willing in any way to jeopardize this international asset . . . for the sake of damaging the UAR's reputation or even to save Yemeni lives. They have also a very important tanker shipping interest which they will not wish to endanger by action directed against Nasser."[80]

When the Norwegian mission to the UN approached UN diplomat Ralph Bunche for advice, he further dissuaded an Egyptian censure and expressed fear "that a resolution might only complicate the Middle East situation."[81] The Norwegian Foreign Minister John Lyng told George Brown that "the Scandinavians considered that their economic and political interests outweighed the moral issues." Other NATO allies similarly shied away from taking an initiative. Delegates from Washington and London broached the subject with the Director-General of the Danish Ministry of Foreign Affairs Gunnar Seidenfaden, who explained that "the Danes would want to avoid any initiative directed against the UAR. Danish shipping and economic interests in the Middle East would in this instance be likely to outweigh any moral feeling about poison gas."[82] Dutch representatives at the NATO Disarmaments Experts meeting in September further justified these economic concerns to George Brown, recognizing that "in light of the passions aroused by the Arab-Israeli war it would be difficult to secure condemnation of a major participant for the use of gas in the Yemen."[83]

MP Emanuel Shinwell then suggested finding a Latin American country to carry out a political censure against the UAR's poison gas use, an idea that failed to take off ,as the United States doubted that any of these countries would take the initiative.[84] In what seems in retrospect an act of sheer desperation, Lee Dinsmore, the acting country director for Yemen in the US State Department, admitted that he was "approaching a number of 'non Anglo-Saxon Nobel prize winners' with a view to organizing a protest against the use of poison gas in Yemen." He told his British counterparts that the approaches were being made indirectly and the State Department was very keen that their part in organizing the protest should if possible not be exposed.[85]

The State Department's "Nobel scheme" was hardly unprecedented, as the British had attempted a similar tactic with South Arabian representatives appealing to the UN. The most willing collaborator to this scheme was Hussein Ali Bayoumi, the pro-British Adeni minister of defence and the secretary-general of the United National Party of Aden. When Bayoumi first learned of the Egyptian use of poison gas, he expressed concern for Egyptian colonialism and tactics following South Yemen's independence from Britain, originally scheduled for 1968: "The people of South Arabia, who have struggled for so long to gain their freedom, are determined not to exchange the miseries of British colonialism for a life of slavery under the Egyptian imperialists."[86]

Hillier-Fry suggested that the British use South Arabian petitioners, like Bayoumi, to publicize local concerns for Egyptian chemical weapons, as the imam's royalist supporters did not have an official public voice. The token South Arabian could appeal to the UN for a mission to save them from the fate of their northern brethren at the hands of the Egyptian air force. Even in the worst possible scenario, if the UAR blocked Bayoumi's petition, "we might be able to get a certain amount of publicity for the suppression of a legitimate petition merely because it criticized the UAR."[87] Neither the Nobel nor the South Arabian scheme ever gained serious traction.

The diplomatic failure was attributed to Egypt's preeminence in the UN: "The Egyptians are not an easy target ... the UAR was, in terms of ability to influence Assembly votes, probably the most powerful member country of the United Nations, not excluding the Soviet Union and the United States." Although events following the Egyptian defeat in June 1967 had dented the country's reputation in the UN, "the Egyptian delegation remains amongst the most efficient of third world delegations and still has a fair chance of swinging the great bloc of Afro-Asian votes the way it wants." A member of the Soviet delegation even remarked in defense of Egypt's war record in Yemen that "since unmarked aircraft have been flying over the Yemen, it may be the CIA who have arranged for the dropping of the bombs!"[88]

George Brown admitted to British MP Duncan Sandys after having approached various governments to intervene in UAR poison gas attacks that "while all the governments we have approached deplore the UAR's use of poison gas, they all seem to feel they have compelling reasons of national interest for not publicly taking the lead in censuring the UAR."[89] When US and British diplomats failed to find another party to lead the attack, George Brown decided to table efforts at obtaining a UN censure of the UAR.[90] Frank Brenchley, the Head of the Arabian Department in the Foreign Office even recommended to Brown that he should omit the issue of poison gas in his upcoming address to the UN General Assembly, as further discussion would be counterproductive. Brenchley was concerned that condemning the UAR would be construed as general hostility to UAR and would "have lessened the chances of getting an overall settlement on the Middle East."[91]

Sandys continued to be Brown's adversary on the poison gas issue and sharply criticized this decision. Sandys questioned Brown's trust in Nasser and why the UK should "allow him to get away with this flagrant breach of the rules of war." Sandys made one final overture to the foreign secretary, asking Britain to take the lead against poison gas in Yemen lest "Britain be afraid to speak alone for humanity."[92] Brown dismissed Sandys' moralistic appeal claiming instead that "were we to raise the matter, it would be widely believed that we were cynically using a humanitarian appeal simply in order to embarrass the UAR."[93]

By November 1967 the withdrawal of Egyptian forces from Yemen was well underway and was expected to be completed by mid-December.[94] British diplomat Norman Hillier-Fry remarked that by this point, "there is no possibility of securing international action to condemn the United Arab Republic."[95] The international initiative and desire to censure Egypt and perhaps force a withdrawal from Yemen had dissipated; the Egyptian troops were already on their way out. Just a few weeks later the Egyptian intervention in Yemen came to an end, leaving the issue of poison gas as only a distant historical memory for most governments and news outlets.

While the United States and Britain had already withdrawn their confrontations with Egypt over chemical weapons, Imam al-Badr and his royalist movement continued their own public relations campaign for many months after the Egyptian troops had left. In 1968 the imam's official printing service released an English-language magazine that highlighted the atrocities committed by Egyptian occupation forces and focused on the use of poison gas. The publication included graphic pictures of Yemeni casualties, copies of ICRC reports, and grossly exaggerated statistics on the number of poison gas attacks, which the royalists numbered in the hundreds. In an attempt to garner support for an international investigation into Egyptian war crimes, the publication ends with the following statement in bold: "You may know personally some of those responsible."[96] However, no Egyptians were ever held accountable for their actions. By the time the royalists began their propaganda effort in earnest, Egyptian forces had already withdrawn and the international community had moved on to other conflicts, leaving the first use of chemical warfare in the Arab world to the backrooms of dusty and neglected archives.

Ignorance of Egypt's use of chemical weapons continued even decades after the civil war had come to an end and the royalists had reconciled with the YAR. Contemporary media analyses and much of the chemical warfare literature tend to overlook the use of poison gas in Yemen.[97] As Walter Benjamin famously remarked, "history is written by the victors." The YAR defeated Imam al-Badr and the royalists, earning the republican leadership the right to dictate national memory of the civil war. During the author's visits to Yemen, there were only a few who could recall the attacks and there was certainly no mention in the limited political archives available in Sana'a. In the National War Museum in Sana'a, as of 2013, there was no reference to Egypt's use of chemical weapons. To date, no monuments have been erected in the targeted villages and no memorial was ever held for the victims of Egypt's chemical attacks. Although many Egyptian military officers published self-serving memoirs of the Yemen campaign, predictably, none of them mentioned the use of chemical weapons, hoping their war conduct would soon be forgotten in the pages of history.

7

The Anglo-Egyptian Rivalry in Yemen

THE AMERICANS, SOVIETS, and Saudis were each secretly pleased to see Nasser rattling in his Yemeni cage with great restraints placed on his plans elsewhere in the region. The British, on the other hand, were not merely content with shackling Nasser's foreign policy. When the first Egyptian troops arrived to Yemen in October 1962, British officials perceived a direct threat to their colonial interests in Aden.[1] Nasser openly declared his malicious intentions toward the British-controlled territories of South Arabia and granted financial support, training, and munitions to anti-British groups. From the British perspective, this was an opportunity to exact revenge on an Arab leader who had singlehandedly delivered the greatest blow to the British Empire in the Middle East with their 1956 defeat in Suez. There was concern that Nasser would try to undermine British control over the Wheelus Air Base in Libya and a pair of bases in newly independent Cyprus. In order to protect these strategically important bases, the official British foreign policy objective was to "keep Nasser locked up in Yemen," without confronting him in open war.[2] The Anglo-Egyptian conflict would eventually encompass elements of the British Special Air Service (SAS), the French Foreign Legion, the Israeli Air Force, the American CIA, and the Iranian *savak* (secret service), among others, adding a clandestine component to the international arena of the Yemen Civil War.

During the 1960s, South Arabia was occupied by two international powers in decline. Following their loss of the Suez Canal in 1956, the British Empire in the Middle East transferred regional military command to the port of Aden. Nasser's gaze, in turn, shifted toward Yemen, whose geography served great strategic interest for Egypt. Yemen overlooked Bab al-Mandeb, the maritime gates of the Red Sea and a vital water passage for the Suez Canal. Yemen's proximity to Arabian oil fields and the remaining imperial possessions of the British Empire which were a source of potential propaganda value, were added bonuses. This Anglo-Egyptian rivalry over regional dominance served as an important backdrop to the Yemen Civil War as their historic struggle had a profound impact on the course of the conflict.

The 1960s was not, however, the first time that British and Egyptian foreign policies clashed in this corner of South Arabia. During the 1830s, both Muhammad Ali, the Khedive of Egypt, and Lord Palmerston of the British Empire had their eyes on this vital region. The rhetoric and circumstances of their first confrontation over Yemen would be recreated 130 years later as Nasser, the inheritor of the country fathered by Muhammad Ali, clashed with the last generation of British imperialists in the same setting. The Yemen Civil War contributed to the decline of both British and Egyptian regional clout and served to close the circle of 130 years of the Anglo-Egyptian rivalry.

British Capture of Aden[3]

Between 1835 and 1837, British Captain Stafford Bettesworth Haines made two expeditionary trips to Aden, noting that the armies of Muhammad Ali, the Khedive of Egypt, had been consolidating their position in Yemen since 1832 and were poised to move southward to capture the port of Aden.[4] Ali's army was sent to Yemen at the behest of the Ottoman Empire to crush the Wahhabi tribal revolt in the Hijaz, an area encompassing the holy cities of Mecca and Medinah. When hundreds of Egyptians were reported to have garrisoned the Yemeni port city of Mocha on June 22, 1837, the British Foreign Office estimated that it was only a matter of time until Muhammad Ali's forces secured the entire Arabian Peninsula.[5] Beyond the Red Sea trade, Yemen itself was estimated to be a valuable asset to Ali as it was, and continues to be, the most populous country on the Arabian Peninsula.[6] The impending Egyptian conquest of Aden would have serious ramifications for British commerce in the Red Sea and the security of India and its trade routes. Moreover, the expansion of Egyptian control on the Arabian Peninsula continued to threaten the relative stability of the Ottoman Empire and the balance of power in the region.

In January 1837 the merchant ship *Deria Dawlat*, owned by the nawab (ruler) of the Carnatic and sailing under the British flag, left India carrying dozens of Muslim passengers on their way to Mecca for the annual Hajj pilgrimage. After the ship crashed into the rocky shores of Aden, tribal members under the leadership of the Sheikh of Aden plundered the British ship and apprehended many of the surviving passengers. In subsequent events, later clarified by detailed testimonies offered to a tribunal in Bombay, the passengers were stripped naked and brought to shore. The men were jailed while the women were harassed by the local inhabitants of Aden. The sheikh forced them, under threat of death, to sign an affidavit declaring that they had not been mistreated. After receiving a coarse waist covering and some food, several passengers found passage to Mocha, where they were forced to beg for food in the streets. The surviving passengers eventually made their way to Jeddah under the protection of a British captain who was passing through the area.[7] The *Deria Dawlat* incident would have far-reaching repercussions for the future of Yemen and the rest of South Arabia.

On March 26, 1838, the British Colonial Council met in Bombay to discuss Muhammad Ali's expanding Egyptian empire and its repercussions for the British Empire. They discussed Captain Haines' "free purchase of Aden" proposal. Although members of the Government of Bombay deemed the military procurement of the Aden to be a dangerous and unnecessary provocation of Egypt, they perceived the situation as an epic confrontation with Egyptian imperialism: "there is but one power in that [Arabia] region, whose views or feelings on that subject are worth a moment's regard; and to that Power it will be a matter of profound indifference whether we gain the port in question by force, fraud, or favor, so as we gain it at all. Probably no sight more hateful could visit the eyes of Muhammad Ali, than that of the British Design flying over the promontory of Aden."[8]

The council viewed Ali as an ambitious ruler equaling, if not surpassing, the global threat of the French and Russian Empires.

> Since first obtaining possession of Egypt by an act of shocking perfidy and cruelty, his career has been uniform. By treason to his acknowledged sovereign, he has extended his sway over the heart of Africa.... His next adventure will be on Baghdad, and on the western shores of the Persian Gulf; and, if once permitted to the Straits of Bab al-Mandib, he never rest till he has stretched his power along the whole cost of Arabia. The object of Muhammad Ali is evident the plans to erect Egypt, Syria, and Arabia, into

an independent Kingdom; and, whenever it suits the views of France or of Russia to abet him in accomplishing that purpose, he will gladly league with either of those powers against England.[9]

The council concluded that the British occupation of Aden was indeed retribution for the embarrassment of the *Deria Dawlat* and could potentially curtail the threat of Egyptian imperialism by blocking Ali's plans for Arabian and Red Sea dominance.

It is distinctively known that as one object amidst his ambitious schemes, Muhammad Ali has for some time contemplated the subjugation of Aden. He cannot therefore but view with great displeasure the anticipation of his design by the British government.... If we withdraw from Aden, and Muhammad Ali plants his foot there, the plea of priority becomes his, and our hopes of superseding him are extinguished forever. We are then at his mercy, and can establish no coal depot for our Red Sea steamers, at a station worth having, which will not be under his control.[10]

Throughout the 1830s, Henry John Temple, Third Viscount, Lord Palmerston, held personal contempt for Ali, whom he accused of establishing state monopolies only to secure a huge profit for himself.[11] As the conflict with Egypt progressed, Palmerston took an increasing vitriolic stance toward the Egyptian *wali*, writing: "I hate Mehmet Ali, whom I consider as nothing but an ignorant barbarian, who by cunning and boldness and mother-wit, has been successful in rebellion; ... I look upon his boasted civilization of Egypt as the arrantest humbug; and I believe that he is as great a tyrant and oppressor as ever made a people wretched."[12]

Having been persuaded by Haines's arguments and by the council's fear of Egyptian imperialism, Sir Robert Grant, the governor of Bombay, issued orders to negotiate with the sheikh of Aden to take possession of the port in compensation for grievances related to the *Deria Dawlat*:[13] "The insult which has been offered to the British flag by the Sultan of Aden has led me to enquiries which leave no doubt on my mind that we should take possession of the port of Aden."[14]

Without a British presence in Aden, it would only be matter of time before Ali conquered Sana'a, the capital of South Arabia, giving him regional political control. Haines believed that the interior tribes looked to the British for support to stop the Egyptian advance and reopen Yemeni roads to commerce.[15] Many of these same tribes later became part of the

Federation of South Arabia (FSA) during the 1960s, a product of British hegemony in twentieth-century South Arabia.

On March 27, 1839, Patrick Campbell, British Consul-General in Egypt, reported to Lord Palmerston that the port of Aden had been secured by the British navy and that he no longer thought that Ali would threaten the British port or British trade routes along the Red Sea.[16] Palmerston's response to Campbell claimed that Ali had marched an expedition force to Mocha with the intention of attacking Sana'a in October 1838 and continuing further south to the tip of the Arabian Peninsula. The British possession of Aden, however, succeeded in halting Ali's advance. Palmerston instructed Campbell to inform Ali that the British did not support continued Egyptian occupation of Yemen and request withdrawal. Campbell was to encourage Ali to "engage in improving the administration of the Provinces confided to His Government instead of employing the energies of his mind and the resources of the countries he governs in, in aggressive expeditions against neighboring districts."[17] Although the occupation of Aden was further justified by the commercial potential of Yemen's coffee trade and of the utility of an Aden coal station, it was clear to all that the real purpose of the British conquest of Aden was primarily to counter Egyptian imperialism.[18] British Aden would serve a similar role during the 1960s.

The Suez Group and the Anti-Nasser Movement

Muhammad Ali's nationalist ambitions were adopted by the Egyptian successor to Ali's dynasty, Gamal Abdel Nasser, when he rose to power in 1954.[19] In his treatise *The Philosophy of the Revolution*, published in 1955, Nasser portrayed himself as the inheritor of a century of incomplete Egyptian revolutions. Beginning with Ali's failed experiment at representing the Egyptian people, Nasser then highlighted Colonel Ahmad Urabi's nationalist revolt in 1881 and Sa'ad Zaghloul's failed 1919 revolution. The Free Officers Revolution on July 23, 1952, Nasser claimed, was the realization of Egyptian dreams for nationhood that began with Ali's founding of the modern Egypt state.[20] Rather than marching an army of conquest through Sudan and the Arabian Peninsula, however, Nasser initially saw the expansion of his influence through anti-imperialist rhetoric and military support for regional allies as manifested in his personal Arab nationalist ideology, Nasserism.

Nasserism has been characterized as an ideology, cult of personality, modernization effort, anticolonialist movement, and even a form of populism. Similar to Ali, Nasser sought to modernize the Egyptian nation state.[21] Under both Ali and Nasser, particular emphasis was given to the modernization of the Egyptian countryside and the local *fellahin*.[22] Walid Khalidi describes Nasserism as an "attitude" of the people, rather than an ideology like Marxism or Socialism.[23] At the core of this "attitude" was an anti-imperialist drive and a sense of pan-Arab identity.

P. J. Vatikiotis argues that, rather than an ideology, Nasserism was an authoritarian cult of personality dependent entirely upon Nasser and "his vision, style, and approach to power."[24] This centrality of Nasser in the Egyptian state is similar to Khaled Fahmy's depiction of Muhammad Ali's dynastic empire.[25] Nasser's ability to appeal to the masses of Egypt, the Arab world, and the developing world was itself a concept of Nasserism.[26] His charismatic authority, however, rested on his heroic performance, necessitating constant success and foreign adventures abroad, an important factor when considering the Anglo-Egyptian rivalry. In an edited volume published fifty years after Nasser's rise to power, Eli Podeh and Onn Winckler argue that Nasser's appeal to Egyptian peasantry and emphasis on mass public appearances resembled the Latin American populist model, and Ali's *fellahin*-directed economic reform and military modernization. Like Ali's, Nasser's populism rested on his ability to appeal to the *fellahin* and the general population through continued efforts against imperialism and the British in particular.[27]

Despite these similarities, Nasser's revolution was not explicitly a reincarnation of Muhammad Ali's empire, aside from elements of historical continuity and a very compelling narrative. After all, the Free Officers Revolution came at the expense of King Farouk, the last ruling member of Muhammad Ali's dynasty. Nonetheless, Nasser's rise to power and his ability to challenge British hegemony in the region helped bring about, once again, the intersection of declining British power and rising Egyptian influence in the Middle East. The reemergence of the Anglo Egyptian clash of equals reintroduced many of the racial, economic, and strategic concerns harbored by British officials during the nineteenth century.

As if echoing Palmerston's concerns about Muhammad Ali, British Prime Minister Anthony Eden considered Nasser an embodiment of all the threats to British hegemony, including the balance of power in the Middle East, British oil supplies, economic export, and general national livelihood.[28] British statesmen during the 1950s and '60s reused much of the Ali-era language to describe Egyptian colonialist involvement in Yemen during the 1960s. During a parliamentary meeting on November 25, 1955,

Conservative MP Julian Amery critiqued that "every Egyptian Government must embark on a policy of foreign adventure."[29] In his maiden speech as an MP on the floor of the House of Commons on March 7, 1956, Colonel Neil 'Billy' McLean observed: "I feel that our Egyptian friends and the Egyptian government must realize that admiration for Egypt is not the same thing as love for Egyptian imperialism."[30]

On July 26, 1956, when Nasser nationalized the Suez Canal Company, British condemnation of the Egyptian President grew more vitriolic. The Suez Canal was immensely important for the British. Every year, six million tons of oil passed through the Suez Canal, with two-thirds allotted for Western European fuel requirements. In 1955, 14,666 ships passed through the canal, with one-third destined for British ports, and three-quarters for NATO countries.[31] British newspapers expressed the views of the British public describing the nationalization as "an act of brigandage,"[32] claiming that "the time for appeasement is over. We must cry 'Halt' to Nasser as we should have cried 'Halt!' to Hitler. Before he sets the Middle East aflame, as Hitler did to Europe."[33]

Given his position as Prime Minister in 1956, Anthony Eden received a great deal of blame in the historical critique of the Suez Crisis. More apologetic and pro-Eden historians have been keen to absolve Eden of complete responsibility for the 1956 fiasco. They argue that Eden did not willingly pursue military options in Egypt. Rather, he was forced into the Suez war by a combination of domestic political pressures, his own failing health, US reluctance to act, and pressure from Israel and France.[34] Whether these reasons account for Eden's decision making in 1956 is a matter of debate. What is not debatable, however, is the political drama that overran Whitehall during the 1950s regarding the Anglo-Egyptian rivalry. At the core of the anti-Nasser coalition in the British government was a group of twenty-six Conservative Party MPs, headed by Captain Charles Waterhouse, a longtime MP and a senior advisor in the Privy Council.[35] Known as the Suez Group, Waterhouse's coalition was a last vestige of swashbuckling British soldiers and administrators who continued to view themselves as global kingmakers through the end of the 1960s.[36]

The Suez Group's image was of "backwoodsmen—a motley collection of colorful, marginal political eccentrics."[37] They formed backbench pressure on the cabinet and were central to Conservative Party thought for two decades. During the 1950s, the group consisted of elderly contemporaries of Churchill including Loran Hankey, the Director of the Suez Canal Company, and Leo Amery, a close confidant of Churchill's anti-appeasement Munich coalition during the 1930s (he died in 1955), who were joined by young Tories such as Enoch Powell, the well-known moral critic of British policy in Kenya, Fitzroy MacLean who had served under Churchill's World War II command in Cairo, and Julian Amery, a Conservative MP and the son of Leo Amery.[38]

The group rose to prominence following the October 19, 1954, British agreement with Egypt to withdraw British troops from the region in exchange for the maintenance of the Suez Canal as a vital British base. The Suez Group believed that their subsequent anti-Egyptian posture was representative of the general sentiments of the British public. The members of the group were intent on maintaining remnants of the British Empire at a time when the United States, under President Eisenhower, was pushing a policy of decolonization. Having grown impatient with the lack of American support for continued British presence in the Middle East, some went as far as proposing an alliance with the Soviet Union, trying to convince the Soviets that a British presence in Middle East would be better than an American takeover.[39] Karl Pieragostini observed that during the 1950s and '60s British politicians, specifically those of the Suez Group, saw themselves as locked in a battle with Nasser for the future of South Arabia and the role of the British in the Middle East.[40] This group, however, was held together by more than their disdain for Nasser. A combination of political intrigue, familial ties, and close friendship brought together the members of the Suez Group to exert influence on a decade of British foreign policy in the Middle East.

The political origins of the Suez Group can be traced back to the anti-appeasement coalition of the 1930s, which included most notably Winston Churchill and his protégé Anthony Eden. Between 1951 and 1955, Eden, who served as foreign secretary and deputy prime minister under Churchill, was instrumental in formulating British foreign policy globally and in the Middle East in particular. On January 29, 1953, Eden returned from a meeting with his Egyptian counterpart during which they had been negotiating the independence of Sudan and the withdrawal from the Suez Canal. Upon hearing news of progress in the negotiations, Churchill reprimanded Eden as a failed foreign secretary and claimed that his former partner in "anti-appeasement" in the 1930s was now practicing a policy of appeasement in the Middle East. Churchill fumed that he "never knew before that Munich was situated on the Nile."[41] After Churchill retired in 1955, Eden succeeded him as Prime Minister, but could not avoid Churchill's continued criticism. Eden's foreign secretary and later chancellor of the exchequer, Harold Macmillan, with his eyes on the prime minister position himself, willingly joined with members of the Suez Group, along with Churchill, in undermining Prime Minister Eden's foreign policy with Egypt. Although not an official member of the Suez Group himself, Churchill acted as the group's ideological and political mentor. In a conversation with his doctor, Lord Maron, Churchill shared a blunt opinion of Nasser: "Whoever he is he's finished after this. We can't have that malicious swine sitting across our communications."[42]

The Suez Group's pressure on Prime Minister Eden continued at the Conservative Party conference in Llandudno, Wales, from October 11–13, 1956, compelling him to further consider military action against Egypt. Waterhouse and Amery introduced a party amendment that stipulated that any agreement with Nasser must ensure the international control of the Suez Canal. The Suez Group's influence did not stop at party headquarters, but gained the sympathy of media figures as well. Malcolm Muggeridge of the *Daily Telegraph* and Randolph Churchill of the *Evening Standard* and *Daily Express*, for example, vilified Eden as a Munich politician (an appeaser) and supported the more hawkish Macmillan.[43]

In his effort to supplant Eden as Prime Minister, Macmillan was able to rely heavily on the support of his son-in-law Julian Amery and the Suez Group in general.[44] Amery's passionate and energetic patriotism is often attributed to the fate of his brother John, who was hanged for treason in a Wandsworth jail in December 1945.[45] MP McLean, a "political soulmate and inseparable friend" of Amery from their time serving together as intelligence officers in the Balkans, also assumed an important role in the group.[46] When Eden resigned in 1957 in the aftermath of the Suez political disaster, Queen Elizabeth took the advice of Churchill and appointed Macmillan as the next prime minister rather than Rab Butler, who was Eden's deputy prime minister.[47]

According to Amery's assessment, Nasser was within forty-eight hours of being overthrown, and the British and French already had alternative government waiting. It was clear that the Soviets had withdrawn military support from Egypt and that Nasser would likely flee Cairo with little resistance. As a consequence of the Suez failure, nicknamed the European "Waterloo" of the Middle East, a major power vacuum emerged. According to Amery, this vacuum was filled by two Arab-Israeli wars, the Egyptian invasion of Yemen, the murder of Prime Minister Nuri al-Said and King Faisal in Baghdad, the rise of Muammar Qadafi in Libya, and the Sovietization of Aden and Ethiopia; in sum all of the region's problems of the late 1950s and throughout the 1960s. He believed this would never have happened if the British and French had been allowed to prevail in Suez.[48]

In 1957, in response to the British retreat from Egypt and Iraq, and the tenuous hold on military bases in Cyprus and Kenya, the Suez Group helped transform the relatively minor British port of Aden into the center of British power in the region. The construction of the British Petroleum (BP) refinery in 1954 helped Aden become the fourth-largest refueling station in the world.[49] The increasing importance of Aden for British regional security inspired the members of the Suez Group to refocus their efforts on the strategic South Arabian port.

The Aden Group and the Secret War with Nasser

In the aftermath of the 1956 Suez War, Nasser was intent on driving the British out of the Red Sea region, and Aden in particular, for fear that it would be used as a British base to reestablish influence over Egypt and the Suez Canal. Nasser later described himself as a "thorn in the British throat."[50] Aden, a port city initially captured as a deterrent to Muhammad Ali's Egyptian nationalism, found itself once again at the forefront of the British-Egyptian imperial struggle. The final Anglo-Egyptian confrontation in Yemen, from 1962 to 1967, marked the bookend to a long history of British and Egyptian power relations in the Middle East.

Having failed to secure the Suez Canal in 1956, the Conservative remnants of the Suez Group turned their political intentions toward the last British military base in Aden. Following the arrival of Egyptian troops to North Yemen in October 1962, the group, under the leadership of Julian Amery and Neil McLean, was renamed the Aden Group. Its anti-Egyptian and anti-Nasser agenda remained the same. In the eyes of the Aden Group, the Yemen Civil War was the second round of the final Anglo-Egyptian confrontation that began with the Suez War in 1956. In the eyes of the historian, however, the history of the Anglo-Egyptian rivalry in Yemen began over a hundred years earlier, with the British capture of Aden in 1839.

In 1869 British colonial officials in Aden formalized strategic relationships with the surrounding tribes, forming the East Aden Protectorate and the West Aden Protectorate which both constituted the area of South Yemen (see Fig. 7.1). Aden High Commissioner Kennedy Trevaskis turned the West Aden Protectorate of fifteen tribes into the Federation of South Arabia (FSA) in April 1962, with Aden joining on January 18,

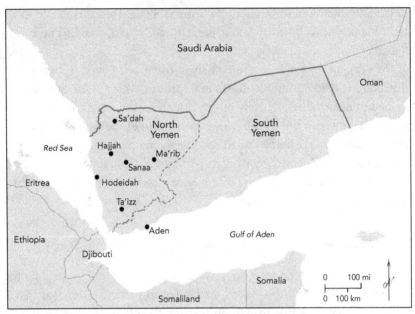

FIGURE 7.1 Map of North-South Yemen. Created by author.

1963, intending it to serve as a permanent barrier from Arab nationalism even after the British withdrew.[51] The East Aden Protectorate, which consisted of those tribes that did not join the FSA, became the Protectorate of South Arabia. The British intent was to grant the FSA independence in 1968, while continuing to maintain defense facilities in Aden. To this end, the Aden Legislative Council formally approved Aden's accession to the Federation on September 24, 1962, only two days before the outbreak of the civil war in what historian William R. Polk described as a "shotgun wedding."[52] Prior to September 1962, it seemed as if Aden and the protectorates were sheltered from pan-Arab nationalism by the "dense curtain of the Imam's Yemen. As the former High Commissioner of Aden, Charles Johnston explained: "The Yemeni revolution brought its bugles on to our doorstep."[53]

Echoing the conversation between Campbell and Palmerston in 1839, Trevaskis explained to the prime minister's office that "the base in Aden is the major obstacle to Nasserite pretensions in the Arabian Peninsula and the Persian Gulf."[54] British Defence Minister Peter Thorneycroft and Secretary of State for the Colonies Duncan Sandys took Trevaskis's words a step further, warning that "the loss of Aden would signal the end of the British Empire."[55] Heeding these words, Prime Minister Macmillan appointed Julian Amery as "minister for Yemen" and entrusted him with the responsibility of supporting royalist forces, with the intention of forestalling Egyptian hegemony in Arabia. Amery's "private war against Nasser" would receive no public recognition or official government approval, as Macmillan's divided cabinet would never have sanctioned open support of the royalists and a confrontation with Nasser.[56]

Subsequent letters from British ambassadors abroad to the Foreign Office reiterated the need to "prevent UAR state from stabilizing in Yemen," and that British intervention should "maintain at least a stalemate if not a royalist victory."[57] For example, in a letter to Amery, Michael Webb, a British undercover journalist fighting with the royalists, explained the shared sentiments felt by many current and former SAS soldiers: "That maniac in Cairo has a complex against Britain, and no amount of diplomacy and tact will ever eliminate it."[58]

Colonel McLean used the crisis in Yemen as a personal opportunity to confront Nasser's imperialism on the Arabian Peninsula, just as Captain Haines had orchestrated the political and military logistics to take possession of Aden during the 1830s. Following his visit to Yemen over Christmas break 1962, McLean explained the measures that were needed to confront Egypt in Yemen: "The objective is to get the Egyptian troops out of the Yemen. If this were not possible then we should at least ensure that the Egyptians in the Yemen are so busy defending themselves against the Yemenis that they will not be able to intervene in Aden and other parts of the Arabian Peninsula. Therefore I believe the maximum possible support should be given to the Imam."[59]

Over the course of the civil war, a total of sixty-six British mercenaries and twenty-four French counterparts aided royalist forces in Yemen. Mercenaries were paid on average $500 per month in addition to airfare, rent, and other expenses. Their responsibilities including weapons training, establishing radio communications, developing guerilla strategy, and mining vital roads. Many of these mercenaries served on the front lines of the royalist battlefield and specifically targeted Egyptian military strongholds and heavy weaponry.[60]

The Saudi royal family financed and supplied the entire mission. Colonel David Smiley, Britain's military advisor on Yemen and an important member of the Aden Group, suspected that the Saudis intended to "keep the pot boiling" in the Yemen without increasing the direct support necessary to openly defeat Egyptian forces in Yemen. Adding to the list of countries machinating to keep Nasser engaged in Yemen, Smiley observed that the Saudis "would no doubt be happy to see 40,000 of Nasser's troops permanently tied down in the Yemen, suffering casualties and costing Nasser a great deal of money." The British, on the other hand, preferred to drive Nasser from the Arabian Peninsula entirely.[61]

Jim Johnson, a central figure of the Aden Group, echoed McLean's observations, claiming that a stalemate that pinned down the Egyptian army "in a war of attrition suited the Saudis nicely." Johnson was skeptical, however, as to the royalists' ability to breach Egypt's strategic triangle. During a 1966 offensive, for example, mercenaries orchestrated a heavy barrage of artillery to cover a royalist advance on Sana'a only to see al-Badr's forces remain in place, noting the "royalists' lack of resolve that went beyond the front line."[62] Mark Millburn, an SAS major who was part of the mercenary group in Yemen, shared a particularly harsh opinion of Yemeni royalists and an honest assessment of why the British intervened in Yemen: "Thank goodness I am nearly finished here. If Nasser wants to occupy such a dud country, the more fool he! . . . . Apart from the obvious importance of safeguarding Aden via Royalists and the comparatively few decent and loyal people excepted, I personally should lose no more sleep if the Egyptians captured all the Yemen killing the men and raping the women. The men are positively asking for this to happen. Yet I would be sorry for the women and children."[63]

Trevaskis argued that royalists could not defeat UAR forces, but might drive Nasser out of Yemen, just as guerillas had driven the British out of Cyprus and Palestine and the French out of Algeria. He advocated open British support for the imam, lest Nasserite supporters rise up as a fifth column against the British in Aden, making the colony untenable.[64] As he explained to Duncan Sandys: "in my view, we should do all in our power to prevent the Yemen Arab Republic from acquiring stability and if possible to rid the Yemen of the UAR and other hostile influences."[65] Open British confrontation with the YAR and Egypt was not, however, a serious option. Several British cross-border attacks from 1963 to 1964 on YAR military positions and against rebels from Radfan were condemned by the US and British press. One air raid on a Yemeni base at Fort Harib in March 1964, in particular, received a great deal of criticism, as it was the first time TV news cameras filmed British counterinsurgency operations in South Arabia.[66]

According to Clive Jones in his book detailing British mercenary operations in Yemen, the post-Suez "malaise" dissuaded London from supporting large-scale efforts to oppose Egypt. Clandestine operations were undertaken as a way to confront Nasser without publicly declaring war on the YAR.[67] According to John Harding, British political officer in Aden during the 1960s, "it was this unofficial campaign, rather than anything mounted by HQ Middle East Command in Aden, that ultimately frustrated Nasser's Yemeni ambitions."[68] The secrecy of these operations was regarded as a useful means to avoid international condemnation of overt military action, particularly from Americans who did not want to be seen as supporting "an old-fashioned colonial campaign."[69] Tony Geraghty, author and journalist who focuses on British intelligence, goes even further in claiming that the secret war in Yemen also "helped prevent an Egyptian or Marxist takeover in Oman and other Gulf States."[70] In the British television series *The Mayfair Set,* which details the clandestine war in Yemen, the English filmmaker Adam Curtis best described the group as "the first example of the 'privatization' of British foreign policy as its worldwide role wound down in the mid-1960s."[71]

On the other end of the political spectrum, British Consul to Ta'iz Christopher Gandy dismissed Amery's alarmism, claiming that the Aden Group's lobbying for royalist support was "moved by nostalgia for lost causes." Gandy suggested recognizing the YAR on December 28, 1962, in an attempt to placate Nasser and stop his attacks on the British position in Aden. These "Tory imperialists," as Gandy termed them, "apparently believed that if only all the King's horses and all the King's men could push hard enough they could put Humpty Dumpty together again and restore the Imamate, provided only that they were not held back by that awkward squad of wets and pussy-footers in the Foreign Office."[72] Despite his ameliorated attitude, Gandy would be expelled by Sallal on February 17, 1963, in response to the nonrecognition of the YAR.[73]

In October 1963, Macmillan was forced to resign and was replaced by Alec Douglas-Home, the previous Foreign Secretary.[74] Douglas-Home maintained a tolerance of the clandestine support for the royalists, as he believed that "the whole history in the Middle East in recent years shows that Nasser has had a series of setbacks in Syria. He has only gotten bogged down in Yemen. Let us leave him alone and let him stew in his own juice."[75]

In November 1963, Deputy Director of CIA Richard Helms explained to Director of MI6 Dick White that he could not sanction official support for the royalists as the White House officially recognized the YAR. NSA director Robert Komer was convinced that London was exaggerating the threat from Nasser to Aden, as Nasser's support for terrorism in

South Yemen was only a "pinprick" and was of no serious concern.[76] Any help given to the British Secret Intelligence Service (SIS) in Yemen would have to be completely "off the record."[77] In aid of his British counterparts, James Fees, a CIA officer in Ta'iz in 1963, organized a network of Arab-born agents who managed to infiltrate the inner-offices of the republic and Egyptian administration obtaining detailed maps of military importance.[78] The clandestine supply of US weapons for the royalists increased American popularity among al-Badr's supporters because the tanks and military hardware used by Egyptians and republicans were all Russian-made. The Irish-born journalist Peter Sommerville-Large explained that "because the Americans did not openly help the republicans it was assumed among the royalists that they secretly supported the Imam, and had only recognized the new regime for devious diplomatic motives."[79]

Nasser did not sit idly as British mercenaries and American agents aided royalist forces against his troops; he instead formed his own anti-British clandestine organization in South Yemen. The group was headed by Qahtan al-Sha'bi, who had fled to Cairo in 1958. During a meeting in Sana'a in June 1963, Sha'bi oversaw the formation of the National Liberation Front (NLF), an anti-British Arab nationalist militant organization supported by Egyptian smuggled weapons across the FSA border.[80] The formation of this organization attracted tribesmen from all over Yemen to join the fight against British imperialism.[81] Egyptian journalist and Nasser confidant Muhammad Heikal justified Egyptian support for the NLF as retaliation for British support for royalists.[82] Mutual border incursions by ground troops, air force, and allied tribes marked the extent of the direct Anglo-Egyptian confrontation in South Arabia. Beihan, a transit point for British-royalist aid, was a frequent target for Egyptian-YAR bombing raids.[83] YAR territory in North Yemen served as a training base for anti-British forces in a way similar to how Aden served as a base for the anti-imam Free Yemeni Movement prior to 1962.[84]

With the looming general elections in England in October 1964, Secretary of State for the Colonies Sandys added a political dimension to the secret war against Nasser, which he thought might discredit Harold Wilson, the leader of the Labour opposition. Sandys argued that "Nasser is probably the most hated man in Britain. But at bottom his policy and the Labour Party's also towards the Middle East are very closely aligned. If we could identify Wilson with Nasser . . . we might greatly strengthen our hand."[85] These political machinations were cut short when in July 1964 the Egyptian newspaper *Al Ahram* published five letters written between

British mercenaries and the central command in England; the letters threatened to uncover the entire operation. The ensuing short-lived media frenzy in the UK and Egypt discredited Conservative party members who were seen as complicit with British clandestine activities in Yemen.[86] The Labour Party won the elections of 1964 and 1966, giving Harold Wilson the premiership. In 1966, Harold Wilson's Labour government published a defense white paper that detailed the withdrawal of British forces "East of Suez," thereby canceling any earlier plans for the British to maintain a military presence in Aden and calling for a complete withdrawal in 1968.[87]

The 1966 decision to withdraw from Aden was based on a number of factors. Beginning in 1964, Sudan forbade British overflights, thereby limiting access to Africa from Aden.[88] The FSA was considered a failure, as the local elite were increasingly unwilling to collaborate with colonial authorities. Egyptian intervention in South Arabia fueled anti-British sentiments and violence, influencing domestic public opinion in the UK against maintaining an empire in the Middle East.[89] Finally, the economic hardships and ensuing Sterling crisis in 1966 forced Prime Minister Wilson to reduce defense expenditures on overseas bases such as Aden.[90]

A report from the British Petroleum refinery in Aden, with a capacity of 150,000 barrels per day, offered an additional consideration for the defense paper of 1966. The investment in the Aden refinery had long since been paid off and therefore the port was expendable from BP's point of view. There was still a danger of Nasser's further plans in the Gulf that constituted a potential threat to BP interests.[91] BP officials felt that it was unlikely that South Yemen had the technical capability to operate the BP Aden refinery, with or without Egyptian help, and would "have little adverse effect on Western interests in the Gulf."[92] The contingency plan in the event that the Aden refinery was closed included new facilities in the French-controlled Djibouti.[93]

The 1966 white paper presented Nasser with an opportunity to emerge victorious in all of South Arabia. The long-breath strategy allowed Nasser to maintain a defensive position in the strategic triangle while dedicating additional resources and attention to South Yemen.[94] In January 1966, Nasser continued to facilitate attacks on Aden and the FSA, by attempting to unite anti-British factions under a single Cairo-controlled Front for the Liberation of Occupied South Yemen (FLOSY).[95] The original members of the NLF rejected this Egyptian-proposed union and the prospects of Egyptian control over their organization and domination over all of South Arabia.[96] From November 1966 through the end of 1967, the NLF and

FLOSY engaged in a heated campaign for control of the anti-imperialist movement.

British complaints to the UN and other international organizations were dismissed, while condemnations of British conduct in Aden were numerous. For example, Amnesty International in a report issued in March 1967 reprimanded colonial officials for allegations of prisoner torture by the British. The British Foreign Office complained that Amnesty International was slanted toward nationalist powers, conducted biased investigations, insisted on interviewing criminal detainees that were not political prisoners, and, in their eyes, issued baseless allegations while Egyptians were committing far greater atrocities in North Yemen.[97] It seemed to British officials in Aden that Egyptian incursions from Yemen into the FSA were condoned by the international community, while British retaliation in Yemen was condemned.[98]

No amount of bickering or finger pointing would have helped the British position in Aden or aided the hapless situation of the Egyptian military against what eventually became a well-trained royalist guerilla force. The Anglo-Egyptian rivalry had already taken its toll on events in both north and south Yemen and contributed to the downfall of both empires. The Aden Group had succeeded in forming an anti-Egyptian force in Yemen while Nasser was satisfied in having contributed to the downfall of his arch British rivalry in Aden. The clandestine war in Yemen would yet have its greatest impact on the history of the modern Middle East on an area outside of Yemen entirely.

Less than twelve months into their campaign to aid the royalists, Tony Boyle, Jim Johnson, and Neil McLean quickly realized that supplying tribesmen in inaccessible mountainous terrain would be equally as difficult for them as it was for Nasser's mechanized army. Taking large caravans through enemy territory was both expensive and impossible to hide from the seeing eyes of the Egyptian air force and UNYOM observers. An airlift, on the other hand, would avoid unpredictable tribal territory and could deliver supplies directly to the frontline, and its effect on Yemeni moral "would be out of all proportion to the equipment dropped."[99] The Aden Group, however, could not find either a neighboring country willing to lend an airfield or an air force willing to undertake a near-suicidal mission. Left with no other option, this last generation of British imperialists turned to Israel, the only country with more to gain from the defeat of Nasser.

Yemen, Israel, and the Road to 1967

THE ARAB-ISRAELI CONFLICT can be added to the list of regional and global conflicts that both influenced the conduct of the civil war in Yemen and was in turn impacted by events in Yemen. Neil McLean was introduced to Brigadier Dan Hiram, the Israeli defense attaché in London, in October 1962. Citing mutual interest in the defeat of Nasser, Hiram promised McLean weapons, money, instructors who could pass as native Arabs, and the support of the Israel Air Force (IAF).[1] In 1964, when French Djibouti, Jordan, and Saudi Arabia withheld permission to host the air support for British mercenaries, McLean, Jim Johnson, and British Royal Air Force veteran Tony Boyle sought the help of the Israeli intelligence services and air force in establishing air supply lines for the royalist army in their struggle against Israel's principal enemy, Egypt.

Chief of the Mossad Meir Amit met with the British group on February 20, 1964, in Tel Aviv, and subsequently with Shimon Peres, the director general of the ministry of defense, and Ezer Weizman, the director of the IAF, to receive official approval for the mission and begin preparations.[2] In approving this mission, Peres and Weizman believed that supporting the royalist forces in Yemen was equivalent to fighting Egyptian forces and diverting their attention from the Sinai border. Imam al-Badr had also promised de-facto recognition of Israel upon a royalist victory in return for their aid during the civil war.[3] Further attempts were made by Israeli officials to establish direct contact with Faisal through the royalists in the faint hopes that the Saudis would commit to recognizing Israel as well.[4]

Ezer Weizman did not trust British intentions for the mission and insisted that Boyle serve as the British supply and liaison officer to the

Israeli counterparts and remain closely involved in the mission planning
and flights.[5] Weizman instructed Arieh Oz, the commander of the Yemen
mission, to keep Boyle close, giving Oz an expense account to take him
out for drinks, dinner, and cabaret to discover any sinister plot to down an
Israeli plane over Yemeni territory. Weizman figured that Boyle would perhaps open up after a few shots of whiskey. Oz became very friendly with
Boyle and found no reason to distrust his intentions and mission plan.
Nonetheless, Weizman insisted that Boyle would have to sit in on every
flight to Yemen, right next to the flight captain, keeping him as a kind of
hostage or insurance policy against any potential ill intentions from the
British. The engineers actually built a chair right next to Oz specifically
for Boyle despite the fact that it blocked the pilot's emergency exit. Boyle
ended up flying twelve out of the fourteen flights with the Israeli mission and made contact with British agents on the ground in Yemen as the
Israeli plane approached.[6]

Israel's International Squadron, established a few months earlier
to transport weapons from France to Israel, assumed responsibility for
the Yemen mission. The squadron consisted of five retired Boeing-377
Stratocruisers that were repurposed as military aircraft. The main concern
of the squadron's staff was potential technical malfunctions to one of the
four Stratocruiser aircraft engines. The engines on the Stratocruiser failed
so often that they referred to it as "the best three engine airplane." It was
decided that if the plane were left with only three engines, the captain
would abandon the mission and land in Asmara, Eritrea. If the plane were
left with only two engines midflight, the crew would ditch out on the coast
of Saudi Arabia in the faint hope that the Israeli navy would be able to
retrieve them from there. Under no circumstances was Oz to bring the
plane down in Yemen, regardless of the malfunction. They were told: "It's
a very bad idea to land near the people who you bombed a minute ago."[7]
After hearing the contingency plans to rescue the crew of a downed aircraft, Boyle admitted to secretly hoping that the IAF would consider him
one of the "rescuable members of the crew."[8]

The supplies transported to Yemen were primarily British munitions
that had been left behind in Mandate Palestine, including guns, rifles,
ammunition, machine guns, mines, fuel, and military supplies as well as
whiskey for the British, cognac for the French, and letters from the wives
of the mercenaries. The flights were to commence only during a full moon
when the moon's light could be relied on for sight. Takeoff time was set for
one hour prior to sunset so that the plane would pass the southernmost

Israeli city of Eilat under cover of darkness. On the return flight, the goal was to have cleared Jeddah, Saudi Arabia, by daybreak.[9]

The first mission took place on March 31, 1964. The irony of this timing is that UNYOM personnel were concurrently endeavoring to curtail Saudi aid to royalists by land and hardly suspected an airlift from Israel, of all places.[10] After seeing the success of the first drop, Imam al-Badr asked for the next drop to be made in front of al-Qarah, the royalist cave base, during a qat-chewing session with local sheikhs on May 26, 1964.[11] The al-Qarah base was on a small mountain with a drop zone of about 50 square meters in front of his cave. The imam gathered those royalist sheikhs loyal to him and announced that supplies would be dropped right in front of them.[12] Moshe Bartov, the mission's navigator, recalled being told by Mossad agents on the ground in Yemen that one of the sheikhs announced: "Look even God is helping the Imam." This and other drops were in such limited areas that even slightly overshooting to the right or left, or failing to take the wind into account, would have jeopardized the entire mission. According to Bartov's account, the squadron lost only one package during the fourteen missions.[13]

After the packages landed on the mountaintop successfully, the tribal leaders cheered and called out, according to British observers: "We are so strong that we will be able to conquer Aden in addition to Sana'a!"[14] While this was hardly an encouraging reaction for British mercenaries aiding the royalists, it was nevertheless a demonstration of the psychological impact of the airlifts, regardless of their origin.

During the flight, there was little concern that the Egyptian air force would notice the Stratocruiser flying toward Yemen over Saudi territory. Oz explained that the plane was equipped with an AWACS-type system to listen to the radio traffic in Egypt and Saudi Arabia. The plane was set to all the frequencies of the Egyptian air force, particularly that of the intercept squadron, which they had stationed in Ghardaqa, along the Egyptian coast between Cairo and Luxor, to give forewarning if the transport was noticed. During one flight, the Egyptians intercepted the Stratocruiser on the radar and the Israeli flight crew overheard the dispatch of several MiGs. Oz turned the plane eastward into Saudi Arabian territory, assuming that the local Ghardaqa commander did not have prior authorization to enter Saudi airspace. When the MiGs finally reached the Saudi border in pursuit of the plane, they were indeed instructed to return to base. This was the only instance when the Egyptians managed to find the Israelis on the radar.[15] An account of the clandestine airlift by British mercenary John

Woodhouse explains that "though the Egyptians knew that supply drops were being made, and though they had complete command of the air, the secret of when, how and by whom the drop was made was always kept."[16]

On later flights, Bartov suggested plotting a flight pattern directly over the Saudi coastline, both making the navigation at night easier and further distancing the aircraft from Egyptian aerial bases.[17] The flight crew was not particularly concerned about flying over Saudi territory and had been assured that the British planning of the air supply mission was done with the knowledge of select Saudi officials who were told to ignore air traffic of this sort.[18] In addition to keeping Saudi officials abreast, Boyle needed to remind Yemeni tribesmen manning the anti-aircraft gun positions around the drop zone to hold their fire that night. In order to placate their curiosity, the tribesmen were told that the aircraft was French in origin and that it would be arriving from Djibouti.[19]

During one of the return flights, the Stratocruiser came under fire from a distance and Oz was forced to reroute to a flight path just north of Sana'a. As they flew over the Egyptian airfield near Sana'a, the crew had a clear vision of rows of MiG fighters parked unprotected along the side of the runway.[20] After returning to Israel, Boyle submitted an official "Proposal for Surprise Attack on Egyptian Aircraft in Yemen."[21] Having seen the Egyptian airfield with his own eyes, Boyle suggested that the Israelis bomb the Egyptian air base in Sana'a on the way back from one of their supply missions to Yemen. Earlier in 1964, Boyle had proposed a similar plan involving himself and other mercenaries using Hunter aircraft based in the Saudi border airfield of Khamis Mushayt for a surprise attack on Egyptian air positions in Yemen.[22] Although such outlandish schemes for attacking Egypt were typical of Boyle's character, they managed to garner a great deal of excitement among his Israeli counterparts.

Oz jumped at the opportunity as he said, "this would have been the highlight of my career." Weizmann and Rabin agreed, but Prime Minister Eshkol rejected the plan, telling them that Israel's role in Yemen was merely to support the imam and not to directly engage Israel in the civil war. Oz recalled "it would have been a piece of cake. In a matter of seconds they would have knocked out 30 MiGs and probably 200 pilots. It would have turned the tide of the war entirely. It would have also changed the Six Day War. The Imam would have surely been victorious as it would have finished off the Egyptians . . ."[23] Furthermore, the Israel Defense Forces were intent on avoiding a crisis either in Yemen or with Syria that might have been used as a diplomatic cover for Egypt's withdrawal from Yemen.[24]

On May 5, 1966, the International Squadron carried out its last airlift to Yemen, marking the end of two years and fourteen missions airlifting military and medical supplies to royalists in the battlefield, as part of two sets of missions codenamed Rotev (gravy) and Dorban (porcupine).[25] On two occasions Israeli airlifts reached royalist commander Abdullah ibn al-Hassan in an isolated and remote mountainous region, saving him from certain defeat.[26] Another drop established a vital fuel dump in the Yemeni wilderness.[27] The Israeli airlift to Yemen had a practical and psychological impact both on Imam al-Badr's war with Egypt and eventually on Israel's decision to attack Egypt in June 1967 after having seen the Egyptian military capabilities firsthand during the course of the mission.

In exchange for its airlifts, Israeli officials asked the British mercenaries for detailed reports on Egyptian military capabilities and troop movements. For example, following the first reported use of Egyptian poison gas on June 8, 1963, in the Yemeni village of al-Kawma, McLean delivered shell casings to his Israeli counterparts for analysis.[28] In a meeting with British counterparts, Golda Meir received reports on Egyptian military performance in Yemen. She expressed concern for the Egyptian missile stockpile and the significant battlefield experience being afforded to Nasser's rotating troops.[29] In a second meeting with British Prime Minister Douglas-Home, Meir expressed additional concern over the Egyptian acquisition of medium-range rockets and the willingness of the USSR to replace the purported 80 million tons of military material expended in Yemen.[30]

Israeli Head of Military Intelligence Aharon Yariv estimated that well-trained and combat-ready Egyptian troops and poison gas bombs could conceivably be transported to Sinai within forty-eight hours. thereby leaving the IDF with limited warning of an impending Egyptian assault. According to Yariv's May 1967 intelligence appraisal, the Egyptian air and ground forces were highly effective and had the potential to increase the UAR offensive capabilities in Sinai, especially after the arrival of updated Soviet aircraft and electronic and navigation systems.[31] Member of Knesset Ya'akov Hazan described the situation in May 1967 as "a storm which had been brewing in Yemen until then and was now moving towards Israel."[32]

From Yemen to Israel, 1967

In May 1967, Neil McLean claimed to have sent a vital piece of intelligence to his Israeli counterparts through unspecified channels, reiterating that there was "no feasible way that Nasser could fight a war with

Israel" with so many of his forces holed up in Yemen for the foreseeable months.[33] By this point, the British had moved up their date of departure to November 1967, leaving the Israelis only a few more months to exploit Nasser's apparent strategic disadvantage. Although this coincidental narrative is compelling, there is no written confirmation that the memo was received by anyone, let alone the Israelis. Furthermore, it is doubtful that the Israelis based their decisions in 1967 on a few lines of intelligence from a nostalgic British MP-turned–Yemeni emissary. Israeli military officials already possessed sufficient intelligence on the Egyptian position in Yemen to make this strategic decision on their own accord. The most revealing aspect of this memo, however, is not the impact that it had on events in Sinai, if any, but in the psyches of British imperialists, even as late at 1967. There was a sense, at least among the members of the Aden Group, that it was still within the power of the British Empire to influence regional events in the Middle East and end this conflict with an Egyptian defeat.

As it happened, events in Sinai in May and June of 1967 turned out much as McLean had predicted. The cost of the Yemeni war economically and politically had taken a toll on Egypt's domestic prosperity and on Nasser's Arab nationalist prestige abroad. The decision to reoccupy the Sinai Peninsula on May 14, 1967, and provoke the Israelis into a war was likely made at the behest of Nasser's poor strategic vision. As Jesse Ferris explains, a successful war with Israel would both restore Nasser's stature in the Arab world and provide him with justification for a military withdrawal from Yemen.[34] Events, however, did not proceed as Nasser envisioned.

Egyptian military officers have readily blamed the Yemen war for their ignominious defeat in the 1967 War with Israel. Egyptian Field Marshal Muhammad 'Abd al-Ghani al-Gamasy claimed that "nearly a third of our land forces, supported by our air force and navy, were engaged in an operation approximately 2,000 kilometers away from Egypt, with no prospects for either a political or a military settlement."[35] Others argued that the Sinai forces were comprised of only 60 percent active forces, with 40 percent reservists. The more experienced fighters were evidently stationed in Yemen, as the economic benefits and opportunities for career advancement were far greater there than on inactive duty in Egypt.[36] Lieutenant General Kamel Mourtagi, the commander in chief of Egyptian armed forces in Yemen, went as far as claiming that Egyptian soldiers had become used to fighting with air superiority against a guerilla force in Yemen and were not prepared to face an army with its own air force.[37] These self-serving accounts do not accurately portray the impact of the ongoing war in Yemen on Egyptian military performance during the Six-Day War.

In reality, by 1967 Nasser's long-breath strategy had consolidated the Egyptian position, allowing for the withdrawal of the great majority of troops who once totaled upwards of 70,000. According to most estimates, there were between 20,000 and 30,000 Egyptian soldiers in Yemen, hardly the one-third described by Gamsay.[38] This number may in fact be even lower, as it likely did not account for the order to withdraw an additional three brigades from Yemen on May 20, 1967. These brigades were destined for Sharm al-Sheikh.[39] According to Israel intelligence estimates at the time, by the end of May 1967, the great majority of combat-ready Egyptian troops had already been stationed along the Sinai border with Israel. The thousands left behind in Yemen were inconsequential, particularly as they were already making plans for further withdrawals.[40] The increasing use of aircraft and chemical warfare compensated for the declining number of soldiers who were being redeployed to Sinai. Rather than an impediment to Egypt's military performance in 1967, the intervention in Yemen and the cycles of troops being deployed acted as training ground for battle experience—much more so than sitting idly in military barracks in Sinai. Even if Nasser had withdrawn all the troops from Yemen prior to June 5, 1967, it is unclear how they would have made a difference, considering the near-total loss of air superiority in Sinai. Indeed, some contemporary accounts of the 1967 war blame the devastating loss on the lack of Egyptian military planning and the difficulties of coordination among Arab countries.[41] Exacerbating the difficulties of coordinating the war with Israel was the fact that Nasser preferred keeping his top brass in Yemen, even after June 1967, in order to avoid a military coup against his own regime.[42]

The official Egyptian national narrative blames the defeat on Field Marshal Amer's reckless behavior, which was convenient, as he was found dead only weeks after the end of the war from an apparent suicide or overdose.[43] Amer had given assurances that his army was ready and more than capable of confronting Israel, perhaps giving Nasser a false sense of confidence.[44] Even as late as May 19, 1967, Amer told Moscow that despite the continued costs of a commitment to Yemen, Egypt was intent on demonstrating that support of the YAR would not preclude support for Syria against Israel.[45] Egyptian generals who were defeated in the field were quick to find Amer culpable, blaming the ill-prepared forces in Sinai on poor military and political planning.[46]

The United States, UK, USSR, and Nasser himself may have surmised that with forces stationed in Yemen, Egypt could not attack Israel. This scenario did not, however, prevent Israel from attacking Egypt. Israeli authorities developed an understanding of Nasser's military capabilities and willingness to use chemical weapons on a civilian population through high-level contact with British mercenaries, airlifts to royalist forces, and intelligence operations in Yemen, all of which were overseen by officials high up in the Israel chain of command. The reluctance of the United States and UN to condemn Egyptian chemical warfare was further evidence that the international community might not rise to the defense of Israel in the aftermath of a poison gas attack. These factors combined to foster a sense of alarm among Israeli military authorities, serving as an additional impetus for a preemptive attack against the Egyptian air force, which was the main mode of chemical weapon delivery. There was no evidence from the Yemen theater of war that Egyptian scientists had managed to retrofit their new rockets with a chemical warhead.

In his seminal work on the 1967 Arab-Israeli War, Ami Gluska explains that a "dread of annihilation" was at the core of Israel's security policy and the decision to preemptively strike Egypt and Syria. The participation of German scientists in the Egyptian medium-range rocket and chemical weapons programs and the publicized deliveries of advanced Soviet weaponry symbolized an existential threat to Israel. In an address to the Israeli Knesset, Foreign Minister Golda Meir expressed alarm at the alliance between German scientists and the Egyptian military, claiming that "the close connection between Cairo and Nazism existed already in Hitler's time, and it is no secret that today Cairo is a haven for the principal Nazis."[47] Many Israeli military authorities feared an Egyptian chemical attack, including the former Chief of Intelligence Brigadier-General Yehoshafat Harkavi, who estimated the potential for casualties with over 100,000 dead.[48]

The fear of chemical attacks was not limited to the Israeli military and political elite, but reached even the teachers association of Tel Aviv. During an emergency meeting in May 1967, teachers debated the safety protocol for the schoolchildren during a potential Egyptian missile attack. Previously, the teachers had been instructed to rush the children to the lower levels of the school. Fearing Nasser's poison gas bombs, some of the teachers began to suggest that the roof would be the safest place for the children, as they would be further away from the toxic fumes. Even the local population of Tel Aviv knew that Nasser was actively using poison gas in Yemen and were concerned that similar weapons would be used against Israeli cities.[49]

This apocalyptic psychology was exacerbated by the "courtside seats" to the Yemen Civil War given to Israeli decision makers from 1964 to 1967. With each passing month in Yemen, the UAR air force gained experience in bombing raids, aerial reconnaissance, and ground support. In 1966 and 1967 in particular, Yemen had become a testing ground for chemical warfare against civilian populations. May 1967, the month before the outbreak of the Six-Day War, saw one of the most intensive bombing and poison gas warfare campaigns of the entire conflict. Egypt's conduct of the war in Yemen had a profound impact on Israel. Nasser, however, was unaware that Israel had become a participant in the Yemen Civil War, a decision that both aided the royalists and provided Israeli politicians with the alarming military intelligence that drove them to war with Egypt.

The decisive Israeli victory in the Six-Day War brought Nasser's imperial expeditions in Yemen to a premature close. By December 1967, just weeks after the British evacuated Aden, Nasser withdrew the last Egyptian soldier from Yemen, marking the end of 130 years of British and Egyptian competition on the Arabian Peninsula. The war in Yemen, however, was far from over. McLean and other British mercenaries remained in Yemen during the ensuing royalist siege of Sana'a, harboring unrealistic hopes that the imam would be victorious.

The Impact of Individuals

AS THE MOUNTAINS of Yemen were overrun by Soviet-equipped Egyptian soldiers, thousands of Saudi-sponsored Yemeni tribesmen, and the diplomatic efforts of the United States and the United Nations, it became increasingly clear that no single foreign or domestic power was able to exercise control over events in Yemen. The relative chaos that emerged opened the doors of Yemen to individuals and organizations that had heretofore not had a presence in South Arabia. Thus, an eclectic American philatelist, the International Committee of the Red Cross (ICRC), and a group of Southern Baptist missionaries were able to make inroads in Yemen, a previously inaccessible area of the world, and play their own roles in the outcome of the civil war and the future of the country.

Postal Wars in Yemen

Beyond the military maneuvers, guerilla tactics, and counterinsurgency strategies, battles between Nasser and Imam al-Badr were being waged through other nontraditional means. Radio Cairo and the *Voice of the Arabs* radio program had without question the farthest reach and greatest impact on the local population, Arabs across the Middle East, and global listeners.[1] Attempts by Saudi Arabia and Israel to broadcast their own radio programs paled in comparison with Nasser's propaganda initiatives. Thousands of free radios were given to Yemeni locals, along with medical care from army doctors, education from Egyptian teachers, and improvements in infrastructure in an attempt to win the "hearts and minds" of Yemeni civilians. In Sa'dah, for example, the Egyptians built a field hospital in which one-third of the beds were reserved for civilians, established a school in which Egyptian teachers taught a hundred boys and fifty girls, and distributed tractors, water pumps, and seeds to local Yemenis.[2] In May 1963, a soccer match between Egyptian pilots and marines in a sports facility in Ta'iz was open to Yemeni spectators at great fanfare.[3] The next month, Egyptian authorities founded a cultural center that afforded patrons the opportunity to play chess and checkers, and to enjoy other leisure activities.[4] Although there are no available statistics on how many Yemenis took up chess or other hobbies in the cultural center, the available programs, which included several lectures a week, gave Yemenis a leisure venue at which to escape from hostilities.

What received less attention, however, were the "stamp wars" waged between Imam al-Badr and the Sallal-Nasser alliance. Stamps were not merely a source of income for al-Badr's Mutawakkilite Kingdom of Yemen, but were a source of legitimacy and pride for an opposition movement that received very little global recognition.[5] In the eyes of the philatelic stamp-collecting community, al-Badr's royalist Yemen was legitimate, heroic, and worthy of their admiration. Nor were stamp collectors the only Westerners to become enamored by the royalist cause. American and European media depicted Imam al-Badr and his northern tribesmen as romanticized anti-imperialists fighting for their country's independence. Photographs, interviews, and press feeds from the northern highlands of Yemen were popular fodder for the Western news media, owing both to the royalist lobbyists and supporters and to the human interest stories of the "simple" farmer taking up arms against the Egyptian invaders. While some Yemeni princes became avid stamp enthusiasts during the 1960s, al-Badr's small stamp victory against Nasser and the YAR can be attributed in part to the role played by Bruce Condé: the first and presumably only American to have aspired to be the postmaster general of Yemen.

Born in California in 1913, Bruce Chalmers Condé served in the US Army counterintelligence service during World War II and studied Arabic at the American University of Beirut on a GI Bill scholarship. One of Condé's greatest passions in life was collecting stamps, particularly from Middle Eastern countries. He became enthralled by Yemen after reading the travelogues of the Lebanese Arab-American Ameen Rihani.[6] In the 1940s, Condé became a pen pal to none other than Crown Prince Muhammad al-Badr, who was himself a philatelist. In 1953, at the invitation of al-Badr, Condé moved to Sana'a and started a business exporting Yemeni stamps to collectors abroad. In 1958, he converted to Islam and changed his name to Abdul Rahman Condé and gave up his American citizenship. In 1960, however, he fell out of favor with Imam Ahmad and the Yemeni Ministry of Communications, was accused of being a spy, and expelled from the country, leaving him a stateless citizen. Condé settled in Beirut and was hired as a Middle East correspondent for *Linn's Weekly Stamp News,* where he worked for the next two decades, sharing detailed descriptions of events unfolding in Yemen. When his old pen pal al-Badr was overthrown, he saw this as an opportunity to find favor with the Hamid al-Din family once again, and made the trip to Najran to meet with the Yemeni princes and their tribal army.[7]

Condé eventually rose to the rank of general in the imam's army and acquired the official title of "Adviser to the Ministry of Communications of the Mutawakkilite Kingdom." As one of the only native English speakers among the royalists, he served as the guide and host by default for American and British officials, reporters, and tourists visiting the royalist frontline. British agents working in Yemen regularly approached Condé for reports on inner royalist politics and used his postal network to communicate with London.[8] Condé in turn tried to recruit additional mercenaries and in one instance tried to persuade the UNYOM radio man Kenneth C. Woskett to join the royalist cause and establish a radio network.[9] David Holden, the Middle East correspondent for the *Guardian,* observed that Condé was "an ardent Yemenophile seeking, it seemed, to ingratiate himself with the Government by acting as their self-appointed public relations man. . . . He was an odd and slightly pathetic figure, somewhat out of both his time and his depth . . . he seemed to belong nowhere, and to be yearning romantically for the impossible . . ."[10] Popular media in the United States referred to him as the American version of Lawrence of Arabia, who dreamed of "worldwide control for Yemeni stamps." Condé would often meet with foreigners while dressed in traditional Yemeni dress, trying his utmost to look and act native. The *New York Herald Tribune* wrote of Condé: "He may not be Peter O'Toole, but his situation is melodramatic enough to throw, say, Malcolm X or Cassius Clay into transports of jealousy."[11]

"The philatelic sideline war," as Bruce Condé referred to the competitive publication of stamps by the imam's Mutawakkilite Kingdom of Yemen and the YAR, became his obsession, and according to Condé, his only source of sanity amid the depressing battlefield. The printed stamps themselves were a manifestation of local religious and political identity and an appeal to international organizations and countries for aid and recognition.[12]

The value listed on Condé's stamps was in *buqsha*, where forty *buq-shas* were equivalent to one of the imam-era riyals. Amongst royalist tribes, the *imadi riyal* (from Imam Yahya's reign), the *Ahmadi riyal* (from Imam Ahmad's reign), and the silver Maria Theresa thaler, a vestige of the Habsburg Empire, were used interchangeably. The YAR introduced the "Yemeni riyal" worth an equivalent amount of forty *buqshas* as part of a broader effort to modernize the economy.[13] The Egyptian occupation forces exhibited a large degree of control over the issuance of currency, replacing the state emblem of arms used under the imam with the Egyptian emblem of Saladin's eagle.[14] This emblem was used on the first paper currency issued in the YAR in February 1964 as part of the broader effort to replace the imam-era currency with a republican alternative. The new bank notes, printed in Egypt, were received reluctantly by republican merchants, yet were completely worthless among royalists, who believed the notes would be useless after the republic's defeat.[15] David Newton, the US Deputy Chief of Mission to Yemen in 1967, explained that printing currency and stamps were considered components of Nasser's effort to establish his own model of "non-Western colonialism," as Egypt did not have the financial resources to fund a European-style colony. The Egyptian occupation was funded by the large-scale printing of paper currency and by a Yemeni puppet regime that gave Egypt free rein over their country's resources. This garnered a great deal of Yemeni animosity toward Egypt.[16] Not only were the Egyptians not sufficiently investing in their colonial endeavors, but UN personnel also observed the Egyptians shipping thousands of silver Yemeni riyals out of the country and replacing them with worthless paper money.[17]

On the other side of this postal war, slogans such as "Loyalist-free Yemen"[18] and "Free Yemen for God, Imam, and Country" figured prominently in Mutawakkilite stamps in a self-identification of the divine-right of the imam's Yemen.[19] Condé described the "romance of the Free Yemen mails," traveling to the war zone in Yemen from Jeddah by truck, in danger of attack.[20] Most of the mail passing through royalist territory was stamped with the phrase "Delayed in transit through enemy lines."[21] The imagery used on the stamps was also a criticism of the Egyptian occupation, as is clear below (see Fig. 9.1) in the "Tank" set of royalist stamps.[22] The capture of an Egyptian T-34 tank in the Jawf battlefield, located 117 miles northeast of Sana'a, and the halting of Egyptian forces 75 miles short of Egypt's goal of reaching the Najran frontier was the inspiration for the "Tank" stamp.[23]

FIGURE 9.1 The two-star UAR flag is shown being torn down by a royalist soldier while another raises the Free Yemen battle flag over the turret, from which is hanging the body of one of the tank crew. Other dead crew members are on and beside the T-34 tank with the Soviet sickle and hammer on the turret, while an Egyptian infantryman is falling to the right of the tank and another is being pursued and bayonetted beside it. On the ground are Soviet Kalashnikov submachine guns while overhead a Soviet plane is falling in flames. (Author's private collection)

Imam al-Badr retained the red flag of the Mutawakkilite Kingdom, decorated with a sword and five stars representing the five natural geographical divisions of Yemen, the five pillars of Islam, and the five daily prayers. The republican flag, on the other hand, was a copy of the UAR version, with red, black, and white stripes, albeit with only one star in the middle rather than two. The flag design was another demonstration of the profound Egyptian influence on state formation and identity in the YAR.[24]

Condé criticized the many typographical and factual errors in the YAR-issued stamps and deemed them mere copies of Egyptian nationalist stamps. The YAR "Freedom from Hunger" stamps (see Figs. 9.2, 9.3 and 9.4), for instance, were close duplicates of Egyptian design, having only changed the country name, indicative of the political reality. According to Condé, "the virtual 'carbon copying' of Cairo by the Sallal regime in Yemen, philatelically as well as politically, has long been one of the charges leveled against the YAR by Yemenites loyal to the Imam."[25] When royalists

FIGURES 9.2 AND 9.3 Egyptian Freedom from Hunger stamps issued in 1963 and labeled with "UAR." (Author's private collection)

"liberated" towns and provinces from the UAR, they ceased using YAR stamps and converted all mail to Mutawakkilite stamps.[26]

In reality, YAR stamp production was more robust and predictably supplied than the Mutawakkilite alternative. Although most of the YAR stamps were Yemeni versions of the Egyptian original, some of the stamps also served as a reflection of national identity and the achievements of the

FIGURE 9.4 Yemeni versions of the "Freedom from Hunger" stamps issued in 1963. The "YAR" and the monetary value were the only differences between the two sets. (Bruce Condé, "Story Of Free Yemen's FFH Set in Tragedy of 'Chickens That Stay at Home to Roost'," *Linn's Weekly Stamp News*, October 14, 1963, 28) (With Permission of Amos Media/Linn's Stamp News)

fledgling Yemeni republic. For example, select 1963 stamps commemorated the founding of the republic and certain 1964 stamps celebrated the opening of spinning and weaving factories and the international airport in Sana'a. In addition to annual commemorations of the revolution, the YAR also used its stamps to appeal to the international community by memorializing President Kennedy and celebrating Soviet space travel achievements.[27] While the variety and number of stamps issued by the YAR and accepted by the international community was significantly larger than those printed by Condé and his Mutawakkilite postal team, greater attention and fanfare were given to the royalist stamps, as they were designed and distributed by the romanticized cave outposts of northern Yemen. Condé (see Fig. 9.5) undertook personal initiative to popularize the royalist stamps, utilizing his network of connections in the Middle East, Europe, and the United States as well as acting as a self-appointed

FIGURE 9.5 Bruce Condé (on left) standing next to Tony "Abu Yusef" Mu'awwad, one of his postal assistants, who is holding the Mauser pistol given to Condé as a gift by Saudi King Faisal's son Muhammad. (With permission of Amos Media/ Linn's Stamp News)[31]

philatelic lobbyist. In addition to dozens of philatelic articles, Condé sent collectors copies of the royalist stamps to many locations, including, for example, Poul Juel Jensen, Denmark's ambassador to Iraq, and to Condé's friends in the ICRC, with both taking a favorable stance to the royalist cause.[28]

Condé depicted the Yemeni battlefield as a war over stamp sovereignty, implying that Egyptian military figures were specifically targeting his stamp project and that the imam was dedicated to its defense. For example, Condé described the imam's capture of the republican post office towns of Barat and Hajjah and stocks of republican stamps in June 1963 as part of the Imam's "philatelic war" against the YAR.[29] His depiction of events was undoubtedly self-absorbed and a gross exaggeration, yet the stamps emerged as an important propaganda tool worthy of some effort to preserve.[30]

Condé also used the stamps to express appreciation to international organizations that had come to the aid of the imam's supporters. In December 1964, the imam signed off on a set of stamps honoring the ICRC and its field hospital in Uqd in the al-Jawf region of northern Yemen (see Fig. 9.6 and 9.7).[32] Dr. J. de Puoz, a stamp collector who ran the

FIGURE 9.6 Stamp honoring ICRC hospital in Uqd (1964). (Author's private collection)

FIGURE 9.7 ICRC Hospital in Uqd. (ICRC Archives. V-P-YE-N-00047-04. 1967)

'Uqd hospital also received a set of stamps from Condé in recognition of the ongoing friendship between the ICRC and royalists.[33] Claude Pillout, director of the ICRC, an avid stamp collector as well, was particularly excited about the prospect of selling copies of these rare and exotic stamp to the philatelic community. He went out of his way to obtain an official document attesting to the validity of the royalist postal network and of Condé's permission to produce these particular 20,000 stamps on behalf of the Mutawakkilite Kingdom of Yemen.[34]

A second set of stamps "Honouring British Red Cross Surgical Team, 1963-64," expressed an appreciation to Doctor William C. Bartlett (an American working with the British), Doctor Colin Wilson-Pepper (a secret informant for British intelligence), and Field Officer Arnold Plummer (forty-year veteran nurse for the Red Cross), who treated wounded royalists only twenty-five miles from Sana'a. The presence of the Red Cross in the royalist camp was no small achievement, especially when the threats issued by YAR vice president Lieutenant-General Hassan al-'Amri to bomb the Red Cross location are taken into consideration; al-'Amri claimed that "anyone opposing the Yemen Arab Republic was a criminal and had no right to medical attention." He specifically threatened members of the Red Cross, saying, "If you establish any kind of hospital or medical attention in the rebel zone, I shall personally order you to be executed." The UAR occupation zone commander Lieutenant-General 'Abd al-Majid Kamal Murtaji, understood the Geneva Convention and personally assured Red Cross that they would not be bombed.[35]

The Red Cross hospital in Uqd served an important role in the health of the surrounding tribal population. In the winter of 1964, for example, teams of doctors traveled to the surrounding areas to treat the wounded and teach general principles of hygiene and first aid. According to their testimonies, local Yemenis regarded them with great respect, assuming that they had some religiously divined power. According to some accounts, locals brought transistors and other car parts to the hospital, assuming that those who could repair a human being could surely repair a car as well.[36]

The royalist memorial stamps for President Kennedy in 1965 (see Fig. 9.8) were a direct appeal to the American people during a pivotal congressional debate over renewing PL-480 wheat sales to Egypt.[37] Other stamps celebrated Saudi support for the imam and Yemen by featuring pictures of al-Badr and King Faisal (see Fig. 9.9).[38]

Nasser was evidently not oblivious to the significance of al-Badr's issuance of royalist stamps. In December 1964, the Mutawakkilite Kingdom of

FIGURE 9.8 Stamp commemorating JFK. (Author's private collection)

FIGURE 9.9 Commemorative postage celebrating Mutawakkilite-Saudi alliance
(September 16, 1965). (Author's private collection)

Yemen printed their last set of stamps with Saikali Press in Beirut, as the
printing house was later pressured by Egypt into imposing a ban on the
printing of stamps issued by the imam.[39] Dar al-Asfhani Press Company
in Jeddah, the former stamp printers of the Saudi government, later
assumed responsibility for printing most Mutawakkilite stamp orders.[40]
After Jordan recognized the YAR on January 22, 1965, Condé claimed
to have been afraid of being arrested in Jordan because the Arab Postal
Union issued a warrant against him for printing "Free Yemen" stamps

"offensive to President Gamal Abdel Nasser." Furthermore, all Arab states had been warned by Egypt not to carry mail affixed with "Free Yemen" stamps.[41]

These six years witnessed the reconstruction of the Mutawakkilite Kingdom's postal system from three tiny post offices in war-torn al-Jawf and the Mashriq eastern provinces in November 1962 to sixty-five post offices and several general post offices servicing 6,000 to 7,000 first-class inland letters daily and 25,000 pieces of outgoing overseas mail monthly. Condé claimed that royalist mail was sometimes faster than Saudi post because "our registry lists are always in correct geographical order." Barring war-related delays, a letter could leave the Yemen border one day and arrive in London three days later via Jizan, Saudi Arabia.[42]

David Newton, the deputy chief of the US Mission to Yemen during the 1960s, provided a somewhat critical depiction of Condé. There is no denying Condé's influence on the international opinion of the Yemeni royalists. His stamp network was extremely popular and Condé always made himself available to the Western media. Condé's availability, however, was a consequence of the fact that he rarely entered the battlefront in Yemen, preferring the relative security of a hotel room in Saudi Arabia. The title of "general" was self-appointed, as was his role as the royalist propagandist. Ibrahim al-Kibsi, known as the "cave director" for the imam, was bemused by the fact that Condé was "more Yemeni than the Yemenis" and certainly more "royalist than the royalists," especially since most of the royalists knew he was a self-promoting farce. Despite his constant hints of connections to the CIA, Newton explained emphatically that Condé had no formal contact with the US government. "We would be crazy to associate with such a flake!" As Newton described it: "Condé just liked to talk," and on occasion there was no harm in listening. Evidently, the only one to truly believe his CIA connections was a Soviet diplomat who tried to gather intelligence on Condé.[43]

Since his time in Lebanon during the 1950s, the US State Department came to regard Condé as "rather a nuisance and an embarrassment." The fact that he considered himself an "American Lawrence of Arabia" served only to justify his amateurish meddling in Arab politics. On one occasion the US embassy needed to intervene after Condé "stuck his nose into some Moslem sectarian quarrel." His time during the 1950s in Yemen was equally unnerving to British officials, as Condé acted "bear-leader" for Western journalist traveling to Yemen to see the "British aggression."

Condé's opportunism earned him the early good graces of the imam and his family in addition to the negative attention of British colonial officials who remained suspicious of him and his related activities and referred to him as the "Middle East crank." There was even concern that Soviet officials might take advantage of his "weakness of character" and his pro-Arab nationalist tendencies.[44]

The greatest harm to Condé came not from his musings, but from his open homosexual activity in Yemen. During his time spent in Yemen during the 1950s, US consular staff would complain about the noise and raucousness emanating from his weekly rendezvous with Yemeni teens in the consular guest house. Yemeni officials eventually lost patience with his outspoken Arab and Yemeni nationalism and his open homosexuality and sent him into exile in 1970 along with his former pen pal Imam al-Badr.[45]

Even years after the demise of the royalist opposition, Condé continued to appeal for historical recognition of the royalist stamps as official state-issued postage in philatelist postal registries.[46] The popularity of Mutawakkilite stamps remained a major topic of the Yemen Philatelic Society under the leadership of the group's Canadian president Blair Stannard.[47] The real victory, however, was Condé's ability to turn the Mutawakkilite stamps and postal system into Western propaganda to attract attention, sympathy, and support for the royalist cause. During a time of tribal divisions, Condé singlehandedly created a national institution that symbolically granted legitimacy to the royalist nonstate actor.

André Rochat and the ICRC

The Yemen Civil War presented the ICRC with an opportunity to expand their medical operations to a previously inaccessible region of the world. Prior to 1962, the ICRC did not have operations anywhere on the Arabian Peninsula. In fact, prior to leading the mission to Yemen, André Rochat, the director of ICRC operations in Yemen, admitted that neither he nor the personnel knew anything about Yemen, assuming incorrectly that "Yemen lay somewhere east of Pakistan!"[48]

The ICRC established its first hospital in Uqd, located in a remote northern region of al-Jawf under the nominal control of royalist tribesmen. At the time the field hospital was established in November 1963, Uqd was included as part of the demilitarized zone established by UNYOM, giving ICRC staff a greater sense of security. The hospital consisted of a

Clinobox, a transportable medical unit equipped with radiology and laboratory services all powered by electric generators and laboriously transported over inhospitable mountains and desert. At its height, the ICRC field hospital treated 160 patients and performed at least one major surgery every day. ICRC personnel ran programs to teach elementary hygiene, prophylaxis, and first aid and by March 1964 had even trained three male Yemeni nurses. ICRC appeals to other national Red Cross organizations were answered by the British Red Cross (BRC), which sent Dr. William C. Bartlett and Arnold Plummer, a nurse. Bartlett led medical missions to the royalist front, accompanied by a varying number of French, German, and Swiss doctors and nurses.[49] Needing to maintain uniform neutrality, however, every member was required to wear ICRC insignia rather than their own national insignias. This was particularly true for BRC personnel, as Nasser was already suspicious of British support for the royalists, and the ICRC was keen on maintaining Nasser's good graces. Plummer criticized Rochat's excessive neutrality, claiming that medical activities to aid northern Yemenis were limited when the ICRC expected the personnel to "be like Caesar's wife."[50]

Aside from the medical care offered to royalists, Rochat assumed the role of a bridge builder between Egypt and the royalists and later was an important witness to Egyptian chemical attacks. For example, in February 1964 he set out to visit Egyptian prisoners in the royalist general headquarters, a fifteen-day journey from Uqd. Rochat succeeded in orchestrating a few small-scale prisoner exchanges and also managed to carry prisoner correspondences back to Egypt, to inform their loved ones of their situation in Yemen. In some cases, these letters were the only official record of Egyptian prisoners who were later executed by tribal leaders. Two other ICRC representatives, Roger du Pasquier and Joseph Gasser, visited Abdullah Sallal in Sana'a and convinced him to sign on to the Geneva Conventions and subsequently provided the YAR with a list of prisoners in royalist hands.[51] As we have already seen, Rochat and the ICRC were also at the forefront of investigating Egypt's use of chemical weapons in 1967, serving as neutral and scientific observers at a pivotal moment in the war.

In 1964, during the course of skirmishes between British forces and rebels in the Radfan region in South Yemen the ICRC saw a need to shift its gaze southward towards Aden and even threatened to inspect the British conduct of the anti-insurgency campaign in Radfan.[52] Rochat tried to use excuse of "fundraising in Beihan," a border region between north and south Yemen, in order to gain access to British prisoners and direct ICRC attention toward Aden. British officials found this hard to believe, as Beihan was not remotely wealthy and was in fact funded primarily by British subsidies. Critics perceived Rochat's meddling as an attempt to gain favor with Egyptian officials who questioned the ICRC's neutrality, a reaction to the extent of medical aid offered to royalist tribesmen in the Uqd hospital.[53] When the British colonial administration refused to sanction ICRC operations in South Yemen in 1965, insisting that Aden was an internal affair, André Rochat approached Roger Gallopin, the Director of the ICRC, pointing out that, "look, I'm only 25 miles from Aden."[54]

As the conflict in Yemen continued, Rochat demonstrated just how close ICRC operations in Yemen were to the British protectorates and to the port city of Aden. In 1967, Rochat crossed the north-south border into Aden, against ICRC directives and British wishes, with the intention of applying the Geneva Conventions to protect prisoners and civilians. He intervened on several occasions to rescue National Liberation Front (NLF) revolutionaries in battle, and, according to Yemeni historian Najib al-Jabeli, Rochat even protected Front for the Liberation of Occupied South Yemen (FLOSY) members by evacuating prisoners to Cairo for political asylum. British officials reprimanded Rochat, who claimed he was operating as a "free agent in Aden." His uninvited and often dangerous interventions in Aden and its environs created a great deal of negative press, as the British administration was cited for torturing Yemeni prisoners and causing civilian casualties. [55] High Commissioner Humphrey Trevelyan complained to the British Foreign Office: "We have suffered here from the fact that M. Rochat is the delegate of the International Committee of the Red Cross.... Rochat's visits have greatly increased our difficulties with the detainees, who are so well treated that we have made ourselves look fools to everyone." A frustrated Trevelyan even tried to petition the ICRC to send in Rochat's place "somebody slightly less eccentric to look after the Detention Camp."[56]

Rochat, however, never left and neither did the ICRC whose operations in Yemen have since continued uninterrupted as the organization played a role protecting prisoners of war and providing medical care in remote regions during subsequent conflicts, including the civil war in 2016. The chaos caused by the Yemen Civil War allowed Rochat and the ICRC to enter a region of the world that had thus far remained outside the purvey of the Geneva Conventions and the Red Cross movement and help Yemen become a participating member of the global community.

Southern Baptist Medical Missionaries

While Bruce Condé was dreaming of becoming postmaster general of
Yemen, another ambitious American dreamed of spreading the gospel
in Yemen. Dr. James D. Young, a Southern Baptist missionary trained
as a surgeon in Irving, Texas, saw the 1962 coup as an opportunity to
bring his religious work to an area of the world that until then had not
been touched by the global networks of American missionaries. Young,
who had previously been part of the Southern Baptist Medical mission to
Gaza during the 1950s, took advantage of the newly opened borders and
made his first trip to Yemen during the early chaotic months of the civil
war. During his trip in 1962, Dr. Young had the good fortune of meeting with Muhammad 'Abd al-Aziz Sallam, the newly instated Yemeni
minister of health, and his director general, Ahmad Mohanny. Sallam
was part of the select group of Yemeni students sent to study abroad
during the 1940s and 1950s and had spent time in America. Although
he had only been a novice in his medical studies abroad, Sallam understood the benefit of bringing American-trained doctors to local Yemenis.
Mohanny spent eight years in America, earned a degree in public health
from Tulane University, and was even married to an American. Much
to the surprise of Dr. Young, Sallam and Mohanny agreed in principle
to a Christian medical mission to Yemen and sent an official written
approval to the Baptist Foreign Mission Board in Richmond, Virginia,
on November 8, 1963.[57]

During a second exploratory trip to Yemen in March 1964, Mohanny
explained to Dr. Young and Dr. John D. Hughey, the Baptist secretary for
Europe and the Middle East, that he was willing to accept medical aid,
even from Christians, as "we are so much in need of medical care that we
cannot be very discriminating."[58] Mohanny's statement could not be more
accurate. At the time of this first meeting, Yemen had among the fewest
doctors per capita in the world, with one doctor for every 150,000 people,
compared to the United States,which during the 1960s had one doctor for
every 790 people.[59]

1962 and the subsequent years marked a unique moment in Yemeni
history as the country's borders were freely open to foreigners for the first
time since the reign of Imam Yahya had begun forty-five years earlier. The
Yemeni government during the civil war was no longer dominated by a
hegemonic and isolationist authority, leaving novice Yemeni officials free
to arrive at agreements even with American Christian groups, something

that may not have been palatable by centralized Arab nationalist agents, religiously conservative groups, or a Soviet satellite state. The Southern Baptist mission to Yemen was all the more unique in that it first began during a decade when other missionaries across the Middle East were being withdrawn.

In September 1964, Dr. Young and his family arrived in the republican-controlled city of Ta'iz, where they established a small clinic, in contrast to the ICRC, which established a hospital in royalist territory. Over an eighteen-month period, the clinic in Ta'iz, located on the second floor of a dilapidated government hospital building, treated over 15,000 Yemeni patients. The popularity and reputation of Dr. Young's medical care drew large crowds of Yemenis to their ward and away from the government hospital on the first floor. In an effort to relocate to a more manageable and isolated rural population, and to avoid an unhealthy competitive environment with the government hospital on the floor below, Dr. Young reached an agreement to lease land in a small rural village of Jibla to serve the Ibb province population of 500,000.[60]

In 1966, the Baptist Charitable Society signed an agreement with the YAR committing themselves to all expenses related to hospital construction and administration in Jibla. The contract stated that Dr. James Young was sent to Yemen by the Baptist Society "to offer medical assistance" and emphasized that proselytization was strictly forbidden. In accordance with the Ibb Regional Department of Endowments, the Baptist Society would contribute a token sum of sixty Yemeni riyals per annum over the total lease term of one hundred years for the 52,000 square meters south-east of the village of Jibla.[61]

From the perspective of the Southern Baptist community in the United States, the members of the medical mission in Yemen were religious messengers carrying their gospel to a remote region of the world. Baker Cauthen, the executive director of the International Mission Board (IMB), wrote to Dr. Young: "You and your family have certainly set a high example of dedication and Christian faith. You have blessed all of us in the way you have laid hand to this very important undertaking, and we are watching each step with joy and thanksgiving."[62]

In a letter to Southern Baptist donors, June Young, Dr. Young's wife, explained the strong evangelical motivations driving the members of their mission in Yemen. She explained: "We have a wonderful opportunity in Yemen to go live as Christians among people in great need, physically and spiritually. In a land with so little medical care, so little education, we have an open door to put Christians in contact with Yemeni people. . . . There is not one Christian witness in the entire area. There is probably not a doctor in the entire area. . . . This is enough to make a follower of Christ want to do something about it."[63]

There were obvious tensions between the religious bent of the mission and the Yemeni government's intentions. Mohanny explicitly warned Dr. Young against proselytizing in Yemen advising them to "stick to your job of treating the sick" and to avoid "causing trouble." The reference to "trouble" in this case was understood by both parties as a form of evangelical missionary work. Shortly after the hospital construction was completed, trouble began to brew. The hospital staff placed scriptures on display in the outpatient clinic and offered copies to patients. One afternoon, the local military commander of Ibb confiscated the scriptures and warned the hospital staff not to let any Yemeni workers or patients read from their personal Christian library housed in the hospital building.[64]

There were additional tensions in relation to the nationality of the Southern Baptist group, as the mission felt compelled to distance itself from its American identity. Upon first arriving in Jibla in November 1966, the missionaries were aided by the USAID program that provided them with trailers and temporary facilities. Aldelmo Ruiz, the head of the USAID water projects in Yemen, offered to draw up initial plans and drill a well for the hospital as well as serve in an advisory capacity for planning and construction of the hospital compound.[65]

Dr. Hughey prophetically observed the dangers of accepting an excess of aid from the US government. In a 1966 letter to Dr. Young, he wrote: "It is fortunate that the AID people are so cooperative. I think, however, you will need to be on guard lest we become involved in the acceptance of government assistance for our mission work. We are now living in an era when government aid is offered very freely. It takes courage to refuse a gift but I think that we should pay our own way. I think that would apply to anything which is done on the property which we have leased."[66]

The foundations of the permanent hospital building were laid in February 1967 by a team of Swedish builders who were given the contract to build the hospital and several residences. In what Dr. Young called "God's doing," similar building contracts were rejected by American and British companies.[67] Sweden's neutrality proved an asset during the post-1967 nadir in Arab-American and Arab-British relations, as the Baptists were able to claim that they were a "Swedish hospital" by highlighting the Swedish company building their hospital.

In the weeks following Egypt's defeat in the June 1967 war with Israel, the YAR was pressured to break diplomatic relations with the United States and evacuate the country of what few American citizens remained.[68] Dr. Young had decided that the mission's Baptist identity and degree of separation from US policy in Yemen would be sufficient to shield them from the deportations.[69] Egyptian soldiers scoured the Yemeni countryside looking for American citizens and eventually arrived at the Baptist Hospital in Jibla. They came to the clinic and confronted Nurse Carolyn McClellan, demanding to know whether the staff was from America. She calmly responded: "We are from Texas." The soldiers nodded, as if they understood, apologized for the intrusion and went on their way.[70] By the end of the month, Southern Baptist missionaries remained the only American representatives in Yemen.[71]

Despite Egyptian and YAR tensions with the United States, local Yemeni leaders had an amenable relationship with the staff at the Baptist hospital. In September 1968, for example, the hospital staff invited to the Jibla Revolution Day celebration at the local school house. While Yemeni women were not invited, a special invitation was granted to the foreign women working in the Baptist clinic.[72] The lack of a restrictive central authority during the civil war gave the missionaries and the Yemeni authorities involved the latitude to found an American Christian medical mission in Arabia during the 1960s, allowing the Southern Baptists to become part of the fabric of the country for the next four decades. This relationship lasted far beyond the chaos of the civil war and until December 2002, when an al-Qaeda operative attacked the hospital, marking the unofficial end of the Southern Baptist presence in Yemen.

The absence of a dominant national power after the 1962 coup opened the country to a new cast of international characters that previously had no access to South Arabia. The conflict was not dictated by US-Soviet machinations alone, nor did Egyptian or Saudi interests solely determine the course of events in Yemen. The three incarnations of Lawrence of Arabia—Bruce Condé, André Rochat, and James Young—are examples of individuals who saw the 1960s as an opportunity to pursue their dreams in the remote deserts of Yemen, play a role in the civil war, and lay the groundwork for continued operations in Yemen inspired by their legacy.

The Siege of Sana'a and the End of the Yemen Civil War

ON AUGUST 29, 1967 at the Arab Summit meeting in Khartoum, Sudan, Nasser and Faisal agreed on a "Yemen peace plan." Egypt committed to withdrawing its troops and in return Saudi Arabia pledged that it would discontinue royalist aid. In return, the oil monarchies agreed to compensate Nasser for Egypt's economic loss as a result of the closure of the Suez Canal.[1] A military intervention that had originally been envisioned by Egyptian Field Marshal 'Abd al-Hakim Amer as taking no more than a few weeks had become a costly five-year war against an underestimated royalist opposition.[2] Efforts at international diplomacy had come full circle. The original withdrawal agreements first proposed by US diplomat Ellsworth Bunker in 1963 continued to serve as the basis for peace negotiations throughout the conflict and were at last implemented at the end of 1967.

On October 10, 1967, Nasser finally released the Yemeni ministers who had been in detention in Cairo since September 1966. After discussing the political situation with Nasser, the opposition group returned to Hodeidah on October 22 with clear intentions to take control of the republic. On November 5, 1967, Abdullah Sallal boarded a plane bound for Moscow, ostensibly to attend the fiftieth anniversary celebrations of the Russian revolution. Sallal's plane never made it to Moscow, as he was diverted to Baghdad, where he would spend the next fourteen years in exile.[3] According to Sallal's unpublished memoirs, this exile was self-imposed as he understood what was awaiting him following Egypt's withdrawal.[4] According to other accounts, Sallal was forced to fly to Baghdad because Egypt had rejected his request for asylum.[5]

Sallal had long fallen out of favor with fellow Yemeni republicans and he would have been deposed earlier were it not for continued Egyptian intervention and support. In Sallal's absence, Qadi 'Abd al-Rahman al-Iryani, a prominent member of the third-force and one of the "Soviet five" orchestrated a bloodless takeover of the YAR. Al-Iryani was joined by fellow members of the third-force, Ahmad Nu'man and Muhammad 'Ali Uthman, to form a triumvirate ruling coalition. Hassan al-'Amri became prime minister and Hassan Makki foreign minister; Soviet-friendly Yemenis thus held influential positions in the new republic.

Aside from Sallal, there were few Yemenis who grieved the departure of the last Egyptian soldier. In fact, during the weeks prior to the Egyptian withdrawal, Yemenis conducted multiple hand grenade attacks against the remaining soldiers. Yemenis hated Egyptians and the Egyptians returned mutual sentiments. The one bright side for Egyptian soldiers returning home were the duty-free imports from Yemen. On the day the Egyptians were scheduled to leave, twenty soldiers returned to Sana'a to complete last-minute shopping before shipping back to Egypt. The group was ambushed by enraged Yemenis who killed at least twelve of them and drove the rest out of the city.[6]

Egyptian aerial and artillery superiority for five years of the conflict had prevented a full-scale royalist advance on the capital city. Nasser's withdrawal, which was to be completed on November 29, 1967, was already in its advanced stages, leaving republican defensive positions and the entire strategic triangle vulnerable to attack. With the republican defenses weakened, Imam al-Badr's counterattack on Sana'a, long expected after the September 1962 coup, finally materialized in December 1967.[7]

Muhammad ibn Hussein, the commander of the royalist armies in 1968, marched an estimated 56,000 tribesmen toward the capital city. The royalist army captured the country's main airport and all major roads leading to Sana'a, placing the city under an effective siege.[8] Both al-Iryani and Makki left the city for purportedly unrelated reasons leaving Hassan al-'Amri, who had only recently been released from political detention in Cairo, in command.[9] Al-'Amri had at his disposal no more than 10,000 republican troops and an equal number of Shafi'i tribesmen from areas south of Sana'a. As was the case throughout the 1960s, the key to the republican victory stemmed from foreign intervention. NLF and FLOSY fighters arrived from Aden to Sana'a in order to defend the revolution and demonstrate solidarity between the two Yemeni nationalist movements.[10] Foreign fighters and other local reinforcements were able to join the defense of Sana'a because the siege started during the month of Ramadan and the royalist tribesmen were not active on the battlefield.[11]

With the onset of the royalist siege of Sana'a in December 1967, al-Iryani turned directly to the Soviets with an urgent request for aid. Makki flew personally to Moscow on December 8 to conclude an economic agreement and arms purchase with the Soviets.[12] Moscow responded with emergency airlifts of medical supplies, food, and ammunition for the besieged city.[13] A total of 10,000 tons of supplies were delivered to Sana'a along with a Soviet squadron of MiG-19s, pilots, and ground crew intended to provide air cover for republican positions.[14] The royalists claimed to have shot down a "red-haired MiG-17 fighter pilot" who was wearing a Russian wristwatch and held Soviet documentation.[15] Hassan al-'Amri even threatened in addresses on Radio Sana'a that "he will summon Soviet warplanes to destroy with poison gas, napalm, rockets, and bombs 'every living thing' in the Royalist two-thirds of Yemen." In response, Condé commissioned a new "Freedom Fighter" set of stamps that portrayed tribesmen with small arms fighting against Soviets, rather than Egyptians, reflecting shifting enemies.[16]

The very decision, however, to place a siege on the city rather than stage a frontal assault while holding the numerical and munitions advantage, was among the underlying reasons for the failed royalist offensive.[17] Royalist tribesmen, unaccustomed to lengthy siege warfare and frustrated by the arrival of foreign reinforcements and Soviet munitions in aid of the YAR, began to drift away from the battlefield and return to their fields before the end of the coffee harvest season. The combination of a lengthy siege with limited funds available, diminishing royalist numbers, as well as an influx of foreign aid and fighters for the YAR eventually broke the siege in February 1968. The siege lasted for seventy days and became a defining moment in Yemeni national history. Al-'Amri's heroic performance at maintaining the city's morale and civil order during the siege and his eventually breaking through royalist lines earned him the moniker of "the general of Yemen."[18] The republican victory and the lifting of the siege marked the practical end of the Yemen Civil War. While sporadic fighting continued for two years, the final outcome had already been decided.

On March 21, 1968, the YAR declared that it had signed a new Soviet-Yemeni friendship treaty that acted to solidify their alliance and continued cooperation. To emphasize the sincerity of their commitment, and in response to renewed hostilities in August 1968, Moscow organized seventy-five to one hundred round-trip flights to Yemen carrying muni-tions and supplies to the last battlefields of the Yemen Civil War.[19]

In March 1969, Prince Muhammad ibn Hussein resigned as the imam's deputy and royalist general. At this point Imam al-Badr realized that continuing the royalist military efforts would only result in more Yemeni bloodshed. According to his own recollections, al-Badr agreed to sever the allegiance between the royalist tribesmen and the Hamid al-Din family, granting political flexibility to negotiate with al-Iryani and the YAR. Official negotiations took place during the Islamic Conference of Foreign Ministers, held in Jeddah from March 23-26, 1969. Both sides agreed to form a unified government with republican and royalist repre-sentation, albeit excluding the Hamid al-Din family. Several weeks later, Saudi Arabia recognized the YAR, officially ending the era of international intervention in Yemen.[20] The YAR Minister of Economics Muhammad Sa'id al-Attar argued that the northern opposition was driven by the pres-ence of a foreign power in Yemen that might infringe upon their tribal independence in the highlands. Once the Egyptians and Soviets had with-drawn from Yemen, the temporary alliance with al-Badr was no longer a necessary measure.[21]

While the royalists and republicans were fighting their final battles in the north, the British-created Federation of South Arabia was quickly col-lapsing. On November 30, 1967, the day after the British withdrew from Yemen, the NLF declared an independent state of the People's Republic of South Yemen (PRSY), taking advantage of the power vacuum created by the simultaneous withdrawal of Britain and Egypt.[22] The NLF sent a del-egation to Moscow and obtained political recognition from the Kremlin. By early 1968 a group of Soviet military advisers arrived in Aden. Political tensions continued in South Yemen as a radical Marxist branch of the NLF gained power and reorganized their party as the Yemeni Socialist Party. On December 1, 1970, South Yemen became the first and only Arab com-munist state, the People's Democratic Republic of Yemen (PDRY).

As the PDRY became a center for Soviet military affairs in the region with a large naval and air presence in Aden, Moscow subsequently allowed their strategic relationship with Sana'a to deteriorate.[23] The USSR decided to abandon Sana'a for a number of reasons. Multiple coup attempts by left-wing Yemeni groups against YAR General Hassan al-'Amri failed, push-ing the republic further to the conservative right and into an alliance with Saudi Arabia and Western powers. This political stance was demonstrated by the YAR decision in July 1969 to resume diplomatic relations with West Germany in exchange for an aid package worth $3.5 million. Saudi Arabia continued to improve its relations with the YAR, offering their recognition in July 1970 along with a renewable aid package worth $20 million.[24] Individual "stipends" or bribes were given to Yemeni tribal sheikhs to maintain their allegiance.[25] Saudi Arabia came to view the YAR as a buffer between the Marxist PDRY and the Saudi border. Furthermore, despite the precarious royalist position and the relative strength of the republican army equipped with Soviet weaponry, the last battle of the civil war was hardly a measure of success. Depleted royalist tribal militias captured the city of Sa'dah from republican forces in February 1970, placing them in a relative position of strength in advance of the conference for national reconciliation.[26]

The Egyptian magazine *al-Jadid* best described the emerging Yemeni state in the north: "the new regime in Yemen will be conservative with some revolutionary glimpses, republican with some monarchical tints, tribal in civil and military framework, progressive compared with the old past and moderate compared with the glaring and boisterous slogans launched by Sallal."[27]

The Personal Sagas Continue

André Rochat, once considered a public enemy of the British colonial administration in Aden for his oversight of British political prisoners, became the guarantor for the remaining British representatives after 1967. Rochat and the ICRC were considered the insurance policy for British subjects and interests in Aden in the event of a national emergency and in the continued absence of a British embassy. The ICRC was committed to protect British hostages who might be in danger from government or radical groups in Aden.[28]

Imam al-Badr left Yemen in 1970 in a self-imposed exile in the UK where he bought a home on St. George's Road in Bromley, Kent. Al-Badr's residence made its way into British news when Scotland Yard seized millions of royalist stamps on July 5, 1971, under the legal pretenses that they were printed without YAR approval and distributed all over the world.[29] On November 8, 1976, al-Badr applied for British naturalization and asked for the former mercenaries to Yemen David Smiley, Julian Amery, and Neil McLean to serve as references for his good character and loyalty.[30]

In 1970, Bruce Condé was exiled from Yemen as well and again found himself stateless, as he had rescinded his American citizenship and the Yemeni government refused to grant him citizenship. Condé finally settled in Spain and later Morocco (Martil and Tangier). In 1984, Condé married another royalist pretender who adopted the persona of Princess Olga Beatrice Nikolaevna Romanovskaya Dolgoroukaya, Princess of the Ukraine, and great granddaughter to Nicholas II of Russia. The two adopted Alexis d'Anjou Dolgorouky, a self-declared prince and author of a controversial and fanciful book, *Moi Petit-Arriere-Fils du Tsar*.[31]

Yet Condé's relationship with al-Badr was not over. Throughout his time in exile, he attested that he maintained close contact with members of the Yemeni royal family, including two of al-Badr's nephews, who brought him various monetary gifts.[32] In September 1975, he published a report issued purportedly by the Mutawakkilite Kingdom of Yemen's Ministry of Communications. Condé had named himself major general and claimed to be an official representative of the imam despite the fact that the war had been officially over for more than five years. Nevertheless, Condé was trying to advocate a new settlement for Yemen that included three states: the YAR, PDRY, and a new state for al-Badr. (see Fig. 10.1)[33]

The Aden Group had been shut down as of May 24, 1967; letters were sent to former members indicating that the "office" in London would be closed for good and that they would be given a new contact for emergencies. The letters ended with the following statement: "As you know, we never did exist and now to prove it we propose to vanish."[34] The group's former members, intent on keeping their mission with Israel a secret, were faced with leaked information in 1971. Jim Johnson concocted a story claiming that Jack Malloch of the Rhodesian Air Services flew weapons to royalists. Johnson ridiculed those who thought Israel was involved, claiming that "no story is too fantastic to be believed in the Middle East."[35]

Two days after Israel's victory in June 1967, Jim Johnson and Tony Boyle were invited by Nahum Admoni to Israel and were flown over the Sinai battlefield to observe hundreds of destroyed Egyptian tanks and airfields. Boyle was given photographs of these scenes of destruction with a note expressing the gratitude of the Israel for the work of British mercenaries in Yemen, claiming that the Six-Day War victory could not have been achieved without him.[36]

Even without the aid of the Aden group, the Mossad continued intelligence operations in Yemen and dispatched an Egyptian-born senior agent named Baruch Zaki Mizrahi to report, ostentibly, on the Egyptian

THE MUTAWAKELITE KINGDOM
OF YEMEN

EXPECTATION: RECONCILLATION BETWEEN BROTHERS OF YEMEN

YEMEN
GEO-POLITICAL
1975

Royal Enclaves in Y.A.R. Territory

1.HAIMATAIN 2.JEBAL BURAH & JEBAL RAIMAH 3.UTOMAH
4.ANIS 5.ANS 6.UDAIN 7.JEBAL MURAIS 8.

(A) TEMPORARY NEW ROUTING VIA RUB AL-KHALI DESERT ROUTE TO OMAN COASTAL PORTS
POSTAL

FIGURE 10.1 Condé's proposed division of Yemen into three states. (Tony Boyle Papers, IWM)

army and on traffic in and out of the Red Sea.[37] He entered the country with a Moroccan passport under the name Ahmad al-Sabbagh and established an espionage ring of Yemenis to observe Palestinian terrorists who were using Hodeidah as a base to launch attack against Israeli shipping.[38] Mizrahi remained in Yemen until his capture by Yemeni authorities in May 1972.[39] In 1972, Israeli officials appealed to US President Richard Nixon to intercede on behalf of Mizrahi, who was still interned in Yemen, as part of a prisoner exchange between Israel and Egypt.[40] When the United States refused to intervene, fearing damage to US-Yemeni relations, the Israelis turned to West Germany and Iran, who in turn appealed directly to Yemeni Interior Minister Sayf 'Ali Khawlani for a delay in Mizrahi's execution and for an official prisoner transfer to Cairo.[41] Negotiations continued after the Yom Kippur War, in October 1973,[42] and Mizrahi was finally released in March 1974 in exchange for Egyptian prisoners of war held by Israel.[43]

According to Nahum Admoni, the prisoner exchange could not have taken place without the intercession of Jim Johnson. There was concern that the lack of order and accountability in Yemen would present insurmountable obstacles to a prisoner swap with Israel. Johnson approached his contacts in Yemen and organized the transfer of Mizrahi to Egypt, where the prisoner exchange was orchestrated.[44]

Arieh Oz developed a long-term friendship with Boyle. On one occasion, after Oz left the air force and went to work for El Al, he met Boyle for dinner during a layover in London. At 11:00 PM that night Oz received a phone call from an Israeli diplomat in Denmark, a former friend from the Mossad who asked how his dinner was, implying that he was being watched. He asked Oz not to see Boyle anymore, as he was "no longer with us." It was not until 2008, after the passing of the ever-cautious chief of the IAF Ezer Weizman, that Oz once again saw Boyle over dinner with Admoni, marking an end to the era of clandestine planning and suspicions. The memories of these individuals and their impact on the history of the modern Middle East live on in the pages of this book.

Legacy of the Yemen Civil War

The Yemen Civil War was a pivotal moment in the history of the Middle East. The decline of Arab nationalism and Nasser's expansionist foreign policy was brought about in part by Egypt's intervention in Yemen.[45] It would be incorrect to assume that Nasser's presence in Yemen was a complete failure. For one, the Yemeni republic remained intact despite eight years of war with the royalists. As part of the Saudi-Egyptian Khartoum agreement, Egypt was given a share of Saudi oil wealth and employment opportunity for hundreds of thousands of Egyptian workers in the Saudi oil industry during the 1970s and 1980s. Finally, Nasser succeeded in securing the Red Sea approach to the Suez Canal by uprooting the imposing British military presence in Aden. Egypt's presence in North Yemen and its support for the NLF and later FLOSY were instrumental in forcing an early British withdrawal from Aden and a collapse of the FSA.[46] Rather than a harbinger of defeat, the war in Yemen gave Nasser an opportunity to further his personal security, economic, and ideological agendas in the region in a relatively low-stakes conflict two thousand miles away from Egypt.

The real victors in the Yemen Civil War were Saudi Arabia and the USSR. Without expending their own troops, the Saudis managed to secure a temporary ally south of their border. The emergent YAR in 1970 represented perhaps the most ideal state the Saudis could have envisioned: the Shi'i monarch in Yemen had been exiled and the state was weak, decentralized, and dependent upon continued Saudi funds. The most populous area on the Arabian Peninsula was split between north and south, allowing Saudi Arabia to maintain its regional hegemony and patronage of the YAR.[47]

The USSR similarly saw its vision of an ideal South Arabian state emerge in the PDRY. As early as June 1968, eighteen Soviet ships docked in Aden, a number that would increase exponentially over the subsequent years.[48] The Marxist country in South Arabia became a Soviet naval and military asset for the interim of the Cold War and served as a strategic base for missions to postcolonial Africa: Angola, Ethiopia, Mozambique, and Somalia, in particular. The increased naval presence in the Indian Ocean occurred as the British withdrew from "east of Suez" in the late 1960s and early 1970s and ushered in a renewed era of Soviet interest in its "internationalist duty" in the developing world.[49] The PDRY gave the USSR a base of operations for intervention in these newly independent territories.

Iraqi political scientist Adeed Dawisha best explains the aftermath of the Yemen Civil War: "Inevitably, the conservative instincts and social customs of the Yemenis, as well as their religious affiliations, meant that sooner rather than later Sana['a] would replace Moscow protection by that of Riyadh." By the 1970s, it had become obvious that the survival of the YAR depended "not so much on the Russian tank as on the Saudi riyal."[50]

As international interest began to wane in 1968, Pavel Demchenko, the senior Middle East correspondent for *Pravda*, observed that September 1962 was not a revolution, but rather "a centuries-old method of Yemeni regime change."[51] When al-Badr's palace was first shelled on September 26, 1962, the conflict was still a localized civil war. Any significant delay in Egyptian intervention may have signified the failure of the republic and the return of the Yemeni imamate, albeit perhaps somewhat reformed. In 1962, the republican model was not a universally accepted concept among local Yemenis. McLean recounted a demonstrative and comical story circulated among the Yemenis during his travels:

> "It is told that that when the great meeting of chiefs was called on the Foundation of the Republic they were informed that 'The Republic will bring you roads, schools, and other benefits which will make the Yemen into a modern country." The chiefs shouted 'Hooray, Long live the Republic," but at the end of the meeting they asked "This is all very fine, but who is going to be the Imam?"[52]

The local "regime change" was overrun by events and conflicts far beyond Yemen's borders. The civil war was prolonged and the sufferings of Yemenis deepened as a result largely of players and forces much larger than themselves. With each additional international intervention, it was easy to lose sight of the fact that this conflict, at its core, was a clash between Yemen's history and its future. The state that emerged in 1970 was starkly different from the isolationist regime of Imams Yahya and Ahmad. The previous generation of autocratic monarchs made every effort to forestall Yemen's entry into the international community. Instead, the civil war brought the international community to Yemen's doorstep and transformed the former kingdom into a modern nation-state. Rather than demonize the individuals who brought destruction, death, and a prolonged international conflict to Yemen, the country continues to celebrate even Abdullah Sallal and 'Abd al-Rahman al-Baydani as national heroes.[53] Yemen's state-issued history and memory focuses on the 1960s as a period of revolution, nationalism, and modernization rather than a trying decade of civil strife and political uncertainty. Even the most culpable collaborators and inept leaders have been granted the status of a national revolutionary heroes.

Epilogue: Echoes of a Civil War

An Arabian Case of Déja vu

The compromise of 1970 marked the official end of the Yemen Civil War. Imam al-Badr and his extended family resettled in the UK and images of the northern Yemeni tribesmen faded from mass media. Over four decades later, those images would reappear along with a modern narrative and international cast of characters starkly similar to those of 1962, and rife with historical ironies. The Yemeni republic is again at war with northern tribesmen, and foreign powers are again intimately involved. Journalists and contemporary scholars have attributed the 2014–15 civil war in Yemen to a "new Arab Cold War" between Iran, which has purportedly given support to a northern tribal alliance, and Saudi Arabia, which is fighting on behalf of the Yemeni republican government in exile, supplanting the role once played by Gamal Abdel Nasser and the Egyptian army. The Egyptian air force, this time as part of a Saudi-led coalition, has returned to the ominous mountainous terrain that bedeviled Nasser's army during the 1960s. The UN has again assumed the role of mediator, with many of the diplomatic shortcomings of UNYOM. The ICRC, which began operations in South Arabia during the 1960s, now finds itself at the center of a growing humanitarian crisis in Yemen. The current war in Yemen even features foreign mercenaries, which summon memories of Neil McLean and the rest of the Aden Group. Dana Adam Schmidt's 1968 journalistic account of the Yemen Civil War, refers to the conflict as "the unknown war." Gabriel Gatehouse, a correspondent for the British Broadcasting Corporation and a modern incarnation of Schmidt, has already termed the new conflict "Yemen's forgotten war."[1]

When the northern tribesmen lay siege to Sana'a in 1968, the republic emerged victorious and established the contemporary model of governance for Yemen. On September 21, 2014, the children of those 1968 tribesmen returned to Sana'a once again, only this time they managed to capture the capital city in the face of a weakened republican government. According Dr. Hassan Abu Taleb, a professor at the Egyptian Al-Ahram Center for Political Studies and Strategy, the 2014 fall of Sana'a marked the symbolic end to the republic that was founded in 1962.[2] The revolutionary leadership of the 1960s has passed on, leaving in its wake the skeleton of a Yemeni republican government whose legitimacy scarcely extends beyond their current hotel quarters in Riyadh.

Rise of the Houthi

The Houthi movement, also known as Ansar Allah, or the "supporters of God," began as a religious educational movement during the 1990s to counter the influence of Saudi proselytizers spreading radical Wahhabi doctrine in North Yemen.[3] Members of the al-Houthi family, one of the early supporters of Imam al-Badr during the 1960s, assumed a central leadership role in the northern tribal opposition group that emerged as a political threat to the Yemeni republic.[4] The Famous Forty and the original revolutionary council of the YAR during the 1960s specifically targeted the hierarchy of the Sayyid families, or the descendants of the Prophet Muhammad. The Houthis, a prominent Sayyid family, had thus been marginalized politically and economically for decades along with the rest of their social class and those among the northern tribes in particular.[5]

Hussein al-Badr al-Houthi, the first leader of the movement, was killed during a 2004 battle with the military forces of the former Yemeni President Ali Abdullah Saleh. His death and subsequent adaption as the movement's martyr marked the expansion of the Houthi movement's armed conflict with the Yemeni government that continued for a decade. Following Saleh's abdication in 2012, the Houthis gradually filled the political void left by the Saleh regime and the decline of the republic's legitimacy more broadly.

Decline of the Revolution

The rise of the Houthi movement coincided with the passing of Yemen's revolutionary generation, which featured a foreign-trained civil service, discussed in chapter 2. The Famous Forty, as they are known in Yemeni national history, returned home either before or during the years following the September 1962 revolution, and represented the core of the country's first modernist and foreign-educated civil service.[6] The country's first foreign minister Mohsin al-'Ayni, for example, was one of the most prominent Yemeni politicians of the twentieth century, tracing his political beginnings to the original Famous Forty group.[7] In the decades following the revolution, nine other members of the Famous Forty became ministers of health, education, economics, state, foreign affairs, finance, and public works. The training they had received abroad translated directly into their designing and staffing the modern state infrastructure of Yemen.[8]

While the great majority of the members of the Famous Forty ended up in the foreign service, in government ministries, in the military, or at the Yemen Bank for Reconstruction and Development, they were not limited to the Yemeni public sector. Several served senior roles in mixed public-private industries, including Yemenia Airlines and the Sana'a Broadcasting Company; a few remained in academia or became national poets.[9] The Famous Forty and their extended cohort became the face of the new republic in every regard, bringing tribal Yemen into the modern era.

On June 3, 2011, six months after the beginning of massive anti-government protests in Sana'a, Yemeni president Ali Abdullah Saleh's palace mosque was targeted by a rocket attack. Although the publicly reviled president was seriously injured in the attack and was forced to travel to Saudi Arabia for medical care, popular jubilation was somewhat tempered, for there was a second, unintended victim. 'Abd al-Aziz 'Abd al-Ghani, one of the original founders of the modern Yemeni republic in 1962, was praying next to Saleh and was mortally wounded in the attack. There was a massive outpouring of grief when the Yemeni public received the news on August 21 that 'Abd al-Ghani, who had served as prime minister again from 1994 to 1997 and had continued to preside as the president of the government's Consultative ("Shura") Council since 2003, had died from his injuries.[10] Al-Ghani's death symbolized the fall of Saleh's regime as well as the passing of a great figure in the history of the Yemeni republic. His funeral marked a unique pause in the months of street protest, when both Saleh's regime and its opposition mourned a casualty of national hostilities. Government employees were given the day off to attend the funeral, and a public day of bereavement was declared. During the height of opposition to Saleh's regime protesters took a one-day hiatus to recognize the tragic loss of one of Yemen's greatest political leaders of the revolutionary era. For many Yemenis, al-Ghani embodied an entire generation of revolutionaries who ran the modern state and continued to represent its legitimacy in the decades after the 1962 revolution.

The death on January 1, 2012, of 'Abd al-Rahman al-Baydani, the former mentor to the Famous Forty students who served as vice-president of the YAR during the 1960s and continued to play a prominent role in Yemeni political society, marked another significant moment in the passing of Yemen's generation of the revolution. Although Baydani was exiled from the country for political conspiracy during the civil war, he was invited back to Yemen during the 1980s to serve in both official governmental and unofficial advisory roles, and even considered a run for president in 2006. Baydani also became a prolific academic writer, garnering a large readership as well as a local following.

An elaborate website dedicated to Baydani's life's work is a testament to the public's perception of him as an embodiment of Yemen's revolution.[11] Until a few months before his death, at the age of eighty-five, Baydani appeared regularly on television shows and radio broadcasts and in newspaper columns, developing a cult of personality rivaled perhaps only by the president himself. Baydani's death was particularly significant, as he had outlived nearly all of the other Famous Forty and was thus one of the last remaining members of Yemen's generation of the revolution who came to political and national prominence during the civil war in the 1960s.

With the passing of the Famous Forty a new generation of Yemenis has assumed the mantle of leadership. While the earlier generation of foreign-educated Yemenis had returned to lead their country into the modern era, the same cannot be said of today's foreign-educated class. Of the original group of the Famous Forty and the approximately five hundred students who studied abroad during the 1950s and 1960s only a small minority remained abroad. 'Abd al-Karim al-Iryani was the starkest example, as he returned to Yemen after earning a PhD in Biochemical Genetics at Yale University in 1968 and served as the country's most prominent statesman until his death in November 2015.

Since the 1970s the trend has been reversed, as Yemenis studying abroad have increasingly declined to return. According to a February 2014 study by the Yemen Ministry of Higher Education and Scientific Research, upward of thirty thousand Yemenis holding undergraduate, graduate, and post-graduate degrees are working in other countries.[12] At a time when local hospitals, universities, and government ministries are struggling to find trained professionals, educated Yemenis continue to leave the country.[13] Yemeni institutions like the universities of Sana'a and Ta'iz have been forced to appoint their own recent B.A. graduates to lecture in place of faculty who have left the country.

The new generation of Yemenis is faced with the difficulty of prolonging a republic that enjoys declining support and validity in the face of tribal and religious alternatives. For example, Yemeni President 'Abd Rabbuh Mansur Hadi, who was deposed by the Houthis in 2014, is a southerner who was studying abroad during the 1968 siege of Sana'a and did not return to South Arabia until the end of the 1970s. Hadi was unable to claim the status of a national hero or an association with the founding fathers of the revolution. The Yemeni republican model and its manufactured national identity have indeed shown signs of serious weakness and decline as the new post-revolutionary generation demonstrates a preference for Yemen's historic clan- and tribal-based affiliations rather than disintegrating national political parties and the remnants of state security.[14]

Saudi Grand Strategy

Since the beginning of the Saudi military campaign against the Houthis in March 2015, the number of Arab, African, and Western coalition members involved has increased. In contrast to Saudi Arabia's reluctant 1962 interventions in Yemen, the current bombing campaign is described as a response to Iranian meddling in Yemeni tribal politics. In actuality, underlying the Saudi interventions of both the 1960s and today is a staunch grand strategy aimed at maintaining control over their southern border. The Saudi monarchy has always feared the instability of its southern border, a remnant of the 1934 Treaty of Ta'if, which ceded the three Yemeni provinces of Asir, Najran, and Jizan to the victorious armies of Saudi founder ibn Saud. During the 1960s, the porous border was a source of regional tension as Imam al-Badr's tribal armies garrisoned soldiers and weapons in the border towns, luring incessant Egyptian air raids over Saudi territory. Serving to exacerbate matters, Baydani and other YAR officials openly declared their intentions to carry the Yemeni revolution over the border into Saudi Arabia. In the current climate, the Houthis have taken up a similar anti-Saudi stance from their native villages in the area surrounding Sa'dah. The prospect of thirty million Yemenis marching across the vast and undefended border continues to serve as a source of anxiety for Saudi leaders. Saudi King Salman therefore is following the short-term tactical strategies set by his predecessors in maintaining Saudi control over a weakened Yemeni state rather than a forward-thinking and long-term solution.

International Follies: The UN, the ICRC, and a New Era of Foreign Mercenaries

UNYOM, which maintained a presence from 1963 to 1964, was hampered by the emergence of the Asia-Africa block, a funding crisis, and the inability of Secretary General U Thant to implement unpopular policies. Although this book has served to debunk many of the historical misrepresentations that have stained the UNYOM legacy, there was no escaping the short-term futility of the mission's diplomacy.

International diplomatic efforts have been similarly plagued by difficulties surrounding the post-Arab Spring governments. Following the overthrow of Arab dictators across the region, a collection of UN diplomats has overseen transitions from dictatorships to democratically elected governments. Jamal Benomar, the UN special envoy to Yemen, was the last of these diplomats to admit failure when he resigned on April 16, 2015, in the face of a complete collapse of Yemen's transitional government. Even as late as 2013, the transition of power in Yemen, orchestrated by the Gulf Cooperation Council and brokered by Benomar, had been praised as a model for peaceful resolutions to regional turmoil. Rather than a model of success, Benomar's efforts in Yemen served only to delay the eventual turmoil in Yemen. President Mansur Hadi, who followed Benomar's prescriptions by forming a national dialogue council, announcing national elections, and attempting to enact overly optimistic political reforms, was nonetheless forced to flee the country in the face of military and political opposition to his government.

Benomar's replacement Ould Cheikh Ahmed has been following the shuttle diplomacy paths marked by Ralph Bunche and Ellsworth Bunker, who traveled between Cairo and Riyadh while largely bypassing the Yemenis themselves. Although he made a brief visit to Sana'a to meet with representatives of the republic, Bunche, along with other UN representatives, was officially barred from meeting with Imam al-Badr and his royalists. The international community recognized only the YAR as the legitimate representatives of the Yemeni people and did not legally sanction the royalist entity. Similarly, Cheikh Ahmed has shuttled between New York, Geneva, Paris, Kuwait, and Riyadh speaking with the small number of representatives of the Houthi government who managed to navigate diplomatic hurdles and arrive for a European-brokered peace conference. The international community and media have easy access to Yemen's government in exile in Riyadh, which is still considered the only legitimate representative of the Yemeni people, despite its illegitimacy in Yemen itself. Similar to the predicament faced by al-Badr and his royalist tribesmen during the 1960s, the Houthi government has not received global recognition, leaving their representatives on the legal periphery of international diplomatic efforts.

When André Rochat was first told of his ICRC mission to Yemen in 1962, he knew nothing of the country, even assuming that it was "east of Pakistan"! Regardless of their organizational ignorance, the ICRC administration recognized the importance of the chaos begot by the civil war in opening for them the opportunity to begin operations in the Arabian Peninsula, an area of the world previously beyond their reach. The ICRC has maintained a continual presence in Yemen since the civil war and is to date one of the few organizations with the knowledge and local network able to address the growing humanitarian crisis.

The British and French mercenaries aiding the royalist armies in northern Yemen during the 1960s were some of the most colorful and influential figures in the civil war. Varying groups of mercenaries have joined the current local conflict, with most supporting the military efforts of the Saudi coalition. Mike Hindmarsh, a former senior Australian army officer, is the public face of this disparate group as the commander of the United Arab Emirate's presidential guard.[15] Hindmarsh and the presidential guard have served an important role in recapturing the port city of Aden on July 17, 2015. While there were many other reports of mercenaries from Australia, Columbia, and Sub-Saharan Africa, none has thus far established a similar public persona.

Arriving at a Historic Solution

In over fifty years since the Yemen Civil War, the country's presence along the vital Bab al-Mandeb waterway to the Suez Canal has not changed, nor it seems has the very public manner in which Yemen transitions regimes and fights its local wars. Egypt's 1962 intervention in Yemen helped legitimize a weak republican government and launched six years of a bloody and costly internationalized conflict. The Yemen Civil War was drawn, in rhetoric and in practice, into regional and global conflicts far beyond its borders. It was not until the withdrawal of British and Egyptian forces at the end of 1967 and the diversion of Soviet attention from Sana'a to Aden at the end of 1969 that the Yemenis found their independent voice to end the civil war, arriving at a compromise that has served as the foundation of the Yemeni government for five decades.

In the current climate, the grand coalition organized by Saudi Arabia is again supporting a weak Yemeni republic. Foreign intervention has served to exacerbate local issues and cloud the true underlying national tensions that spawned the current Houthi rebellion. The current war in Yemen has been couched as a manifestation of the Saudi-Iranian rivalry or as part of the West's global war against terror. At its core, the current Yemen conflict, similar to the civil war during the 1960s, is nothing more than "a centuries-old method of regime change," a fact that will emerge only after foreign interests are withdrawn.[16] For the sake of innocent Yemenis, one can only hope that this date arrives with great expediency, lest fifty years from now another historian sits down to write a sequel entitled the International History of the Yemen Civil War, 2014–...

Notes

INTRODUCTION

1. Robert W. Stookey, *Yemen: The Politics of the Yemen Arab* Republic (Boulder, CO: Westview Press, 1978), 2. Robin Bidwell, *The Two Yemens* (Boulder: CO: Westview Press, 1983). Bidwell argues that the concept of the unified state of Yemen dates back to 1229 CE, when the Yemeni region entered two centuries of a golden age under the Rasulid Dynasty, which ruled over most of South Arabia.

2. Harold Ingrams, *The Yemen: Imams, Rulers, & Revolutions* (London: John Murray, 1963), 4.

3. Mohammed A. Zabarah, "The Yemeni Revolution of 1962 Seen as a Social Revolution," in *Contemporary Yemen: Politics and Historical Background*, ed. B.R. Pridham (London: Croom Helm, 1984), 80. In a more abstract sense, Zabarah highlighted the importance of new roads in carrying modern ideas to formerly isolated areas of the country. (Mohammed Ahmad Zabarah, *Yemen: Traditionalism vs. Modernity* (New York: Praeger Publishers, 1982), 85). Roads were constructed mainly by American, Chinese, and Soviet companies. Burrowes argues that the YAR was defined by its roads, which served as "foci of change." (Robert D. Burrowes, *The Yemen Arab Republic: The Politics of Development, 1962–1986* (Boulder, CO: Westview Press, 1987), 7.)

4. Fred Halliday, *Arabia Without Sultans* (London: Saqi Books, 2002), 27. Halliday argues that Soviet foreign intervention in South Arabia presented a fourth obstacle to the Yemeni state following the end of the civil war in 1968.

5. Gamal Abdel Nasser, *The National Charter* (Cairo: Information Department, 1962).

6. Interview with David Newton, November 5, 2015. The phrase "non-Western colonialism" was coined by an UN employee from India who was stationed in Yemen. Rather than Egypt's colony, James Cortada, the US chief of mission in Yemen (1963–64) referred to Yemen as "Egypt's zone of influence." James N. Cortada Oral History, *The Association for Diplomatic Studies and Training Foreign Affairs Oral History Project*, September 1, 1992.

7. Malcolm Kerr, *The Arab Cold War: Gamal 'Abd Al-Nasir and his Rivals*—1958–1970 (London: Oxford University Press, 1971). Kerr published three editions of his book, maintaining the same central thesis and only expanding the period of his evidence to account for the passage of time.

8. For example: Fawaz A. Gerges, *The Superpowers and the Middle East: Regional and International Politics, 1955–1967* (Boulder, CO: Westview, 1994); Roby C. Barrett, *The Greater Middle East and the Cold War: US Foreign Policy Under Eisenhower and Kennedy* (London: I.B. Tauris, 2007); and Jeffrey A. Lefebvre, "Middle East Conflicts and Middle Level Power Intervention in the Horn of Africa," *Middle East Journal* 50 (1996), 387–404.

9. For example: Robert McNamara, *Britain, Nasser, and the Balance of Power in the Middle East, 1952–1967: From the Egyptian Revolution to the Six Day War* (London: Frank Cass, 2003), 131.

10. Curtis Ryan, "The New Arab Cold War and the Struggle for Syria," *Middle East Report 271* (2014); Hilal Khashan, "The New Arab Cold War," *World Affairs* 159 (1997), 158–169; Morten Valbjorn and Andre Bank, "The New Arab Cold War: Rediscovering the Arab Dimension of Middle East Regional Politics," *Review of International Studies* 38 (2012), 3–24; F. Gregory Gause, "Beyond Sectarianism: The New Middle East Cold War," *Brookings Doha Center* 11 (2014).

11. Tariq Habib, *Milaffat thawrat yuliyu shahadat 122 min sunnaiha wa-maasiriha* (Cairo: Al Ahram, 1997), 242. Avraham Sela, "Nasser's Regional Politics," in *Rethinking Nasserism: Revolution and Historical Memory in Modern Egypt*, eds. Elie Podeh and Onn Winkler (Gainesville, FL: University Press of Florida, 2004), 200. Sela made similar observations about the limitations of Kerr's ideological Arab Cold War. He refers to the 1960s as a transition from political symbols to "negotiated order."

12. Wallerstein dismisses as mere fantasy the notion that everything that happened during those years was initiated by either the United States or the USSR. Immanuel Wallerstein, "What Cold War in Asia? An Interpretative Essay," in *The Cold War in Asia: The Battle for Hearts and Minds*, eds. Zheng Yangwen, Hong Liu, and Michael Szonyi (Boston: Brill, 2010), 4–5.

13. John Lewis Gaddis, *The Cold War: A New History* (New York: Penguin Press, 2005). Gaddis introduced a theory of "dogs wagging tails" to describe the relationship of small nonaligned nations, including Nasser's Egypt, to the two superpowers. Michael E. Latham, "The Cold War in the Third World, 1963–1975" in *The Cambridge History of the Cold War*, eds. Melvyn P. Leffler and Odd Arne Westad (Cambridge: Cambridge University Press, 2010), 5–6.

   Soviet Premier Nikita Khrushchev's "wars of liberation speech" on January 6, 1961, affirmed the USSR's support for nationalist movements in Africa, Asia, and Latin America. (CIA, Current Intelligence Weekly Review, January 26, 1961, *Foreign Relations of the United States* (hereafter FRUS), 1961–1963, Vol. V, Soviet Union (Washington: GPO, 1998): doc. 39. Also cited in Robert B.

Rakove, *Kennedy, Johnson, and the Nonaligned Movement* (New York: Cambridge University Press, 2013), 62.)

14. Odd Arne Westad, *The Global Cold War* (Cambridge, UK: Cambridge University Press, 2007). Westad is known for his division of the Global Cold War into an ideological rivalry. Matthew Connelly, *A Diplomatic Revolution: Algeria's Fight for Independence and the Origins of the Post-Cold War Era* (Oxford: Oxford University Press, 2002) and Matthew Connelly, "Taking Off the Cold War Lens: Visions of North-South Conflict during the Algerian War for Independence," *The American Historical Review* 105 (2000): 739–69. Manela suggests the concept of bifocals rather than getting rid of the lens entirely. Erez Manela, "A Pox on Your Narrative: Writing Disease Control into Cold War History," *Diplomatic History* 34:2 (2010): 299–323.

CHAPTER 1

1. Kevin Rosser, "Education, Revolt, and Reform in Yemen: The 'Famous Forty' Mission of 1947" (M.Phil diss. St. Antony's College, Oxford, 1998), 53. FRUS 1961-1963, Vol. XVIII, 51, Paper by the Person in charge of Arabian Peninsula Affairs (Seelye), September 20, 1962. Y. Aboul-Enein, "The Egyptian-Yemen War (1962–67): Egyptian Perspectives on Guerilla Warfare," *Infantry*, January–February 2004.

2. Ali Abdel Rahman Rahmy, *The Egyptian Policy in the Arab World: Intervention in Yemen 1962–1967 Case Study* (Washington, DC: University Press of America, 1983).

3. Edgar O'Ballance, *The War in Yemen* (Hamden, CT: Archon Books, 1971), 68.

4. Khadija al-Salami, *The Tears of Sheba: Tales of Survival and Intrigue in Arabia* (Chichester, UK: Wiley, 2003), 198–199. This account is based on a version of events as told by Yahya al-Mutawakil to the author.

5. The historian Gregory Gause claims emphatically that there is no disputing Egyptian foreknowledge and involvement in the coup, citing Baydani and two other Egyptian military memoirs as evidence (Gause, *Saudi-Yemeni Relations*, 59).

6. A. I. Dawisha, "Intervention in the Yemen: An Analysis of Egyptian Perceptions and Policies," *Middle East Journal* 29 (1975), 47.

7. Jesse Ferris, *Nasser's Gamble: How Intervention in Yemen Caused the Six-Day War and the Decline of Egyptian Power* (Princeton: Princeton University Press, 2013), 28.

8. Tariq Habib, *Milaffat thawrat yuliyu shahadat 122 min sunnaiha wa-maasiriha* (Cairo: Al Ahram, 1997), 244.

9. Anthony Nutting, *Nasser* (New York: E.P. Dutton & Co., 1972), 351.

10. Nutting, *Nasser*, 338.

11. Dawisha, "Intervention in the Yemen," 50.

12. TNA, CO 1015/2150, 4. January 6, 1961, C. Johnston (Aden) to FO. It was not clear who these two individuals were. The British were the target of Arab nationalist rhetoric as well during a 1961 Arab League meeting when Nasser boasted that he would soon have a consulate in Aden.

13. Tony Geraghty, *Who Dares Wins: The Special Air Service, 1950 to the Falklands* (London: Arms and Armour Press, 1980), 63. Geraghty and other British historians take any opportunity to blame unrest on Soviet agent Kim Philby.

14. Churchill Archives Centre, Interview with R. W. Bailey, British Diplomatic Oral History Program.

15. TNA, CO 1015/2150, 561, February 2, 1962.

16. TNA, CO 1015/2150, 534, February 2, 1962, C. Johnston (Aden) to FO.

17. Imperial War Museum Archives (hereafter IWM), Tony Boyle Papers, Box 1, Notebook.

18. TNA, CO 1015/2150, 559A, February 8, 1962, C. Johnston (Aden) to FO.

19. Ahmad Yusuf Ahmad, *Al-Dawar al-Misri fi al-Yaman* (The Role of Egypt in Yemen) (Cairo: Muaissasit Dar al-Nasir al-Misriya, 1981), 110.

20. Clive Jones, *Britain and the Yemen Civil War* (Brighton: Sussex Academic Press, 2004), 27.

21. Saudi Radio Mecca, February 14, 1967 (taken from the O'Brien communiqué in IWM, Neil McLean Files. Box A). McLean would later quote additional circumstantial evidence that the Egyptians had departed for Yemen before the revolution began. Among other points, he notes that Egyptian heavy artillery and armory arrived only one day after Sallal shelled the palace. (IWM, Neil McLean Files, Box 39)

22. James, *Nasser at War*, 58–59; 'Abd al-Rahman al-Baydani, *Misr wa Thawrat al-Yaman* (Egypt and the Yemen Revolution) (Cairo: Dar al-Maarif, 1993), chaps. 1 and 2. Baydani's tales grew more hyperbolic over time, as evidenced by his 2001 interview with *al-Jazeera* in which he claimed sole responsibility for the revolution (Nawaf Madkhli, *"Nasser's Vietnam"—The Egyptian Intervention in Yemen 1962–1967* (master's thesis, University of Arkansas, 2003), 15).

23. Telegram from the legation in Yemen to the Department of State, December 22, 1962, FRUS 1961–1963, Vol. XVIII, Near East, ed. Nina Noring (Washington DC: GPO, 1994), doc. 119. Since the 1960s, Baydani had been banished from both Egyptian and Yemeni politics, although he attempted a return to politics on a number of occasions. His political aspirations might explain his outlandish retrospective account of heroism and leadership during the Yemeni coup (Robert D. Burrowes, *Historical Dictionary of Yemen* (Lanham, MD: Scarecrow Press, 1995), 52).

24. Yael Vered, *Hafikhah u-milhamah be-Teman* (Coup and War in Yemen), (Tel Aviv: Am 'oved, 1967), 100. Baydani continued to operate on the fringes of Yemeni politics during the 1960s, traveling often to Germany, Aden, Cairo, and Baghdad. George M. Haddad, *Revolution and Military Rule in the Middle East: The*

Arab States. Vol. 3 Pt. 2: Egypt, The Sudan, Yemen and Libya (New York: Speller, 1973), 267.

25. Habib, *Milaffat thawrat yuliyu,* 240–41. According to this version, Nasser sent a full platoon only fifteen days after the original coup. Baghdadi would later describe Nasser's intervention as "100% a mistake."

26. Salah al-Din al-Hadidi, *Shahid 'ala Harb al-Yaman* (Cairo: Maktabat Madbūlī, 1984), 21.

27. Duff Hart-Davis, *The War that Never Was* (London: Century, 2011), 25. This account was based on British intelligence material from the IWM.

28. al-Hadidi, *Shahid 'ala Harb al-Yaman,* 38.

29. J. Leigh Douglas, *The Free Yemeni Movement 1935–1962* (Beirut, Lebanon: The American University of Beirut, 1987), 25.

30. Muhammad Ali Luqman and Faruq Muhammad Luqman, *Qissat al-Thawra al-Yamaniyya* (Aden: Dar Fatat al-Jazira), 82.

31. Douglas, *The Free Yemeni Movement,* 63.

32. O'Ballance, *The War in Yemen,* 43.

33. J. Leigh Douglas, "The Free Yemeni Movement: 1935–1962," in *Contemporary Yemen: Politics and Historical Background,* ed. B. R. Pidham (London: Croom Helm, 1984), 34.

34. Douglas, *The Free Yemeni Movement,* 34. Imam Yahya eventually uncovered their organization and imprisoned or exiled their members.

35. Paul Dresch, *Tribes, Government, and History in Yemen* (Oxford: Clarendon Press, 1989), 237.

36. Douglas, *The Free Yemeni Movement,* 39. Among this group were Qadi Yahya Muhammad al-Iryani, Qadi Abdullah al-Jirafi, and many others who would assume important roles in the 1948 coup.

37. Douglas, *The Free Yemeni Movement,* 43.

38. Douglas, *The Free Yemeni Movement,* 86.

39. Rosser, "Education, Revolt, and Reform in Yemen," 35.

40. Robert D. Burrowes, "The Famous Forty and their Companions: North Yemen's First-Generation Modernists and Educational Emigrants," *Middle East Journal* 59 (2005), 82. Burrowes explains that although moving abroad for employment opportunities was common for Yemenis, going abroad for education was relatively unheard of. This cohort was even more unique in the fact that with few exceptions they all returned to Yemen, rather than act as a "brain-drain" for the country.

41. Rosser, "Education, Revolt, and Reform in Yemen," 28.

42. Rosser, "Education, Revolt, and Reform in Yemen," 46.

43. Burrowes, "The Famous Forty." Burrowes estimates that between one-third and one-half of all Yemeni cabinet appointments since 1967 originated from the original Famous Forty.

44. Douglas, *The Free Yemeni Movement,* 122–139.

45. Paul Dresch, *A History of Modern Yemen* (Cambridge, UK: Cambridge University Press, 2000), 56.

46. John Hewitt, "First footsteps in Yemen, 1947," *The British-Yemeni Society* 2005, 3. Jamal Jamil was an Iraqi artillery officer assigned to the Yemeni army in Sana'a. He was the father of Ra'is Jamal Jamil, the Iraqi artillery officer wanted in Baghdad for his role in the 1940 Iraqi Golden Carpet revolution. Jamil was later executed along with other co-conspirators.

47. Rosser, "Education, Revolt, and Reform in Yemen," 58. Al-Fusayyil considered the 1962 coup to be a popular uprising with a greater number of educated supporters.

48. *Yemen Under the Rule of Imam Ahmad (Documents on the History of Arabia, Volume VII)*, ed. Ibrahim al-Rashid (Chapel Hill, NC: Documentary Publications, 1985), 107–11. The list was included in a Foreign Service Dispatch from Hermann Eilts to Department of State, February 20, 1953.

49. Douglas, *The Free Yemeni Movement*, 162. The prison was located in the Qahera Fortress (Qula'at al Qahera), which dates from the eleventh century. The fortress and its large underground prisons were used for centuries to house the imam's hostages from rebel tribes.

50. Ali Abdel Rahman Rahmy, *The Egyptian Policy in the Arab World: Intervention in Yemen 1962–1967 Case Study* (Washington, DC: University Press of America, 1983), 84. According to Sallal's recollections, he returned to the army after his time in prison with the objective to remove all imams, including al-Badr.

51. Douglas, *The Free Yemeni Movement*, 171.

52. Dresch, *Modern Yemen*, 79. The pamphlet was first printed in Aden. Dresch argues that Ahmad Nu'man, who was Muhammad Nu'man's son, likely wrote the actual pamphlet.

53. Rosser, "Education, Revolt, and Reform in Yemen," 37, 43.

54. Douglas, *The Free Yemeni Movement*, 190.
    Haddad, *Revolution and Military Rule*, 232.

55. Rahmy, *Egyptian Policy*, 90.

56. "The Real Yemeni Revolution and History," Ahmad Jaaber, *Al Thawra* (December 31, 1962). Copies of *Al Thawra*, an official government-funded newspaper, can be found in the Yemeni presidential compound. At least according to the archivist's account, other copies of Yemeni newspapers were destroyed during the siege of Sana'a in 1968.

57. Boals, *Modernization and Intervention*, 254.

58. According to British observers, in addition to economic aid, al-Badr also developed a drinking problem, perhaps over the course of his Eastern European excursions (Stephen Dorril, *MI6: Inside the Covert World of Her Majesty's Secret Intelligence Service* (New York: The Free Press, 2000), 678).

59. Jones, *Britain and the Yemen Civil War*, 24. Al-Badr's uncle Prince Hassan believed as well that his nephew was unfit to rule as imam.

60. Vsevolod Aleksandrovich Galkin, *V Temene; zapiski sovetskogo vracha* (*In Yemen: A Soviet Doctor's Notes*) (Moscow: Oriental Literature Publishing House, 1963), 68. Galkin was a Soviet doctor serving in Sana'a, Hodeidah, and other Yemeni villages. He documents his interactions with Yemeni patients, daily routine, and the details of each city or village.
    All translations are those of the author, unless otherwise indicated.

61. Stephen Page, *The Soviet Union and the Yemens: Influence in Asymmetrical Relationships* (New York: Praeger Special Studies, 1985), 4. Page suggests that by the end of 1961, Imam Ahmad was no longer the ideal Soviet third world leader, because he broke with Nasser, made an alliance with Chinese, accepted economic aid from the US, and ceased attacks on British Aden. Page describes the September 1962 coup as the revitalization of Soviet-friendly Yemeni leaders.

62. Adeed Dawisha, "The Soviet Union in the Arab World: The Limits to Superpower Influence," in *The Soviet Union in the Middle East: Policies and Perspectives*, eds. Adeed Dawisha and Karen Dawisha (London: Heinemann Educational Books, 1982), 16.

63. Vladimir Sakharov and Umberto Tosi, *High Treason* (New York: G.P. Putnam's Sons, 1980), 147–149.

64. Charles B. McLane, *Soviet-Middle East Relations* (London: Central Asian Research Centre, 1973), 113.

65. AVPRF, Fond 585, Opis 5, Papka 4, Dela 6, March 1962—Soviet Delegation to Yemen Report. The delegation included Al-Badr who was the Minister of Defense and Commander in Chief of Armaments and Strength), Hassan bin Ibrahim (Foreign Minister), 'Abd al-Rahman al- Sayigi (Minister of Internal Affairs), Seif al Islam Abduh Rahman (Minister of Health), Abduh Rahman Abu Taaleb (Minister Economics and Trade), Muhammad 'Abd al-Amuv (Minister of Education), Prince Hassan ibn Ali (Minister of Social Labor and Manufacturing), Sheikh Muhammad Ali Osman (Finance Minister), Zeid Akabat (Minister of Agricultural Economy), Abdel Qader Abdullah (Postal Minister), Abdullah al Hadjari (Minister of Communications), Abdullah Abdel Karim (Minister of State), Qadi Nasser al Zuravi (Minister of Land). Stanko Guldescu, "War and Peace in Yemen," *Quenn's Quarterly* Vol. 74 Is. 3 (1967), 475.

66. Fred Halliday, *Arabia Without Sultans* (London: Saqi Books, 2002), 97.

67. RGANI, Fond 5, Opis 30, Dela 452, List 30–38, June 1964, Brief Yemeni history written by V. Kornev. In February 1961 the Yemenis would open their own mission in Moscow staffed by a Yemeni charge d'affaires.

68. GARF Fond 4459, Opis 24, Dela 2125, File 5, November 1, 1959, TASS-Peking.

69. Page, Stephen, *The USSR and Arabia: The development of Soviet policies and attitudes towards the countries of the Arabian peninsula 1955–1970* (London: The Central Asian Research Centre, 1971), 49.

70. RGANI, Fond 5, Opis 30, Dela 452, List 30–38, June 1964, Brief Yemeni history written by V. Kornev. Port Ahmad was named after Imam Ahmad who served as monarch of Yemen from 1948 through his death in 1962.

71. GARF, Fond 4459, Opis 24, Dela 2555, File 7, April 1, 1961, TASS-Ahmad and AVPRF, Fond 585, Opis 5, Papka 4, Dela 6, January 1962, notes from the Soviet Mission to Yemen.

72. Page, *The USSR and Arabia*, 48.

73. IWM, Neil McLean Files, Box 20, Green Envelope.

74. GARF, Fond 4459, Opis 24, Dela 2555, File 24–25, April 7, 1961, TASS-Ahmed.

75. AVPRF, Fond 585, Opis 5, Papka 4, Dela 62, June 14, 1962, Report of the Soviet Mission to Yemen. The majority of al-Badr's speech consisted of religious rhetoric and talk of creating a new and more socialist Yemeni society. Port Ahmad was seen as the first of many municipal projects in his new Yemeni society.

76. AVPRF, Fond 585, Opis 14, Papka 7, Dela 10, File 1, September 21, 1962, "The New Imam's Reforms."

77. Page, *The USSR and Arabia*, 64. Despite Nasser's call in December 1961 for revolution in Yemen, the Soviets continued to remain friendly to Ahmad until his death in September.

78. Department of State, Central Files, DEF 19-8 US-Iran, Telegram From the Embassy in Iran to the Department of State, July 11, 1966. Evidently Meyer's interest in Yemen peaked around October 1962 and he never discovered that al-Badr was not actually killed.

79. David Holden, *Farewell to Arabia* (New York: Walker and Company, 1966), 89.

80. Clive Jones, *Britain and the Yemen Civil War*, 33.

81. Xan Fielding, *One Man in His Time: The Life of Lieutenant-Colonel NLD ('Billy') McLean, DSP* (Macmillan: London, 1990), 136.

82. Rosser, "Education, Revolt, and Reform in Yemen," 45.

83. Rosser, "Education, Revolt, and Reform in Yemen," 49.

84. Rosser, "Education, Revolt, and Reform in Yemen," 53.

85. IWM, Neil McLean Files, Box 20, Green Envelope.

86. Anwar Sadat's presidential resort was located in Borg el-Arab as well. The town would become an industrial city in later decades.

87. IWM, Neil McLean Files, Box 20, Green Envelope. When al-Badr tried to convince his father of the "benign" intentions for hosting a Soviet naval fleet in Hodeidah, Ahmad refused to grant permission.

88. Jonathan Walker argues that the Yemen Civil War cannot be separated from the anti-British insurgency in South Arabia. Nasser's sponsorship of the revolution in North and South Yemen was a testament to his plans of uniting the two halves of Yemen and incorporating the country as a member of the UAR. (Jonathan Walker, *Aden Insurgency: The Savage War in South Arabia, 1962–67* (S pellmount: Staplehurst, 2005).

89. IWM, Neil McLean Files, Box 6. This version was based on Imam Al-Badr's testimony and was confirmed by other Royalists as well.

90. IWM, Neil McLean Files, Box 4.

91. Editorial Note, April 1959, FRUS 1958-1960, Vol. XII, Near East Region, ed. Edward Keefer (Washington D.C.: GPO, 1992), doc. 370. Al-Badr was deemed to have been very unpopular with the Yemeni tribes. The US believed in addition that the Soviets were unpopular with the Yemeni people as a consequence of Nasser's anti-communist campaign.

92. Page, *The USSR and Arabia,* 48.

93. IWM, Neil McLean Files, Box 20, Green Envelope.

94. David Holden, *Farewell to Arabia* (New York: Walker and Company, 1966), 94. In the last twelve months of his reign, there were at least seven attempts on Ahmad's life. On one occasion in March 1962, he was found lying on the floor with four bullets in his body.

95. IWM, Neil McLean Files. Box 20. Green Envelope.

96. Rahmy, *The Egyptian Policy in the Arab World,* 59.

97. Bodleian Library: Oxford University, Papers of Sir Kennedy Trevaskis, MSS.Brit Emp. S 367,5/14, File 65, April 20, 1961.

98. Rahmy, *The Egyptian Policy in the Arab World,* 59.

99. Salim Yaqub, *Containing Arab Nationalism: The Eisenhower Doctrine and the Middle East* (Chapel Hill: University of North Carolina Press, 2004), 145, 142.

100. Yaqub, *Containing Arab Nationalism,* 270

101. John S. Badeau, *The Middle East Remembered* (Washington, DC: The Middle East Institute, 1983), 201.

102. Parker T. Hart, *Saudi Arabia and the United States: Birth of a Security Partnership* (Bloomington: Indiana University Press, 1998), 117.

103. Hart, *Saudi Arabia and the United States,* 144.

104. Chester L. Cooper, *In the Shadows of History: Fifty Years Behind the Scenes of Cold War Diplomacy* (Amherst, NY: Prometheus Books, 2005), 182.

105. Robin Bidwell, *The Two Yemens* (Boulder, CO: Westview Press, 1983), 20.

106. "Forbidden Yemen Yields to a Yankee's Offer," *Life Magazine,* December 5, 1955.

107. Telegram from Embassy in Saudi Arabia to the Department of State, October 31, 1955, FRUS 1956-1957, Vol. XIII, Near East, ed. Will Klingman, Aaron Miller, and Nina Noring, (Washington DC: GPO, 1988), doc. 422.

108. Phil H. Shook, "Yemen Oil Fields, Dallas Feud," *Dallas Star,* March 20, 1988. In 1981, Hunt Oil Company, discovered oil in the same region where Crichton and his team had obtained concessions. A fierce legal battle ensued to determine the owner of the Yemeni oil proceeds.

109. Jack Crichton and E. J. Anderson, *The Middle East Connection (Yemen)* (Bloomington: Author House, 2003). Crichton, who was among the first to

recognize the importance of oil deposits in the Middle East, later published this
book based partially on his experiences in Yemen as part of the YDC.

110. El-Khalide, Hatem, *Sojourn in a Dreadful Land* (*Yemen Chronicles*) (Pittsburg:
Dorrance Publishing, 2011). The book itself focuses around a fictional character that observes events in Yemen during the 1955. In his introduction, we learn
of a CIA character operating under the cover of a geologist for an American
oil firm. Portions of his own tale match the activities of the YDC as they actually occurred. Although the majority of the book reads like a fanciful novel-
ette, Khalide provides additional material to fill out the thickening plot of US
intelligence.

111. TNA, FO 371/149223, BM 1531/1, November 24, 1960, Oil Concessions
in Yemen.

112. TNA, FO 371/149223, BM 1531/1, November 29, 1960, R.W. Bailey to D. J.
Wyatt (Arabian Department).

113. Memorandum for the record by Thomas A. Cassilly of the Executive Secretariat,
November 13, 1957, FRUS 1955–1957, Vol. XIII, doc. 434. There was additional
concern that if oil would actually be found, the State Department would have to
explain why they used tax payer money to finance the ventures of a private oil
company.

114. GARF, Fond 4459, Opis 43, Dela 195, File 15, March 6, 1961, "American
Business Concessions in Yemen," French Press Correspondent. The American
Overseas Investment Corporation was a State Department organization that
recruited private company to invest overseas as part of a broader American
Foreign Policy mission.

115. TNA, FO 371/149223, BM 1531/1, November 6, 1960, R.W. Bailey to D.J. Wyatt
(Arabian Department).

116. AVPRF, Fund 585, Opis 5, Papka 4, Dela 6, File 35, April 19, 1962, Report of
Soviet Mission to Yemen. During a conversation that lasted for one hour, Hassan
ibn Ali and the Yemeni envoy to Rome Sa'id Muhammad 'Abd al-Qadus al-Bazir
were present. Exploration rights in this area had previously been granted to a
German oil company.

117. O'Ballance, *The War in Yemen*, 54.

118. AVPRF, Fund 585, Opis 14, Papka 7, Dela 9, File 89, May 3, 1962, *Al Nasser*
published interview.

119. GARF, Fond 4459, Opis 43, Dela 195, File 73, March 6, 1961, French Press
Correspondent in Hodeidah reported the arrest. Muhammad Galeb Farakh had
previously worked for the U.S. diplomatic mission in 1959.

120. Special National Intelligence Estimate: The Yemen Situation, November 12,
1958, FRUS 1958-1960, Vol. XII, doc. 366.

121. Mawby, *British Policy in Aden*, 56.

122. El-Khalide, *Sojourn in a Dreadful Land*.

123. Zaid al-Wazir, *Muhawalat li-Fahm al-Mashkelah al-Yamaniah* ("An Attempt to Understand the Yemeni Problem") (Beirut: Mu'assasat al-Risālah, 1971), 197.

124. Paper by the Person in charge of Arabian Peninsula Affairs (Seelye), September 20, 1962, FRUS 1961-1963, Vol. XVIII, doc. 51. It seems that Hassan's anti-Soviet stance was not sufficient to warrant American support.

CHAPTER 2

1. Aboul-Enein, "The Egyptian-Yemen War." In addition to the radio and telephone stations, Sallal's troops captured Qasr al-Silaah, the main armory and Central Security Headquarters. His followers were instructed to attack their respective sites when they heard the shelling on al-Badr's palace.

2. Oleg Gerasimovich Gerasimov, *Iemenskaia revoliutsiia, 1962-1975 gg.: Probl. i suzhdeniia* (Moscow: Nauka, 1979), 44.

3. al-Salami, *The Tears of Sheba*, 199.

4. Saeed M. Badeeb, *The Saudi-Egyptian Conflict over North Yemen 1962–1970*, (Boulder, CO: Westview Press, 1986), 118, Al-Badr Interview (December 21, 1983). Supposedly Hussein al-Shukeiri was still alive during the 1980s, albeit with a disfigured face. 'Abd al-Ghani is a reference to a prominent Yemeni political family. Al-Badr's nonspecific reference may be an indication of the dubious nature of certain parts of his account. During the time of this interview, Abdel Aziz Abdel Ghani was the acting Prime Minister of the YAR, perhaps explaining why al-Badr chose his family name as the head of the conspirators.

5. Sebastian O'Kelly, *Amedeo: The True Story of an Italian's War in Abyssinia* (London: Harper Collins, 2002), 306.

6. Claude Deffarge and Gordian Troeller, *Yemen 62–69: De la révolution "sauvage" a la trêve des guerriers,"* (Paris: Robert Laffont, 1969), 18.

7. "Fierce Fighting in Yemen," *Pravda* October 12, 1962 (No. 285, 1).

8. Deffarge and Troeller, *Yemen*, 47. The authors were skeptical of Baydani's dismissal because al-Badr's body was not found under the rubble of the palace.

9. "Events in Yemen: With the rotten monarchy ended forever," *Izvestia*, October 15, 1962, 1.

10. Rosser, "Education, Revolt, and Reform in Yemen," 56.

11. "Hassan is Dead," *Pravda*, October 20, 1962, 1. Bidwell, Robin, *The Two Yemens* (Essex and Boulder: Longman Group and Westview Press, 1983), 198.

12. Deffarge and Troeller, *Yemen*, 94.

13. Badeau, *The Middle East Remembered*, 215.

14. Ibid.

15. AVPRF, Fond 585, Opis 14, Papka 7, Dela 10, File 12–21. Reports on YAR-UAR telegram exchange, September 29 and October 4, 1962.

16. Aboul-Enein, "The Egyptian-Yemen War."

17. AVPRF, Fond 585, Opis 5, Papka 4, Dela 6, File 126, October 1, 1962, Report of Soviet Mission to Yemen.

18. AVPRF, Fond 585, Opis 5, Papka 4, Dela 6, File 112, October 6, 1962, Report of Soviet Mission to Yemen. The arrival of Egyptian troops was accompanied by the Algeria, Tunisia, Yugoslav, Hungary, Sudan, Libya, Bulgaria, Democratic Republic of Germany recognitions of the YAR.

19. *Arab Political Encyclopedia: Documents and Notes* (vol. 11, 1962–63).

20. TNA, FO 371/16883/BM 1071/54 (I), June 21, 1963, UAR letter to UN.

21. Rahmy, *Egyptian Policy*, 102.

22. Mark Robertson, "Twentieth Century Conflict in the Fourteenth Century: Intervention in Yemen" (*The Fletcher Forum*, Winter 1989, 95–111).

23. *Al Ahram*, November 16, 1962.

24. Meir Ossad, "Legal Aspects of the Egyptian Intervention in Yemen," *Israel Law Review* 5 (1970), 226. Nasser used the Jeddah agreement despite the fact that it was renounced by both Egypt and Yemen during the 1961 political tensions between the two countries. On November 10, 1962, the YAR and UAR concluded a new military agreement that presumably annulled or replaced the previous Jeddah agreement.

25. Deffarge and Troeller, *Yemen*, 88.

26. Eli Podeh, "'Suez in Reverse': The Arab response to the Iraqi Bid for Kuwait," *Diplomacy and Statecraft* 14:1 (2010), 103–130.

27. Habib, *Milaffat thawrat yuliyu*, 244.

28. Muhammad Fawzi, *Thiwar Yuliyu Yitahaddithun* (Cairo, 1987), 126.

29. Dan Hofstadter, *Egypt & Nasser Volume 2, 1957–1966* (New York: Facts on File, 1973), 180.

30. "Sallal traveled by plane to Hodeidah while an economic conference was held in Sana'a; 'Nasser our Ally'," *Al Thawra*, December 31, 1962.

31. Gamal Abdel Nasser, *Speeches and Press-Interviews*, January–December 1963 (Cairo: UAR Information Department, 1964), 102–103, Joint Communique on Talks in Cairo between President Abdullah al-Sallal and President Gamal Abdel Nasser, June 10, 1963.

32. Habib, *Milaffat thawrat yuliyu*, 240.

33. James, *Nasser at War*, 66.

34. Badeeb, *The Saudi-Egyptian Conflict* , 133. Baydani's outlandish tales seem to have made him the favorite scapegoat for Egyptian, Yemenis, and Saudis.

35. John S. Badeau, *The American Approach to the Arab World* (New York: Harper & Row, 1968), 127.

36. "The June Challenge," *Al Ahram Weekly*, February 6, 2013.

37. "Ta'if Agreement, 1934," accessed March 13, 2016, www.al-bab.com/yemen/pol/int1.htm.

38. Badeeb, *The Saudi-Egyptian Conflict*, 16. Badeeb's assessment of the Yemen Civil War is written from a Saudi perspective. While the Ta'if Agreement was certainly

invoked, it is unclear how seriously the articles of the agreement factored into actual decision-making.

39. Zayd is a Shi'i Muslim school of thought whose followers are known as "fivers." The majority of Yemen's northern country adheres to Zaydi Islam while the southern half of the country belong predominantly to the Shafi'i school of Sunni thought. The twentieth-century Yemeni imams and the Hamid al-Din family date back to 1918 with Yemen's independence from the Ottoman Empire under Imam Yahya. Yahya was Imam al-Badr's grandfather and the father of Imam Ahmad.

40. Badeeb, *The Saudi-Egyptian Conflict*, 10.

41. Robert Lacey, *The Kingdom: Arabia and the House of Saud* (New York: Avon Books, 1981), 346.

42. JFK Library, Parker Hart, Oral History, 39

43. Badeeb, *The Saudi-Egyptian Conflict*, 53. The Yemeni army in the beginning of October did not have the capability to invade Saudi Arabia. These threats were entirely empty and were likely intended to garner foreign support for the Yemeni war effort (Bidwell, *Two Yemens*, 198).

44. Haddad, *Revolution and Military Rule*, 260.

45. Central Intelligence Bulletin. October 11, 1962, FOIA. Baydani's declaration was cited from a Middle East News Agency dispatch.

46. Vered, *Hafikhah U-Milhama be-Teman*, 36.

47. Lacey, *The Kingdom*, 346.

48. UN High Commissioner for Refugees Archive, 15/S.AR/Yem, UNHCR, London to Geneva, May 3, 1966. The number of refugees might have numbered as much as 500,000, although no official census was taken during the war and the Saudi-Yemeni border was notoriously porous.

49. See Lacey, *The Kingdom* for a full account of the Saudi succession crisis. King Saud's health was declining along with his mental faculties, leaving most of the governing responsibilities to his brother Faisal. Periodic legal attempts to replace Saud as king were met with continued resistance from Saud and his supporters. It wasn't until 1964 that Faisal was officially named king.

50. Lacey, *The Kingdom*, 346.

51. Nasser, *Speeches and Press-Interviews*, 35. Address by President Gamal Abdel Nasser at the Popular Rally in Aswan on the Occasion of the High Dam Celebrations, January 9, 1963.

52. Paul Dresch, *Tribes, Government, and History in Yemen* (Oxford: Clarendon Press, 1989), 238.

53. Ibid., 243. Additional hostility was related to Ahmad's tribal hostage system and forcing tribes to return al-Badr's bribes from 1961.

54. al-Salami, *The Tears of Sheba*, 234.

55. Bidwell, *Two Yemens*, 198.

56. Vered, *Hafikhah u-milḥamah be-Teman*, 39.

57. Muhammad Sa'id al-Attar, *Le Sous-Développement Economique et Social du Yemen* (Algiers: Tiers-Monde, 1964). Al-Attar fell out of favor with the right-leaning government that emerged after the civil war and accepted a position as a diplomat to the UN for the next fifteen years.

58. *Frankfurter Allgemeine Zeitung*, May 2, 1964, Interview with Imam Al Badr.

59. Helen Lackner, *PDR Yemen: Outpost of Socialist Development in Arabia* (London: Ithaca Press, 1985).

60. AVPRF, Fond 585, Opis 5, Papka 4, Dela 6, File 155, October 8, 1962, Report of Soviet Mission to Yemen.

61. Dresch, *Tribes, Government, and History*, 245. One wonders how many tribal truces were undertaken as a result of these wartime *qat* chews.

62. Deffarge and Troeller, *Yemen*, 73.

63. Deffarge and Troeller, *Yemen*, 97. This opinion was based on their conversation with an unspecified American official in Beirut.

64. GARF, Fond 4459, Opis 43, Dela 2310, File 294, French Journal *Perspective*, January 13, 1963.

65. P. J. Vatikiotis, "The Soviet Union and Egypt: The Nasser Years," in *The Soviet Union and the Middle East: The Post-World War II Era*, edited by Ivo J. Lederer and Wayne S. Vucinich (Stanford: Hoover Institute Press, 1974), 131. Galia Golan agreed with this perception as well claiming that the goal of Soviet relations with Egypt was to obtain a strategic location to open a Mediterranean Squadron to counter the US Sixth Fleet. (Golan, Galia, *Soviet Policies in the Middle East from World War Two to Gorbachev* (Cambridge: Cambridge University Press, 1990), 56–57).

66. "Port Ahmad-Beacon of Light," *Pravda*, April 12, 1961, 1.

67. "Yemen in Peril," *Izvestia*, October 10, 1962, 2.

68. Alan R. Taylor, *The Superpowers and the Middle East* (Syracuse: Syracuse University Press, 1991), 133. Taylor cites Fred Halliday's assessment in formulating his opinion of Soviet opportunism.

69. RGANI, Fond 5, Opis 30, Dela 452, List 6, 1961, Brief Yemeni history written by V. Kornev. National assessment was written by V. Kornev, Deputy Head of the Department of Middle East-Soviet Relations.

70. RGANI, Fond 5, Opis 30, Dela 452, List 12–13, June 1963, Brief Yemeni history written by V. Kornev.

71. CIA Intelligence Weekly Summary, "Yemeni Rebel Regime Gaining Strength," October 19, 1962, FOIA.

72. Richard E. Bissell, "Soviet Use of Proxies in the Third World: The Case of Yemen," *Soviet Studies* (vol. XXX (1978), 87–106), 92.

73. RGANI, Fond 5, Opis 30, Dela 452, List 4, October 3, 1963, Brief Yemeni history written by V. Kornev.

74. Bissell, "Soviet Use of Proxies in the Third World," 92.

75. RGANI, Fond 5, Opis 30, Dela 452, List 33, June 1964, Brief Yemeni history written by V. Kornev. A Chinese road building team completed a Sana'a-Hodeidah road in January 1962.

76. RGANI, Fond 5, Opis 30, Dela 452, List 36, June 1964, Brief Yemeni history written by V. Kornev. By the beginning of 1964, the Egyptians had already spent 35 million pounds sterling and had suffered five to six thousand casualties battling royalist opposition.

77. Peter Somerville-Large, *Tribes and Tribulations: A Journey in Republican Yemen* (London: Robert Hale, 1967), 123. When Somerville told American Charges d'affaire Cortada that he paraded as an American journalist for his safety, Cortada responded: "We can take it. . . . If the Royalists regard us as allies, it's all to the good – you can't have too many friends." (161)

78. Stookey, *America and the Arab States*, 1975, 183.

79. JFK Library, Talbot, Oral History 2, 10.

80. Frank Leith Jones, *Blowtorch: Robert Komer, Vietnam, and American Cold War Strategy* (Annapolis: Naval Institute Press, 2013), 3. Komer, who later serve as LBJ's adviser and head of US counterinsurgency efforts under General William Westmoreland in Vietnam, was aptly nicknamed "Blowtorch" as a description of his aggressive personality and brash self-confidence. He was also described as "a caricature, a self-important sycophant, or a person so outlandishly optimistic that he is of no importance other than to serve as comic relief or a symbol of American hubris."

81. JFK Library, Komer, Oral History 2, 17.

82. JFK Library, Hart, Komer, Oral History, 31. Komer's illustrative and emotional memos eventually antagonized enough senior diplomats in the State Department that Johnson exiled him to Vietnam to work on the pacification program. (Jonathan Colman, *The Foreign Policy of Lyndon B. Johnson: The United States and the World, 1963–69* (Edinburg: Edinburgh University Press, 2010), 13.)

83. JFK Library, Komer, Oral History 2, 9.

84. Badeau, *The American Approach*, 185.

85. JFK Library, Box 208a, Folder 2, July 1963, CIA Summary. In 1957, the Soviet Bloc introduced an economic and military aid program, supplying Yemen with heavy artillery, tanks, small arms, and aircraft. On the economic front, the Soviets built the new port in Hodeidah and began construction on the new Sana'a. The Chinese built a new highway from Hodeidah to Sana'a.

86. Hart, *Saudi Arabia and the United States*, 120.

87. JFK Library, Box 207, Folder 3, 55, October 1962, Stookey to State.

88. Badeeb, *The Saudi-Egyptian Conflict*, 52. In fact, in 1963, Nasser paid some Yemeni workers to carry out acts of sabotage in Saudi Arabia that potentially threatened to undermine the Saudi regime.

89. JFK Library, Box 207a, Folder 1, 10, November 1962, Macomber to State. In an interview with William Macomber, the U.S. Ambassador to Jordan, on November 18, 1962, King Hussein spoke his thoughts aloud: "I wonder who will be next King Saud or me!"

90. Macro, *Yemen and the Western World*, 128.

91. JFK Library Box 207a, Folder 2, 23, February 1962, Brubek to Bundy.

92. Hart, *Saudi Arabia and the United States*, 117.

93. Ibid., 119. There is doubt that the Saudis even had that many battle-ready troops.

94. Badeau, *The American Approach*, 192.

95. JFK Library, Box 207a, Folder 1, 70, November 1962, Yemen Summary.

96. Badeeb, *The Saudi-Egyptian Conflict*, 60.

97. Peterson, *The Decline of Anglo-American Middle East*, 33 and 43. This "jealousy" was symptomatic of a general suspicion that Nasser had of any Arab leader whom he thought might be trying to build his own "Arab" credentials and perhaps force unity upon Egypt.

98. *La Gazette*. October 10, 1962.

99. Christopher McMullen, *Resolution of the Yemen Crisis, 1963: A Case Study in Mediation* (Washington DC: Institute for the Study of Diplomacy School of Foreign Service Georgetown University, 1980), 3.

100. Mordechai Gazit, *President Kennedy's Policy Towards the Arab States and Israel: Analysis and Documents* (Tel Aviv: Shiloah Center for Middle Eastern and African Studies, 1983), 26.

101. Badeau, *The American Approach*, 123.

102. JFK Library, Box 209, Folder 2, 54a, 2, Komer to Kennedy, October 1963.

103. JFK Library, Box 208, Folder 5, 25, February 1963, Rusk to State, Summary of UAR incursion into Saudi Arabia and Aden Federation.

104. "UAR, Saudi Arabia, and Yemen," Central Intelligence Weekly Review, March 15, 1963, FOIA.

105. JFK Library, Box 208a, Folder 1, 33, June 10, 1963, Badeau to State.

106. JFK Library, Box 208a, Folder 3, 8, July 2, 1963, Sherman Kent, CIA Civil War Summary.

107. JFK Library, Box 208a, Folder 3, 8, September 18, 1963, Jones (London) to Dept. of State.

108. JFK Library, Box 208a, Folder 3, 23, July 2, 1963, Komer to Kennedy. After 1961, the UAR referred only to Egypt.

109. McMullen, *Resolution of the Yemen Crisis*, 7.

110. Ibid, 9. Ellsworth Bunker was chosen for his experience in mediating Dutch-Indonesian West Irian dispute in 1962, rather than his Middle East qualifications. He also served in India during the 1950s and greatly improved American relations with Nehru's government.

111. Ibid, 32.

112. Ibid, 17.

113. Brian Urquhart, *Ralph Bunche: An American Life* (New York: W.W. Norton, 1993), 363.

114. Little, "The New Frontier on the Nile," 520. Edward Weintal and Charles Bartlett, *Facing the Brink: an intimate study of crisis diplomacy* (New York: Charles Scribner's Sons, 1967), 43.

115. JFK Library, Box 209, Folder 5, 2, Brubeck to McGeorge Bundy. February 28, 1963. Komer claims that Kennedy originally hoped to have the planes withdrawn within sixty days (Jones, *Blowtorch*, 68).

116. JFK Library, Box 209, Folder 5, 9, Komer to Kennedy. March 11, 1963. Air Force Chief of Staff Curtis LeMay protested the mission as the Dharan airfield had been deactivated in April 1962. The absence of a modern airfield not only ensured the inability of the Hard Surface planes to respond to Egyptian incursions, but also made them sitting ducks for enemy fire (Weintal and Bartlett, *Facing the Brink*, 45). Little, "The New Frontier on the Nile". Operation Hard Surface was intended as a symbolic deterrent and was under strict orders from Kennedy to remain idle, lest the United States be drawn into a large-scale military confrontation with Nasser.

117. JFK Library, Robert Komer, Third Oral History Interview, 2.

118. Weintal and Barlett, *Facing the Brink*, 45. Although Kennedy was not dragged into the war, Operation Hard Surface had an unintended consequence. Rumors spread by Radio Cairo claimed that American Jews were among the pilots sent to Saudi Arabia, creating a media storm and public relations issues for the administration both domestically among Jewish groups and among Arab allies abroad (Hart, *Saudi Arabia*, 195).

119. JFK Library, Box 209, Folder 6, 74, April 3, 1963, Badeau to Dept. of State.

120. JFK Library, Box 209, Folder 6, 102, April 19, 1963, Dept. of State: Bunker Mission Summary.

121. McMullen, *Resolution of the Yemen Crisis*, 43.

122. JFK Library, Box 208a, Folder 3, 60, August 19, 1963, Komer to Kennedy.

123. JFK Library, Box 208a, Folder 1, 78, June 26, 1963, Ball to State.

124. JFK Library, Box 208a, Folder 2, July 1963, CIA Summary.

125. JFK Library, Box 208, Folder 4, 43, April 17, 1963, Cortada to State.

126. JFK Library, Box 208a, Folder 2, 1, July 1963, CIA Summary.

127. JFK Library, Box 208a, Folder 2, 6, July 1963, CIA Summary.

128. JFK Library, Box 209, Folder 1, 23, September 20, 1963, Komer Yemen Summary.

129. Bent Hansen, *The Political Economy of Poverty, Equity, and Growth: Egypt and Turkey* (Washington DC: Oxford University Press, 1991). Hansen is the best resource on Nasser's economic reform during the 1960s.

130. Tom Little, *Modern Egypt* (New York: Frederick A. Praeger, 1968), 266.

131. John Waterbury, *The Egypt of Nasser and Sadat: The Political Economy of Two Regimes* (Princeton: Princeton University Press, 1983), 95, 100.

132. Alaini, *Fifty Years*, 83.

CHAPTER 3

1. Milton Bearden, "Afghanistan, Graveyard of Empires," *Foreign Affairs* (December 2001), accessed January 6, 2016, https://www.foreignaffairs.com/articles/afghanistan/2001-11-01/afghanistan-graveyard-empires.

2. Kathryn Boals, *Modernization and Intervention: Yemen as a Case Study* (Princeton University, PhD., 1970), 278.

3. Schmidt, *Yemen: The Unknown War* (London: Bodley Head, 1968), 210. Schmidt claims that Nasser suffered political and military embarrassment prior to the 1964 conference and was not prepared to withdraw.

4. The British saw Nasser's presence as an epic Anglo-Egyptian battle and could not believe that Nasser's commitments to withdrawal were sincere (Karl Pieragostini, *Britain, Aden, and South Arabia: Abandoning Empire* (Hampshire: Macmillan, 1991)). The anti-Nasser lobbyist and politicians in America depicted Nasser as benefitting from a policy of appeasement, receiving American aid while continuing hostilities and making a mockery of diplomatic efforts. Alan R. Taylor, *The Superpowers and the Middle East* (Syracuse: Syracuse University Press, 1991).

5. Intelligence and Terrorism Information Center (ITIC), Imam's Forces, 25. Egyptian servicemen found sixteen rusting Ilyushin-10 planes left out in the open and six Ilyushin-14 planes that were in serviceable condition. Once repaired and reconstructed, these were used for domestic transport. Four additional planes were found in Ta'iz; they were repaired by Egyptian technicians and used for reconnaissance.

6. ITIC, Yemen Aerial, 56. The military airport in Sana'a had a 1,000-meter runway and was 7,200 meters above sea level. The civilian airport in Sana'a was 1,200 meters long and 7,200 meters above sea level. The Hodeidah civilian airfield had an 800-meter runway and was at sea level. The Ta'iz civilian airport had an 800-meter runway and was at 4,000 meters above sea level.

7. ITIC, Artillery Lessons, 11. Caves around Sana'a remain inaccessible and are deemed a restricted military zone.

8. ITIC, Artillery Lessons, 10. David Mitty likens the Egyptian program of transferring military and security responsibility over to Yemeni republicans to the American program of Vietnamization. (David M. Mitty, "A Regular Army in Counterinsurgency Operations: Egypt in North Yemen, 1962–1967," *The Journal of Military History* 65 (2001), 415).

9. ITIC, Yemen Overview, 13–15. Although Yemen was the most fertile region in the Arabian Peninsula, the country was nonetheless covered with large swaths of desert and limited water resources. According to Anwar al-Qadi, the commander of the Egyptian forces in Yemen, the terrain in Yemen was so difficult, that distance was measured in hours rather than in kilometers. (Vered, *Hafikhah u-milhamah be-Teman*, 63.)

10. Vered, *Hafikhah u-milhamah be-Teman*, 54–58.

11. ITIC, Battlefield: Sa'dah, 38.

12. ITIC, Battlefield: Sa'dah, 39.

13. ITIC, Battlefield: Sa'dah, 40.

14. ITIC, Battlefield: Sa'dah, 41.

15. ITIC, Battlefield: Sa'dah, 42. Egyptian estimates claimed that three hundred royalists were killed with only six Egyptian casualties. Accurate statistics from the Yemen Civil War are difficult to ascertain. See Ferris, *Nasser's Gamble,* for an overview of memoirs of Egyptian officers and soldiers serving in Yemen and their own casualty estimates ranging anywhere from ten thousand to sixty thousand, with an undetermined number of maimed or injured.

16. Interview with David Newton, November 5, 2015.

17. Schmidt, *Yemen: The Unknown War,* 64.

18. Bruce Condé, "Odd Battle Of Stamp Orders Punctuates Conflict In Yemen, Philately Safe After Close Call," *Linn's Weekly Stamp News,* January 18, 1965, 16. Condé added that the "royal motor pool" also carried the mail. Bruce Condé, an American philatelist serving as a military commander in Yemen, published many of his observations during the 1960s in *Linn's Weekly Stamp News,* for which he served as a Middle East correspondent.

19. Schmidt, *The Unknown War,* 65.

20. Bruce Condé, "Free Yemen POD Carries On, Resumes Operations In West, North And East As Loyalists Repel Rebels In These Areas," *Linn's Weekly Stamp News,* April 1, 1963, 26. British MP McLean was witness to these royalist victories, leading him to conclude that recognition of YAR would be premature.

21. Bruce Condé, "Free Yemen's First Definitives In Pictorial Theme Appear In Perf, Imperf, and Sheet Form," *Linn's Weekly Stamp News,* June 15, 1964, 13. Condé's history is notoriously inaccurate, citing the early-twentieth-century artillery as Turkish rather than Ottoman and misquoting Yemen's date of independence from the Ottoman Empire as 1926 rather than 1918.

22. Schmidt, *Yemen: The Unknown War,* 130.

23. ITIC, Artillery Lessons, 7.

24. IWM, Boyle/Johnson Papers—64/89/5, The Diaries and Papers of Mark Millburn.

25. ITIC, Battlefield: Sana'a-Hodeidah, 53.

26. George de Carvalho, "Yemen's Desert Fox," *Life Magazine,* February 19, 1965, 103.

27. IWM: Tony Boyle's Papers, May 16, 1964.

28. Patrick Seale, "The War in Yemen," *The New Republic,* January 26, 1963.

29. Mordechai Gazit, *President Kennedy's Policy Toward the Arab States and Israel: Analysis and Documents* (Tel Aviv: Shiloah Center for Middle Eastern and African Studies, Tel Aviv University, 1983), 26.

30. Rahmy, *The Egyptian Policy,* 246–247. Salah al-Din Al-Hadidi, *Shahid 'ala Harb al-Yaman* (al-Qāhirah: Maktabat Madbūlī, 1984), 55–56. Many of these items

were later sold on the black market in Egypt and were a source of financial corruption as detailed in Ferris, *Nasser's Gamble*, 199–205.

31. Vered, *Hafikhah u-milhamah be-Teman*, 142.
32. Nasser, *Speeches and Press-Interviews*, 126, Address by President Gamal Abdel Nasser on the Occasion of the 11th Anniversary of the Revolution at the Republican Square, Cairo, July 22, 1963 and 164, Address by President Gamal Abdel Nasser on the 11th Anniversary of the Revolution at Alexandria, July 26, 1963. It seems more likely that these letters, which were passed along to Amer, served as evidence for the role that the Yemen battlefield played in Nasser's patronage network.
33. Andrew McGregor, *A Military History of Modern Egypt: From the Ottoman Conquest to the Ramadan War* (Westport, CT: Praeger Security International, 2006), 261, 264. McGregor explains Amer's personal fiefdom: "loyalty to the commander came to outweigh success on the battlefield."
34. Mitty, "A Regular Army in Counterinsurgency Operations," 417.
35. Hofstadter, *Egypt & Nasser*, 189–190.
36. 'Abd al-Latif al-Baghdadi, *Mudhakkirat 'Abd al-Latif al-Baghdadi* Vol. 2 (Cairo: al-Maktab al-Misri al-Hadith, 1977), 123. Sami Sharaf, Sanawat wa-ayyam ma'a Gamal Abdel Nasser: shahadat Sama Sharaf (Cairo, Egypt: Dār al-Fursān lil-Nashr, 2005), 409–420.
37. ITIC, Overview, 30–39. Although the 1962 port was never intended for large-scale military shipments, the 1958 Hodeidah-Sana'a road and the existing port facilities were sufficient for Egyptian military purposes.
38. ITIC, Naval Forces, 73. Ironically, the large number of ships in and around the Hodeidah port created an added layer of difficulty for enemy forces to discern the Egyptian military vessels from the neutral commercial ones.
39. ITIC, Naval Forces, 74.
40. ITIC, Yemen Aerial, 58. The time bombs also facilitated multiple rounds of over flights unobstructed by premature explosions on the ground.
41. ITIC, Yemen Aerial, 57.
42. ITIC, Yemen Aerial, 59.
43. ITIC, Yemen Aerial, 63–67.
44. ITIC, Battlefield: Jawf, 44. The Egyptian offensive was a response to enemy attacks on roads leading from Sana'a to Ta'iz and the coastal city of Zabid under the pretext of cutting supplies in preparation for an attack on Sana'a.
45. Bruce Condé, "Loyalist Yemen Mail Continues; Operations Through Territory Held By Invaders To Reach Free World At Post Of Aden," *Linn's Weekly Stamp News*, June 10, 1963, 1.
46. ITIC, Artillery Lessons, 3.
47. ITIC, Airborne Troops, 25–27.
48. ITIC, Artillery Lessons, 5. Digging ditches to protect the artillery was also a challenge in the rocky mountainside, and the army engineers opted instead to pile sand bags and rocks for protection, further increasing the need for transport. Artillery pieces stored in makeshift bunkers would often break upon firing and required extra maintenance.

49. ITIC, Artillery Lessons, 4.

50. ITIC, Artillery Lessons, 8.

51. ITIC, Artillery Lessons, 9.

52. ITIC, Artillery Lessons, 12.

53. Anwar Sadat, *In Search of Identity: an Autobiography* (New York: Harper Row, 1978), 162. Al-Qadi did not have much of a chance to respond for at the end of 1963 he was injured during an ambush on his convoy in northeast Yemen and was evacuated to Egypt for treatment (Mitty, "A Regular Army in Counterinsurgency Operations," 415).

54. Mitty, "A Regular Army in Counterinsurgency Operations," 418.

55. Bruce Condé, "Loyalist Yemen Salutes Flight of Mariner 4 with Release of Overprints on Astronaut Issue," *Linn's Weekly Stamp News*, January 3, 1966, 22.

56. ITIC, Enemy Weapons, 28. The two main routes of infiltration from Saudi Arabia and the southern Federation of South Arabia led directly into Yemeni border villages, which became royalist bases and targets for the Egyptian air force. Supplies from the northern border with Saudi Arabia came directly to the regions of Amara and Wadi Amlach (about fifty miles from Sa'dah). Supplies from the eastern border with the tribe of Bayhan led to the southern Harib region, three miles from the border.

57. Bruce Condé, "Free Yemen's First Definitives in Pictorial Theme Appear in Perf, Imperf, and Sheet Form," *Linn's Weekly Stamp News*, June 15, 1964, 13. These have replaced the .50 caliber American machine guns received before UNYOM. Their bullets could penetrate armor of Russian Ilyushins and MiGs, posing a threat to low flying planes.

58. Schmidt, *Yemen: The Unknown War*, 159.

59. ITIC, Enemy Tactics, 27.

60. Bruce Condé, "Free Yemen's First Definitives In Pictorial Theme Appear In Perf, Imperf, and Sheet Form," *Linn's Weekly Stamp News*, June 15, 1964, 12.

61. Bruce Condé, "Story of Free Yemen's FFH Set in Tragedy of 'Chickens That Stay at Home to Roost,'" *Linn's Weekly Stamp News*, October 14, 1963, 29.

62. IWM, Boyle/Johnson Papers—64/89/5, The Diaries and Papers of Mark Millburn. IWM, Boyle/Johnson Papers—64/89/7, Record of Mines.

63. O'Ballance, *The War in the Yemen*, 129–130.

64. Bruce Condé, "Odd Battle of Stamp Orders Punctuates Conflict in Yemen, Philately Safe After Close Call," *Linn's Weekly Stamp News*, February 1, 1965, 36.

65. Vered, *Hafikhah u-milḥamah be-Teman*, 198.

CHAPTER 4

1. These include: Dana Adams Schmidt, "The Civil War in Yemen," in *The International Regulation of Civil Wars*, ed. Evan Luard (London: Thames and Hudson, 1972). Schmidt argues that the UN presence was actually detrimental as it gave Yemenis an excuse to avoid finding their own solution to the conflict, preferring instead to tell their people: "It is in the hands of the United Nations now"

(145). Alan James, *Peacekeeping in International Politics* (London: MacMillan, 1990), 305. O'Ballance, *The War in Yemen*.

2. For example, see Ferris, *Nasser's Gamble*.

3. Bodleian Library Archive, Oxford University, Michael Crouch Papers, File 102, May 29, 1963. It is somewhat ironic that several years later, the anti-British nationalist organizations in South Arabia, NLF and FLOSY, would refer to a subsequent UN mission as "UN Puppets of British imperialism" (Julian Paget, *Last Post: Aden 1963–1967* (London: Faber and Faber, 1969), 190).

4. Bernard J. Firestone, *The United Nations under U Thant, 1961–1971* (Lanham, MD: Scarecrow Press, 2001), 32.

5. Ann G. Livingstone, "Canada's policy and attitudes towards United Nations Peacekeeping, 1956–1964", PhD diss., Keele University, 1995. Livingstone argues that Canada's "middlepowermanship" gave the country significance in a foreign policy dominated by the great powers. Canadians saw themselves as a "fire-brigade" for international crisis. Pearson was awarded the Nobel Peace Prize in 1957 for his work on resolving the Suez Crisis and envisioning the UN peacekeeping force in Sinai.

6. C. V. Narasimhan, *Regionalism in the United Nations* (New York: Asia Publishing House, 1977), 43.

7. Brian Urquhart, *A Life in Peace and War* (New York: Harper and Row, 1987), 171.

8. The principles of the Non-Aligned Movement were agreed upon during a preliminary conference in Cairo in April 1961. Imam Ahmad's Yemen was one of the founding nations of NAM in 1961.

9. The first ministerial meeting of this group of seventy-seven countries occurred in October 1967 in Algeria. To date, there are 133 members in the Group of 77, making it one of the most powerful and influential groups in the UN.

10. Firestone, *The United Nations under U Thant*, xvii, xx. April 1963, was to have been the end of Hammarskjöld's term. Firestone explains that Thant envisioned the coming decades to be characterized by the North-South conflict of developed-undeveloped nations, rather than the East-West Cold War conflict of the previous decade. The General Assembly, dominated by countries of the developing world, would serve as the "prime arena" for these future conflicts.

11. *The Blue Helmets: A Review of United Nations Peacekeeping* (New York: United Nations Department of Public Information, 1996), 175.

12. Peter Bishop, "Canada's Policy on the Financing of U.N. Peace-Keeping Operations," *International Journal* 20 (1965): 463–483.

13. Michael K. Carroll, *Pearson's Peacekeepers: Canada and the United Nations Emergency Forces, 1956–67* (Vancouver: UBC Press, 2009).

14. Karl Th. Birgisson, "United Nations Yemen Observation Mission," in *The Evolution of UN Peacekeeping: Case Studies and Comparative Analysis*, ed. William J. Durch (New York: Henry L. Stimson Center, 1993), 211.

15. TNA, FO 371/16831/BM 1071/9, March 7, 1963.

16. Firestone, *The United Nations under U Thant*, 31.
17. Peter Jones, "UNYOM: The Forgotten Mission," *Canadian Defence Review Quarterly* 22 (1992), 18–22.
18. "The Mess in Yemen," *Time Magazine*, vol. 82, issue 11, p. 41, September 13, 1963. Von Horn remarried in 1964 to Elisabeth Liljenroth, a Swedish movie actress thirty years his junior, perhaps the reason why he needed to leave UNYOM early and take personal leave in July 1963.
19. Schmidt, *Yemen: The Unknown War*, 196. Practically the only creature comforts of prestige offered to von Horn were Imam Ahmad's old white horse and Daimler.
20. Carl Von Horn, *Soldiering for Peace* (New York: David McKay Company, 1966), 307.
21. Jones, "UNYOM: The Forgotten Mission."
22. UN Archives (hereafter UNA), S-5794, Report by the Secretary-General to the Security Council on the functioning of UNYOM, July 2, 1964. Thant presented this speech to the entire Security Council, evidently trying to appease the cost-conscious peacekeeping advocates.
23. "Yemen-UNYOM Background, accessed March 13, 2016, http://www.un.org/en/peacekeeping/missions/past/unyombackgr.html.
24. Ellsworth Bunker blamed UNYOM delays for losing his diplomatic momentum in the interim between his report to the UN on April 12, 1963, and the beginning of the mission in the end of June. Howard B. Schaffer, *Ellsworth Bunker: Global Troubleshooter, Vietnam Warhawk* (Chapel Hill: University of North Carolina Press, 2003), 126.
25. UNA, S-0656-0002, Folder 2, June 15, 1963, von Horne to Bunche.
26. "Yemen-UNYOM Background, accessed March 13, 2016, http://www.un.org/en/peacekeeping/missions/past/unyombackgr.html.
27. TNA, FO 371/168833/BM 1071/42, May 21, 1963.
28. The Soviet Union pressured the Security Council to accept only renewable two-month terms for the observer mission, contingent upon available financial resources for its continuation.
29. United Nations General Assembly, 18th session, 1,235th plenary meeting, October 9, 1963.
30. Library and Archives Canada (hereafter LARC), RG 24—Volume 21494, September 4, 1963. The mission consisted of a reconnaissance unit of 114 Yugoslav officers who had been serving as part of UNEF.
31. Ian Umbach, "134 ATU in Yemen," accessed March 13, 2013, http://www.115atu.ca/yem.htm.
32. LARC, RG 24,Volume 21494, June 12, 1964. The Canadian aircraft and personnel had been part of UNEF originally created to maintain the demilitarization of the Sinai Peninsula and uphold the agreed-upon armistice lines after the 1956 War.

33. Canada House of Commons Debates—Volume II, 1963.

34. Canada House of Commons Debates—Volume II, 1963.

35. LARC, RG 25,Volume 6144, June 19, 1963.

36. UNA, S-0656-0002, Folder 5, June 17, 1963, von Horn to U Thant.

37. LARC, RG 25,Volume 21592, June 19, 1963.

38. LARC, RG 25—Volume 6144, June 21, 1963.

39. TNA, C.T. Crowe, FO 371/16885/ BM 1071/98, August 7, 1963.

40. LARC, RG 25,Volume 6144, July 2, 1963. During the 1960s, it was assumed that one had to boil water for a longer period of time in higher elevations in order to rid the water of harmful bacteria. More recent studies indicate that almost all of the harmful bacteria would have already been killed off at temperatures lower than that of the boiling point, even at high elevations.

41. Holden explains that many Americans and Europeans mistakenly assumed that Yemen was a flat desert like the rest of Arabia and were dismayed to find rugged mountains (David Holden, *Farewell to Arabia* (New York: Walker and Company, 1966), 101–102).

42. UNA, S-0656-0003, Folder 2, August 21, 1963, von Horn to U Thant.

43. UNA, S-0656-0003, Folder 1, September 3, 1963, Rikhye to Bunche. Mas'ud further elucidated on Saudi thinking: "Yemenis have classical pattern of civil war, revolt, counter-revolt." Saudis have "no special love for Imam nor for republicans", and only want to have Yemenis left to find their own solution."

44. UNA, S-0656-0003, Folder 4, September 19, 1963, UNYOM commander to Secretary General.

45. LARC, RG 24,Volume 21494, August 26, 1963.

46. UNA, S-0656-0002, Folder 2, July 12, 1963, Pavlovic to Rolz-Bennett.

47. UNA, S-5325, "Report of the Secretary-General on the latest developments on the proposal to send a UN observation mission to Yemen," June 7, 1963.

48. LARC, RG 24, Volume 21494, August 26, 1963.

49. LARC, RG 24, Volume 21494, July 23, 1963.

50. George E. Mayer, "134 ATU (Air Transport Unit), Sana'a Yemen 1962–3," accessed March 13, 2016, http://www.115atu.ca/yem.htm. Mayer claims that "dodging the Russian made Yak fighters flown by Egyptian pilots was almost suicidal."

51. Fred Gaffen, *In the Eye of the Storm: A History of Canadian Peacekeeping* (Toronto: Deneau & Wayne Publishers, 1987), 80.

52. UNA, S-0656-0003, Folder 7, November 21, 1963, Paulson testimonial.

53. LARC, RG 24,Volume 21494, August 26, 1963. There were rumors that U Thant was purposely ignoring von Horn's reports entirely (Edward Weintal and Charles Cartlet, *Facing the Brink: An Intimate Study of Crisis Diplomacy* (New York: Charles Scribner's Sons, 1967), 51).

54. UNA, S-0656-0001, Folder 2, January 1964, McLellan to UN, was written as a formal letter on behalf of himself and other members of his cohort.

55. Pavlovic would later serve as the UN Chief of Staff for the mission. While serving as the Commander and Chief of Staff of the mission, Saudis were often suspicious of Pavlovic and of the Yugoslav contingency of the mission, and were hesitant to work with them. Although the Yugoslav presence was less than desirable for the Saudis it prevented Nasser from accusing UN mission of partiality.

56. LARC, RG 24, Volume 21494, November 12, 1963.

57. UNA, S-0657-007, Folder 1, November 1, 1963, Colonel Branko Pavlovic, Chief of Staff UNYOM, "UNYOM Operations Instructions."

58. UNA, S-0656-0003, Folder 7, January 2, 1964, U Thant to Security Council.

59. UNA, S-0656-0003, Folder 10, August 27, 1964, Sabharawal to Spinelli and Bunche. The governor of Jizan submitted an official complaint, claiming that UAR planes were returning to the area in an attempt to intercept transports.

60. UNA, S-0656-0003, Folder 10, September 3, 1964.

61. LARC, RG 24, Volume 21494, August 5, 1964.

62. LARC, RG 24, Volume 21494, August 7, 1964.

63. Schmidt, "The Civil War in Yemen," 141.

64. Jones, *Britain and the Yemen Civil War 1962–1965*, 71. Jones claims a "paucity in manpower and equipment that reflected the styptic nature of the mandate" and that "Von Horn was prohibited from establishing contact with forces loyal to the Imam."

65. Schmidt, "The Civil War in Yemen," 146. He claims that UN should have suspended recognition until after the conclusion of the mission so as to keep the diplomatic channel open to both parties. In his memoirs, *Soldiering for Peace*, Von Horn, does not mention that extensive contacts with royalists, yet laments U Thant's restrictions regarding contact with royalists. Yael Vered, *Hafikhah u-milḥamah be-Teman* (Tel Aviv: Am 'oved, 1967), 128, claims that UNYOM made no contact whatsoever with royalists and pretended they did not exist. Fred Gaffen claims the mission was hampered by the inability to make contact with royalists (Gaffen, *In the Eye of the Storm*, 81). Birgisson argues that UNYOM officials could not make contact or accept complaints made by royalists, for fear that the mission would compromise its impartiality (Birgisson, "United Nations Yemen Observation Mission," 213). Other accounts accused the UN of "acting as if the Royalists did not exist." (Meir Ossad, "Legal Aspects of the Egyptian Intervention in Yemen," *Israel Law Review* 5, 1970).

66. UNA, S-0657-0012, Folder 5, August 24, 1963, Major L.P. David to Deputy Commander UNYOM.

67. UNA, S-0657-0012, Folder 5, October 13, 1963, Doughty, Najran to Operations. Doughty did not pass this statement about tribal behavior to the Canadians, because "it may spread alarm and despondency."

68. UNA, S-0657-0012, Folder 5, October 13, 1963, Doughty, Najran to Operations. Doughty described the dances as a mixture of "the Twist and Hop Step and Jump."

69. UNA, S-0656-0001, April 25, 1964. Spinelli refused to meet with al-Badr in al-Hayat, Yemen because Cairo had criticized the timing and intentions of the meeting.

70. UNA, S-0656-0003, Folder 10, August 5, 1964, weekly operations.

71. Richard Deming, *Heroes of the International Red Cross* (New York: ICRC, 1969), 196. ICRC visits to al-Badr's mountain stronghold were to be limited to once per month. André Rochat, *L'homme á la Croix: une anticroisade* (Geneva: Editions de l'Aire, 2005), 77.

72. ICRC, DMO Yemen 1-002, Boisard (ICRC) to Kennen (UNYOM), August 12, 1964.

73. UNA, S-5412, September 4, 1963.

74. UNA, S-0057-0001, Folder 12, 1963, Chronological Action Files of Complaints.

75. Ibid.

76. UNA, S-0057-0001, Folder 3 and 4, June 1963.

77. UNA, S-0057-0001, Folder 11, August 31, 1963, Captain Ibrahim Hamad, Saudi Liaison Officer to Major B. Schaathun UNYOM liaison officer. Twelve bombs were dropped and the bombing continued after UNYOM withdrawal. Major David threatened to leave Yemen along with von Horn, but was convinced to stay on until October 23, 1963 (Parker T. Hart, *Saudi Arabia and the United States: Birth of a Security Friendship* (Bloomington, Indiana: Indiana University Press, 1998), 218).

78. UNA, S-0656-0003, Folder 7, November 24, 1963, Captain Ibrahim Hamad, Saudi Liaison Officer to Major C.F. Wrede UNYOM liaison officer.

79. Von Horn, *Soldiering for Peace*, 383. In discussion with media during the mission, von Horn claimed that the personnel was near starvation and occasionally survived only on their doses of iron. (Vered, *Hafikhah u-milḥamah be-Teman*, 129).

80. Gaffen, *In the Eye of the Storm*, 83.

81. Mayer, "134 ATU." In Mayer's recollections he compares the gastrointestinal condition in El Arish, known as "Gyppo gut" with that equivalent while serving on UNYOM, claiming that the illness in Yemen was much worse.

82. Doug Poole, "My 115 ATU RCAF Yemen Adventure," accessed March 13, 2016, http://www.115atu.ca/yem.htm. Following the coup, this old palace had been converted into the Liberty Hotel, one of the few hotels in the city 1960s and presumably better than alternative options (UNA, S-0656-0002, Folder 5, June 22, 1963, von Horn to U Thant). The Liberty Hotel, however, could not accommodate the entirety of the UN staff, leaving a group of others to stay at the Viceroy Hotel, also a former palace that had since been converted into an American/European style bed and breakfast. (UNA, S-0656-0002, Folder 5, June 17, 1963, von Horn to Bunche).

83. Gaffen, *In the Eye of the Storm*, 81.

84. UNA, S-0656-0001, Folder 2, January 1, 1964, Gyani to Spinelli.

85. UNA, S-0656-0002, Folder 7, September 30, 1964.

86. UNA, S-0656-0001, Folder 6, January 27, 1964.

87. BM 1721/27, Evelyn Bark's letter from visit to Yemen, July 12, 1964.

88. UNA, S-0656-0001, Folder 6, January 27, 1964. Tuborg refers to the Danish beer company.

89. UNA, S-0656-0001, Folder 6, January 23, 1964, Sana'a to Hodeidah, Vanderboon. Order for increase in whisky rations. The other two examples occurred January 18 and 21.

90. UNA, S-0656-0001, Folder 5, December 24, 1963, from Jizan to Jedda. UN radioman Kenneth Woskett believed that Paulson's request was more of a joke than a serious order. No Rémy Martin was ever received and the notions of receiving a Christmas tree anywhere in Yemen was ridiculous (Interview with Kenneth Woskett, January 8, 2016).

91. UNA, S-0656-0001, Folder 1, December 1, 1963, from Jizan to base (Major Moe).

92. Poole, "My 115 ATU." The blonde Poole referred to was Dorothy Stevens, UNYOM's secretary and "a remarkable Scottish lady who was efficiency and dignity itself but could drink and swear like a trooper when necessity arose" (von Horn, Carl, *Soldiering for Peace*, 329).

93. Interview with Kenneth C. Woskett, January 8, 2016.

94. Mayer,"134 ATU." Mayer added that although he retells several humorous anecdotes, life in Yemen was not all fun and games. The missions were difficult and the conditions were less than ideal . . . but the beer was always in stock.

95. UNA, S-0657-007, Folder 6, April 1964.

96. Poole, "My 115 ATU."

97. Mayer, "134 ATU."

98. Poole, "My 115 ATU." Wing Commander Olsen left Yemen shortly after this episode. (Von Horn, *Soldiering for Peace*, 368). Von Horn's outburst does not differ from military talk in general, but was sufficiently harsh to be noted with surprise by UNYOM personnel.

99. Interview with Kenneth Woskett, July 2, 2015.

100. Poole, "My 115 ATU."

101. Umbach, "134 ATU in Yemen."

102. Poole, "My 115 ATU."

103. UNA, S-0656-0001, Folder 4, November 1, 1963, Samper to Spinelli. The opinion was a reaction to a *Daily Telegraph* editorial.

104. UNA, S-0656-0003, Folder 2, September 11, 1963, Bunche to Gyani. Bunche further elaborated that "UNYOM has no mediation, investigation, inspection functions not directly related to the observation responsibilities."

105. UNA, S-0656-0003, Folder 2, October 2, 1963, Gyani to Bunche.

106. Jones, "UNYOM: The Forgotten Mission."

107. Vered, *Hafikhah u-milḥamah be-Teman*, 87–88.

108. UNA, S-0656-0003, Folder 7, September 24, 1963, Thant to Security Council.

CHAPTER 5

1. Adeed Dawisha, *Arab Nationalism in the Twentieth Century: From Triumph to Despair* (Princeton: Princeton University Press, 2003), 246. The Cairo and Alexandria Summits were photo-ops for Arab "reconciliation" between Egypt, Iraq, Jordan, and Saudi Arabia, creating a massive media spectacle.

2. *Blizhnevostochnyĭ konflikt: iz dokumentov arkhiva vneshneĭ politiki Rossiĭskoĭ Federatsii*, vol. 2 (Moscow: Mezhdunarodnyĭ fond "Demokratiia", 2003), 440–441. AVPRF, Fond 059, Opis 50, Papka 49, Dela 204, List 188–195, Erofeev UAR telegram to USSR Foreign Office, September 13, 1964. Saudi Arabia was clandestinely supporting British-royalist efforts while openly preaching an anti-British rhetoric.

3. Bruce Condé, "British Committee for Relief of Yemeni Wounded Honored by Overprints on Three Air," *Linn's Weekly Stamp News*, March 21, 1966, 10.

4. George de Carvalho, "Yemen's Desert Fox," *Life Magazine*, February 19, 1965,

5. Abdullah bin Ahmad al-Wazir had been declared Imam, albeit only for several weeks, following the 1948 assassination of Imam Yahya.

6. Burrowes, *Historical Dictionary of Yemen*, 19. Members of the third-force established a center for operations in exile in Lebanon that featured members of the al-Wazir clan and another prominent Egyptian-opposition leader Ahmad Jabr al-Afif, who would serve as the Yemeni Education Minister during the 1970s.

7. Ibid., 197. Iryani was nicknamed the "republican Imam" and was given a hero's burial upon his death in 1998. The term *qadi* is both a profession and a hereditary designation. The Iryani family is one of the most prominent *qadi* families in Yemen.

8. Schmidt, *Yemen*, 226. Two suspects were arrested and implicated Egypt in the assassination.

9. Vered, *Hafikhah u-milḥamah be-Teman*, 220.

10. Manfred W. Wenner, "The Civil War in Yemen, 1962–70," in *Stopping the Killing*, ed. Roy Licklider (New York: New York University Press, 1993), 105.

11. Embassy in Yemen to the DOS, April 30, 1965, FRUS, 1964–1968 Vol. XXI, Near East Region; Arabian Peninsula, ed. Nina Howland (Washington DC: GPO, 2000), doc. 369.

12. Alaini, *Fifty Years in Shifting Sands*, 104.

13. Zaid al-Wazir, *Mu'tamar Khamir* (The Khamir Conference) (Beirut: Ittihad al-Gowa al-Sha'biah al-Yamaniah, 1965), 9.

14. Bruce Condé, "Free Yemen's ICY Set Pays Tribute to Saudi Arabian Aid; First of Haradh Rush Series," *Linn's Weekly Stamp News*, June 20, 1966, 33.

15. O'Ballance, *The War in Yemen*, 150.

16. Stanko Guldescu, "Yemen: The War and the Haradh Conference," *The Review of Politics* 28, 1966, 323.

17. Mahmud Adil Ahmad, *Dhikriyat Harb al-Yaman 1962–1967* (Remembrances of the Yemen War) (Cairo: Dar al-Ikwa, 1992), 316–318.

18. Bruce Condé, "Free Yemen's ICY Set Pays Tribute to Saudi Arabian Aid; First of Haradh Rush Series," *Linn's Weekly Stamp News*, June 20, 1966, 33. Condé reported hearing about the shooting and the popular protests on Radio Sana'a.

19. O'Ballance, *The War in Yemen*, 155.

20. al-Salami, *The Tears of Sheba*, 200.

21. IWM, Tony Boyle Papers, Boyle/Johnson—64/89/4, light brown notebook.

22. al-Salami, *The Tears of Sheba*, 201.

23. International Committee of the Red Cross Archives (hereafter ICRC), BAG 229 064-014, Gaillard to Rochat, March 20, 1967.

24. O'Ballance, *The War in Yemen*, 156.

25. Gause, *Saudi-Yemeni Relations*, 69.

26. Schmidt, *Yemen*, 210. Badeeb blamed Yemeni corruption for undermining Saudi-Egyptian peace efforts (Badeeb, *The Saudi-Egyptian Conflict*, 133).

27. Nadav Safran, *Saudi Arabia: The Ceaseless Quest for Security* (Cambridge, MA: Harvard University Press, 1985), 120.

28. Zayd ibn 'Alī Wazīr, *Muḥāwalah li-fahm al-mushkilah al-Yamanīyah* (Beirut: Mu'assasat al-Risālah, 1971), 173. Ferris bases his analysis on a single article from *The Observer* in 1965 (Ferris, Jesse *Nasser's Gamble*, 254).

29. Wenner, "The Civil War in Yemen," 106.

30. Safran, *Saudi Arabia*, 201–202.

31. Alan Hoe, *David Stirling: The Authorized Biography of the Founder of the SAS* (London: Little, Brown and Company, 1992), 388. Stirling estimated that the system would be operational in February 1967.

32. IWM, Neil McLean Files, Box 36, Brown Book, Jan–Jun 1965, McLean's diary of 1965 visit to Yemen. Imam al-Badr's original appeal to the shah of Iran in 1963 was used as leverage to obtain a greater level of support from Saudi Arabia who was reluctant to allow the expansion of Iranian influence on the Peninsula.

33. IWM, Neil McLean Files, Box A, Green Government of Aden File. McLean had this conversation with Prince Muhammad when he returned from Iran in November 1966.

34. Bissell, "Soviet Use of Proxies in the Third World," 97. Iranian involvement was not merely a matter of military aid and supremacy. The religious component, or the Shi'ite network on Iranians and Zaydi Yemenis was of particular concern to the Saudis, who were Sunni.

35. Jones, *Britain and the Yemen Civil*, 219.

36. O'Ballance, *The War in Yemen*, 156.

37. Rory Cormac, *Confronting the Colonies: British Intelligence and Counterinsurgency* (London: Hurst & Company, 2013), 134.

38. Badeau, John S., *The American Approach to the Arab World* (New York: Harper & Row, 1968), 145.

39. Guldescu, "Yemen: The War," 327.

40. *Al Nadwa*, April 7, 1966. *Al Nadwa* was Mecca's official newspaper. Al-Wazir blamed Israel as well for a conspiracy to keep Nasser occupied in Yemen.

41. Adeed Dawisha, "The Soviet Union in the Arab World: The Limits to Superpower Influence," in *The Soviet Union in the Middle East: Policies and Perspectives*, eds. Adeed Dawisha and Karen Dawisha (London: Heinemann Educational Books, 1982), 16. Sana'a and Hodeidah were perfectly situated as a refueling station en route to East Africa (Page, *The USSR and Arabia*).

42. RGANI, Fond 5, Opis 30, Dela 452, List 4, October 3, 1963, Brief Yemeni history written by V. Kornev. Both in response to and in an effort not to be outdone by American efforts to court the Yemeni regime, the Soviet team of technicians undertook the expansion of the Yemeni international airport in Sana'a, a project that was also completed by October.

43. United Nations, *Treaty Series*, vol. 553, 1966, 272–274. Copied in its entirety in Rahmy, *The Egyptian Policy in the Arab World*, 311–313.

44. al-Salami, *The Tears of Sheba*, 201.

45. Donald Chipman, "Admiral Gorshkov and the Soviet Navy," *Air and Space Power Journal*, July–August 1982.

46. S. G. Gorshkov, *The Sea Power of the State* (Annapolis: Naval Institute Press, 1979), 39.

47. Robert G. Patman, *The Soviet Union in the Horn of Africa: The Diplomacy of Intervention and Disengagement* (New York: Cambridge University Press, 1990), 82.

48. Y. Tomilin, "Indiyskiy Okean v agressivnykh planakh imperializma," MEiMO, 8, 1971, 27.

49. Alexei Vassiliev, *Russian Policy in the Middle East: From Messianism to Pragmatism* (Reading: Ithica Press, 1993), 195. Vassiliev also attributes the importance of the Hodeidah port to the anti-British stance in Moscow.

50. *Blizhnevostochnyĭ konflikt* vol. 2, 461. AVPRF, Fond 087, Opis 28, Papka 75, Dela 5, List 71–74, February 23, 1965. Marshal Amer appealed to Gorshkov for an increase in the Egyptian navy size in advance of their meeting in the UAR.

51. Talal Nizaemeddin, *Russia and the Middle East: Towards a New Foreign Policy* (London: Hurst & Company, 1999), 24.

52. Aryeh Yodfat, *Arab Politics in the Soviet Mirror* (Jerusalem: Israel Universities Press, 1973), 13.

53. Guldescu, "Yemen: The War," 325.

54. Muhammad Haykal, *The Sphinx and the Commissar: The Rise and Fall of Soviet Influence in the Middle East* (New York: Harper & Row, 1978), 146–147. Haykal claims this number to be $500 million.

55. Moussa, *al-Ishtirakiya al-Misriya*, 90. Moussa argues that the United States exercised a similar policy of supporting Egypt in order to keep Nasser's army away from the Sinai border with Israel.

56. Stephen Page, *The USSR and Arabia: The development of Soviet policies and attitudes towards the countries of the Arabian peninsula 1955–1970* (London: The Central Asian Research Centre, 1971), 75.

57. Rahmy, *The Egyptian Policy*, 235.

58. Oles M. Smolansky, *The Soviet Union and the Arab East Under Khrushchev* (Cranbury, NJ: Associated University Presses, 1974), 263. Smolansky explains that Sino-Soviet tensions were a major factor in the Soviet decision to maintain a close alliance with Egypt.

59. Alexei Vassiliev, *King Faisal of Saudi Arabia: Personality, Faith and Times* (London: Saqi Books, 2012), 291.

60. RGANI, Fond 5, Opis 30, Dela 452, List 43, June 1964, Brief Yemeni history written by V. Kornev. *Blizhnevostochnyĭ konflikt*: iz dokumentov arkhiva vneshneĭ politiki Rossiĭskoĭ Federatsii, vol. 2 (Moscow: Mezhdunarodnyĭ fond "Demokratiia", 2003), 461. AVPRF, Fond 087, Opis 28, Papka 75, Dela 5, List 71–74, Erofeev memorandum following UAR Vice President Marshal Amer's visit to Yemen, February 23, 1965.

61. Anthony Nutting, *Nasser* (New York: E.P. Dutton & Co., 1972), 350.

62. RGANI, Fond 5, Opis 30, Dela 451, List 75 and 76, March 31, 1964, assessment written by V. V. Kuznetsova.

63. RGANI, Fond 5, Opis 30, Dela 452, List 14–19, June 1964, intelligence report compiled by V. Kornev.

64. RGANI, Fond 5, Opis 30, Dela 452, List 24, June 1964, Intelligence report on Iryani.

65. RGANI, Fond 5, Opis 30, Dela 452, List 20, June 1964, Intelligence report on Makki. Makki also spoke fluent English and Italian.

66. RGANI, Fond 5, Opis 30, Dela 452, List 21, June 1964, Intelligence report on Dafa'i.

67. RGANI, Fond 5, Opis 30, Dela 452, List 22–23, June 1964, Intelligence report on Dobbi. The Soviet intelligence report attributed his early absence from the YAR government to initial hesitancy to join the revolution. He was also married, had four children, and spoke a little bit of English.

68. Oleg Gerasimovich Gerasimov, *Iemenskaia revoliutsiia, 1962–1975: Probl. i suzhdeniia* (Moskva: Nauka, 1979), 43. Among this group were Muhammad Hassan, chief of the presidential bureau, Galeb Ali Sha'ri, the director of the Peoples Court, Ahmad Jalil, head of security in Sana'a, and Abdullah Barakam who also worked in national security. All four served under Dobbi during his time as national security director in Hodeidah and were among the group that accompanied Sallal to Moscow. (RGANI, Fond 5, Opis 30, Dela 452, List 28, June 1964, report on Sallal's trip to Moscow.)

69. RGANI, Fond 5, Opis 30, Dela 452, List 25–6, June 1964, Intelligence report on Ashwal. Ashwal also headed the YAR delegation to the DPRK.

70. RGANI, Fond 5, Opis 30, Dela 452, List 28, June 1964, report on Sallal's trip to Moscow.

71. GARF, Fond 4459, Opis 24, Dela 3084, File 74, October 24, 1964, "Soviet Tourists in Yemen."

72. GARF, Fond 4459, Opis 24, Dela 3084, File 114, November, 1964, TASS-Sana'a. Prior to the concert, the Yemeni minister of information addressed the audience and gave thanks to the USSR for the concert.

73. GARF, Fond 4459, Opis 24, Dela 3084, File 75, October, 1964.

74. GARF, Fond A2306, Opis 75, Dela 3997, File 2, 1964, Education Plan and Construction Plan for Hodeidah.

75. GARF, Fond A2306, Opis 76, Dela 1764, File 32, 1967, report from Hodeidah. The first diesel generators were installed in Sana'a by Italian (1961) and Yugoslav (1963) companies. The Soviet electrification proposal also included plans for an intricate sewer system in Sana'a and Hodeidah.

76. GARF, Fond A2306, Opis 75, Dela 3997, File 11, 1964 Education Plan and Construction Plan for Hodeidah.

77. GARF, Fond A2306, Opis 75, Dela 3997, File 16, 1964, Education Plan and Construction Plan for Hodeidah. Most of the teachers in these schools were Soviet-trained Egyptians.

78. GARF, Fond A2306, Opis 75, Dela 3997, File 7, 1964 Education Plan and Construction Plan for Hodeidah.

79. Richard E. Bissell, "Soviet Use of Proxies in the Third World: The Case of Yemen," *Soviet Studies* vol. XXX (1978), 94.

80. Vassiliev, *Russian Policy in the Middle East*, 196. Oleg Peresypkin made similar observations.

81. Ambassador David G. Newton Oral History, *The Association for Diplomatic Studies and Training Foreign Affairs Oral History Project*, November 1, 2005.

82. Interview with Aldelmo Ruiz, June 25, 2015.

83. Aldelmo Ruiz, "Efforts of US Agency for International Development to Supply Water to People of Yemen," *Journal of the American Water Works Association*, Vol. 58, No. 10 (OCTOBER 1966), pp. 1247–1259.

84. USAID Archives, File PD-AAR-646, John F. Kennedy Water System for Taiz, Yemen Rehabilitation, February 7, 1973.

85. Interview with Aldelmo Ruiz, June 25, 2015.

86. World Health Organization Archives, YES-HSD-002, December 1967 Report. Within a month of Egypt's departure, there was a noticeable drop in national water consumption.

87. Interview with Marjorie Ransom, November 5, 2015.

88. Interview with David Newton, November 5, 2015. As a junior officer in 1966, Newton was instructed to deliver the news to Hariz that he had been declared persona non grata.

89. Interview with Marjorie Ransom, November 5, 2015.

90. Interview with David Newton, November 5, 2015. Newton, who was deputy chief of mission at the time, recalls that the USAID office had a large freezer full of meat that all spoiled when the Egyptians cut the compound's electricity.

91. Interview with Aldelmo Ruiz, June 25, 2015.

92. Marjorie Ransom Oral History, *The Association for Diplomatic Studies and Training Foreign Affairs Oral History Project*, December 18, 2000.

93. James Cortada, *The Yemen Crisis* (Los Angeles, CA: University of California, 1965), 11.

94. Quotes of Senate Foreign Relations Committee. Oct 13, 1965 (LBJ Library, NSF UAR Files, Box 159, Vol. 1, 176a).

95. Johnson, "The Origins of Dissent." The Gruening targeted both Nasser and Indonesian President Sukarno.

96. Warren Bass, *Support Any Friend: Kennedy's Middle East and the Making of the US-Israeli Alliance* (Oxford, UK: Oxford University Press, 2003), 140.

97. Gerges, "The Kennedy Administration and the Egyptian-Saudi Conflict in Yemen."

98. Barrett, *The Great Middle East and the Cold War*, 298. It was clear that Nasser was not involved in either Ba'thist coup.

99. DOS to US Embassy in Saudi Arabia, December 19, 1963, FRUS, Vol. XVIII, doc. 389. LBJ Library, NSF Files of Robert Komer, Box 3, 57, RWK-LBJ, Dec 16, 1963.

100. Douglas Little, "Nasser Delenda East: Lyndon Johnson, the Arabs, and the 1967 War," in *The Foreign Policies of Lyndon Johnson: Beyond Vietnam*, ed. H.W. Brands (College Station, Tex.: Texas A&M University Press, 1999), 152.

101. William J. Burns, *Economic Aid and American Policy Towards Egypt, 1955–1981* (Albany: SUNY Press, 1985), 160.

102. Gamal Abdel Nasser Speech in Port Sa'id on Victory Day celebration, December 23, 1867, accessed January 15, 2013, nasser.bibalex.org/speeches.

103. Burns, *Economic Aid*, 144. By 1962, 99 percent of Egyptian wheat imports were coming from the United States, amounting to 53 percent of Egyptian wheat requirements.

104. RWK-Bundy, April 24, 1964, FRUS, Vol. XXI, doc. 331.

105. LBJ Library, NSF Files of Robert Komer, Box 4, 365, RWK-LBJ. Mar 9, 1964.

106. LBJ Library, NSF Saudi Arabia Files, Box 155, Volume 1, 175, RWK-LBJ. Apr 15, 1965. Komer made this statement only weeks after spending a month in Israel negotiating an agreement with Israeli Prime Minister Levi Eshkol, signed on March 10, 1965, reiterating commitment to Israeli security and territorial integrity in return for an Israeli commitment not to manufacture nuclear weapons (Ami Gluska, *The Israeli Military and the Origins of the 1967 War: Government, Armed Forces, and Defence Policy 1963–1967* (New York: Routledge, 2007), 30).

107. IWM, Neil McLean Papers, Box 20, Brown Book (Diary of visit to Yemen—Jan-May 1965).

108. Michael Oren, *Six Days of War: June 1967 and the Making of the Modern Middle East* (New York: Ballantine Books, 2003), 40.

109. Tewfik Moussa, *Al-Ishtirakiya al-Misriya wal Qadiya al-Falastinia*, 90.

110. Oren, *Six Days of War*, 15. The term "Nasser's Vietnam" may have been coined by David Holden, the Middle East correspondent for the *Guardian* on December 1, 1965 (David Holden, *Farewell to Arabia* (New York: Walker and Company, 1966), 110).

111. Guldescu, *The War and the Haradh Conference*, 326.

112. Embassy Saudi Arabia to DOS, August, 19, 1964, FRUS, Vol. XXI, doc. 344.

113. Summary of UN meeting on Yemen, December 11, 1964, FRUS, Vol. XXI, doc. 356.

114. LBJ Library, Social Files, Bess Abell, Box 15, King Faisal Dinner.

115. CIA Summary: "Nasser's Problems and Prospects in Yemen, February 18, 1965, FRUS, Vol. XXI, Doc. 360.

116. Faisal-Rusk Conversation transcript, June 22, 1966, FRUS, Vol. XXI, doc. 402.

117. LBJ Library, NSF National Intelligence Estimates, Box 6, Folder 36.1, National Intelligence Estimate: UAR, May 19, 1966.

CHAPTER 6

1. McGregor, *A Military History of Modern Egypt*, 263.

2. Richard Price, "A Genealogy of the Chemical Weapons Taboo," *International Organization* Vol. 49, No. 1 (1995): 73–103.

3. *Conference on the Limitation of Armaments* (New York: American Association for International Conciliation, 1922), 387.

4. Barbara Keys, *Reclaiming American Virtue: The Human Rights Revolution of the 1970s* (Cambridge: Harvard University Press, 2014), 14.

5. Richard M. Price, *The Chemical Weapons Taboo* (Ithica: Cornell University Press, 1997), 1.

6. Memorandum from the Secretary of State to the President, August 23, 1962, FRUS 1961–1963, Volume II, Vietnam, 1962, eds. John P. Glennon, David M. Baehler, Charles S. Sampson Document (Washington: GPO, 1990), doc. 270.

7. Seymour M. Hersch, "Poison Gas in Vietnam," *New York Review of Books*, May 9, 1968.

8. John R. Walker, *Britain and dDsarmament: The UK and Nuclear, Biological and Chemical Weapons Arms Control and Programmes, 1956–1975* (Farham: Ashgate, 2012).

9. IWM, Neil McLean Papers, Box 3, Green Folder, Dec 1967.

10. Keys, *Reclaiming American Virtue*, 49.

11. Power, *A Problem from Hell*, Preface.

12. George W. Baer, *Test Case: Italy, Ethiopia, and the League of Nations* (Stanford: Hoover Institution Press, 1976).

13. Joost Hiltermann, *A Poisonous Affair: America, Iraq, and the Gassing of Halabja* (New York: Cambridge University Press, 2007).

14. Kenneth Cmiel, "The Recent History of Human Rights," *The American Historical Review* 109 (2004): 117–135.

15. Jonathan B. Tucker, *War of Nerves: Chemical Warfare from World War I to al-Qaeda* (New York: Pantheon Books, 2006), 191. Price, *The Chemical Weapons Taboo*, 5.

16. TNA: DEFE 55/418/E101. The Egyptian Use of CW Agents in Yemen, July 1967.

17. Richard Beeston, "Nasser's Planes Use Poison Gas," *Daily Telegraph*, July 8, 1963. Richard Beeston, *Looking for Trouble: The Life and Times of a Foreign Correspondent* (London: Brassey's, 1997), 83–84.

18. TNA: DEFE 55/418/E101, The Egyptian Use of CW Agents in Yemen, July 1967. TNA: DEFE 55/418/E1, December 11, 1963. Desmond Stewart, "Whose Poison Gas?," *The Spectator*, July 19, 1963, 5–6.

19. TNA: DEFE 55/418/E35, Raymond A. Titt, Munitions Research Division, "Weapons Fragments from Overseas," July 26, 1963.

20. TNA: WO 188/2058, E.E. Haddon, Director CDEE Porton report November 26, 1963.

21. TNA: DEFE 55/418/E34, July 26, 1963, "Examination of Objects from Overseas." Copy of US analysis of poison gas bomb fragments sent to them by UN on August 23, 1963 (UNA, S-1071-03-10 General Narasimhan letter to UN Geneva, August 2, 1963).

22. Embassy UAR to DOS, July 11, 1963, *FRUS 1961–1963*, Volume XVIII, Near East, 1962–1963, ed. Nina Noring (Washington: Government Printing Office, 1994), doc. 294.

23. JFK Library, NSF, UAR, 6/63–8/63, RWK to Bundy, July 15, 1963.

24. Edwin A. Martini, *Agent Orange: History, Science and the Politics of Uncertainty* (Amherst: University of Massachusetts Press, 2012), ch. 1.

25. USIA to Embassy Vietnam, March 11, 1963, FRUS 1961-1963, Vol. III, January–August 1963, eds. Edward C. Keefer and Louis J. Smith (Washington: GPO, 1991), doc. 55.

26. Central Intelligence Agency, Intelligence Information Cable, "Activities Affection the United Nations: Attitude of Permanent United Nations Representatives to the Vietnam Conference," March 26, 1965.

27. D. Hank Ellison, *Chemical Warfare During the Vietnam War* (London: Routledge, 2011), ch. 2.

28. UNA, S-1071-03-10, U Thant response to William Yates (House of Commons, London), December 4, 1963.

29. UNA, S-1071-03-10, UAR Statement in response to poison gas charges—July 8, 1963.

30. Tom Spacey, "Nasser Poison Gas Attacks—Tories Press for Action," *Evening Standard*, January 30, 1965.

31. IWM, Neil McLean Papers, McLean Yemen (2), Notes on Gas Bombs in Yemen, January 23, 1967.
32. TNA: FCO 8/712/129, W.N. Hillier-Fry, "Mr. Mulley's Address to the Disarmament Committee of the United Nations Association," July 31, 1967.
33. TNA: PREM 13/1625/2, "Poison Gas in Yemen," August 2, 1967.
34. Richard Beeston, "Paris Tests on Gas used in Yemen," *Daily Telegraph*, January 20, 1967.
35. International Red Cross Society—Annual Report 1967 (Geneva, 1968).
36. TNA: FCO 8/710/24, W.P. Cranston (Foreign Office) to Jeddah, February 1, 1967.
37. TNA: FCO 8/710/10, Foreign Office to Beirut and Jeddah, January 30, 1967.
38. TNA: FCO 8/710/37, ICRC Press Release, "The ICRC and Events in Yemen," January 31, 1967.
39. *Humanitarian Citadel*, directed by Frederic Gonseth (Geneva, Switzerland, 2009), DVD.
40. TNA: FCO 8/718/4, F.J. Burlsce, Ministry of Defence to T.F. Brenchley, Foreign Office, February 9, 1967.
41. TNA: FCO 8/718/10, Hillier-Fry, "Gas Masks for Yemen," February 1967.
42. Dana Adams Schmidt, "British Group Sends Gas Masks to Yemenis," *New York Times*, February 28, 1967.
43. TNA: FCO 8/710/41, UAR Use of Gas in the Yemen and Bombing Attacks on Saudi Arabia, Feb 23, 1967.
44. TNA: FCO 8/710/15, UK Mission to NY, January 31, 1967.
45. UNA, S-1071-03-10, U Thant to Baroody, February 18, 1967.
46. TNA: FCO 8/710/41, UAR Use of Gas in the Yemen and Bombing Attacks on Saudi Arabia, Feb 23, 1967.
47. TNA: FCO 8/710/46, UK Mission to UN, February 14, 1967.
48. US-UK Talks on UN Affairs, August 9, 1967, FRUS 1964–1968. Vol. XXI, doc, 101.
49. TNA: FCO 8/710/41, UAR Use of Gas in the Yemen and Bombing Attacks on Saudi Arabia, Feb 23, 1967.
50. TNA: FCO 8/710/32, House of Lords Discussion, February 3, 1967.
51. TNA: FCO 8/713/192, Stephen L. Egerton, August 4, 1967.
52. TNA: FCO 8/710/19, Baghdad to Foreign Office, February 2, 1967.
53. TNA: FCO 8/710/60, D. J. McCarthy, UAR Use of Poison Gas in the Yemen and the International Red Cross, March 6, 1967.
54. TNA: FCO 8/710/60, Peter W. Unwinn, UAR Use of Poison Gas in the Yemen, February 28, 1967.
55. TNA: FCO 8/710/43, MP Patrick Wall (Haltemprice) to Secretary of State for Foreign Affairs, 20 February 1967.
56. "Jamil the Irrepressible," *Time*, December 13, 1971, Vol. 98, Iss. 24.
57. TNA: DEFE 55/418/E99, Jamil Baroody, Saudi representative to UN to UN Secretary General, April 6, 1967.

58. TNA: FCO 8/710/35, House of Lords Discussion, February 7, 1967.

59. TNA: FCO 8/710/51, UN Mission to Foreign Office, Feb 24, 1967.

60. TNA: FCO 8/711/67, Baroody to U Thant, April 1, 1967.

61. TNA: DEFE 55/418/E99, Jamil Baroody, Saudi representative to UN to UN Secretary General, April 6, 1967.

62. TNA: FCO 8/711/109, Report on Poison Gas, July 13, 1967.

63. TNA: FCO 8/711/114, Poison Gas in Yemen, June 29, 1967.

64. Spencer Mawby, "The 'Big Lie' and the 'Great Betrayal': explaining the British collapse in Aden," in *The Cold War in the Middle East: Regional Conflict and the Superpowers, 1967–73*, ed. Nigel J. Ashton (New York, NY, 2007), ch. 8.

65. TNA: FCO 8/711/101, D.J. McCarthy to Brenchley, June 26, 1967.

66. TNA: FCO 8/711/100, W.N. Hillier-Fry to A. Campbell (Minister of Defense), July 3, 1967.

67. TNA: FCO 8/712/146, Foreign Office to Washington, August 2, 1967.

68. TNA: FCO 8/712/133, "Early Day Motion: Gas in the Yemen," August 8, 1967.

69. John Finnley, "US is Disturbed by Yemen Reports of Poison-Gas Use," *New York Times*, July 28, 1967.

70. Embassy Saudi Arabia to DOS, July 23, 1967, *FRUS 1964–1968*. Vol. XXI, doc. 454.

71. DOS to the Mission to the European Office of the United Nations, July 22, 1967, FRUS 1964–1968, Volume XXI, doc. 453.

72. Memorandum of Conversation, June 2, 1967, *FRUS 1964–1968*, Vol. XIX, Arab-Israeli Crisis and War, 1967, ed. Harriet Dashiell Schwar (Washington: GPO, 2004), doc. 130.

73. TNA: FCO 8/712/151, United States is Disturbed by Yemen Reports of Poison-Gas Use, July 28, 1967.

74. Martini, *Agent Orange*, 39.

75. Ellison, *Chemical Warfare During the Vietnam War*, 64, 74.

76. NARA, Agent Orange Litigation Files, Box 184, 1945-63, "Defoliant Operations in Vietnam," Memo, Secretary of State to JFK, November 24, 1961.

77. TNA: FCO 8/713/196, Harold Beeley to P.T. Hayman—"Poison Gas in Yemen," September 5, 1967.

78. Roscoe Drummond, "A Plea to Goldberg—Poison Gas in Yemen," *Washington Post*, August 9, 1967.

79. TNA: PREM 13/1625/2, Foreign Office to UK Mission Washington DC, August 2, 1967.

80. TNA: FCO 8/712/160, Foreign Office to Oslo, August 13, 1967.

81. TNA: FCO 8/712/172, Oslo to Foreign Office, August 16, 1967.

82. TNA: FCO 8/712/171, Copenhagen to Foreign Office, August 16, 1967.

83. TNA: FCO 8/713/201, D. Thomas (UK Delegation to NATO) to D. J. McCarthy, Aden Department Foreign Office, September 16, 1967.

84. TNA: FCO 8/712/130, D.J. McCarthy to Sir R. Beaumont, "Poison Gas in Yemen," August 1, 1967.

85. TNA: FCO 8/713/184, A.B. Urwick (UK Embassy Washington) to Ann Warburton, UN Foreign Office, August 22, 1967.
86. TNA: FCO 8/302/3, Aden to Foreign Office, February 19, 1967.
87. TNA: FCO 8/302/1, C.P. Hope to T.F. Brenchley (Arabian Department), February 1967.
88. TNA: FCO 8/713/195, C.P. Hope (UK mission to UN), August 24, 1967.
89. TNA: FCO 8/712/205, George Brown to Duncan Sandys, September 15, 1967.
90. TNA: FCO 8/713/205, Hayman to Harold Beeley (UK Delegation to the 18 Nation Disarmament Conference), September 17, 1967.
91. TNA: FCO 8/713/202, Brenchley, "Poison Gas in the Yemen," September 22, 1967.
92. TNA: FCO8/713/211, Duncan Sandys to George Brown, September 19, 1967.
93. TNA: FCO8/713/210, George Brown to Duncan Sandys, September 19, 1967.
94. Battle to Rusk, October 3, 1967, FRUS 1964–1968, Vol. XXI, doc. 459.
95. TNA: FCO 8/713/229, Hillier-Fry to Brenchley (Parliamentary Office), November 17, 1967.
96. Neil McLean Papers, IWM. A copy of this magazine is found in McLean's personal papers.
97. For example: Hiltermann, *A Poisonous Affair*; Price, *The Chemical Weapons Taboo*; "The Shadow of Ypres: How a Whole Class of Weaponry Came to Be Seen as Indecent," *The Economist*, August 31, 2013.

CHAPTER 7

1. Spencer Mawby, *British Policy in Aden*. Mawby argues that colonial officials assumed that Aden was far enough on the fringes of the Middle East to make it safe from Arab nationalist subversion.
2. TNA, Foreign Office Memo, DEFE 13/570/49, July 1964.
3. Sections of this chapter were previously published in: Asher Orkaby, "The Yemeni Civil War: The Final British-Egyptian Imperial Battleground," *Middle Eastern Studies* Vol. 51 Is. 2 (2015), 195–207.
4. Eric Marco, *Yemen and the Western World* (London: Hurst, 1968), 27.
5. British Library, R/20/E/1, June 22, 1837.
6. R.J. Gavin, *Aden Under British Rule: 1839–1967* (London: C. Hurst & Company, 1975), 25. The British began warning Muhammad Ali about his expeditions in Arabia as early as 1825 for fear that he would endanger the route to India. Ibrahim's troops entered Yemen in 1831 with the intention of conquering South Arabia.
7. British Library, R/20/E/1, July 6, 1837. Some historical accounts have assumed the wrecked ship to have been an early case of insurance fraud (David Ledger, *Shifting Sands: The British in South Arabia* (London, UK: Peninsular Publishing, 1983), 12). Haines first attempted to negotiate the lease of Aden, but was met with

gun shots. (Zaka Hanna Kour, *The History of Aden, 1839–1872* (London: Frank Cass & Co., 1981), 8–11).

8. British Library, R/20/E/1, March 26, 1838.
9. Ibid.
10. Ibid.
11. Sir Charles Webster, *The Foreign Policy of Palmerston, 1830–1841: Britain, the Liberal Movement and the Eastern Question* (London: G. Bell and Sons, 1951), 275. Written on June 23, 1838.
12. Letitia W. Ufford, *The Pasha: How Mehmet Ali Defied the West, 1839–1841* (London: McFarland & Company, 2007), 85.
13. British Library, R/20/E/1, October 16, 1837.
14. *Parliamentary Papers, House of Commands and Commands.* 1839, Volume XL, 54.
15. TNA, FO 78/373, 101, February 28, 1839.
16. British Library, R/20/E/3, March 27, 1838.
17. British Library, R/20/E/3, May 12, 1838.
18. Pieragostoni, *Britain, Aden, and South Arabia*, 21. Pieragostoni agrees that the occupation of Aden was a check to Ali's expansion in Syria and the Arabian Peninsula. He adds that the geographic location of Aden added a level of importance in protecting the route to India.
19. Elie Kedourie, "Egypt, the Arab State and the Suez Expedition, 1956," in *Imperialism and Nationalism in the Middle East: The Anglo-Egyptian Experience 1882–1982*, ed. Keith M. Wilson. (London: Mansell Publishing Limited, 1983), 123–24.
20. Gamal Abdel Nasser, *The Philosophy of the Revolution* (Cairo: Dar al-Maaref, 1955).
21. Maxime Rodinson, "The Political System," in *Egypt Since the Revolution*, ed. P. J. Vatikiotis (London: George Allen and Unwin, 1968), 87–113.
22. James B. Mayfield, *Rural Politics in Nasser's Egypt: A Quest for Legitimacy* (Austin: University of Texas Press), 1971.
23. Walid Khalidi, "Political Trends in the Fertile Crescent," in *The Middle East in Transition*, ed. Walter Z. Laqueur (New York: F.A. Praeger, 1958).
24. Vatikiotis, *Nasser and his Generation*, 298.
25. Khaled Fahmy, *All the Pasha's Men: Mehmed Ali, His Army, and the Making of Modern Egypt* (Cambridge: Cambridge University Press, 1997).
26. Elie Podeh and Onn Winckler, *Rethinking Nasserism: Revolution and Historical Memory in Modern Egypt* (Gainesville: University of Florida Press, 2004), 2.
27. Podeh and Winckler, *Rethinking Nasserism*, 18.
28. Jonathan Pearson, *Sir Anthony Eden and the Suez Crisis: Reluctant Gamble* (Palgrave Macmillan: London, 2003), 18.
29. Macmillan Papers, Oxford Bodleian Library, MS Macmillan.dep.C.431. November 23, 1955. Julian Amery later served as Minister of Aviation from 1962 to 1964 and was fundamental in orchestrating mercenary operations in Yemen.

30. Xan Fielding, *One Man in His Time: The Life of Lieutenant-Colonel NLD ('Billy') McLean, DSP* (Macmillan: London, 1990), 103. McLean made his first speech fifteen months after first being elected to office. This was indicative of his shadowy style of politics as he preferred the adventurous exploration to the parliamentary debate. (Sue Onslow, "Unreconstructed Nationalists and a Minor Gunboat Operation: Julian Amery, Neil McLean and the Suez Crisis," *Contemporary British History* 20 (2006): 73–99.)

31. Robert Rhodes James, "Eden," In *The Suez-Sinai Crisis 1956: Retrospective and Reappraisal*, eds. Selwyn Ilan Troen and Moshe Shemesh, 100–109 (London: Frank Cass, 1990), 106.

32. *The Times* 28 July, 1956.

33. *Daily Mail* 28 July, 1956. Populist-Conservative newspaper.

34. Pearson, *Sir Anthony Eden*. Pearson combines all of these arguments in his defense of Eden's actions in 1956.

35. Julian Amery, "The Suez Group: A Retrospective on Suez" in *The Suez-Sinai Crisis 1956: Retrospective and Reappraisal*, eds. Selwyn Ilan Troen and Moshe Shemesh, (London: Frank Cass, 1990), 110. Julian Amery met him by chance in Cape Town in January 1953. Although the core group had twenty-six members, there was a total of forty MPs associated with the Suez Group.

36. Jones, *Britain and the Yemen Civil War*, 18.

37. Ibid., 69.

38. Keith Kyle, *Suez: Britain's End of Empire in the Middle East* (London: IB Tauris, 2011), 40.

39. Ibid., 112, 119.

40. Pieragostoni, *Britain, Aden, and South Arabia*, 5. His argument is somewhat overstated in that he does not substantiate the significance of Aden for British global strategy other than the historical coincidence that the war with Nasser took place during the final years of the British Empire.

41. Evelyn Shuckburgh, *Descent to Suez: Diaries 1951–56* (London: W.W. Norton and Company, 1986).

42. Sir Charles Watson, *Winston Churchill: The Struggle for Survival* (New York: Carroll and Graf Publishers, 2006), 735.

43. Pearson, *Sir Anthony Eden*, 140.

44. Kyle, *Suez*, 42.

45. Sue Onslow, "Julian Amery and the Suez Operation," in *Reassessing Suez 1956: New Perspectives on the Crisis and its Aftermath*, ed. Simon C. Smith (Hampshire: Ashgate, 2008), 76.

46. Onslow, "Unrestricted Nationalists and a Minor Gunboat Operation," 73. Onslow, "Julian Amery and the Suez Operation," 70.

47. Harold Macmillan, *The Macmillan Diaries, The Cabinet Years, 1950–1957*, ed. Peter Catterall (Aldershot: Macmillan, 2003).

48. Amery, "The Suez Group," 120.

49. Tom Bower, *The Perfect English Spy: Sir Dick White and the Secret War 1935–90* (London: Heinemann, 1995), 242.

50. Nasser, *Speeches and Press-Interviews*, 306, Address by Nasser on the Occasion of the Seventh Anniversary of Victory Day at Port Said, December 23, 1963.

51. Bodleian Library, Papers of Kennedy Trevaskis, MSS.Brit Emp. S 367, 6/1, October 31, 1962. In 1839, Captain Haines wrote that the tribes surrounding the port of Aden were looking to the British to protect them from the rapid expansion of Muhammad Ali's empire.

52. John Harding, *Roads to Nowhere: A South Arabian Odyssey 1960–1965* (London: Arabian Publishing, 2009), 143. Following the war's outbreak, riots and protests broke out in Aden as the population presumably regretted the September 24 vote. William R. Polk, *The Arab World* (Cambridge: Harvard University Press, 1980), 210.

53. Charles Hepburn Johnston, *The View from Steamer Point: Being an Account of Three Years in Aden* (London: Collins, 1964), 125. Vitaly Naumkin argues that this "shelter" from Pan-Arabism was one of the factors that allowed Marxism to take hold in South Yemen (Vitaly Naumkin, *Red Wolves of Yemen* (Cambridge, UK: The Oleander Press, 2004).

54. TNA. PREM 11/4928, October 14, 1963.

55. Bower, *The Perfect English Spy*, 244.

56. Bower, *The Perfect English Spy*, 249.

57. TNA, J K Watkins to FO, CO1055/3/61, January 23, 1963, for example.

58. TNA, Michael Webb to Julian Amery, DEFE 13/570, August 20, 1963.

59. IWM, Neil McLean Files, Box 20.

60. IWM, Tony Boyle Files, Boyle/Johnson 64/89/3, Green Folder. IWM, Tony Boyle Files, Boyle/Johnson 64/89/7.

61. IWM, Neil McLean Files, Box 6, Green Folder, David Smiley's report on visit to Yemen 7/3–3/4/64.

62. Tony Geraghty, *Black Ops: The Rise of Special Forces in the CIA, the SAS, and Mossad* (New York: Pegasus Books, 2010), 170.

63. IWM, Boyle/Johnson Papers, Box 64/89/5, *The Diaries and Papers of Mark Millhurn*, May 15, 1964.

64. Bodleian Library, Papers of Kennedy Trevaskis, MSS.Brit Emp. S 367, 6/1, March 31, 1964. This statement was made in relation to sending support to royalists through Federation territory. Bodleian Library, Papers of Kennedy Trevaskis, MSS.Brit Emp, S 367, 6/1, October 14, 1963.

65. TNA, Kennedy Trevaskis to Secretary of State for the Colonies, Duncan Sandys, FO 371/174635 BM/1041/64, April 23, 1964.

66. David French, *The British Way in Counter-Insurgency, 1945–1967* (Oxford: Oxford University Press, 2011), 240. The rebels in Radfan, noted for their skill in battle, earned the British nickname "Radfan red wolves" (Naumkin, *Red Wolves of Yemen*, 89.)

67. Jones, *Britain and the Yemen Civil War*. Jones notes that the intelligence from the Aden Group was ignored by the British government, particularly in 1965 when Nasser was weakest. This led to the premature withdrawal announcement by the Labor Government.

68. Harding, *Roads to Nowhere*, 174.

69. Spencer Mawby, "The Clandestine Defence of Empire: British Special Operations in Yemen, 1951–1964," *Intelligence and National Security* 17:3 (2002), 107.

70. Geraghty, *Who Dares Wins*, 66. Geraghty observations are purely speculative.

71. McNamara, *Britain, Nasser and the Balance of Power*, 187.

72. Cormac, *Confronting the Colonies*, 137.

73. Jones, *Britain and the Yemen Civil War*, 53.

74. Bower, *The Perfect English Spy*, 253. Home was replaced by Richard "Rab" Butler. Butler, closely associated with the defeatist (appeasement was the term used during the 1930s) attitude toward Hitler in 1940, seemed eager to pursue a similar policy toward Nasser by opposing any British policy that might anger the Egyptian leader.

75. TNA, PREM 11/4679, 56, April 8, 1964.

76. TNA, FO 371/174636/ BM 1041/17, May 11, 1964, Komer conversation with Eilts (UK-US Embassy).

77. Bower, *The Perfect English Spy*, 252.

78. FRUS, 1964-68, Vol. XXI, doc. 441, Fees exercised a cover as a humanitarian aid worker.

79. Peter Sommerville-Large, *Tribes and Tribulations: A Journey in Republican Yemen* (London: Robert Hale, 1967), 123, 161. American charge d'affaire to Yemen James N. Cortada remarked when hearing Sommerville's story of pro-American royalists: "we can take it ... if the Royalists regard us as allies, it's all to the good—you can't have too many friends."

80. Walker, *Aden Insurgency*, 72.

81. Dresch, *A History of Modern Yemen*, 91.

82. TNA. FO 371 174636. BM1041/130, May 12, 1964. Conversation between Canadian Ambassador Robert Ford and Heikal.

83. Glen Blafour-Paul, *The End of Empire in the Middle East: Britain's Relinquishment of Power in Her Last Three Arab Dependencies* (Cambridge: Cambridge University Press, 1991), 81.

84. Jeffrey R. Macris, *The Politics and Security of the Gulf: Anglo-American Hegemony and the Shaping of a Region* (New York: Routledge, 2010), 133–34.

85. Churchill Archives Centre, Duncan Sandys Papers, 8/16, Julian Amery to Alec Douglas-Home with note on Aden/Yemen problems, 7 May 1964.

86. Johnny Cooper, *One of the Originals: The Story of a Founder Member of the SAS* (London: Pan, 1991), 181. Tony Boyle had written three of those letters hinting at some activities in Yemen. One letter was addressed to Lady Birdwood, the director of the Yemen Relief Committee in Great Britain and Johnny Cooper

regarding the transfer of medical supplies to Yemen, thereby underscoring the Egyptian distrust of the ICRC in Yemen.

87. Jeffrey R. Macris, *The Politics and Security of the Gulf: Anglo-American Hegemony and the Shaping of a Region* (New York: Routledge, 2010), 137.
88. *The Times*, September 29, 1965. Pieragostini quotes this article as well in an effort to justify the British 1966 decision to withdrawal from Aden.
89. Jacob Abadi, "Britain's Abandonment of South Arabia—A Reassessment," *Journal of Third World Studies* vol. 12, no. 1, 1995, 152–80.
90. Jones, *Britain and the Yemen Civil War*, 190.
91. British Petroleum Archives, 28693, A H Dutton, April 15, 1966.
92. British Petroleum Archives, 9910, Middle East General—Aden, D F Mitchell, June 28, 1966. British Petroleum Archives, 9910, Middle East General—Aden, A H Dutton, June 16, 1966. Soviet involvement, however, later called this conclusion into question.
93. British Petroleum Archives, 9910, Middle East General—Aden, A H Dutton, August 16, 1965.
94. Trevaskis, *Shades of Amber*, 189–190.
95. British Petroleum Archives. 28693, A H Dutton, May 6, 1966. Walker, *Aden Insurgency*, 176.
96. Paget, *Last Post: Aden*, 165.
97. TNA, UN HRC, FCO 61/219/3, February 20, 1967.
98. TNA, Baghdad to Foreign Office, FO 371/174627/ BM 1022/62, April 2, 1964.
99. IWM, Tony Boyle Papers, Box 2/7.

CHAPTER 8

1. Portions of this sections were previously published in Asher Orkaby, "The 1964 Israeli Airlift to Yemen and the Expansion of Weapons Diplomacy," *Diplomacy and Statecraft*, Vol. 26 Is. 4 (2015), 659–677. Dorril, *MI6: Inside the Covert World*, 680. Tony Boyle had worked as the aide de camp to Aden Governor Charles Johnston and had the most intimate knowledge of Yemeni terrain amongst the group (John Harding, *Roads to Nowhere: A South Arabian Odyssey 1960–1965* (London: Arabian Publishing, 2009), 174).
2. Hart-Davis, *The War that Never Was*, 138 and 185. Sayyid Ahmad Bin Muhammad Al-Shami, the head of Yemen's delegation in London and Imam al-Badr's Foreign Minister, was the direct contact for the Israeli representatives organizing the mission. Moshe Ronen, *Tehomot u-shehakim* (Tel Aviv: Yedioth Ahronoth, 2013), 180.
3. Aryeh Oz, *Shema' Yisrael* (Tel Aviv: Ofir Publishing, 2011), 130–131. It is not clear how seriously Israeli officials took this offer for recognition, although Herzog makes reference to this in a letter to Julian Amery.
4. Michael Bar-Zohar, *Yaacov Herzog: A Biography* (London: Halban, 2005), 239.

5. Interview with Moshe Bartov, June 30, 2014.

6. Interview with Arieh Oz, June 30, 2014.

7. Interview with Arieh Oz, June 30, 2014. Everyone had a cover story related to a South American airline. They flew to Yemen in civilian clothes that were purchased for them from the UK department store Marks and Spencer by their British counterparts.

8. IWM, Tony Boyle Papers, Box 1.

9. Interview with Shaya Harsit, June 25, 2014.

10. IWM, Tony Boyle Papers, Box 2/7.

11. Hart-Davis, *The War that Never Was*, 150–151.

12. Interview with Arieh Oz, June 30, 2014.

13. Interview with Moshe Bartov, June 30, 2014.

14. "Hamarkiv Hasodi Shel Harotev," *IAF Magazine*, Vol. 180, January 2008.

15. Interview with Arieh Oz, June 30, 2014.

16. IWM: Tony Boyle Papers, Box 1, Notebook.

17. Interview with Moshe Bartov, June 30, 2014. Bartov recalled a crowded Jeddah market which they would have to avoid, but otherwise the flight path was clear.

18. Interview with Yithak Biran, June 26, 2014.

19. IWM Archives, Tony Boyle Papers, Box 2.
    Interview with Nahum Admoni, March 16, 2015.

20. Oz, *Shema' Yisrael*, 144–45.

21. Hart-Davis, *The War that Never Was*, 211. IWM, Tony Boyle Papers, Box 64/89/3.

22. IWM, Tony Boyle Papers, Box 64/89/3, Folder: Leopard, Proposal for Surprise Attack on Egyptian Aircraft in Yemen (1964).

23. Interview with Arieh Oz, June 30, 2014. Oz, *Shema' Yisra'el*, 145.

24. *Israel's Clandestine Diplomacies*, ed. Clive Jones and Tore T. Petersen (London: Hurst & Company, 2013), 114.

25. "The Secret Ingredient of the Sauce," *Israeli Air Force Magazine*, April 4, 2008.

26. IWM, Neil McLean Files, Box 9.

27. IWW, Tony Boyle Paper, Box 1, Notebook.

28. Dorril, *MI6*, 689. Porton Down, the UK Government's military science park determined that the shells contained nothing more than tear gas while the Israeli laboratories found traces of mustard gas. David Smiley believed that the lab results were obscured because government officials wanted to avoid a confrontation over chemical use.

29. TNA, PREM 11/4928, October 7, 1963.

30. TNA, PREM 11/4928, October 7, 1963, Home conversation with Golda Meir.

31. Gluska, *The Israeli Military*, 200.

32. "Political and Security Situation," May 22, 1967, Sitting 176 of the Sixth Knesset, in *Major Knesset Debates 1948–1981*, vol. 4, ed. Netanel Lorch (Lanham, Maryland: University Press of America, 1993), 1561.

33. IWM, Neil McLean Files, Box 3, May 1967. According to McLean, Nasser's blockade of the Gulf of Aqaba in May 1967 was part of the Russian orchestrated plan of turning the Red Sea into an Egyptian "Mare Nostrum" after the British withdrawal from Aden. The parallels between the legitimate fears of Muhammad Ali and Nasser's efforts to dominate the Red Sea are further testament to the similarities between the two eras.

34. Ferris, *Nasser's Gamble*, 268.

35. Muḥammad 'Abd al-Ghanī Jamasī, *Mudhakkirāt al-Jamasī* (*The October war: memoirs of Field Marshal El-Jamasi of Egypt*) (Cairo, Egypt: American University in Cairo Press, 1993), 36. Muhammad Heikal explains that the Egyptian military debacle in Yemen was the cause of Israeli collusion with oil states and companies intent on weakening the Egyptian position in Sinai (Mohamed Heikal, *Secret Channels: The Inside Story of Arab-Israeli Peace Negotiations* (London: Harper Collins Publishers, 1996), 124.

36. Rahmy, *The Egyptian Policy in the Arab World*, 251.

37. Ibid., 252. This opinion was quoted from an interview in *Ros al-Youssef*, Cairo, October 10, 1977, 19.

38. TNA, Foreign Office, FCO 8/840, June 1967. British intelligence records report an estimated 22,000 by the end of June 1967. Some estimates go as high as 30,000 (Huwaydī, Amīn, *Ḥarb 1967: asrār wa khabāyā* (al-Qāhirah: al-Maktab al-Miṣrī al-Ḥadth, 2006), 51) or as low as 20,000 (al-Hadidi, *Shahid ala harb 57–58*, 155). Haddad claims there were 27,000 troops remaining in Yemen (Haddad, *Revolutions and Military Rule*, 286).

39. Ian Black and Benny Morris, *Israel's Secret Wars: A History of Israel's Intelligence Services* (New York: Grove Weidenfeld, 1991), 217. This order was intercepted by Israeli intelligence.

40. Interview with Nahum Admoni, March 16, 2015.

41. Eugene Rogan and Tewfik Aclimandos, "The Yemen War and Egypt's Preparedness," in *The 1967 Arab-Israeli War: Origins and Consequences*, ed. Avi Shlaim and William Roger Louis (Cambridge, UK: Cambridge University Press, 2012), 164.

42. Stanko Guldescu, "War and Peace in Yemen," *Quenn's Quarterly* Vol. 74 Is. 3 (1967).

43. Ferris, *Nasser's Gamble*, 273.

44. Sadat, *In Search of Identity*, 172 and Tariq Habib, *Milaffat thawrat yuliyu: Shahadt 122 min san'ha wa mu'asiriyyha* (Cairo: al-Ahram, 1997), 320. Laura James provides additional sources on Amer's misleading statements (James, *Nasser at War*, 98–99).

45. *Blizhnevostochnyĭ konflikt: iz dokumentov arkhiva vneshneĭ politiki Rossiĭskoĭ Federaṭsii*, vol. 2 (Moscow: Mezhdunarodnyĭ fond "Demokratiia", 2003), 558. AVPRF, Fond 087, Opis 30, Papka 89, Dela 6, List 140–145, Pozhidaev memorandum following meeting with Marshal Amer, May 19, 1967.

46. For example: Chief of Land Forces, 'Abd al-Muhsin Kamil Murtagi (Murtagi, 'Abd al-Muhsin Kamil, *al-Fariq Murtagi yarwi al-haqa'iq* (Cairo: Dar al-Watan al-'Arabi, 1976) and Chief of Operations Lieutenant General Anwar al-Qadi (Oren, Michael, *Six Days of War*, 58). Ferris cites these examples and several others in his discussion of the opinions of Egyptian military officers (Ferris, *Nasser's Gamble*, 285).

47. "Activities of German Scientists in Egypt," March 20, 1963, Sitting 234 of the Fifth Knesset, in *Major Knesset Debates 1948-1981*, vol. 4, ed. Netanel Lorch (Lanham, MD: University Press of America, 1993), 1347.

48. Gluska, *The Israeli Military and the Origins of the 1967 War*, 6.

49. Bar-Zohar, *Ha-Hodesh he-'arokh be-Yoter*, 154.

CHAPTER 9

1. Meir Ossad, "Legal Aspects of the Egyptian Intervention in Yemen," *Israel Law Review* 5, (1970), 225. International law prohibits the use of radio waves to incite the population of another state to violence. The "Voice of Arabs" radio program was in constant violation of this convention even before the September 1962 coup when it called for revolution in Yemen (December 29, 1961) and an overthrow of the imam (April 26, 1962).

2. Kathryn Boals, *Modernization and Intervention: Yemen as a Case Study* (Princeton University, PhD., 1970), 149.

3. AVPRF, Fond 585, Opis 15, Papka 8, Dela 9, File 39, May 30, 1963, news summary.

4. AVPRF, Fond 585, Opis 16, Papka 9, Dela 5, File 51, June 8, 1963, news summary.

5. Edward B. Proud, *The Postal History of Aden & Somaliland Protectorate* (East Sussex, UK: Proud-Bailey Co., 2004). The British colonial authorities in Aden oversaw an alternate set of postal stamps dating from the mid-nineteenth century. Richard R. John, *Spreading the News: The American Postal System from Franklin to Morse* (Cambridge: Harvard University Press, 1998). John explains that beyond the ordinary functions of transferring information and commerce, the postal system has the ability to foster a unified national society out of a loose union of confederate states.

6. "L'affaire «Moslem Today», en 1953 - Bruce Condé, un personnage énigmatique," *L'Hebdo Magazine*, March 29, 2013.

7. Schmidt, *Yemen the Unknown War*, 127–129. Condé communicated with the magazine through several handwritten sheets of paper, because his typewriter was destroyed during airing in transit between Ma'rib and al-Jawf. (Bruce Condé, "Free Yemen PO Carries On, Resumes Operations an West, North and East As Loyalists Repel Rebels In These Areas," *Linn's Weekly Stamp News*, April 15, 1963, 15.

8. IWM, Tony Boyle Papers, Box 2.

9. Interview with Kenneth C. Woskett, August 10, 2015. Woskett, *Puberty at Eighty*, 186. Woskett declined the offer, preferring not to be hunted down by Egyptians.

10. Holden, *Farewell to Arabia*, 83.

11. Bill Richardson, "New Lawrence of Arabia Gallops into Yemen War," *New York Herald Tribune*, June 9, 1964.

12. Yemen was by no means the exception in terms of postal significance in the Middle East. Stamps were used as propaganda in the Arab-Israeli conflict as well (Harvey D. Wolinetz, *Arabic Philatelic Propaganda Against the State of Israel* (Ann Arbor, Michigan: LithoCrafters, 1975).

13. Peter Symes, Murray Hanewich and Keith Street, *The Bank Notes of Yemen* (Canberra: The Authors, 1997), 13.

14. Ibid., 16–17. After 1965, the second set of YAR state emblems differed from the Egyptian version of Saladin's eagle.

15. Ibid., 21. The Egyptians introduced paper notes for three reasons: The imam-era silver coins could often be sold for more than the currency's value. Coinage was heavy to transport and impractical in a modern economy. By exchanging paper bank notes with silver coins, the Egyptians could then use silver riyals to bribe local tribal sheikhs during the civil war.

16. Interview with David Newton, November 5, 2015.

17. Woskett, *Puberty at Eighty*, 172.

18. Bruce Condé, "'Free Yemen' Overprints are First Philatelic Varieties to Come out of Latest Revolution," *Linn's Weekly Stamp News*, December 24, 1962, 10.

19. Bruce Condé, "Free Yemeni Mail Continues; Operations through Territory Held by Red Backed Invaders," *Linn's Weekly Stamp News*, June 17, 1963, 16.

20. Bruce Condé, "Free Yemen POD Carries On, Resumes Operations in West, North and East as Loyalists Repel Rebels in These Areas," *Linn's Weekly Stamp News*, April 1, 1963, 26.

21. Bruce Condé, "Free Yemen's Red Cross Set Has Rough Sledding, Consular Stamp Overprinted as Airmail," *Linn's Weekly Stamp News*, April 6, 1964, 39.

22. Bruce Condé, "Free Yemen's First Definitives in Pictorial Theme Appear in Perf, Imperf, and Sheet Form," *Linn's Weekly Stamp News*, June 8, 1964, 14. The inscription on the bottom of the "Tank" stamp in Arabic and English: "The Free Mutawakkilite Kingdom of Yemen Fights Egyptian Imperialist Agression." The word aggression is misspelled with only one "g," perhaps a testament to Condé's poor editorial skills while working from a dimly lit cave in Yemen.

23. Bruce Condé, "Free Yemen's First Definitives in Pictorial Theme Appear in Perf, Imperf, and Sheet Form," *Linn's Weekly Stamp News*, June 15, 1964, 29.

24. Vered, *Hafikhah u-milḥamah be-Teman*, 41.

25. Bruce Condé, "Story Of Free Yemen's FFH Set in Tragedy of 'Chickens That Stay at Home to Roost'," *Linn's Weekly Stamp News*, October 14, 1963, 28.

26. Bruce Condé, "YAR 'Sallal Coup' Commem Set Includes Map Errors and Soldier Now Back with Imam," *Linn's Weekly Stamp News*, November 15, 1965, 78.

27. *Yemen Stamp and Postal Stationary Index*, accessed on February 25, 2014, http://www.ohmygosh.on.ca/stamps/yemen/ryemen.htm.

28. Andreas Abitz, "A Bundle of Historic Letters Tells Yemen's History," *Gibbons Stamp Monthly*, September 2009, 71–75.

29. Bruce Condé, "Story Of Free Yemen's FFH Set in Tragedy of 'Chickens That Stay at Home to Roost'," *Linn's Weekly Stamp News*, October 14, 1963, 29.

30. Bruce Condé, "Free Yemen's Red Cross Set Has Rough Sledding, Consular Stamp Overprinted as Airmail," *Linn's Weekly Stamp News*, April 20, 1964, 41.

31. Bruce Condé, "Odd Battle of Stamp Orders Punctuates Conflict in Yemen, Philately Safe after Close Call", *Linn's Weekly Stamp News*, February 1, 1965, 36.

32. Bruce Condé, "Loyal Forces Keep Freedom Fire Blazing in Free Yemen; Red Cross Set Late But Is Issued," *Linn's Weekly Stamp News*, December 21, 1964, 6. Delegate General of the Swiss Red Cross and hospital André Rochat was reported to have been delighted with issue of Swiss Hospital stamps.

33. Bruce Condé, "Loyal Forces Keep Freedom Fire Blazing in Free Yemen; Red Cross Set Late But Is Issued," *Linn's Weekly Stamp News*, January 4, 1965, 35.

34. ICRC, BAG 251 016-010, Claude Pilloud, Deputy Director for General Affairs to André Rochat, note regarding Yemen Stamps, November 27, 1964. ICRC, BAG 251 016-014, Pilloud to Rochat, Yemeni Stamps, January 12, 1965.

35. Bruce Condé, "Two Yemen Overprints Honor Valiant British Surgical Team for Services In Battle Area," *Linn's Weekly Stamp News*, April 19, 1965, 14.
   British Red Cross Archives (hereafter BRC), RCC/1/12/4/105 (18/09/10A, Conflict in Yemen, Vol. 1). Wilson-Pepper reported agitation when he was initially barred from venturing far from 'Uqd and was the first to volunteer for battlefield service.

36. Vered, *Hafikhah u-milḥamah be-Teman*, 135.

37. Bruce Condé, "British Committee for Relief of Yemeni Wounded Honored by Overprints on Three Air," *Linn's Weekly Stamp News*, March 21, 1966, 10.

38. Bruce Condé, "Free Yemen's ICY Set Pays Tribute To Saudi Arabian Aid; First of Haradh Rush Series," *Linn's Weekly Stamp News*, June 20, 1966, 32.

39. Bruce Condé, "'Phantom Philately' Sprouts in Free Yemen; Two Singles and Sheet Junked by Officials," *Linn's Weekly Stamp News*, December 28, 1964, 21. The stamps were previously shipped from Lebanon to the Saudi port of Jizan, from where they were shipped to the royalist base of al-Qarah.

40. Bruce Condé, "Yemen Wartime Postal Stationery," *The Arab World Philatelist*, 1978, 22.

41. Bruce Condé, "Odd Battle of Stamp Orders Punctuates Conflict in Yemen, Philately Safe after Close Call," *Linn's Weekly Stamp News*, January 25, 1965, 22.

42. Bruce Condé, "The Matter of Yemen Postal Use Vs. the Stolow Criteria; Detailed Report from Abroad," *Linn's Weekly Stamp News*, June 17, 1968, 1.

43. Interview with David Newton, November 5, 2015.

44. TNA: FO 371/127066, W. Morris, Eastern Department to British Embassy Washington DC, February 27, 1957.

45. Interview with David Newton, November 5, 2015.

46. *Linn's Weekly Stamp News* Archive. Bruce Condé letter to Charles W. Prichett (*Linn's Weekly*), April 24, 1985.

47. Blair Stannard, "Yemen: Booklet Panes," *The Arab World Philatelist* 4 (1979), 35.

48. *Humanitarian Citadel*, directed by Frederic Gonseth, (2009: Lausanne, Switzerland: Frederic Gonseth Productions), DVD.

49. The French Red Cross would later send Drs. Maximilien Recamier and Jean-Pascal Grellety-Bosviel to establish mobile surgical unit. Drs. Wolfgang Schuster, Guido Piderman, Georg Muller, and Edwardo Ermano Leuthold led teams of doctor-nurses to the battlefront throughout the course of the civil war.

50. BRC, Yemen in Conflict, 18/09/10, Vol. 1, Notes on Yemen Civil War and ICRC, February 1964; BRC, RCC/1/12/4/105 (18/09/10A, Conflict in Yemen, Vol. 1), Plummer's letter April 29, 1964.

51. *The ICRC and the Yemen Conflict*, International Committee of the Red Cross (Geneva, 1964).

52. TNA: CO 1055/260, Acting High Commissioner to Monson, 29 August 1964.

53. TNA: FO to Geneva, International Committee of the Red Cross, May 29, 1964. TNA: BM 1721/12, Jeddah to Foreign Office, May 31, 1964

54. *Humanitarian Citadel*, directed by Frederic Gonseth.

55. *Humanitarian Citadel*, directed by Frederic Gonseth.

56. TNA: FCO 8/494/26A—Trevelyan to Denis Allen (FO), June 10, 1967.

57. James D. Young, "Gods Miracles for Yemen," *Royal Service*, December 1966.

58. John D. Hughey, "Yemen," *The Commission*, March 1965.

59. Art Toalstom "Yemen Accepted Doctor's Office," *Baptist Press*, February 21, 1985.

60. International Mission Board (hereafter IMB) archives, Brief History of Jibla Baptist Hospital 1964–1986.

61. IMB Archives, Agreement between Yemen Government and Baptist Charitable Society (February 19, 1966).

62. IMB Archives, Baker J. Cauthen to James Young, December 31, 1964.

63. IMB Archives, June Young letter, December 2, 1971. The letter was written at the behest of the IMB, a fact that June mentions several times.

64. IMB Archives, June Young letter, December 2, 1971.

65. Aldelmo Ruiz, *Reflections: An Engineer's Story* (XLIBRIS, 2013).

66. IMB Archives, J.D. Hughey to Dr. James Young, April 6, 1966.

67. Interview with James D. Young, May 2015.

68. IMB Archives, John D. Hughey, "Hospital in Yemen," *The Commission*.

69. Interview with June Young, May 2015.

70. Interview with Star Good, May 2015.

71. Telegram from the Department of State to the Embassy in Italy, December 14, 1967, FRUS, 1964-1968, Volume XXI, Near East Region, Doc. 467.

72. IMB Archives, June Young, "Let me tell you about Yemen," 1969.

CHAPTER 10

1. Yevgeny Primakov, *Russia and the Arabs: Behind the Scenes in the Middle East from the Cold War to the Present* (New York: Perseus Books Group, 2009), 100. Despite the title, no plans were put into place for an oversight of local Yemeni reconciliation.
2. Rahmy, *The Egyptian Policy*, 195.
3. Ferris, *Nasser's Gamble*, 293.
4. Rahmy, *The Egyptian Policy in the Arab World*, 238–289.
5. George M. Haddad, *Revolutions and Military Rule in the Middle East: The Arab States PT. II: Egypt, the Sudan, Yemen and Libya* (New York: Robert Speller, 1973), 287.
6. Interview with David Newton, November 5, 2015.
7. Schmidt, *Yemen: The Unknown War*, 295. Over the course of five years, the royalist radio station had announced an attack on Sana'a so often that listeners hardly took these claims seriously anymore.
8. "The Siege of San'a," *Time*, December 15, 1967, 53.
9. Andrew McGregor, *A Military History of Modern Egypt: From the Ottoman Conquest to the Ramadan War* (Westport, CT: Praeger Security International, 2006), 264.
10. Dresch, *A History of Modern Yemen*, 114.
11. Ledger, *Shifting Sands*, 215.
12. IWM, Neil McLean Files, Yemen (1)–63/1/21.
13. Primakov, *Russia and the Arabs*, 99.
14. Peter Mangold, *Superpower Intervention in the Middle East* (London: Croom Helm, 1978).
15. Schmidt, *Yemen: The Unknown War*, 296.
16. Bruce Condé, "Yemen Stamp Roundup Sorts Recent 'Crop'; Only Postally Available Material Recognized" in *Linn's Weekly Stamp News*, February 26, 1968, 46.
17. O'Ballance, *The War in the Yemen*, 189–202.
18. Burrowes, *Historical Dictionary of Yemen*, 29–30. Although al-'Amri may have been mentally unstable, he managed to repel the "Sana'a Mutiny" of left-wing factions, ensuring that the emerging republic would remain conservative. After al-'Amri murdered a journalist in 1971, al-Iryani exiled him to Egypt when he died in 1989.
19. Rahmy, *The Egyptian Policy in the Arab World*, 239-240.
20. Badeeb, *The Saudi-Egyptian Conflict*, 86-87.
21. Muhammad Said al-Attar, *Le Sous-Développement Economique et Social du Yemen* (Algiers: Tier Monde, 1964). Al-Attar argues that the presence of a foreign power in Yemen served as a uniting force for the tribes of North Yemen.
22. Fred Halliday, *Revolution and Foreign Policy: The Case of South Yemen, 1967–1987* (Cambridge, UK: Cambridge University Press, 1990), 17.
23. Stephen M. Walt, *The Origins of Alliances* (Ithaca, NY: Cornell University Press, 1990), 1967.

24. Page, *The USSR and Arabia*, 99.

25. Dresch, *A History of Modern Yemen*, 124. Stipends were also given to leaders exiled from South Yemen after the British withdrawal.

26. Bruce D. Porter, *The USSR in Third World Conflicts: Soviet Arms and Diplomacy in Local Wars, 1945–1980* (Cambridge, UK: Cambridge University Press, 1984), 85.

27. *al-Jadid*, November 10, 1967.

28. TNA: FCO 8/494/37, H. Trevelyan (Aden) to FO, November 25, 1967

29. IWM, Boyle/Johnson Papers, Box 64/89/5.

30. IWM, Neil McLean Files, Box Yemen (2).

31. Alan Rush, "Obituary: Bruce Condé," *The Independent*, August 5, 1992. Don Meadows Collection, MS-R001, University of California, Irvine.

32. Alfonso Yorba Collection, Blas Aguilar Adobe, San Juan Capistrano, CA.

33. IWM, Neil McLean Files, Yemen (1)–63/1/21.

34. IWM, Boyle/Johnson Papers, Box 64/89/5, copy of the letter sent to Kerry Stone on May 24, 1967.

35. Ian Clovin, "Rhodesia plane flew Iron Curtain arms to Yemen Royalists," *Daily Telegraph*, February 5, 1970.

36. IWM, Boyle/Johnson Papers, Box 64/89/7. Interview with Nahum Admoni, March 2015.

37. Dan Raviv and Yossi Melman, *Every Spy a Prince: The Complete History of Israel's Intelligence Community* (Boston: Houghton Mifflin, 1990), 149. Prior to being transferred to Yemen, Mizrahi was stationed in Syria where he had been serving as the principal of a foreign language school, before his cover was blown in February 1965 forcing him to flee the country.

38. Nixon Library, NSC 5551, July 17, 1972, Cairo 02818. One of the Yemenis Mizrahi recruited was referred to as Saleh al-Sukkari.

39. Black and Morris, *Israel's Secret Wars*, 269. According to Shmuel Segev, Mizrahi was arrested while the Egyptian authorities were still stationed in Yemen. (Shmuel Segev, *Boded BeDamesek* (Jerusalem: Keter, 1986), 14.

40. Nixon Library, NSC 5551, Harold Saunders to Henry Kissinger, "US involvement in Israeli Spy Case in Yemen," July 17, 1972.

41. Nixon Library, NSC 5551, Tel Aviv Embassy to Department of State, July 17, 1972.

42. Backchannel Message From Secretary of State Kissinger to the Egyptian Presidential Adviser for National Security Affairs (Ismail), November 28, 1973, FRUS, 1969-1976, Vol. XXV, Arab-Israeli Crisis and War 1973, ed. Nina Howland and Craig Daigle (Washington, D.C.: GPO, 2011), doc. 362.

43. Efraim Halevy, *Man in the Shadows: Inside the Middle East Crisis with the Man Who Led the Mossad* (New York: St. Martin's Press, 2006), 198-200. Mizrahi's release was a contentious point in Israeli-Egyptian negotiations, as he was a spy rather than a captured soldier. Zvi Zamir, the director of the mossad in 1974, threatened to resign if Prime Minister Golda Meir did not press the negotiations for Mizrahi's release.

44. Interview with Nahum Admoni, March 16, 2015.

45. Ferris, *Nasser's Gamble*. Ferris argues in his book that the Yemen Civil War played a role in Nasser's downfall and the Egyptian defeat in 1967.

46. TNA, Prendergast (Director of Intelligence) to T. Oates Deputy High Commissioner of Aden, FCO 8/169/78, May 6, 1967. As a reaction to an increased number of FLOSY assassinations in 1967, NLF officials were "increasingly of the opinion that the Egyptians are assisting in keeping interactional tensions alive so as to render impossible any stable government in South Arabia."

47. Gause, *Saudi-Yemeni Relations*, 73.

48. Robert G. Patman, *The Soviet Union in the Horn of Africa: The Diplomacy of Intervention and Disengagement* (New York: Cambridge University Press, 1990), 82. One third of those ships that visited were considered combatants.

49. Patman, *The Soviet Union*, 71. This Soviet ideology was based on Lenin's concept of "Proletarian Internationalism" and the solidarity of the international working class.

50. Adeed Dawisha, "The Soviet Union in the Arab World: The Limits to Superpower Influence," in *The Soviet Union in the Middle East: Policies and Perspectives*, eds. Adeed Dawisha and Karen Dawisha (London: Heinemann Educational Books, 1982), 16.

51. P. Demchenko, 'Khozyaeva yemenshikh got' *Aziya I Afrika segodnya*, 1968.

52. IWM, McLean Files, Box 6, October 1964.

53. Burrowes, *Historical Dictionary of Yemen*, 333–334. Sallal was invited back to Yemen in 1981, where he became an elder statesman until his death in 1994. He was celebrated as a war hero. The first anniversary of Baydani's death in January 2013 was similarly sponsored by the Yemeni embassy and hosted in the Cairo Opera House ("Anniversary of Yemeni Politician's Death to be Marked in Cairo," in *The Cairo Post*, January 3, 2014.

EPILOGUE

1. "Yemen's Forgotten War," *Newsnight*, British Broadcasting Corporation (London, UK: BBC, September 10–11, 2015)

2. Hassan Abu-Taleb, "The State Crisis in Yemen and Libya," Arab Center for Research and Studies, Al-Ahram Foundation, 2015.

3. Portions of this Epilogue have previously been published in Asher Orkaby, "A Passing Generation of Yemeni Politics," *Middle East Brief*, Crown Center for Middle East Studies, Vol. 90 (2015) and Asher Orkaby, "The UN's Yemen Problem: The International Community and an Elusive Peace," *Foreign Affairs*, May 11, 2015.

4. IWM, Neil McLean Files, Box A (Yemen 1960s).

5. Gabriele vom Bruck, *Islam, Memory, and Morality in Yemen: Ruling Families in Transition* (New York: Palgrave Macmillan, 2005).

6. Douglas, *The Free Yemeni Movement*, 162.

7. See Alaini, *Fifty Years in Shifting Sands*. Al-'Ayni served four terms as prime minister from 1962 to 1975, after which he became a career diplomat.

8. Burrowes, "The Famous Forty and Their Companions," 87.

9. Rosser, "Education, Revolt, and Reform in Yemen," 77–78. Al-Sayyid 'Ali al-Saqqaf never returned to Yemen; he worked as a medical librarian at New York Medical College and then at Johns Hopkins University (Burrowes, "The Famous Forty and Their Companions," 89).

10. "The Death of the President of Yemen's Shurah Council," *Al Jazeera*, August 22, 2011.

11. Accessed March 14, 2016, http://www.elbaydany.com.

12. The complete study is available through the Ministry of Higher Education and Scientific Research at http://www.yemen.gov.ye/portal/mohe.

13. Murad Alazzany and Robert Sharp, "Yemen's Brain Drain," *Yemen Times*, August 28, 2014. They report that Yemeni university professors are applying for a sabbatical year abroad and not returning to their positions the following year.

14. Roby Barrett, *Yemen: A Different Political Paradigm in Context* (Tampa: Joint Special Operations University, 2011). According to Barrett, Yemen never existed as a nation-state in the Weberian sense, as it was always forced to share central authority and territorial control with tribes and competing political groups, and had to reckon with foreign influence as well.

15. "Revealed: The Mercenaries Commanding UAE Forces in Yemen," *Middle East Eye* (http://www.middleeasteye.net/news/mercenaries-charge-uae-forces-fighting-yemen-764309832, accessed December 24, 2015.)

16. P. Demchenko, 'Khozyaeva yemenshikh got' *Aziya I Afrika segodnya*, 1968.

Bibliography

BIBLIOGRAPHICAL NOTES

The goal of presenting this international history of the Yemen Civil War is to draw from multiple historical viewpoints and construct a single comprehensive analysis of a landmark conflict. This study uses archives from Britain, Canada, Israel, Russia, Switzerland, the UN, the United States, and Yemen along with the secondary literature from each, in an effort to explain how and why the Yemen Civil War became an arena for global involvement and what the implications were of international participation in the conflict.

When *New York Times* correspondent Dana Adams Schmidt published his book on the Yemen Civil War in 1968, he was justified in referring to the conflict as "the unknown war." Relatively little media attention had been given to this remote region of Arabia. Around the time of Schmidt's book three additional media accounts were published by British, Israeli, and French journalists, collectively providing a thorough chronological description of the war. Since the publication of these four journalistic accounts, other works have focused on various aspects of the conflict such as Saudi-Egyptian rivalry and the history of Saudi-Yemeni relations.

Firsthand accounts and analyses of the final years of British occupation in Aden represent the largest single body of literature on Yemen during the 1960s. There are dozens of memoirs written by former British diplomats, Special Air Services (SAS) members, and colonial officials in Aden, and an equal number of historical studies. Two recent books by Clive Jones and Duff Hart-Davis have focused on the British covert war in Yemen. The collection of books and articles on the end of the British Empire are singularly focused on internal British politics, border wars with Yemeni tribes, and nationalist terrorism in Aden and do not, for the most part, contextualize British policies within an international framework.

Significantly less attention has been devoted to original research on US policy toward the Yemen war, with only a few articles or chapters devoted to Kennedy and

Johnson's policy toward the conflict. Perhaps a reflection of the minimal attention given to Yemen by the US State Department, the Yemen Civil War appears as a footnote or at most a small section in studies of the Arab-Israeli conflict and relations with Nasser. Multiple works in English provide a history of Yemen, covering the civil war from a domestic perspective as a chapter within a larger work without studying the conflict as a topic in its own right.

Literature in Arabic and Russian on the Yemen Civil War is extensive, but lacking in sources and academic analysis. Several Russian books focus on the Yemen Arab Republic, the September 1962 Revolution, and Soviet involvement in South Arabia. Recently declassified documents compiled on Soviet-Egyptian relations from 1957 to 1967, collectively titled "The Near East Conflict," focus mostly on the Arab-Israeli conflict, while devoting only minor attention to events in Yemen.

The great majority of Arabic writing on the civil war was published in Yemen. Dozens of eyewitness and historical accounts provide an interesting local perspective, albeit with few, if any, verifiable sources. Mohsin al-'Ayni and 'Abd al-Rahman al-Baydani, two former YAR prime ministers, published the most organized and well-known recollections of the first decades of the YAR. As is the case with political memoirs generally, the recollections of al-Ayni and al-Baydani are intended to unabashedly whitewash their involvement in the civil war. Yemeni government-financed historical accounts of September 1962 portray the years of the civil war as an idealistic struggle for Yemeni nationalism. For example, from 2003 to 2010, the Yemeni Department of Moral Guidance based in Sana'a released a seven-volume series following a national conference to commemorate the forty-year anniversary of the revolution. The volumes include selected essays, speeches, and original documents. The historic analysis, however, amounts to little more than propaganda for Yemeni nationalism and the idealized life of Yemeni revolutionaries, while the most substantial archival sources in this series are merely translations of documents from the British National Archives.

A significant number of Egyptian war veterans have written historic recollections and assessments of the Egyptian occupation of Yemen. The most well-known among these books, written by Egypt's former chief of intelligence Salah al-Din al-Hadidi and Mahmud 'Adil Ahmad, are used in this book to elucidate elements of Egyptian politics and decision making. The two best overviews and incorporations of these Egyptian memoirs were compiled by Jesse Ferris in his work on Nasser's intervention in Yemen and its impact upon the Egyptian political class, and by Laura James in her book on Nasser's foreign policy. While extensive, Egyptian literature does not venture beyond the immediate confines of military barracks and the political world of Cairo. In addition to these accounts, this book's analysis of Egypt's military strategy is based on captured Egyptian military manuals held at the Intelligence and Terrorism Information Center (ITIC) located at the Gelilot army base in Israel.

Furthermore, this international history of the Yemen Civil War makes use of recently available multinational and multilingual archives which both complement previous accounts of the war and allow for a more comprehensive synthesis of the multitude of perspectives involved. US national archives and the presidential libraries serve a central role in presenting official US government policy in Yemen. The Soviet perspective is based on the Russian Archive of the Foreign Policy of the Russian Federation (AVPRF), Government Archive of the Russian Government (GARF), and the Russian Government Archive of Contemporary History (RGANI). Gleaned from these sources are governmental cables, expert analyses of Yemen, reports of the communist committees operating in Yemen, commentary on news reports, and news briefs.

Given the vantage from Aden and the sheer number of individuals involved in the Yemen conflict, British archives feature prominently in this work. In addition to the plethora of Yemen files in the National Archives at Kew and the nineteenth-century India Office Records accounts of the British landing in Aden at the British Library, this book relies on a number of important collections of personal papers. These include the personal papers of Neil McLean, Tony Boyle, and other mercenaries at the Imperial War Museum; the papers of Julian Amery and Duncan Sandys at the Churchill Archives Centre in Cambridge University; and the papers of Kennedy Trevaskis, Michael Crouch, and other British administrators at the Bodleian Library and Middle East Centre at Oxford.

The role of international organizations featured prominently in the conflict. ICRC records in Geneva elucidate the impact of Rochat and his medical team on events in South Arabia. The UN mission to Yemen 1963-64 has received scant scholarly attention. The analysis of the UN mission in this book makes use of recently declassified UN and Canadian national archives to clarify the historical account of this forgotten mission. Interviews conducted by the author with UN radioman Kenneth Woskett, who was stationed in the region during the civil war, further add to our understanding of the UN mission to Yemen and the dispositions of the mission head Carl von Horn.

In addition to interviews with Woskett, the author has conducted interviews with many other individuals who played a role in the civil war in order to shed light on previously neglected perspectives. Interviews with former Southern Baptist missionaries to Yemen, for example, reveal the backstory behind the establishment of a medical mission to Ta'iz in 1964. The details and significance of Israel's clandestine airlifts to Yemen between 1964 and 1966 were best understood from interviews with the Israeli pilots and navigators who flew these missions. In another instance, the author analyzed dozens of articles written by Bruce Condé in *Linn's Weekly Stamp News*, which were further supplemented by interviews with US diplomatic personnel who were stationed in Yemen during the 1960s in order to add detail to the mysterious story of a homosexual American philatelist in Yemen.

This introduction of new perspectives goes beyond the current accounts of the Yemen Civil War, often still referred to as the "Unknown War," in the both scope of its historical time period and the extent of its archival resources. Through an extensive narrative of international participation in this conflict, it is the intention that

Yemen during the 1960s will no longer remain an obscure and "unknown" conflict. Rather, it will be seen as a significant moment in history with ramifications for the Yemeni state, the Middle East, and the broader international community.

ARCHIVES

Alfonso Yorba Collection, Blas Aguilar Adobe. San Juan Capistrano, CA, USA.

Archive of the Foreign Policy of the Russian Federation (AVPRF). Moscow, Russia.

Bodleian Library, Oxford University. Oxford, UK.

British Library, India Office. London, UK.

British Museum (Captain Rundle Collection). London, UK.

British Petroleum Archives, University of Warwick. Coventry, UK.

British Red Cross Archives. London, UK.

The Churchill Archives Centre, Cambridge University. Cambridge, UK.

Don Meadows Collection. University of California, Irvine. Irvine, CA, USA.

Government Archive of the Russian Government (GARF). Moscow, Russia.

Imperial War Museum Archives. London, UK.

Intelligence and Terrorism Information Center (ITIC). Gelilot, Israel.

International Committee of the Red Cross Archives (ICRC). Geneva, Switzerland.

Israel State Archives (ISA). Jerusalem, Israel.

John Fitzgerald Kennedy Presidential Library. Boston, MA, USA.

Library and Archives Canada (LARC). Ottawa, Canada.

Linn's Weekly Stamp News Archives. Sidney, Ohio, USA.

Lyndon Baines Johnson Presidential Library. Austin, TX, USA.

The Middle East Centre, St. Antony's College. Oxford, UK.

The National Archives (TNA). Kew, Surrey, UK.

National Archives and Records Administration (NARA). College Park, MD, USA.

Republic of Yemen Presidential Archive. Sana'a, Yemen.

Republic of Yemen Military Museum. Sana'a, Yemen.

Richard Milhous Nixon Presidential Library. Yorba Linda, CA, USA.

Russian Government Archive of Contemporary History (RGANI). Moscow, Russia.

Southern Baptist International Mission Board Archive. Richmond, VA, USA.

United Nations Archives. New York, NY, USA.

United National High Commissioner for Refugees Archive (UNHCR). Geneva, Switzerland.

United States Agency for International Development Archive (USAID). Washington DC, USA.

World Health Organization Archives (WHO). Geneva, Switzerland.

Interviews Conducted for this Book

Nahum Admoni, former chief of Mossad and Israeli liaison to Aden Group, March 16, 2015.

Moshe Bartov, Israeli navigator who flew missions to Yemen, June 30, 2014.

Yithak Biran, Israeli pilot who flew missions to Yemen, June 26, 2014.

Star Good, daughter of Reverend Merrell Callaway, who served as part of the Southern Baptist medical mission to Yemen, May 18, 2015.

Shaya Harsit, Israeli navigator who flew missions to Yemen, June 25, 2014.

David Newton, US deputy chief of mission to Yemen during the 1960s, November 5, 2015.

Arieh Oz, Israeli commander on missions to Yemen, June 30, 2014.

Marjorie Ransom, served with USIS in Yemen during 1960s, November 5, 2015.

Aldelmo Ruiz, USAID engineer during the 1960s, June 25, 2015.

Kenneth C. Woskett, chief radioman for UNYOM, August 10, 2015.

James D. Young, head of Southern Baptist medical mission to Yemen, May 20, 2015.

June Young, married to James Young, May 20, 2015.

PUBLISHED COLLECTION OF DOCUMENTS

Arab Political Encyclopedia: Documents and Notes.

Blizhnevostochnyĭ konflikt: iz dokumentov arkhiva vneshneĭ politiki Rossiĭskoĭ Federatsii, vol. 2 (Moscow: Mezhdunarodnyĭ fond "Demokratiia", 2003).

British Parliamentary Papers, House of Commands and Commands, Vol. XL, 1839.

Cairo, Documentation and Research Centre, State Information Services. *Arab Political Encyclopedia: Documents and Notes,* 1962–63.

Canada House of Commons Debates, vol. II, 1963.

Major Knesset Debates, vol. 4, edited by Lorch, Netanel. Lanham. Maryland: University Press of America, 1993.

Macmillan, Harold. *The Macmillan Diaries: The Cabinet Years, 1950–1957,* edited by Peter Catterall. London: Macmillan, 2003.

President Gamal Abdel Nasser's Speeches and Press-Interviews: 1962–1964. Cairo: Information Department, UAR.

Thawrat 26 September 1962 (7 Volumes). Sana'a: Department of Moral Guidance, 2004.

United Nations. *Treaty Series.* Vol. 553, 1966.

United Nations Peacekeeping 1946–1967: Documents and Commentary, Vol. 1: Middle East, edited by Rosalyn Higgins. London: Oxford University Press, 1969.

US Department of State. *Foreign Relations of the United States* (FRUS).

JOURNALS, NEWSPAPERS AND PERIODICALS

The Arab World Philatelist

The Asiatic journal and monthly register for British and foreign India, China and Australasia

Daily Mail

Dallas Star

Der Fischer Weltalmanach

Frankfurter Allgemeine Zeitung
La Gazette
Gibbons Stamp Monthly
The Independent
Israeli Air Force Magazine
Izvestia
Life Magazine
Linn's Weekly Stamp News
Al Nadwa
The New Republic
New York Herald Tribune
The Observer
Pravda
Ruz al-Youssef
Al Thawra (Yemen)
The Times

SECONDARY SOURCES

Abadi, Jacob. "Britain's Abandonment of South Arabia—A Reassessment." *Journal of Third World Studies* 12.1 (1995): 152–180.

Aboul-Enein, Y. "The Egyptian-Yemen War (1962–67): Egyptian Perspectives on Guerilla Warfare." *Infantry* January–February 2004.

Aclimandos, Eugene Rogan and Tewfik. "The Yemen War and Egypt's Preparedness." *The 1967 Arab-Israeli War: Origins and Consequences.* Eds. Avi Shlaim and William Roger Louis. Cambridge, UK: Cambridge University Press, 2012. 149–164.

Ahmad, Mahmud 'Adil. *Dhikrayat Harb al-Yaman, 1962–1967.* Cairo: Maṭba'at al-Ukhuwwah, 1992.

Alaini, Mohsin A. *50 Years in Shifting Sands: Personal Experience in the Building of a Modern State in Yemen.* Beirut, Lebanon: Dar An-Nahar, 2004.

al-'Amri, 'Abdullah. *Tarikh al-Yaman al-Hadith wa-l-mu'asir.* Damascus: Dar al-Fikr, 2001.

al-Attar, Muhammad Sa'id. *Le Sous-Développement Economique et Social du Yemen.* Algiers: Tiers-Monde, 1964.

Al-Haddad, Abdul-Rahman. *Cultural Policy in the Yemen Arab Republic.* Paris: UNESCO, 1982.

Al-Hadidi, Sallah al-Din. *Shāhid 'alá ḥarb al-Yaman.* Cairo: Maktabat Madbūlī, 1984.

Al-Salaimi, Khadija. *The Tears of Sheba: Tales of Survival and Intrigue in Arabia.* Chichester: Wiley, 2003.

Al-Wazir, Zaid. *Muhawalat li-Fahm al-Mashkelah al-Yamaniah* ("An Attempt to Understand the Yemeni Problem"). Beirut: Mu'assasat al-Risālah, 1971.

Al-Wazir, Zaid. *Mu'tamar Khamir* ("The Khamir Conference"). Beirut: Ittihad al-Gowa al-Sha'biah al-Yamaniah, 1965.

Almadhagi, Ahmed Noman Kassim. *Yemen and the United States: A Study of Small Power and Super-state Relationship 1962–1994.* London: I.B. Tauris, 1996.

Amery, Julian. "The Suez Group: A Retrospective on Suez." *The Suez-Sinai Crisis 1956: Retrospective and Reappraisal.* Eds. Selwyn Ilan and Shemesh, Moshe Troen. London: Frank Cass, 1990. 110–126.

Ashton, Nigel J. "Introduction: The Cold War in the Middle East, 1967–73." In *The Cold War in the Middle East: Regional Conflict and the Superpowers, 1963–73,* edited by Nigel Ashton, 1–15. London, UK: Routledge, 2007.

Badeau, John S. *The American Approach to the Arab World.* New York: Harper & Row, 1968.

Badeau, John S. *The Middle East Remembered.* Washington, DC: The Middle East Institute, 1983.

Badeeb, Saeed M. *Saudi-Iranian Relations, 1932–1982.* London: Centre for Arab and Iranian Studies, 1993.

Badeeb, Saeed M. *The Saudi-Egyptian conflict over North Yemen, 1962–1970.* Boulder, CO: Westview Press, 1986.

Baer, George W. *Test Case: Italy, Ethiopia, and the League of Nations.* Stanford: Hoover Institution Press, 1976.

Balch-Lindsay, Dylan and Enterline, Andrew J. "Killing time: The World Politics of Civil War Duration, 1820–1992." *International Studies Quarterly* 44 (2010): 615–642.

Bar-On, Mordechai. "The Generals' 'Revolt': Civil-Military Relations in Israel on the Eve of the Six Day War." *Middle Eastern Studies* 48.1 (2012): 33–50.

Barrett, Roby Carol. *The Greater Middle East and the Cold War: US Foreign Policy Under Eisenhower and Kennedy.* London: IB Tauris, 2007.

Barrett, Roby Carol. *Yemen: A Different Political Paradigm in Context.* Tampa: Joint Special Operations University, 2011.

Bar-Zohar, Michael. *Yaacov Herzog: A Biography.* London: Halban, 2005.

Bass, Warren. *Support Any Friend: Kennedy's Middle East and the Making of the US-Israeli Alliance.* Oxford, UK: Oxford University Press, 2003.

Beeston, Richard. *Looking for Trouble: The Life and Times of a Foreign Correspondent.* London: Brassey's, 1997.

Bidwell, Robin. *The Two Yemens.* Boulder: CO: Westview Press, 1983.

Birgisson, Karl Th. "United Nations Yemen Observation Mission." *The Evolution of Peacekeeping: Case Studies and Comparative Analysis.* Ed. William J. Durch. New York: Henry L. Stimson Center, 1993. 206–218.

Bishku, Michael B. "The Kennedy Administration, the UN, and the Yemen Civil War." *Middle East Policy* 1.4 (1992): 116–128.

Bishop, Peter. "Canada's Policy on the Financing of U.N. Peace-Keeping Operations." *International Journal* 20 (1965): 463–483.

Bissell, Richard E. "Soviet Use of Proxies in the Third World: The Case of Yemen." *Soviet Studies* XXX (1978): 87–106.

Black, Ian and Morris, Benny. *Israel's Secret Wars: A History of Israel's Intelligence Services.* New York: Grove Weidenfeld, 1991.

Blafour-Paul, Glen. *The End of Empire in the Middle East: Britain's Relinquishment of Power in Her Last Three Arab Dependencies.* Cambridge: Cambridge University Press, 1991.

Boals, Kathryn. *Modernization and Intervention: Yemen as a Case Study.* Princeton University, PhD, 1970.

Bower, Tom. *The Perfect English Spy: Sir Dick White and the Secret War 1935–90.* London: Heinemann, 1995.

Burns, William J. *Economic Aid and American Policy Towards Egypt, 1955–1981.* Albany, NY: State University of New York Press, 1985.

Burrowes, Robert D. *Historical Dictionary of Yemen.* Lanham, MD: Scarecrow Press, 1995.

Burrowes, Robert D. "The Famous Forty and their Companions: North Yemen's First-Generation Modernists and Educational Emigrants." *Middle East Journal* 59 (2005).

Carroll, Michael K. *Pearson's Peacekeepers: Canada and the United Nations Emergency Forces, 1956–67.* Vancouver: UBC Press, 2009.

Chipman, Donald. "Admiral Gorshkov and the Soviet Navy." *Air and Space Power Journal* (1982).

Cmiel, Kenneth. "The Recent History of Human Rights," *The American Historical Review* 109 (2004): 117–135.

Colman, Jonathan. *The Foreign Policy of Lyndon B. Johnson: The United States and the World, 1963–69.* Edinburg: Edinburgh University Press, 2010.

Conference on the Limitation of Armaments. New York: American Association for International Conciliation, 1922.

Connelly, Matthew. *A Diplomatic Revolution.* Oxford: Oxford University Press, 2002.

Connelly, Matthew. "Taking Off the Cold War Lens: Visions of North-South Conflict during the Algerian War for Independence." *The American Historical Review* 105 (2000): 739–769.

Cooper, Chester L. *In the Shadows of History: Fifty Years Behind the Scenes of Cold War Diplomacy.* Amherst: Prometheus Books, 2005.

Cooper, Johnny. *One of the Originals: The Story of a Founder Member of the SAS.* London: Pan, 1991.

Cormac, Rory. *Confronting the Colonies: British Intelligence and Counterinsurgency.* London: Hurst & Company, 2013.

Cortada, James. *The Yemen Crisis* (Los Angeles: University of California, 1965).

Crichton, Jack and Anderson, E. J. *The Middle East Connection (Yemen).* Bloomington: Author House, 2003.

Darwin, John. *The End of the British Empire: The Historical Debate.* Oxford: Basil Blackwell, 1991.

Dawisha, Adeed. "Intervention in the Yemen: An Analysis of Egyptian Perceptions and Policies." *Middle East Journal,* vol. 29 (1975), 47–64.

Dawisha, Adeed. *Arab Nationalism in the Twentieth Century: From Triumph to Despair.* Princeton: Princeton University Press, 2003.

Dawisha, Adeed. "The Soviet Union in the Arab World: The Limits to Superpower Influence." In *The Soviet Union in the Middle East: Policies and Perspectives,* edited by Adeed and Karen Dawisha, 18–23. London: Heinemann Educational Books, 1982.

Deffarge, Claude and Troeller, Gordian. *Yemen 62–69, de la Révolution Sauvage à la Trêve des Guerriers.* Paris: R. Laffont, 1969.

Demchenko, Pavel. "Khozyaeva yemenskikh got." *Aziya I Afrika Segodnya* (1968): 100–108.

Dixon, William J. "Third-party Techniques for Preventing Conflict Escalation and Promoting Peaceful Settlement." *International Organization* 50 (1996): 653–681.

Dorril, Stephen. *MI6: Inside the Covert World of Her Majesty's Secret Intelligence Service.* New York: The Free Press, 2000.

Douglas, J. Leigh. *The Free Yemeni Movement 1935–1962.* Beirut, Lebanon: The American University of Beirut, 1987.

Douglas, J. Leigh. "The Free Yemeni Movement: 1935–1962." *Contemporary Yemen: Politics and Historical Background.* Ed. B.R. Pidham. London: Croom Helm, 1984. 34–45.

Dresch, Paul. *A History of Modern Yemen.* Cambridge: Cambridge University Press, 2000.

Dresch, Paul. *Tribes, Government, and History in Yemen.* Oxford: Clarendon Press, 1989.

El-Khalide, Hatem. *Sojourn in a Dreadful Land (Yemen Chronicles).* Pittsburg: Dorrance Publishing, 2011.

Fahmy, Khaled. *All the Pasha's Men: Mehmed Ali, His Army, and the Making of Modern Egypt.* Cambridge: Cambridge University Press, 1997.

Fain, W. Taylor. "'Unfortunate Arabia': The United States, Great Britain and Yemen, 1955-63." *Diplomacy & Statecraft* 12.2 (2001): 125–152.

Fawzi, Muhammad. *Thiwar Yuliyu Yitahaddithun.* Cairo, 1987.

Fearon, James D. and Laitin, David D. "Ethnicity, Insurgency, and Civil War." *American Political Science Review* 97 (2003): 75–90.

Ferris, Jesse. *Nasser's Gamble: How Intervention in Yemen Caused the Six-Day War and the Decline of Egyptian Power.* Princeton: Princeton University Press, 2013.

Fielding, Xan. *One Man in His Time: The Life of Lieutenant-Colonel NLD ('Billy') McLean, DSP.* London: Macmillan, 1990.

Firestone, Bernard J. *The United Nations under U Thant, 1961–1971.* Lanham, Maryland: Scarecrow Press, 2001.

French, David. *The British Way in Counter-Insurgency, 1945–1967*. Oxford: Oxford University Press, 2011.

Gaddis, John Lewis. *The Cold War: A New History*. New York: Penguin Press, 2005.

Gaffen, Fred. *In the Eye of the Storm: A History of Canadian Peacekeeping*. Toronto: Deneau & Wayne Publishers, 1987.

Galkin, Vsevolod Aleksandrovich. *V Iemene; zapiski sovetskogo vracha (In Yemen: A Soviet Doctor's Notes)*. Moscow: Oriental Literature Publishing House, 1963.

Gause, F. Gregory. "Beyond Sectarianism: The New Middle East Cold War." *Brooking Doha Center* 11 (2014).

Gause, F. Gregory. *Saudi-Yemeni Relations: Domestic Structures and Foreign Influence*. New York: Columbia University Press, 1990.

Gavin, R. J. *Aden Under British Rule: 1839–1967*. London: C. Hurst & Company, 1975.

Gazit, Mordechai. *President Kennedy's Policy Towards the Arab States and Israel: Analysis and Documents*. Tel Aviv: Shiloah Center for Middle Eastern and African Studies, 1983.

Geraghty, Tony. *Black Ops: The Rise of Special Forces in the CIA, the SAS, and Mossad*. New York: Pegasus Books, 2010.

Geraghty, Tony. *Who Dares Wins: The Special Air Service, 1950 to the Falklands*. London: Arms and Armour Press, 1980.

Gerasimov, O. G. and L.V. Val'kova, *Noveĭshaia istoriia Iemena, 1917–1982*. Moscow: Izd-vo "Nauka," Glav. red. vostochnoĭ lit-ry, 1984.

Gerasimov, O. G. *Iemenskaia revoliutsiia, 1962–1975*. Moscow: Nauka, 1979.

Gerges, Fawaz A. "The Kennedy Administration and the Egyptian-Saudi Conflict in Yemen: Coopting Arab Nationalism." *Middle East Journal* 49.2 (1995).

Gerges, Fawaz A. *The Superpowers and the Middle East: Regional and International Politics, 1955–1967*. Boulder, CO: Westview, 1994.

Gluska, Ami. *The Israeli Military and the Origins of the 1967 War: Government, Armed Forces, and Defence Policy 1963–1967*. New York: Routledge, 2007.

Golan, Galia. *Soviet Policies in the Middle East from World War Two to Gorbachev*. Cambridge: Cambridge University Press, 1990.

Gorshkov, S. G. *The Sea Power of the State*. Annapolis, Maryland, 1979.

Guldescu, Stanko. "Yemen: The War and the Haradh Conference." *The Review of Politics* 28 (1966).

Haber, Eitan. *ha-Yom tifrots milḥamah: zikhronotav shel Tat-aluf Yiśra'el Li'or, ha-mazkir ha-tseva'i shel rashe ha-memshalah Levi Eshkol ve-Goldah Me'ir*. Tel Aviv: Edanim: Sifre Yedi'ot aḥaronot, 1987.

Habib, Tariq. *Milaffat thawrat yuliyu shahadat 122 min sunnaiha wa-maasiriha*. Cairo: Al Ahram, 1997.

Haddad, George M. *Revolution and Military Rule in the Middle East: The Arab States*. Vol. III Pt. 2: Egypt, The Sudan, Yemen and Libya. New York: Speller, 1973.

Halevy, Efraim. *Man in the Shadows: Inside the Middle East Crisis with the Man Who Led the Mossad*. New York: St. Martin's Press, 2006.

Halliday, Fred. *Arabia Without Sultans*. London: Saqi Books, 2002.

Halliday, Fred. "The Middle East and the Great Powers." In *The Cold War and the Middle East*, edited by Avi Shlaim and Yezid Sayigh, 6–26. Oxford: Clarendon Press, 1997.

Halliday, Fred. *Revolution and Foreign Policy: The Case of South Yemen, 1967–1987*. Cambridge, UK: Cambridge University Press, 1990.

Hansen, Bent. *The Political Economy of Poverty, Equity, and Growth: Egypt and Turkey*. Washington, DC: Oxford University Press, 1991.

Harding, John. *Roads to Nowhere: A South Arabian Odyssey 1960–1965*. London: Arabian Publishing, 2009.

Harris, Robin. *The Conservatives—A History*. London: Bantam, 2011.

Hart, Parker T. *Saudi Arabia and the United States: Birth of a Security Partnership*. Bloomington: Indiana University Press, 1998.

Hart-Davis, Duff. *The War that Never Was: The True Story of the Men Who Fought Britain's Most Secret Battle*. London: Arrow, 2012.

Haykal, Muhammad. *The Sphinx and the Commissar: The Rise and Fall of Soviet Influence in the Middle East*. New York: Harper & Row, 1978.

Hewitt, John. "First footsteps in Yemen, 1947." *The British-Yemeni Society* (2005).

Hiltermann, Joost. *A Poisonous Affair: America, Iraq, and the Gassing of Halabja*. New York: Cambridge University Press, 2007.

Hofstadter, Dan, ed. *Egypt & Nasser 1956–1966*. Vol. 2. New York: Facts on File, Inc., 1973.

Holden, David. *Farewell to Arabia*. New York: Walker and Company, 1966.

Humanitarian Citadel, directed by Frederic Gonseth (Geneva, Switzerland, 2009), DVD.

Ingrams, Harold. *The Yemen: Imams, Rulers, & Revolutions*. London: John Murray, 1963.

Jamasī, Muḥammad 'Abd al-Ghanī. *Mudhakkirāt al-Jamasī (The October war: memoirs of Field Marshal El-Jamasi of Egypt)*. Cairo, Egypt: American University in Cairo Press, 1993.

James, Alan. *Peacekeeping in International Politics*. London: MacMillan, 1990.

James, Laura M. *Nasser at War: Arab Images of the Enemy*. New York: Palgrave Macmillan, 2006.

James, Robert Rhodes. "Eden." *The Suez-Sinai Crisis 1956: Retrospective and Reappraisal*. Ed. Selwyn Ilan Troen and Moshe Shemesh. London: Frank Cass, 1990. 100–109.

John, Richard R. *Spreading the News: The American Postal System from Franklin to Morse*. Cambridge: Harvard University Press, 1998.

Johnson, Robert. "The Origins of Dissent: Senate Liberals and Southeast Asia, 1959–1964." *Pacific Historical Review* 65 (1996): 249–275.

Johnston, Charles. *The View from Steamers Point: Being an Account of Three Years in Aden*. London: Collins, 1964.

Jones, Clive and Tore T. Petersen, *Israel's Clandestine Diplomacies*. London: Hurst & Company, 2013.

Jones, Clive. *Britain and the Yemen Civil War, 1962–1965: Ministers, Mercenaries, and Mandarins: Foreign Policy and the Limits of Covert Action*. Brighton, UK: Sussex Academic Press, 2004.

Jones, Frank Leith. *Blowtorch: Robert Komer, Vietnam, and American Cold War Strategy*. Annapolis, Maryland: Naval Institute Press, 2013.

Jones, Peter. "UNYOM: The Forgotten Mission." *Canadian Defence Review Quarterly* 22 (1992): 18–22.

Kedourie, Elie. "Egypt, the Arab State and the Suez Expedition, 1956." Wilson, Keith M. *Imperialism and Nationalism in the Middle East: The Anglo-Egyptian Experience 1882–1982*. London: Mansell Publishing Limited, 1983. 123–124.

Kerr, Malcolm. *The Arab Cold War: Gamal 'Abd Al-Nasir and his Rivals—1958–1970*. London: Oxford University Press, 1971.

Keys, Barbara. *Reclaiming American Virtue: The Human Rights Revolution of the 1970s*. Cambridge: Harvard University Press, 2014.

Khalidi, Rashid. *Sowing Crisis: The Cold War and American Dominance in the Middle East*. Boston: Beacon Press, 2009.

Khalidi, Walid. "Political Trends in the Fertile Crescent." *The Middle East in Transition*. Ed. Walter Z. Laqueur. New York: F.A. Praeger, 1958. 121–128.

Khashan, Hilal. "The New Arab Cold War." *World Affairs* (1997): 158–169.

King, Gillian. *Imperial Outpost—Aden: Its Place in British Strategic Policy*. London: Oxford University Press, 1964.

Kingston, William Henry G. *Our Sailors: Anecdotes of the British Navy During the Reign of Queen Victoria*. Charleston: Nabu Press, 2010.

Kotlov, Lev Nikolaevich. *Īemenskaīa Arabskaīa Respublika*. Moscow: Nauka, 1971.

Kour, Zaka Hanna. *The History of Aden, 1839-1872*. London: Frank Cass & Co., 1981.

Kyle, Keith. *Suez: Britain's End of Empire in the Middle East*. London: IB Tauris, 2011.

Lacey, Robert. *The Kingdom: Arabia and the House of Saud*. New York: Avon Books, 1981.

Lackner, Helen. *PDR Yemen: Outpost of Socialist Development in Arabia*. London: Ithaca Press, 1985.

Latham, Michael E. "The Cold War in the Third World, 1963–1975." *Cambridge History of the Cold War*. Ed. Melvyn P. Leffler and Odd Arne Westad. Cambridge: Cambridge University Press, 2010. 258–280.

Lefebvre, Jeffrey A. "Middle East Conflicts and Middle Level Power Intervention in the Horn of Africa." *Middle East Journal* 50 (1996): 387–404.

Lerner, Daniel. *The Passing of Traditional Society: Modernizing the Middle East*. Glencoe: The Free Press, 1958.

Little, Douglas. "Nasser Delenda East: Lyndon Johnson, the Arabs, and the 1967 War." *The Foreign Policies of Lyndon Johnson: Beyond Vietnam.* Ed. H.W. Brands. College Station, TX: Texas A&M University Press, 1999. 140–155.

Little, Douglas. "The Cold War in the Middle East: Suez Crisis to Camp David Accords." Ed. Melvyn P. Leffler and Odd Arne Westad. Cambridge: Cambridge University Press, 2010. 305–326.

Little, Douglas. "The New Frontier on the Nile: JFK, Nasser, and Arab Nationalism." *Journal of American History* 75.2 (1988): 501–527.

Livingstone, Ann G. "Canada's policy and attitudes towards United Nations Peacekeeping, 1956–1964." PhD diss. 1995.

Luqman, Muhammad Ali and Faruq Muhammad Luqman. *Qissat al-Thawra al-Yamaniyya.* Aden: Dar Fatat al-Jazira, 1997.

Macris, Jeffrey R. *The Politics and Security of the Gulf: Anglo-American Hegemony and the Shaping of a Region.* New York: Routledge, 2010.

Macro, Eric. *Yemen and the Western World.* London: C. Hurst & Co., 1968.

Manela, Erez. "A Pox on Your Narrative: Writing Disease Control into Cold War History." *Diplomatic History* 34:2 (2010): 299–323.

Mangold, Peter. *Superpower Intervention in the Middle East.* London: Croom Helm, 1978.

Marco, Eric. *Yemen and the Western World.* London: Hurst, 1968.

Mawby, Spencer. *British Policy in Aden and the Protectorates, 1955–67: Last Outpost of a Middle East Empire.* London: Routledge, 2005.

Mawby, Spencer. "The Clandestine Defence of Empire: British Special Operations in Yemen, 1951–1964." *Intelligence and National Security* 17.3 (2002).

Mayer, George E. "Royal Canadian Air Force in UN Operations." 24 June 2013. *134 ATU.* <www.134atu.ca>.

Mayfield, James B. *Rural Politics in Nasser's Egypt: A Quest for Legitimacy.* Austin: University of Texas Press, 1971.

McGregor, Andrew. *A Military History of Modern Egypt: From the Ottoman Conquest to the Ramadan War.* Westport, CT: Praeger Security International, 2006.

McLane, Charles B. *Soviet-Middle East Relations.* London: Central Asian Research Centre, 1973.

McMullen, Christopher. *Resolution of the Yemen Crisis, 1963: A Case Study in Mediation.* Washington DC: Institute for the Study of Diplomacy School of Foreign Service Georgetown University, 1980.

McNamara, Robert. *Britain, Nasser, and the Balance of Power in the Middle East, 1952–1967: From the Egyptian Revolution to the Six Day War.* London: Frank Cass, 2003.

Mitty, David M. "A Regular Army in Counterinsurgency Operations: Egypt in North Yemen, 1962–1967." *The Journal of Military History* 65 (2001).

Moussa, Tewfik. *al-Ishtirakiya al-Misriya wal Qadiya al-Falastiniya* (Egyptian Socialism and the Palestinian Question). 1966.

Muḥrizī, Ṣalāḥ al-Dīn. *al-Ṣamt al-ḥāʾir wa-thawrat al-Yaman.* Cairo, 1998.

Murtagi, 'Abd al-Muhsin Kamil. *al-Fariq Murtagi yarwi al-haqa'iq.* Cairo: Dar al-Watan al-'Arabi, 1976.

Narasimhan, C. V. *Regionalism in the United Nations.* Nbagdew York: Asia Publishing House, 1977.

Nasser, Gamal Abdel. *The National Chater.* Cairo: Information Department, 1962.

Nasser, Gamal Abdel. *The Philosophy of the Revolution.* Cairo: Dar al-Maaref, 1955.

Nasser, Gamal Abdel. *Speeches and Press-Interviews, January–December 1963.* Cairo: UAR Information Department, 1955.

Nizaemeddin, Talal. *Russia and the Middle East: Towards a New Foreign Policy.* London: Hurst & Company, 1999.

Nutting, Anthony. *Nasser.* New York: E.P. Dutton & Co., 1972.

O'Ballance, Edgar. *The War in Yemen.* Hamden, CT: Archon Books, 1971.

O'Kelly, Sebastian. *Amedeo: The True Story of an Italian's War in Abyssinia.* London: Harper Collins, 2002.

Onslow, Sue. "Julian Amery and the Suez Operation." *Reassessing Suez 1956: New Perspectives on the Crisis and its Aftermath.* Ed. Simon C. Smith. Hampshire: Ashgate, 2008. 67–78.

Onslow, Sue. "Unreconstructed Nationalists and a Minor Gunboat Operation: Julian Amery, Neil McLean and the Suez Crisis." *Contemporary British History* 20 (2006): 73–99.

Oren, Michael. *Six Days of War: June 1967 and the Making of the Modern Middle East.* New York: Ballantine Books, 2003.

Orkaby, Asher. "The 1964 Israeli Airlift to Yemen and the Expansion of Weapons Diplomacy," *Diplomacy and Statecraft,* Vol. 26 Is. 4 (2015), 659–677.

Orkaby, Asher. "A Passing Generation of Yemeni Politics," *Middle East Brief,* Crown Center for Middle East Studies, Vol. 90 (2015).

Orkaby, Asher. "The Yemeni Civil War: The Final British-Egyptian Imperial Battleground," *Middle Eastern Studies* Vol. 51 Is. 2 (2015), 195–207.

Ossad, Meir. "Legal Aspects of the Egyptian Intervention in Yemen." *Israel Law Review* 5 (1970): 216–248.

Page, Stephen. *The Soviet Union and the Yemens: Influence in Asymmetrical Relationships.* New York: Praeger Special Studies, 1985.

Page, Stephen. *The USSR and Arabia: The Development of Soviet Policies and Attitudes Towards the Countries of the Arabian Peninsula 1955–1970.* London: The Central Asian Research Centre, 1971.

Paget, Julian. *Last Post: Aden 1964–1967.* London: Faber and Faber, 1969.

Patman, Robert G. *The Soviet Union in the Horn of Africa: The Diplomacy of Intervention and Disengagement.* New York: Cambridge University Press, 1990.

Pearson, Jonathan. *Sir Anthony Eden and the Suez Crisis: Reluctant Gamble.* London: Palgrave Macmillan, 2003.

Peterson, John E. *Yemen: The Search for a Modern State.* London: Croom Helm, 1982.

Peterson, Tore T. "Post-Suez Consequences: Anglo-American Relations in the Middle East from Eisenhower to Nixon." *Reassessing Suez 1956: New Perspectives on the Crisis and its Aftermath.* Ed. Simon C. Smith. Hampshire: Ashgate, 2008. 215–226.

Peterson, Tore T. *The Decline of the Anglo-American Middle East, 1961–1969.* Brighton, UK: Sussex Academic Press, 2006.

Pieragostoni, Karl. *Britain, Aden, and South Arabia: Abandoning Empire.* New York: Macmillan, 1991.

Podeh, Eli. "Suez in Reverse: The Arab response to the Iraqi Bid for Kuwait." *Diplomacy and Statecraft* 14.1 (2010): 103–130.

Podeh, Elie and Winckler, Onn. *Rethinking Nasserism: Revolution and Historical Memory in Modern Egypt.* Gainesville: University of Florida Press, 2004.

Polk, William R. *The Arab World.* Cambridge: Harvard University Press, 1980.

Poole, Doug. "115 ATU RCAF Yemen Adventure." 24 June 2013. *Royal Canadian Air Force in UN Operations.* <www.115atu.ca/yem.htm>.

Porter, Bruce D. *The USSR in Third World Conflicts: Soviet arms and Diplomacy in Local Wars, 1945–1980.* Cambridge, UK: Cambridge University Press, 1984.

Powers, Thomas. *The Man Who Kept the Secrets: Richard Helms and the CIA.* New York: Alfred A. Knopf, 1979.

Pratt, R.W. *The Postal History of British Aden (1839-1967).* East Sussex, UK: Proud-Bailey, Co., 1985.

Price, Richard M. *The Chemical Weapons Taboo.* Ithica: Cornell University Press, 1997.

Price, Richard M. "A Genealogy of the Chemical Weapons Taboo," *International Organization* Vol. 49, No. 1 (1995): 73–103.

Pridham, B.R., ed. *Contemporary Yemen: Politics and Historical Background.* London: Croom Helm, 1984.

Primakov, Yevgeny. *Russia and the Arabs: Behind the Scenes in the Middle East from the Cold War to the Present.* New York: Perseus Books Group, 2009.

Proud, Edward B. *The Postal History of Aden & Somalialand Protectorate.* East Sussex, UK: Proud-Bailey Co., 2004.

Rahmy, Ali Abdel Rahman. *The Egyptian Policy in the Arab World: Intervention in Yemen 1962–1967 Case Study.* Washington, DC: University Press of America, 1983.

Rakove, Robert B. *Kennedy Johnson and the Nonaligned Movement.* New York: Cambridge University Press, 2013.

Raviv, Dan and Melman, Yossi. *Every Spy a Prince: The Complete History of Israel's Intelligence Community.* Boston: Houghton Mifflin, 1990.

Regan, Patrick M. and Aydin, Aysegul. "Diplomacy and Other Forms of Intervention in Civil Wars." *The Journal of Conflicts Resolution* 50 (2006): 736–756.

Regan, Patrick M. and Noron, Daniel. "Greed, Grievance, and Mobilization in Civil Wars." *Journal of Conflict Resolution* 49 (2005): 319–336.

Regan, Patrick. "Third Party Interventions and the Duration of Intrastate Conflicts." *Journal of Conflict Resolution* 46 (2002): 55–73.

Roberts, John. "The Saudi-Yemeni Boundary Treaty." *IBRU Boundary and Security Bulletin* (2000).

Robertson, Mark. "Twentieth Century Conflict in the Fourteenth Century: Intervention in Yemen." *The Fletcher Forum*. Winter 1989. 95–111.

Rochat, André. *L'homme á la Croix: une anticroisade*. Geneva: Editions de l'Aire, 2005.

Rodinson, Maxime. "The Political System." Vatikiotis, P. J. *Egypt Since the Revolution*. London: George Allen and Unwin, 1968. 87–113.

Ronen, Moshe. *Tehomot u-shehakim*. Tel Aviv: Yedioth Ahronoth, 2013.

Rosser, Kevin. *Education, Revolt, and Reform in Yemen: The 'Famous Forty' Mission of 1947*. M.Phil diss. St. Antony's College. Oxford, 1998.

Ruiz, Aldelmo. "Efforts of US Agency for International Development to Supply Water to People of Yemen," *Journal of the American Water Works Association*, Vol. 58, No. 10 (1966), 1247–1259.

Ruiz, Aldelmo. *Reflections: An Engineer's Story* (XLIBRIS, 2013).

Ryan, Curtis. "The New Arab Cold War and the Struggle for Syria." *Middle East Report* 271 (2014).

Sadat, Anwar. *In Search of Identity: an Autobiography*. New York: Harper Row, 1978.

Safran, Nadav. *Saudi Arabia: The Ceaseless Quest for Security*. Cambridge, MA: Harvard University Press, 1985.

Sakharov, Vladimir and Umberto Tosi. *High Treason*. New York: G. P. Putnam's Sons, 1980.

Sayigh, Yezid and Avi Shlaim. "Introduction." In *The Cold War and the Middle East*, edited by Avi Shlaim and Yezid Sayigh, 1–5. Oxford: Clarendon Press, 1997.

Schaffer, Howard B. *Ellsworth Bunker: Global Troubleshooter, Vietnam Warhawk*. Chapel Hill: University of North Carolina Press, 2003.

Schmidt, Dana Adams. "The Civil War in Yemen." In *The International Regulation of Civil Wars*, edited by Evan Luard. London: Thames and Hudson, 1972.

Schmidt, Dana Adams. *Yemen: The Unknown War*. London: Bodley Head, 1968.

Segev, Shmuel. *Boded Be Damesek*. Jerusalem: Keter, 1986.

Shahari, Muhammad Ali. *'Abd al-Nasirwa-thawrat al-Yaman*. Cairo: Maktabat Madbuli, 1976.

Shahari, Muhammad Ali. *Tarīq al-thawrah wa-al-wahdah al-Yamanīyah*. Beirut, Lebanon: Dar al-Farabi, 1987.

Sharaf, Sami. *Sanawat wa-ayyam ma'a Gamal Abdel Nasser: shahadat Sama Sharaf*. Cairo, Egypt: Dār al-Fursān lil-Nashr, 2005.

Shoham, Dany. "The Evolution of Chemical and Biological Weapons in Egypt." Policy Paper. 1998.

Shu'aybī, Muhammad. *Mu'tamar Harad wa-muhāwalāt al-salām bi-al-Yaman*. Damascus: Matba'at Dār al-Kitāb, 1980.

Shuckburgh, Evelyn. *Descent to Suez: Diaries 1951-56*. London: W.W. Norton and Company, 1986.

Smiley, David. *Arabian Assignment*. London: Cooper, 1975.

Sommerville-Large, Peter. *Tribes and Tribulations: A Journey in Republican Yemen.* London: Robert Hale, 1967.

Stookey, Robert. *America and the Arab States: An Uneasy Encounter.* New York: Wiley, 1975.

Stookey, Robert W. *Yemen: The Politics of the Yemen Arab Republic.* Boulder, CO: Westview Press, 1978.

Symes, Peter, Murray Hanewich and Keith Street. *The Bank Notes of Yemen.* Canberra: The Authors, 1997.

Taylor, Alan R. *The Superpowers and the Middle East.* Syracuse: Syracuse University Press, 1991.

Terrill, W. Andrew. "The Chemical Warfare Legacy of the Yemen War." *Comparative Strategy* 4 (1991): 109–121.

Tomilin, Y. "Indiyskiy Okean v agressivnykh planakh imperializma." *MEiMO* 8 (1971).

Tucker, Jonathan B. *War of Nerves: Chemical Warfare from World War I to al-Qaeda.* New York: Pantheon Books, 2006.

Trevaskis, Kennedy. *Shades of Amber: A South Arabian Episode.* London: Hutchinson & Co, 1968.

Ufford, Letitia W. *The Pasha: How Mehmet Ali Defied the West, 1839–1841.* London: McFarland & Company, 2007.

Umback, Ian. "Royal Canadian Air Force in UN Operations." 2013. *134 ATU in Yemen.* <www.115atu.ca/yem.htm>.

Urquhart, Brian. *A Life in Peace and War.* New York: Harper and Row, 1987.

Urquhart, Brian. *Ralph Bunche: An American Life.* New York: W.W. Norton, 1993.

Valbjorn, Morten and Andre Bank. "The New Arab Cold War: rediscovering the Arab dimension of Middle East regional politics." *Review of International Studies* (2012): 3–24.

Vassiliev, Alexei. *King Faisal of Saudi Arabia: Personality, Faith and Times.* London: Saqi Books, 2012.

Vatikiotis, P. J. "The Soviet Union and Egypt: The Nasser Years." *The Soviet Union and the Middle East: the Post-World War II Era.* Ed. Lederer, Ivo J. and Vucinich, Wayne S.. Stanford: Hoover Institute Press, 1974.

Vatikiotis, P. J. *Nasser and His Generation.* New York: Croom Helm, 1978.

Vered, Yael. *Hafikhah u-milhamah be-Teman (Coup and War in Yemen).* Tel Aviv: Am 'oved, 1967.

Vladimirov, Leonid Sergeevich. *Maīak druzhby: port Akhmedi, Īemen.* Moscow: Gos. izd-vo polit. lit-ry, 1962.

Vom Bruck, Gabriele *Islam, Memory, and Morality in Yemen: Ruling Families in Transition.* New York: Palgrave Macmillan, 2005.

Von Horn, Carl. *Soldiering for Peace.* New York: David McKay Company, 1966.

Walker, John R. *Britain and Disarmament: The UK and Nuclear, Biological and Chemical Weapons Arms Control and Programmes, 1956–1975.* Farham: Ashgate, 2012.

Walker, Jonathan. *Aden Insurgency: The Savage War in South Arabia, 1962–67.* Spellmount: Staplehurst, 2005.

Wallerstein, Immanuel. "What Cold War in Asia? An Interpretative Essay." *The Cold War in Asia: The Battle for Hearts and Minds.* Ed. Zheng Yangwen, Hong Liu and Michael Szonyi. Boston: Brill, 2010. 1–21.

Walt, Stephen M. *The Origins of Alliances.* Ithaca, NY: Cornell University Press, 1990.

Waterbury, John. *The Egypt of Nasser and Sadat: The Political Economy of Two Regimes.* Princeton: Princeton University Press, 1983.

Watson, Sir Charles. *Winston Churchill: The Struggle for Survival.* New York: Carroll and Graf Publishers, 2006.

Wazīr, Zayd ibn 'Alī. *Muḥāwalah li-fahm al-mushkilah al-Yamanīyah.* Beirut: Mu'assasat al-Risālah, 1971.

Webster, Sir Charles. *The Foreign Policy of Palmerston, 1830–1841: Britain, the Liberal Movement and the Eastern Question.* London: G. Bell and Sons, 1951.

Weintal, Edward and Bartlett, Charles. *Facing the Brink: an intimate study of crisis diplomacy.* New York: Charles Scribner's Sons, 1967.

Wenner, Manfred W. "The Civil War in Yemen, 1962–70." *Stopping the Killing.* Ed. Roy Licklider. New York: New York University Press, 1993.

Westad, Odd Arne. "The Cold War and the International History of the Twentieth Century." *The Cambridge History of the Cold War.* Ed. Melvyn P. Leffler and Odd Arne Westad. Cambridge: Cambridge University Press, 2010. 1–19.

Westad, Odd Arne. *The Global Cold War.* Cambridge, UK: Cambridge University Press, 2007.

Wolinetz, Harvey D. *Arabic Philatelic Propaganda Against the State of Israel.* Ann Arbor, Michigan: LithoCrafters, 1975.

Woskett, Kenneth C. *Puberty at Eighty: Kenneth C. Woskett Autobiography.* Kenneth Woskett, 2009.

Yaqub, Salim. *Containing Arab nationalism: The Eisenhower Doctrine and the Middle East.* Chapel Hill: University of North Carolina Press, 2004.

Yodfat, Aryeh. *Arab Politics in the Soviet Mirror.* Jerusalem: Israel Universities Press, 1973.

Zabarah, Mohammed A. "The Yemeni Revolution of 1962 Seen as a Social Revolution." *Contemporary Yemen: Politics and Historical Background.* Ed. B.R. Pridham. London: Croom Helm, 1984. 76–84.

Zabarah, Mohammed A. *Yemen: Traditionalism vs. Modernity.* New York: Praeger Publishers, 1982.

Index